The LEGENDS Of LANDOVER

Long-Lost Stories of the Washington Capitals

Glenn Dreyfuss

THE LEGENDS OF LANDOVER
Long-Lost Stories of the Washington Capitals

> **Landover?**
> *"Friends would call and say, 'Where's Landover?'"*
> *- Caps goalie Bernie Wolfe.*
>
> *This book derives its title from the suburban Maryland city, 14 miles east of the White House, which the Capitals called home for their first 23 seasons.*

Copyright © 2020 by Glenn Dreyfuss
All rights reserved. This book or any portion thereof may not be reproduced or used in any manner whatsoever without the express written permission of the publisher except for the use of brief quotations in a book review.

Printed in the United States of America

ISBN 978-0-578-68546-5

Contact author & publisher Glenn Dreyfuss:
notapwplfan@yahoo.com

Galleries, audio and video:
capitals-legends.blogspot.com

THE LEGENDS OF LANDOVER

✪ *PREGAME:* My Team and Me – How We Met ... 1
Washington Gets The Vote (For Hockey) ... 3

First Period: Capsized

✪ *1st Shift:* Loss Leaders: 1974-75 ... 6
Terrible Twos ... 44
3rd Time's A Charm ... 58
✪ *2nd Shift:* Expansion Era: Skaters ... 65
Goalies ... 79
Coaches & G.M. ... 85
✪ *3rd Shift:* The Stuff Legends Are Made Of ... 98
✪ *4th Shift:* Games Of Note 1977-1982 ... 115

Second Period: Capi-Pedia

✪ *5th Shift:* They Could've Been Pandas ... 132
✪ *6th Shift:* Pride & Prejudice & Pucks ... 139
✪ *7th Shift:* Comedy Club, Fight Club, Health Club ... 147
✪ *8th Shift:* Hockey Sticks and Politics ... 169
✪ *9th Shift:* Exhibitions Of Note ... 175
✪ *10th Shift:* Media ... 182
✪ *11th Shift:* Capital Centre ... 193
✪ *12th Shift:* Save The Caps! ... 202

Third Period: Capital Gains

✪ *13th Shift:* Montreal Seasoning ... 216
✪ *14th Shift:* The Playoff '80s: Skaters ... 224
Retired Numbers ... 236
Goalies ... 240
Coaches & G.M. ... 249
✪ *15th Shift:* '70's and '80's, By The Numbers ... 260
✪ *16th Shift:* More Stuff Legends Are Made Of ... 268
✪ *17th Shift:* Games Of Note 1982-1989 ... 275
✪ *18th Shift:* Playoffs: Faceoff Circle of Hell ... 294
✪ *19th Shift:* Hunter's Shot: 1988 Playoffs ... 298

✪ *OVERTIME:* Still Crazy - About the Caps ... 303
✪ *DOUBLE OT:* From Stanley Can To Stanley Cup ... 305

Dedicated to the memory of
my mother Ruth,
my father Don,
and my brother Gavin.

THE LEGENDS OF LANDOVER

PREGAME:
My Team and Me – How We Met

As a childhood fan of the 1960's New York Mets, I became intimately acquainted with sports futility. Then, after seven years of laughable efforts, something amazing happened. The 1969 Miracle Mets erased a 9½ game lead by the Cubs, swept Hank Aaron's Braves in the playoffs, and stunned the heavily favored Orioles to win the World Series.

Having seen the Mets through to a successful outcome, my family moved to suburban Maryland. In 1974, I adopted the new hometown team – the fledgling Washington Capitals of the NHL. My father and I attended our first hockey game in February, 1975. For $8.50 per ticket, we scored seats along the goal line in the third row from the glass. During warmups, an errant slapshot found the forehead of a woman five seats down the row from us, knocking her unconscious. Perhaps I should have taken that as a sign, and avoided a lot of future heartbreak.

Regardless, we stayed for the match between the Capitals and K.C. Scouts. Stan Gilbertson's beautiful individual effort gave the Caps the lead; Mike Marson doubled it on a power play. And I was almost close enough to celebrate with Ace Bailey, after he roofed a goal under the crossbar in the 2nd period. The Capitals won, 3-0 – the first shutout in team history, one of only eight wins they would register that inaugural season – and I was hooked.

✪ **Me, Ber-nie and Maroook!**

The Caps are one of the great star-crossed teams in sports history. Even before the playoff collapses, consider this: the team set a record for losses (67!) in a season. And they missed the playoffs on the final night twice (Twice!) in consecutive seasons – 1980 and 1981. Even when they clinched their first playoff berth, was it at home to the revelry of the long-suffering fans? No, it was at midnight Eastern in Calgary (Calgary!), with me and about four others listening to the broadcast.

Even so, some of my fondest memories growing up were spent in the red seats high above the rink at the Capital Centre. It was the crowd chanting *"Ber-nie"* for a Bernie Wolfe save, and *"Maroook"* for a Dennis Maruk score. It was P.A. man Marv Brooks: "Ladies and Gentlemen, the Washingtaaaaaaan Capitals!" It was the strains of Pat Benatar, belting out *Hit Me With Your Best Shot* during warmups. It was my friend Matt standing and exhorting the Caps to "Make Them Pay!" And my friend Robert exhorting Matt to "Sit down. I can't see the game."

THE LEGENDS OF LANDOVER

✪ Time Circuits On... Flux Capacitor... Fluxing...

Now, fast forward, it's the 21st century, and I live on the West Coast. Odd thing is, with cable TV and the Web, it's far easier for me to follow the Capitals from 3,000 miles away than it ever was living in suburban Maryland back in the day. Not only can I watch every game live; all the behind-the-scenes stories are as close as the click of a mouse.

That got me wondering – what was my favorite team really like when I was growing up? During the '70's and '80's, newspaper columnists and local TV sports anchors were criminally negligent about reporting on the Caps, and before blogs and TV hockey channels, there weren't any other options. So I dug into it. Now, like Marty McFly in *Back To The Future*, you're invited to buckle up your DeLorean and set the Flux Capacitor for Landover, Maryland and 1974, to read what I uncovered.

Deep-dive research (**more than 170 unique sources**) revealed that beyond the historically wretched expansion season, the decade-and-a-half climb out of the wreckage was also worthy of sharing – and hadn't previously been shared. The book's filter is that each entry should make the reader smile or reflect. In other words, dry recitations of games and numbers wouldn't cut it. There's no mandate to be comprehensive, because year-by-year results, player statistics and scores are easily found online. This is a volume about people and their circumstances, that just happened to revolve around a hockey franchise.

The '70's and '80's Capitals are also a jumping-off point to larger topics of American society. Issues examined include bigotry (*Pride, Prejudice & Pucks*); the ethics of hockey fighting, and disregard for player safety (*Comedy Club, Fight Club, Health Club*); the political class (*Hockey Sticks and Politics*); foreign relations (*Exhibitions of Note*); media relations, and lack of same (*Media*); arena issues (*Capital Centre*); and the business of sports (*Save The Caps!*). As a public service, when you reach the '80's, discussion of the playoff meltdowns are kept mercifully short - and limited to one chapter. However, if you're the sort who likes walking barefoot on broken glass, by all means, go there now (*18th Shift*, page 294).

Luckily, tales of the early Caps are not only abundant, but in turns hilarious, moving, and thought-provoking. This book is both a wild ride and a cautionary tale for fans and sports leagues alike. That's the goal; bite-sized stories which are interesting, funny, or poignant – even if you're not a Caps fan. I hope you agree.

THE LEGENDS OF LANDOVER

Washington Gets The Vote (For Hockey)

In June of 1972, NHL governors gathered at a Montreal hotel to select two expansion franchises from among 10 applicants. Besides construction magnate Abe Pollin, hockey in Washington had a pair of champions inside the meeting rooms. One was Flyers owner Ed Snider, who had two reasons to back D.C.'s bid. First, Snider was born in the District and graduated from the University of Maryland. Second, a former partner of Pollin's with the basketball Bullets was Snider's brother-in-law.

The other ally was L.A. sports titan and Redskins owner Jack Kent Cooke. Pollin, as an NBA owner, had helped Cooke secure the Lakers franchise. Cooke, having since acquired the NHL Kings, now stood ready to return the favor. As Juan Williams wrote in the *Washington Post*, Cooke came prepared. "When Pollin arrived in Montreal, there was a message from Cooke: 'Don't go to your room. Come to my suite immediately.' Cooke told Pollin whom to see, whom to talk to, whom to court."

Borrowing from his beloved NBA, Pollin employed a full-court press at the Board of Governors meeting. "We got to Montreal on a Sunday and didn't get to sleep until Thursday," Abe recalled. "We went from one owner's suite to the next, begging, pleading, lobbying." Pollin later recited his pitch, which went like this: "I had a location for an arena, as a builder I could get it built, I was an experienced sports person, and it would be a plus for hockey to have a franchise in the Nation's Capital."

Abe's wife Irene pitched in, too. "For three days and three nights we were up," she told *AP*. "I was in a nightgown typing letters to the president and everybody to have them send letters to the league because they kept saying, 'Washington is a southern city, it'll never be a hockey town.'"

Sports Illustrated noted Pollin's "support from 17 U.S. Senators and 42 representatives, who wrote to the governors over the weeks leading to its vote." The U.S. Senators' letter: "We… join in urging you to grant a hockey franchise to the national capitol area… One of the nation's largest urban areas is anxiously awaiting word of your decision." The letter from U.S. House members: "Your action would provide major league hockey and basketball for this sports-starved community and also insure a beautiful facility… to celebrate the Nation's bicentennial."
(From Irene Pollin's book, *Irene and Abe: An Unexpected Life*.)

Rangers president William Jennings told the *Toronto Globe & Mail*, "We've been besieged. I must have received 80 telegrams from people in Washington." The *Globe* story added, "Walter Bush, governor for the North Stars, commented that it didn't hurt to have friends in Washington."

THE LEGENDS OF LANDOVER

✪ Beating The Odds

Bookmaker Jimmy the Greek placed 600-1 odds against Pollin pulling it off. Other bidders knew the real percentages were much better for D.C., due to Abe's formidable will. Future Caps G.M. Max McNab shared this nugget with *The Hockey News*: "Less than two weeks before the NHL meeting, Bob Breitbard (representing San Diego) came in and told me, 'Our chances are slim and none; I just found out Abe Pollin is after one.'"

The voting by NHL governors continued through four very close rounds of secret ballots, with Kansas City certain of obtaining one of the two available slots. Ultimately, Pollin bested the San Diego bid, as well as groups from Dallas, Cincinnati, Phoenix, Indianapolis, and Cleveland. When the voting was over and D.C. was in, Jack Kent Cooke told the *Post*, "I couldn't be happier. It is truly a major league city again."

FIRST PERIOD:
Capsized

The Titanic Struggles of the Expansion Capitals (1974-1982)

THE LEGENDS OF LANDOVER

1st Shift: *Loss Leaders: 1974-75*

"Hockey has arrived in the land of Watergate"
Bob Verdi, Chicago Tribune

The 1974-75 Washington Capitals were handcuffed, blindfolded, and had their skate laces tied together - at least it felt that way - then were sent out for slaughter by eager opponents.

A callous NHL, a hungry rival league, and front office gaffes left a roster that one writer called "castoffs and malcontents." The predictably horrid results: 8 wins, 5 ties, 67 losses - still the worst record in a century-plus of National Hockey League campaigns. With the league providing better pre-natal care for recent expansion franchises, the futility mark may last another century. So read on for sympathetic reflections on the people and events of that historically forlorn season, and the two that followed.

✪ No Mercy

If the NHL employed a Mercy Rule in 1974-75, more than a few Caps games from that first season would have ended early. Some of the lopsided losses: 11-1, 9-2, 12-1, 10-0, 10-3, 8-0, 12-1, 10-2. "I knew it was going to be a bad season," general manager Milt Schmidt said, "but not this bad." (*San Mateo Times*)

In early December, G.M. Schmidt traveled to Chicago in a mood of despair. The night before, fewer than 9,000 watched his team fall meekly, 6-0 to visiting Pittsburgh. The *Washington Star* game story began, "One day, National Hockey League play will come to Capital Centre. Until then, there are the Washington Capitals." The shutout increased their winless streak to 14, being outscored 91-34 after 18 games.

The crisis was starkly summarized by *The Hockey News* in a front page banner headline: "Washington Begs For Player Help." Now, as he rose to speak at a meeting of fellow NHL general managers, Schmidt's words had to catch in his throat. "Look, for the good of the whole league," Milt began, "the Washington franchise could use some help. Many of you have players sitting in the stands who could help in Washington. Our team is willing to deal a first round draft choice in return."

Schmidt never thought he'd wave that white flag, vowing on the day he was hired, "Nobody, but nobody, will get draft choices from us. I have seen teams trade away their draft choices," Schmidt said to *AP*. "I refuse to do it." Now, he explained to *Hockey Digest*, "The situation has changed tremendously. My scouts report there won't be much in next year's draft, certainly nobody better than a player we could get in trade now for our No.1 pick."

THE LEGENDS OF LANDOVER

Milt's damning assessment of his roster went beyond talent level. Read what he told *The Hockey News*: "If we are unable to motivate the players on our roster, we'll have to make moves." Motivate? Apparently, burdened by a 1-15-2 record, the Caps not only didn't have the skill to compete, many had lost the desire to try. And there were still 62 games left! Goalie Ron Low later would concede there were "times when this team absolutely quit. We've had some of the most ridiculous practice sessions, and I mean thoroughly disorganized and worthless. There was hardly any contact or hard work at all." (*Washington Star*)

✪ Sure They Were Having Fun; The Season Hadn't Started

How much grander this new voyage seemed before the good ship Capitals left port. On March 28, 1974, NHL expansion team bosses Sid Abel and Milt Schmidt convened at Toronto's Royal York Hotel to hash out rules for the various player drafts. "Rather than holding a home-and-home, with the rubber match along I-70 in Indiana, Toronto appeared to be convenient neutral ground." (*K.C. Times*)

Visitors to room 13111 witnessed those two impish gents mugging for photographers. Kansas City general manager Abel recreated mock amazement at losing a coin toss to his D.C. counterpart. Schmidt, having thus secured the first pick in the amateur draft, reveled in his good fortune with a knowing wink for the camera.

Why shouldn't they kid around? Both men were already Hall-of-Famers. Abel won three Stanley Cups with Detroit, while Schmidt won four with Boston - two as a player, two as G.M. Abel expressed the optimism both men felt, telling *AP* that Kansas City would be "a great hockey city." Abel won a second toss, determining first pick of expansion goalies. Was it an omen that when Abel called "heads," the first toss came up tails, and when Schmidt called "tails" on the second toss, the coin came up heads?

Milt and Sid tag-teamed some negotiations on the eve of the expansion draft. Of one confab with New York, the *K.C. Times* reported, "Emile Francis, the Ranger general manager, will ask both clubs to lay off a certain player so he can get him through the draft. The deal will require the cooperation of both Schmidt and Abel. The payoff was not revealed." The player not selected was Nick Beverly, a defenseman who would have played on the top pair in either expansion city; instead, Beverly skated two more seasons in New York, and later was named captain in Minnesota.

Milt and Sid's optimism is haunting, akin to pictures of happy passengers boarding the Titanic. Few laughs lay ahead for these members of hockey royalty. Abel's Scouts suffered two malnourished seasons (27-110-23). In June, 1976, the Scouts ran out of money, Sid was laid off, and the franchise abandoned its "great hockey city" for a move to Denver.

THE LEGENDS OF LANDOVER

Milt's season-and-a-half at the helm left the Caps even more starved for wins (11-95-10). At the time, a rueful Schmidt admitted, "My pride is hurting something awful." In Jason Farris' book *Behind The Moves*, Milt elaborated. "It wasn't easy to get personnel. I never even tried to trade because I didn't have anybody to trade." Later, he described leaving Boston for Washington as one of his "worst moves." Time - four decades worth - didn't heal the wounds. "I don't wish to discuss that (season). It's still too painful to think about," Schmidt told *bleacherreport.com*... in April of 2015.

✪ No Chance

The Capitals never had a chance of fielding a competitive squad, mostly for reasons beyond their control. The World Hockey Association raided talent that would have stocked the Washington and Kansas City rosters. A record 32 pro clubs opened training camp for 1974-75, 18 in the NHL, 14 in the WHA. Moreover, Canada almost exclusively was expected to fill the burgeoning player pool. Non-Canadians represented a tiny fraction of NHL (9.2%) and WHA (11.5%) lineups, according to *quanthockey.com*. Quite simply, demand for qualified pros far exceeded supply.

The amateur draft had been diluted, top prospects plundered as teens in prior seasons. "The NHL did this to stymie the rival WHA, and the Caps just got caught in the crossfire." (*Hockey Digest*) Mismanagement hurt, too. High Caps draft picks Greg Joly and Mike Marson were pressed into service too soon, and forced to play against top opposition, stunting their development. Meanwhile, the Caps didn't have, or didn't choose to spend, the cash that would have attracted veterans.

On top of everything else, the Caps were born too late. Existing rosters had already been over-harvested in the 1970 expansion to Buffalo and Vancouver, and Long Island and Atlanta in 1972. To prevent further losses of quality talent, NHL teams hoarded players like never before. Rules were egregiously altered, allowing teams to place off-limits almost any player worth protecting.

On the day of the 1974 expansion draft, *Windsor Star* columnist Jim McKay assessed available draftees as, "Little more than a bag of bones." McKay then imagined a story from a near-future sports section: "Washington and Kansas City met last night in hockey for the first time. Hockey lost."

Stunned and dismayed Caps owner Abe Pollin asked, "When will someone on an established club admit that the expansion draft as it's run now is a disgrace? The old clubs don't give away a thing." *(N.Y. Times)* "It's not fair," general manager Milt Schmidt agreed. "We paid $6 million to join the league, and look how little other teams have left for us." Schmidt had been equally miserly as G.M. of the Bruins, admitting, "I'm on the other side of the fence now."

THE LEGENDS OF LANDOVER

Years later, Schmidt told *bleacherreport.com* that, "NHL President Clarence Campbell gets the most blame. He told us we were supposed to have first choice of any player sent to the minors. That wasn't so. We didn't get the players we were supposed to get." Within the shallow talent pool, Schmidt made a tactical blunder. "We went for big guys and Kansas City went for skaters in the expansion draft," Milt said. "I figured the big thing was not to get pushed around. The trouble was, the big guys I drafted – they don't like to fight."

Opponents knew it, too. One night, Montreal's Murray Wilson laid a thunderous hit on one of Washington's biggest forwards. A *Montreal Gazette* reporter wondered what accounted for Wilson's uncharacteristic aggressiveness. Habs teammate Glenn Goldup gleefully chimed in, "You knew he wouldn't hit you back." As Caps defenseman Yvon Labre pointed out, "We had guys that wanted to play, but were easily intimidated."

✪ Comedy Column Could Have Used More Comedy

For all the reasons enumerated, taking shots at the expansion Capitals was as unfair as mocking a high school track team at the Olympics. Some NHL scribes, though, found big yuks in traveling the low road. Summoning his inner Henny Youngman, *Maclean's* columnist John Robertson actually wrote, right after the expansion draft, "Take Washington. Please."

Robertson's comedy stylings: Capitals players were "only vaguely recognizable in their own mirrors." To avoid humiliation, they should "wear unlisted numbers." To keep them from playing in his country, Canada should "tighten up our immigration laws." Although the Caps' 22 draftees scored just 40 combined NHL goals, "Mind you, several of them hit the goalpost." More Robertson: nine drafted left-wingers "sounds like a communist plot." Concerning one of those left wings, "Who is Bob Gryp? Is he excess baggage?" Montreal and Washington, in the same division, will be playing "four-point games... reduced to two-ninety-eight."

Most of these one-liners didn't deserve time on a fourth line. *Rimshot!* Don't forget to tip your waitress. Anyway, what's up with all the animosity towards the team representing the Nation's Capital? Possibly because 24 years earlier, Robertson, then a teenage lefty pitcher, failed a tryout with... *Dun-Dun-Duuun!*... the Washington Senators.

✪ The Beginning Of The Beginning

Probably, a long-ago printing error was just an honest mistake - although it proved to be depressingly prophetic. A 1974 exhibition game program from the Capitals' first training camp in London, Ontario, mistakenly listed the new team as the "Washington Generals." That, of course, being the fictional basketball foils who always lost to the Harlem Globetrotters.

THE LEGENDS OF LANDOVER

Win a bet from even the most die-hard Caps fan with obscure facts from their first exhibition - the first time Washington players hit the ice in competition. *Date:* Sept. 22, 1974; *Opponent:* Buffalo; *Site:* St. Catharine's, Ontario; *Final:* Sabres 4, Caps 2. One oddity from the game: Washington played all three of their goaltenders, one per period. John Paddock scored the first goal, a slapshot 4:36 into the first period. "I was so excited that I almost went in the net after it." Defenseman Gord Smith delivered the first on-ice zinger to an official: "If you'd open your eyes, you would make a pretty good linesman." (*Hockey News, Washington Star*)

Preseason hockey at Capital Centre, tilts with Montreal & Philadelphia, was promoted by a curious newspaper ad. The giant, bold, one-word headline read "Kerrrrack!" What did "Kerrrrack!" mean? The sound of stick on puck? The sound of puck on skull? The sound of a fan breaking a molar on an unpopped kernel of popcorn? The fine print read, "How good is this scrappy new team of fast-skating wild men?" As Jerry Seinfeld once asked, who were the ad wizards that came up with that one?

The first NHL hockey in Washington, a preseason affair vs. Montreal on Sept. 28, 1974, got off to a good start - even if it started a half-hour late. Tommy Williams scored 11 seconds in, and someone in the press box joked, "They'll outscore the Bullets." Fans saw a bizarre rule experiment, intended to speed up play: a free shot from the faceoff circle when the opposition froze the puck. Guy Lafleur scored on the gimmick, which was thankfully rejected by the board of governors. Steve Atkinson's goal with 1:23 left, scored the traditional way, sent 8,119 home happy with a 4-4 tie.

✪ Too Many Cooks Spoil The Roster

The Caps had a "Y'all Come" attitude at their first training camp; 56 more or less warm bodies accepted. Flawed as the eventual roster was, consider the pedigree of players who didn't make the cut. These included Jiri Bar and Florian Lampert, Europeans more experienced with heat than with ice. As explained in the *Baltimore Sun*, "Bar returned to his job as executive chef of the Sheraton Airport Inn in Philadelphia. Lampert now can go back to puffing pastry for the residents of Watergate."

"A complete farce," was Russ White's assessment in the *Washington Star*. "Players walked around moping, cursing the fate that had brought them to an expansion team. A couple of rookie phenoms captured most of the publicity, and the older players resented it. Milt Schmidt had to send the RCMP after a rookie who stole a pair of skates. A rookie coach failed to gain any respect. Practices produced nothing." One of those campers, Jim Hrycuik, didn't disagree, although some of the issues were endemic to any expansion team. "It was brutal. We had never met each other. We didn't have any idea what was happening on the ice, and I remember coming back to the hotel each night wondering who I would eat dinner with. We were a bunch of lost sheep."

THE LEGENDS OF LANDOVER

Then there's Ron Poole, who holds a draft-day distinction which will never be duplicated. In the 1970's, the NHL didn't place a limit on the duration of the amateur draft; teams could keep making selections until they tired of the exercise. By the 25th round in 1974, every club had dropped out except the Capitals! Washington made Poole, a center with the Kamloops Chiefs, the 247th and final member of the '74 draft class.

The NHL later shortened its draft to 12 rounds, eventually truncating it further to seven rounds. So Ron Poole will likely be the only hockey player ever chosen as late as the 25th round. Now Ron, understanding the odds, never tried turning pro. But in one way, he would have felt a certain familiarity on the expansion Caps. In a February, 1973 game, Poole scored two goals – to help his junior team snap a 17-game winless streak.

✪ Gracious Sam Pollock

Montreal G.M. Sam Pollock, like a loan shark, each year trolled the NHL's poor neighborhoods, offering the illusion of quick help. "I've always traded for futures - not pasts," explained Pollock. Time and again, Montreal would give up an older player, or one who couldn't crack their lineup, in exchange for high draft picks, which fueled the Habs' dynasty.

The expansion Capitals were offered one of Pollock's baubles. "Trader Sam" lent a talented farmhand named Peter Sullivan to the Caps for a preseason tryout. Sullivan skated circles around the rest of the campers, showing flashy moves that would later make him a star in the WHA. The infant Capitals, though in dire need of skilled youngsters, wisely returned Sullivan to Montreal. Why? The *Winnipeg Free Press* revealed, "Pollock, who so graciously offered (Sullivan) to the Caps, decided $100,000 and a first round draft choice would be ample compensation. Little wonder Washington reneged."

✪ Unrealistic Goals

Right before the season, G.M. Milt Schmidt and coach Jim Anderson - on a dare? - allowed the same absurd claim to be printed. "We're as good as anyone in goaltending," Schmidt told the *Washington Star*. "We've got the best goaltending in the league," Anderson said to the *Washington Post*.

They weren't alone; at a team-welcoming event, D.C. Council president John Neivus hailed Ron Low as "the next Walter Johnson of our community." (Huh?) Make no mistake - the Low/Michel Belhumeur tandem made goaltender the strongest position on the Caps. But in a league populated by goalies named Dryden, Parent, Esposito, and Vachon, Caps management – and politicians – fell victim to blind optimism. Here's the truth: even the league's best couldn't have stopped enough pucks to make the Caps competitive.

THE LEGENDS OF LANDOVER

✪ Broadway Premier - October 9, 1974 at New York

"Tonight, for the first time ever, the Washington Capitals play a regular league game in the National Hockey League." With those words, TV-9's Hal Kelly welcomed D.C. viewers to Madison Square Garden, and the first game in Capitals history. Kelly predicted a lot of "nervous Nellies" with so many first-time NHLers on the visitors' bench. Indeed, each game would prove an uphill climb akin to scaling the Empire State Building.

AP's game story recounts a jittery opening night: "'It could've been worse – but not much,' said weary, sweat-soaked Ron Low. The Washington goaltender faced a 19-shot barrage almost alone in the third period. Ed Giacomin, his counterpart, faced only one. The result was a four-goal burst by New York and a 6-3 victory. 'We're brand new,' Low said between swallows of salt tablets. 'Half the time we didn't know what we were doing. Still, I think we've got a pretty good team. It's just that we played a better one.'"

"The worst moments," winger Jim Hrycuik said to the *Hockey News*, "were when we got trapped in our own zone and couldn't move the puck out. They swarmed all over us. They hit us, they muscled us. I never realized how strong some of the guys are who are in this league."

Hrycuik gave Washington an early 1-0 lead, the first goal in Caps history. At 5:06 of the first period, Hrycuik, #25 in the infamous white pants, walked out of the corner and pushed a backhand past Ed Giacomin. "It was super," Hrycuik said. "I got so excited I didn't know what to do with myself." When Ron Anderson's power play goal gave the Caps a 2-1 lead in the middle period, and Bruce Cowick almost scored seconds later, Rangers fans filled the Garden with boos.

Despite a meager 12 shots on goal, and exactly zero during the final 18 minutes of play, the Capitals actually maintained a 3-3 tie early in the 3rd period before wearing down. "We did better than I expected," defenseman Doug Mohns told *UPI*. "When these guys play together a bit more, they'll gain cohesion." Coach Jimmy Anderson added, "These kids really looked like they belonged out there. We're going to give teams a lot of trouble."

✪ Fashion Faux Pas

Everyone knows you don't wear white pants after Labor Day. Everyone except the 1974 Capitals. Before Milt Schmidt became their G.M., he played and coached in Boston. Schmidt remembered Bruin goalies saying that defenders' black pants made it hard to locate the puck. Milt put that tidbit to use. The Capitals skated into Madison Square Garden for their first-ever game sporting white pants.

THE LEGENDS OF LANDOVER

Sadly, they proved an off-color choice, laughably silly, hardly a competitive edge. As described by the *Washington Star*, "The white pants looked just like underwear under the bright lights. And as the game progressed, they looked very much like dirty underwear." Players found to their distress that white also shows stains, and when wet, reveals what's underneath.

Goalie and fashion critic Ron Low told Evan Weiner of *nhl.com*, "It was a joke. The pads get rubbed against the boards and it gets filthy. After 10 games you couldn't tell if it was white or not." Defenseman Jack Lynch provided an unflattering counterpoint. "In Detroit, before I got traded to Washington, the joke was that the Caps never had to worry about getting those pants dirty because they never went in the corners." (*SI*)

Only Joan Rivers would applaud the cruelty in Howard Erickson's *Detroit Free Press* fashion review. "The Washington Capitals looked like the sissy team of the NHL. What else would you make of the Capitals' red sweaters, white pants, and red stockings? It appeared they were playing in their shorts." (Sissies? Howard must have gotten his writing diploma from the *Little Rascals'* "He-Man Woman-Haters Club.")

Infamous as the white pants are, the Caps only wore them in four regular season road games. The final indignity came at Chicago Stadium on October 23, 1974. According to a team-issued history, the pants became discolored... brown. Fans taunted players with insults of, shall we say, a gastrointestinal nature.

The NHL overlooked its own rules to authorize an in-season uniform change. When the Capitals next hit the road, they had red pants to go with their red sweaters. This retina-straining combo also lasted just four games. The Caps then settled on blue pants with red sweaters, the familiar away kit used for 20 years. The kicker: the team switched pants color again in 1995, to... wait for it... *Black!* We're guessing Milt was not consulted.

✪ Caps "Cooked" In Home Opener - October 15, 1974 vs. L.A.

Believe it or not, Redskins owner Jack Kent Cooke and coach George Allen conspired against the Capitals before their first-ever home game. Cooke also owned the Los Angeles Kings, who would christen Capital Centre against the Caps on October 15, 1974.

Before the team bus left for the rink, Allen boarded to give the Kings a pep talk. As Bob Miller recounts in *Tales From The Kings*, Allen clapped his hands as he talked. "Aware the Kings were unbeaten in three straight, Allen said, 'Remember men, four is better than three,' and left the bus." Not exactly "Win one for the Gipper."

THE LEGENDS OF LANDOVER

Cooke gets a pass; he helped shepherd Washington's bid for a franchise through the NHL's finance committee in 1972, "Under the aegis of one of the most capable sports owners in America, Abe Pollin." Other dignitaries on hand - though not as saboteurs - included NHL President Clarence Campbell and Maryland Governor Marvin Mandel.

They saw Yvon Labre score at 4:35 of the 2nd period, as the Caps and Kings tied, 1-1. Goalie Ron Low turned aside two breakaways among his 33 saves, and the Caps survived a pair of 5-on-3 disadvantages. Kings netminder Rogie Vachon told the *Washington Post* afterward, "They look plenty good to me. They worked like hell." The sport received a glowing review on the *Washington Star* editorial page. "With its blinding speed, ballet-like grace and bruising jousts, big league hockey is a great addition to the rich sports life of the metropolitan area."

If it seemed like time flew by, that's because the clock didn't always stop when play did. A computer glitch caused 90 seconds to be lost. (At a game more than a decade later, referee Denis Morel ordered the scoreboard plug pulled because the seconds were ticking off too slowly. "They should check out the clock. It's not as if it hadn't happened before," Morel told the *Post*.)

Fans took home a commemorative certificate. It says the bearer "Attended the first regular season National Hockey League game ever played in the Washington area." It concludes, "With Appreciation For Your Support," signed "Abe Pollin, President" and "Milt Schmidt, General Manager."

Chances are a whole lot more certificates were printed than were needed. *UPI* described attendance at the inaugural NHL game in Washington as "sparse." Three factors contributed to just 8,093 fans - less than half of capacity - clicking the turnstiles. First, the sales department overestimated interest in the new team and sport. Second, they didn't "paper the house" with free tickets, or, say, bus inmates to the game from the jail in Upper Marlboro, just so the arena would appear full.

Lastly, there's the matter of the World Series, which still was a big deal nationally in 1974. These days, Series broadcasts routinely draw fewer than 15 million viewers. But on D.C. hockey's grand opening, 30 million Americans - including many within driving distance of Landover - stayed home to watch Game 3 between the Dodgers and A's. In light of that, *UPI* called the small Capital Centre crowd "explainable."

Not to Jack Kent Cooke, raised in Hamilton, Ontario and a hockey player as a youngster. A disenchanted Cooke sold the Kings in 1979, lamenting that transplanted Canadians in Southern California didn't buy enough tickets. "Now I know why they left Canada - they hate hockey!" As older Washington sports fans know, he took controlling ownership of the Redskins later in 1974.

THE LEGENDS OF LANDOVER

✪ First Franchise Victory - October 17, 1974 vs. Chicago

"Not far from our nation's capital, where earth-shaking events are daily propositions," Bob Verdi wrote in the *Chicago Tribune,* "a landmark of sorts was established when the Capitals recorded their first victory." (On draft day, Verdi had dubbed the Caps, "Athletes Anonymous.") Assistant G.M. Lefty McFadden described a jubilant locker room after the Hawks were vanquished, 4-3. "They were measuring one another for ring sizes. It was like they took the Stanley Cup." Ron Low stopped all 18 3rd period shots, 33 in total, for the milestone win. Chicago coach Bill Reay said, "No question – Low beat us."

Denis Dupere scored twice, on shots Willie Mosconi would admire. The first, while behind the net, banked in off the skate of Hawks goalie Mike Veisor. "Dupere's next goal," *The Hockey News* reported, "was a carom off the rear end of Chicago defenseman Doug Jarett. 'No big deal,' said Jarett. 'I have the biggest rump in the league.'" Jack Egers potted the winner with 11 minutes left. Egers' blazing shot earned him the nickname "Smokey." So it was pre-ordained that his post-hockey career would be as a fire department captain. Come to think of it, a novel way for Jack to say he wore a "C" on a uniform!

Beating the Hawks represented, "A reward for hard work," coach Jim Anderson told the *AP*. "Now they know they can do it, so if the guys don't win more, I'll be able to kick their butts." Jim would've needed Manchester United and the Rockettes to do that much kicking – the Caps didn't win again for more than a month.

✪ "Shoot, Dupy, Shoot!" - November 7, 1974 at Boston

Less than a month in, merciless schedule-makers demand a three-match stretch against the Bruins, Flyers and Canadiens, who would whip the Caps by a combined 27-7. "Those are character builders," claimed coach Jimmy Anderson to *AP*.

Boston has Bobby Orr, Phil Esposito, and two Stanley Cups in the past five years. The Caps have a 1-9-1 record, including four losses by shutout. "Bobby Orr can't beat the Capitals by himself. It just looked that way tonight," marveled Bob Fachet in the *Washington Post*. "Orr collected 3 goals and 3 assists to trigger a Boston massacre, 10-4."

Twenty minutes in, Washington had already yielded 17 shots and four goals. An embarrassing homecoming for Caps G.M. Milt Schmidt, who spent almost four decades with the Bruins as player, coach, and general manager. "Schmidt charged into the dressing room after the first period and tore into his players," reported the *Washington Star*. "The sight of cigarette butts on the floor intensified his anger, and he finally had to be restrained by coach Anderson."

THE LEGENDS OF LANDOVER

Years later, Jack Egers revealed to Fachet what happened late in the game. "I passed to Denis Dupere and Orr just kept backing in on Gerry Cheevers and saying, 'Shoot, Dupy, shoot.' He backed in so close Cheevers was screened and Denis put it in. That's how sympathetic other teams looked at us." Cheevers wasn't feeling as generous, scolding Orr as he skated by, "You can be such a prick."
(*Cheevers quote from Sports Illustrated*)

✪ Misery Loves Company

Expansion bosses Sid Abel and Milt Schmidt talked nearly every day during the long, long season. "We had both been trying to make some trades, and weren't having any luck," Abel told the *Kansas City Times*. "I told him I'd put down six or seven players from my roster, and he could do the same with his roster." Did Sid mean "put down," as in what you do to injured animals? Thankfully, no. "We'd make some kind of deal," Abel said. "Sometimes just moving a player will cause him to play better." Talks fizzled when Sid purloined talented Guy Charron from Detroit, leaving an envious Schmidt to ask, "How did you make that deal?"

✪ Welcome... Don't Bother Unpacking

"Insulting" was one way to describe trade offers from other teams. "People who see us down are throwing garbage in my face," G.M. Milt Schmidt told *The Hockey News*. Milt also couldn't catch a break. "Schmidt has talked with Minnesota about center Fred Stanfield, sitting out early games. Stanfield finally dressed, and enjoyed a hat trick against Detroit. 'I was happy for Stanfield,' Schmidt said, 'but his timing was awful.'"

A month into the season, the Capitals did engineer an insanely complex trade involving four teams. First, Schmidt sent $30,000 - the waiver fee – to the Rangers in exchange for underperforming star defenseman Rod Seiling. Schmidt raved to *THN*, "We'll build our defense around him." Well, for one game, anyway. Capital Center patrons might have believed Rod was an apparition, because after suiting up for one home game on Halloween night, *poof*, Seiling was gone, shipped (along with his six-figure salary) to the Maple Leafs for forward Tim Ecclestone and defenseman Willy Brossart.

Assistant G.M. Lefty McFadden later confessed the Caps never intended to retain Seiling. Rod, reportedly near tears upon hearing of his trade to Washington, soon learned the truth. "Milt told me, 'I don't want you to move your family down here,'" Seiling recalled to *nhl.com*. "I stayed in a hotel and hardly got to know my teammates. We had a practice, played a game (a 3-0 loss to Montreal), then I was gone." Curiously, younger brother Don Seiling became Capitals property several months later. He would play one fewer game with the Caps than older brother Rod, which is to say, none.

THE LEGENDS OF LANDOVER

The same day Rod Seiling departed, wheeler-dealer Milt traded Ecclestone to the Flames for cash, more than he had sent to the Rangers. When the dust settled, the Caps had Brossart and a fatter bank account, while giving up nothing. Viewed another way, they did relinquish Seiling, who played another 333 NHL games, and Ecclestone, who scored 13 goals and finished +7 for Atlanta in '74-'75.

Brossart recorded a minus-63 in two injury-plagued seasons. It was all too much for columnist Bob Fachet, who in *The Hockey News* scorched the organization for not retaining a superior player. "(Brossart) wore the same Halloween costume – Caps uniform No. 17 – Seiling had worn in his one brief game as a Capital."

✪ When You Wish Upon A Star - November 24, 1974 vs. Minnesota

We suspect Caps fan John A. Kling was hardly capable of disappointment. Not if his soup was cold, his bus was late, or his TV lost horizontal hold. We surmise this from a November, 1974 newspaper advertisement featuring Mr. Kling. In the ad, titled, "Why I'm going to the Capitals-North Stars game Sunday night," John explains, "The Capitals are playing better consistently than I thought they would."

At the time, the Caps had won just two of their first 20 games, outscored 103-43, shut out five times, and coming off a 7-3 drubbing in Buffalo. Those results could exceed only expectations the size of subatomic particles. On the other hand, Mr. Kling was prescient in ignoring the dismal numbers. Against the North Stars, Washington rallied from a one-goal deficit three times. Minnesota played like the expansion team, taking four minor penalties and a misconduct in the final 8:30 of the second period.

The home side, meanwhile, took three minors the entire game, and killed them all off. Denis Dupere scored twice on the power play, the Caps outshot Minnesota 36-27, and John and 8,896 fellow Capital Centre believers relished a 4-4 tie. "We're getting better all the time and working as a team," coach Jimmy Anderson told *AP*. "We're putting out a little extra because we all hate losing." Mr. Kling undoubtedly would be too polite to add, "Told ya."

✪ I'll Gladly Score A Goal Tuesday For A Hamburger Today

In the mid-'80's, 81-year-old Clara Peller gained nationwide fame for uttering three iconic words in a fast-food commercial: "Where's the beef?" (Peller, incidentally, was a manicurist by trade.) A decade earlier, 56-year-old Milt Schmidt gained nothing but derision, shouting four forgotten words on the team bus: "Who took my cheeseburger?" (Schmidt, incidentally, was the Capitals' general manager by trade.)

THE LEGENDS OF LANDOVER

The phrase, "Who took my cheeseburger?" didn't catch on as well as the other one, though Caps players were known to jokingly repeat it. As explained in *The Hockey News*, "(It) became a code word that had everyone erupting in laughter; everyone except rookie Paul Nicholson, who thought the cheeseburger was up for grabs." The obvious lesson here is to never leave your food unattended around puppies or hockey players.

✪ Doug Mohns (1974-75)

Trivia Time: Who was the first captain of the Capitals? Prior to Zdeno Chara joining the franchise in 2021, who was the oldest player, and who had the longest NHL career? One player scored an answer hat trick: Doug Mohns. The Caps' inaugural season was Mohn's last of an illustrious 22-year run. Rather than pull rank or expect special treatment, Doug arrived early at Washington's training camp alongside rookies half his age.

"He was a mentor-type guy you looked up to," Nelson Pyatt told *Sports Illustrated*. "I had one suit, an old corduroy suit. Dougie pulled me aside and said, 'You're in the big leagues, you've got to dress accordingly.' He knew a tailor in Montreal, we went out, he made me three designed suits."

Small wonder that the Capitals appeared rudderless from October through December; they had no captain. For 37 games - three of them wins - only assistant captains were assigned. Finally, the "C" was stitched to Mohn's sweater on January 2, 1975. The decision paid dividends, when, with the Caps mired in an 18-game winless streak, Mohns called a team meeting. "I don't want my name on anything like that," Doug later said to *AP*. Sure enough, the Caps beat the visiting Red Wings that night, 6-3.

(Hard-working winger Bill Lesuk got Washington off to a fast start against the Wings, scoring 24 seconds in. Then he exercised the power of not-negative thinking. "Detroit had a shot before we did and it took a whale of a save by Ronnie Low to keep it from going in. I hate to think what would have happened if Detroit had beaten us to that first goal. No... I just won't think about it." [*The Hockey News*])

Mohns was noteworthy for donning a helmet, even before all goaltenders did. Smart idea - he was over 40 during his season in Washington. But safety wasn't the only factor. Mohns, "used to carry a curious red box with him on road trips," reported the *Washington Star*. "There was a big furor when it got lost one night. He kept his toupee inside the box."

Doug's regular practice was saluting during the anthem, as removing his headgear could prove risky. Goalie Ron Low explained, "One night we're heading off the ice. He takes his helmet off on the way back and his toupee's stuck in his helmet." Mohns kept his sense of humor about the toupee, too. A Canadian columnist wrote, "It makes him look younger, but he wishes it made him feel younger."

THE LEGENDS OF LANDOVER

✪ Steve Atkinson (1974-75)

No hockey player goes un-nicknamed. Forward Steve Atkinson received his during the second game in franchise history, a 6-0 blanking at Minnesota. Displeased with Atkinson's effort, G.M. Milt Schmidt shouted, "Get moving, you f***ing snail!" From then on, it was Steve "The Snail" Atkinson – on more formal occasions, "L'Escargot." (*nhl.com*)

In a February game at Vancouver, Steve earned a penalty shot. Recalling his moniker, Atkinson skated with a leisurely pace toward Canucks goalie Ken Lockett – and scored! "No player ever approached the exciting play quite as casual as Atkinson, who made a couple of stops in an already too-slow-to-be-true advance," reported the *Washington Star*. "Perhaps Atkinson put the guy to sleep, but he beat him." Steve joked, "They'll have to speed that up (on TV replays) to play in slow motion."

✪ Bruce Cowick (1974-75)

"We waited a whole season for Cowick to intimidate people. He had his chance here but didn't come through." The scouting report by Caps G.M. Milt Schmidt on winger Bruce Cowick's one season in D.C. (5 goals, 6 assists) before being released. Concurred Russ White in the *Washington Star*, "Cowick played in 65 games for Washington without much notice."

Absolutely everbody noticed Cowick on March 4, 1986, by which time he'd become a police constable in Esquimalt, B.C. "Cowick stripped to his undershorts and did a bump-and-grind for 100 cheering women before he pushed a fellow officer down a flight of stairs." So began a *Canadian Press* story, which should be studied by future generations of journalism students as a lead paragraph guaranteed to make readers want to know more.

It was ladies' night at a local club, you see, and Cowick was inspired to follow the performance of a male stripper. "10 minutes later, Cowick and Randhawa (an officer from neighboring Victoria) became embroiled in an argument about beer." Cowick allegedly threw Randhawa down the stairs, broke his arm, and threatened to break the other one. Clearly, if the Caps wanted livelier play out of Cowick, the Centre organist should have belted out "The Stripper" while Bruce was on the ice.

✪ Diaries Of Despair From Leo Monahan's *Sporting News* Columns

♦ *Dec. 14, 1974:* "An interviewer asked Henri Richard, Montreal captain, if the Caps would improve. 'No,' replied honest Henri. 'Not a chance.'"
♦ *Dec. 28, 1974:* "Caps' Coach Jimmy Anderson admitted, 'There's probably nobody on our club who could make the Sabres' team.'"
♦ *Feb. 8, 1975:* "The Caps declined so-called help from other teams because they would have to assume heavy contracts."

THE LEGENDS OF LANDOVER

✪ Dave Kryskow, Shortening Expectations (1974-75)

Opponents sometimes offered brutal honesty. Caps forward Dave Kryskow recalled a center ice conversation the night of January 4, 1975 at the Montreal Forum. "Habs defenseman Larry Robinson was there and he looked at me," Kryskow told the *Toronto Globe & Mail*. "I smiled and asked, 'What's the over-under on tonight's game?' He said, 'Ten.' I said, 'Sounds about right.'"

The Canadiens went on to score five power play goals, outshoot the Caps 47-17, and win by a score of, yes, 10-0. The Caps, lacking an appreciation for witty banter, traded Kryskow to Detroit one month later. We picture Kryskow smiling on his way out of town; Beltway drivers in rush hour snowstorms enjoy their time in Washington more than Dave did.

The season before, Kryskow lived large as a Blackhawks rookie, scoring in both game five and game six of the 1973 Stanley Cup Final. When you begin your career in a penthouse, it's no fun relocating to a tenement. In 51 games with his new expansion team, the Caps won just four. "I couldn't take this s**t anymore," Kryskow told Stephen Laroche for his book, *Changing The Game*. "It was tough, especially if you came from a winning team. I was disappointed with no structure or plan. After 20 games you were wondering how much time was left in the season."

A West Coast road trip further soured Kryskow's mood. On December 19, Los Angeles outshot the Caps 42-15 and outscored them 4-1. The next night in Oakland, Bill Lesuk and Ron Lalonde scored shorthanded goals 32 seconds apart during the same Yvon Labre penalty - and Washington still lost convincingly, 5-2. Kryskow decided the time had come to confront coach Jimmy Anderson about the use of his inexperienced teammates. "I said he should send these young bastards down to the minors and get some guys who knew how to play the game."

For a player shy of his 23rd birthday, Dave was unusually sure that youth was wasted on the young. "Building around draft choices was wrong," he said. Dave, don't hold back; tell us how you really feel. "It was one of those times you wish you could have input in how things were done."

As Kryskow recognized, G.M. Milt Schmidt wasn't about to install a suggestion box inside the dressing room. "Milt was old school and it was his way or the highway." So Kryskow hit that highway – where he found Red Wings management no more accommodating. "They weren't going to play me much," he was told, "because they wanted to give the younger guys more time. I was only 23!" The *Detroit Free Press* had a different take, saying Kryskow "showed a lack of hustle and aggressiveness."

THE LEGENDS OF LANDOVER

✪ Bloom Off The Rose - January 5, 1975 at Atlanta

Officially, Mike Bloom engaged in four fights during the 1974-75 season. His fifth bout – actually more of a one-sided ambush – occurred inside the visitors' dressing room in Atlanta. The first period at the Omni really hadn't gone badly for the Capitals. Sure, they failed on a couple of power plays and were outshot 15-8 by the Flames. But considering the Caps had surrendered ten goals the previous night in Montreal, ending the opening stanza with a scoreless tie represented a moral victory.

The problem was that coach Jimmy Anderson had kept Bloom, a 6-3, 206 pound left wing, mostly plastered to the bench. Teammate Ron Lalonde recalled what happened once the Caps filed off the ice. "We're in the dressing room. Mike Bloom is sitting in the corner and he's seething. Coach comes in to give us his pep talk. (Bloom) exploded and grabbed Jimmy Anderson by the collar, had him up against the wall. He was not a happy camper. Anderson was shocked." The coach was also giving up five inches, 40 pounds, and 22 years to Bloom.

Apparently, that was the last fight the Caps had in them on this evening. Atlanta outshot Washington 30-12 over the final 40 minutes, and despite Michel Belhumeur's 42 saves, the Flames coasted to a 3-0 victory. "I wish all the games were this easy," winning goalie Phil Myre gushed to the *Canadian Press*. "Nowhere has it been written that the meek shall inherit the National Hockey League," wrote Vic Dorr in the *Atlanta Journal-Constitution*. "Just ask the shell-shocked Washington Capitals, by far the meekest team in the NHL."

Despite his team's 20th straight road loss, and Bloom's physical insubordination, coach Anderson stayed publicly supportive. "Sure we're struggling. But the league could have helped us more in the expansion draft. I know one thing - I don't have one quitter on this club."

Anderson claimed benching Bloom was done purposely to agitate him. Mike's response, to the *Washington Star*: "I'd rather be angry playing. I've sat on my behind too much already." Years later, a more contrite Bloom told *Sports Illustrated*, "It wasn't (Anderson's) fault. That was a horrible job." Both coach and winger were jettisoned in the next few weeks, Anderson given the heave-ho in February, Bloom traded to Detroit in March.

(The Lalonde quote is from King Kaufman's podcast, *Can't Win 4 Losing*. Kaufman interviewed Ron Low, Jack Lynch, and Lalonde. Can it be coincidence that he chose three players whose surnames start with "L"?)

THE LEGENDS OF LANDOVER

✪ The Expansion Coach Blues: Jimmy Anderson (1974-75)

What's more thankless in sports than coaching an expansion team? Saddled with fringe players and impatient fans; losing a lot, and by a lot; knowing you won't be around by the time it gets better. Jimmy Anderson coached the Caps for their first 54 games, winning four. Like all members of his woebegone fraternity, Anderson suffered through the five stages of Expansion Coach Grieving:

Hope: "I had two goals in life," Anderson told his introductory news conference. "One was to play in the NHL, and one was to coach in the NHL. It took me 36 years to play seven games. I hope it doesn't take me that long to get a winner in Washington." Years later, he'd admit, "I had stars in my eyes. I couldn't see anything wrong with them."

Depression: The Capitals' record sank to 2-23-4 when Jim observed, "It's tough being an expansion team. You get in your mind you can't win." A tight game in Chicago turned when officials whistled Yvon Labre for a pair of borderline 3rd period penalties. Down two men, the Caps surrendered the winning Hawks goal. An exasperated Anderson said, "This was such a miscarriage of justice, it defied imagination."

Self-Depreciation: As a Dallas-Washington NFL epic was concluding at RFK Stadium, the Caps took to the ice on a Sunday night. After losing 6-0, Anderson asked, "Did anyone hear the score of the Redskins game? I meant to watch it. But I had to go to a hockey game." At the finish of another shutout loss, a writer asked, "Any good points?" The coach's answer: "The end of the game."

Dismissal: With zero road wins in 28 games, and a zero-for-60 stretch on the power play, the Capitals relieved Anderson on February 11, 1975. Ray Fitzgerald of the *Boston Globe* wrote in Jim's defense, "The job was impossible. You can't take hockey players named Flotsam and Jetsam and win games. You can't make an apple pie out of a barrel of lemons."

Contentment: 20 years later, Anderson still wore a Capitals ring. "It was a great experience. It was my one NHL head coaching job, and, sure, the record was a disaster, but it wasn't anybody's fault." (Quotes from *Wash. Star, Pgh. Post-Gazette, Baltimore Sun, Anchorage Daily News*)

✪ Delay Of Game - February 11, 1975 vs. New York Rangers

The blessing (and curse) of Capital Centre was that it provided a venue for every conceivable form of entertainment. Consider this manic scheduling in February, 1975: Ice Capades Sunday, Metallica show Monday, Capitals game Tuesday! The ice show had left "an overdose of blue paint on the surface." (*UPI*) Because of setup and teardown for the heavy-metal concert, staff had no chance to reconfigure the ice for hockey.

THE LEGENDS OF LANDOVER

Even with workers putting in 12 hours of overtime, removing the 1½ inches of blue ice - which obscured the hockey markings - caused a two hour delay. However, the cash-strapped Caps literally couldn't afford to cancel the game. New York's Derek Sanderson, still wearing an overcoat and street clothes, could be seen conferring on ice with an NHL official.

If fans and the visiting Rangers were antsy, that was nothing compared with Caps goalie Ron Low. "All I know is I'm hungry," Ron announced in the dressing room to a *Weekend Magazine* reporter. "I don't eat the day of a game and I'm starved." Low had further reason to grouse. The Capitals had made a coaching change that very afternoon. "I don't even know if I'm starting tonight," he fumed. "Who the hell knows anything around here?"

The only beneficiaries of the delay: new Caps coming from out of town. Chief scout Red Sullivan had been at home in suburban Toronto enjoying his morning paper when the team called and asked him to take over as coach. "When do you want me?" Red recalled of his conversation with G.M. Milt Schmidt. "He said, 'Tonight.' I had to drive through two blizzards to get to the Toronto airport."

Meanwhile, Blues winger Ace Bailey, traded with Stan Gilbertson for Dennis Dupere, was fighting those same snowstorms. He couldn't even find a flight out of St. Louis until 4 p.m., so he never could have arrived in time under normal circumstances. Aided by the delay, Ace not only dressed for the Caps, he contributed three assists!

Early on, it seemed like just another exercise in Capitals futility, as the Rangers led 4-1 midway through the game. Remarkably, the Caps scored twice before the end of the 2nd period, then poured in four scores on just seven shots in the 3rd, to win for their new coach, 7-4 (and improve their record to 5-45-5). Who cared if the game ended after midnight! When asked if all Capitals home games should be rescheduled for 10 p.m. starts, Sullivan laughed and said, "That might be a good idea." (*AP*)

✪ Network TV Blackout

NBC, the U.S. network partner of the NHL in the mid-70's, refused to show the Capitals. "On the grounds," wrote Dan Proudfoot in *Weekend Magazine*, "that hockey ratings were bad enough without the Caps."

Oh, NBC once scheduled a Capitals telecast, a Sunday afternoon home game against Pittsburgh. But it was removed, reported the *Pittsburgh Press*, "Because the Capitals would be an embarrassment to both the network and the NHL." Ouch. The shame is that the Caps played a competitive game, scoring twice in the 3rd period before falling, 3-2.

THE LEGENDS OF LANDOVER

✪ 19 Games, 17 Losses, 1 Ulcer: Red Sullivan, Coach (1975)

Pinned onto Caps' uniforms should have been a cigarette-box warning: *Coaching this team may be hazardous to your health*. Instead, Red Sullivan learned the hard way. "It's been rough," he told the *New York Times*. "I tried laying on them, I tried being nice to them. Nothing seems to work. I don't know. I just don't know."

Good-guy Red showed up as Washington rode a five game losing streak, pulverized 38-12 in goals. The Caps had hung tough, trailing by one goal late before dropping a February game at Pittsburgh. In the locker room, Sullivan invited the team back to his hotel room. Except Red wasn't there when the team arrived - just a bellboy wheeling in a cart. Ron Lalonde told the rest to *Sports Illustrated's* Alex Prewitt: "Sullivan walks in and says, 'Congratulations, boys. You tried hard. Unfortunately, we didn't make it.' He uncovers the cart, and it was cases of beer." Jack Lynch was appreciative. "For a coach to do that was unheard of. I thought it was so cool."

Taskmaster Red showed up at morning skates, trying to whip the less well-conditioned members of his team into shape. "Three guys got sick to their stomach in one practice," captain Doug Mohns recalled to the *Washington Post*. "One guy got cramps, another guy got so tired he fell to the ice and couldn't get up."

Ace Bailey provided Red a rare moment of levity. Losing 5-1 to the Flyers and listening to Sullivan's between-periods pep talk, the room was silent. But when Sullivan said, "They're not that good," Ace chimed in, "That's right, Red. But they're not that bad." Sullivan told the *Post's* Bob Fachet, "That broke up the room. I had to walk out, because it even got to me."

Less than two months after taking over from Jimmy Anderson, Sullivan watched Bobby Orr score another hat trick as Boston crushed the Caps, 8-2. Red's 15th consecutive loss behind the bench would be his *no mas* moment. Nelson Pyatt recalled the words Sullivan spoke inside the visitors' room at Boston Garden, as Red announced his departure. "You've got to admit gang, the only thing you guys set on fire this year was my stomach. I tried to kill it with beer, booze. It just went out, gang."

He made an urgent call to Capital Centre, according to the *Washington Star*. "Sullivan's ulcers got so bad that he pleaded to be returned to his job as head scout. 'You guys got to come up here', Sullivan begged Milt Schmidt. 'I can't do this anymore.'" Red told *AP*, "The old stomach is all buggered up. I'm not eating properly. I'm not sleeping properly." He then made a startling admission. "I can't do it anymore at my age." Sullivan, at least in calendar years, was only 45. His age in coach-years was much higher.

THE LEGENDS OF LANDOVER

General manager Milt Schmidt, age 57, agreed to coach the final seven games of the season. It was a mission of mercy. "Sully was in bad shape. I saw his hands shaking," Schmidt said to *The Hockey News*. "I didn't want him to have a breakdown. I didn't want to do that to a man." Besides, "If anyone suffers, it should be me. I have been sitting upstairs and cursing all year. I had to go down to the bench and try to do something myself." Noting the lack of talent on his roster, Schmidt mused, "If I was 10 years younger, I'd come back as a player, too."

✪ No Good Way To Say This

Content created by sports teams is like investor brochures; carefully constructed messaging, with skeletons deeply buried. So the Capitals showed refreshing candor in 1994, publishing an unvarnished article about their Shakespearian tragedy of a first season. Retired *Post* Caps beat man Robert Fachet - nobody's idea of a shill - was commissioned to write it.

Many of his most stinging memories involved the men leading their motley crew. Coach Jimmy Anderson announced, "I'm fed up with hockey" - before the season even started. And this: "I had seven lefthanded defensemen. What are you going to do with seven lefthanded defensemen?"

Anderson's replacement, Red Sullivan, once tossed a water bottle 100 feet across the Capital Centre ice to protest a call; another time, he pitched a phone across his hotel room. "It didn't make a bit of difference who played with whom or who was in goal," Sullivan said. "There just wasn't anything anyone could do." General manager and glutton for punishment Milt Schmidt subjected himself to a newspaper account of a 12-1 loss, until he threw down the sports section in disgust. He once asked a reporter, "Do you mind if I wring your neck to relieve the tension?"

✪ Yvon Labre, Heart of the Capitals (1974-81)

Perhaps you've stared at the "Labre 7" banner hanging from the Capital One Arena rafters and wondered, "Who's that?" Even those who know he was an Original Capital may wonder, "How did he get up there?" Bill Simmons of *espn.com* noted (obnoxiously) that the retired numbers in Capitals history included "some guy named Yvon Labre, who was apparently the team chef back in 1978."

Eh, no. Labre richly deserves his recognition, although achieved in unorthodox fashion. Virtually all number retirements fit one of two categories: superior achievement or tragic circumstances. Yvon didn't fit into either category, despite seven seasons of reliable defense on the Capitals blueline.

THE LEGENDS OF LANDOVER

"Thank God there are guys who don't use their abilities," Labre once observed, "so guys who don't have much – guys like me – can stay in this great game." He also prospered into middle age, despite repeatedly ignoring his body's pleas. Labre, describing one shoulder injury: "It sounded the way it does when you crack your knuckles."

So, what elevated Yvon to the rafters?

- "Labre wouldn't quit. There may be those with more talent, but few with as big a heart." (Russ White, *Washington Star*)

- "He threw every ounce of his heart into clearing creases and engaging in fights." (*legendsofhockey.net*)

- "The guts of a burglar, the heart of an elephant." (Robert Fachet, *Washington Post*)

The heart Labre exhibited wasn't just admirable; on the 1970's Caps, it was super-human. Wrote Fachet, "In sports history, few franchises match the Capitals for ineptitude. With very few exceptions – Labre is an obvious one – the Capitals were saddled with malcontents and fringe players. While teammates often went through the motions, Labre skated at full speed on every shift. Patrons at Capital Centre were guaranteed of a 100% effort from the man with the No. 7 and the 'C' on his chest."

Yvon first demonstrated his toughness early in life. After his father died in a mining accident, he supported three brothers as an electrician and played junior hockey. While injuries forced him to retire in 1981, Labre continued working in the Capitals front office through the rest of the 20th century.

If the reasons for Labre's sweater retirement were unusual, so was the ceremony itself. For one thing, Yvon wasn't informed about it beforehand. For another, he hadn't retired yet! As detailed by *sudbury.com*, the stated presentation was for Ron Weber, broadcasting his 500th game.

Owner Abe Pollin asked Labre to accompany him onto the ice. "He opened up his jacket and pulled out my jersey. That's when Pollin went on with a speech about how I was the heart of the team and then he retired my jersey right then and there," Labre recalled. Pollin addressed Yvon before 17,921 jammed in for the Caps-Bruins game. "This is in recognition for what you've done over the years for this franchise."

As *sudbury.com* pointed out, Labre then played the game in the jersey that had just been retired. "At the ceremony, I dedicated it to all the muckers, the workers, and the grinders, to all the guys who just won't get this opportunity. It was the best moment of my life."

THE LEGENDS OF LANDOVER

Purists (snobs) will argue this still doesn't merit a place in the rafters. Hogwash! Brian Costello of *The Hockey News* provides a more elegant rebuttal. "The franchise retired Labre's No. 7 because of his resilience and unconditional dedication on a bunch of dreadful teams. Honoring players and their numbers is all about the passionate feeling between the team, player and fans, not about Hall of Fame standards."

Labre earned immortality for *surviving* under conditions few athletes could have endured. Now, as generations of 21st century Caps followers look up at "Labre 7," I like to think it's also a tribute to the fans who bravely stuck with the team from its most humble of beginnings. Yvon, Washington's hockey ambassador, would surely agree.

✪ Bill Mikkelson Knew About Being In Deep Water (1974-75)

During the Capitals' woeful first season, defenseman Bill Mikkelson was on ice for 82 more even-strength goals by the opposition than by the Caps. That's "minus 82" in hockey speak, a mark that still stands. "For myself, I don't mind the record," Mikkelson told the *Toronto Sun*. "We were a minor league team playing in a run-and-gun era against some truly great teams."

Retired in Edmonton, Bill's children were occasionally teased about it. But the good-natured Mikkelson had a ready-made comeback. "I would always tell them to ask the kid who was bothering them what *their* father's NHL plus-minus had been." Here's more ammunition for your kids, Bill: Mario Lemieux was -35 as a rookie, and Wayne Gretzky was a minus player for seven of his last eight seasons. Phil Esposito once was minus 39, Gil Perreault -40, Reggie Leach -61. So there.

A third of a century after Mikkelson hung up his skates, the number remains a subject of fascination. So much so that *Sports Illustrated* dispatched writer Michael Farber to ask Bill about minus-82... *again*. "The number was earned," Bill said. "Still, it's a question of circumstances. Like when you're crossing the street and get hit by a car because the driver runs a red light. You're still hit, but it's not your fault."

Most people will consider that the money quote from the article. However, Mikkelson, a retired IBM executive whose son and daughter both went on to successful hockey careers, had an even more revealing observation about the record. "In the grand scheme of life it's so far down there you can't even see it. It's in the Marianas Trench."

Whoa. The Marianas Trench is the deepest spot under the ocean, near Guam, seven miles beneath the Western Pacific. If Bill Mikkelson is smart enough to pull up this obscure analogy - along with his business and family accomplishments - he deserves a +1.

THE LEGENDS OF LANDOVER

✪ Mike Marson (1974-78)

Even if you know Mike Marson was the NHL's second black player when he joined the Capitals in 1974 - and even if you know he was the first since Willie O'Ree's final game with the Bruins 13 years earlier - you have no idea how tough it was for this small-town Canadian teenager.

In Cecil Harris' book *Breaking The Ice*, Marson revealed, "I was called n****r and every other bad name in the book, along with stuff I didn't even know was in the book." Details of the gut-wrenching racism Marson had to combat both on and off the ice are examined in the *6th Shift, Pride & Prejudice & Pucks*, Page 140.

Undeniably, Marson was news because of his skin color. An October, 1974 front page photo in *The Hockey News* accompanied the cover line, "Mike Marson: First Black To Crack NHL In 15 Years." Bigots failed, or refused, to grasp that Marson detested special attention, which he didn't solicit. "I'm not a freak. I'm just another rookie trying to make it in the big leagues," Marson told the *N.Y. Times*. "What I don't need is someone pointing and saying, 'Hey look! There's a black hockey player.' If I was brought up because I was black, I wouldn't want to be here."

Mike's only self-inflicted wounds came from a knife and fork. "I came in (to training camp) at 222 pounds. Too much home cooking. Too much relaxing. But now I've cleaned up my act," he told the *Boston Globe* in November. "I'm through messing around. I'm down to 200 pounds." Thoughtful and patient beyond his years, Mike indulged a never-ending series of reporters in every road city, even to his hotel room. Jim Hrycuik once implored his roommate, "Mike, we have to get to bed for a couple of hours. We need our rest."

Remember, Marson was barely 19. "I found myself looking in awe at guys like (Bobby) Orr and (Phil) Esposito instead of playing my game," Marson admitted to the *Lowell Sun*. "Rookies have to battle these feelings, but it's not something you can control." He did muster gumption to challenge Orr in a one-on-one puck duel. "And then I must have caught him off balance," Marson told *CBC Radio*. "We go to the corner and he gives me a cuff on the back of my helmet. I turned to Yvon Labre and said, 'What was that for?' Yvon says, 'You don't come into Boston and do that to Bobby Orr.'"

Mike persevered, scoring 16 goals as a rookie. A high point came in a January 3-3 tie with those Bruins, when Marson outshined the Boston superstars. In front of 15,222 at Capital Centre, Marson scored to tie the game in the first period, scored again to tie the game in the second period, and in the last frame assisted on what would prove to be the game's final score. The third star on this night was Esposito, the second star was Orr, and the first star was Mike Marson.

THE LEGENDS OF LANDOVER

He ultimately played 196 NHL games. "I was, if I may say in a humble way, a trail blazer," Marson shared with *washingtoncaps.com* senior writer Mike Vogel. That blazed trail for future minority players led off the ice, too. "Players would say to me, 'Y'know, I never met a black guy before. I never had a friend who was a brother.' Traveling with the team, you're going places traditionally people of color don't go." Marson also can take pride in helping the NHL craft fines, penalties, and suspensions for on-ice slurs.

After retiring, Marson became a karate black belt, teaching "hockey fighting like it's a martial art. Marson's instruction wipes away the mystery of combat. Students know they can take a punch without collapsing because Marson has punched them, and they haven't collapsed." (*toromagazine.ca*) The same can be said about Mike Marson. On the eve of a 2016 Verizon Center ceremony in his honor, Mike told *colorofhockey.com*, "For me, it's interesting to have put away all the negative things that transpired so many years ago – 40 years ago – when the world was a totally different place."

✪ Chase Scene

Road Runners are sneaky fast. Ask Wile E. Coyote - or Mike Marson, who recalled the team's first trip into Montreal, "playing against Yvon Cournoyer, the 'Roadrunner,' one of the fastest people ever on skates. We went into the Montreal end, they started to work their magic coming up the ice, I shifted, he shifted again, I stayed with him. We hit the Washington blue line. Cournoyer suddenly cut left, I could not believe this superhuman activity where he was cutting across in front of me, staying onside, and being the first man in to get the puck. It was like, 'whoa,' could we back that up please, I gotta have another look at this." *(CBC Radio)*

✪ They Beat 'Em, Then They Joined 'Em

The Capitals spent a mid-November Saturday night getting drubbed in Pittsburgh, 8-1. The teams reconvened Sunday night in Landover, and the Caps were thumped again, 6-0. Sometime during the twin killings, Pens center Ron Lalonde's thoughts drifted to a member of the opposition. "Washington had selected my friend Yvon Labre in the expansion draft," Lalonde said to the *Canadian Press*. "I'm sitting on the bench looking over at Yvon and I'm saying, 'Geez that poor bugger. This is going to be a long season.' A few weeks later I was there with him in the dressing room."

Like Lalonde, defenseman Jack Lynch joined the Capitals mid-season (from Detroit). "I was shocked. Losing was so entrenched," Lynch said. "Guys were counting down how many games were left, how many practices, how many periods. They just really wanted to get the season over with." Off-ice promotional events proved no more successful, like Lynch's foray to a mall in Columbia, Md. "The kids thought we were air hockey players. That was a little bit of a shot to the ego."

THE LEGENDS OF LANDOVER

What frustrated baseball players occasionally resort to when they strike out, Jack did one night in celebration. He scored, and promptly broke his stick over his knee! "I almost broke it in my hands just by squeezing," said Jack, "and I'm not hardly that strong." The Caps no doubt aggravated his medical history of hypertension and anxiety. Oh, Jack was fine once the game started – "The initial contact relieves all the tension that has built up inside," he told the *Washington Star*. "I dread the hours before. I dread the drive to the arena and the wait inside the dressing room before we go out. Usually only the goaltenders go through an ordeal like mine."

✪ Even The Highlights Were Lowlights

This *UPI* excerpt recalls Ace Bailey in misery during a game in 1975: "The winger falls to his knees as his opponent skates around him and scores. Bailey brings his stick above his head and slams it to the ice in a picture of absolute frustration. The end of the stick splinters into a half dozen pieces and Ace Bailey looks at it sadly and shakes his head."

In the article, the *UPI* reporter also mentions where he saw this scene play out: the Capitals' 1974-75 promotional highlight film! How bad does a team have to be to include abject despair in its marketing? On a cheerier note, "In their highlight film, the Capitals score 10 goals, while allowing only two." (*Washington Star*)

✪ Greg Joly (1974-76)

Picture this: you're a high school valedictorian. A tech startup hires you. The boss compares you to Bill Gates, your product competes against Google and Apple, and oh by the way, they expect to see immediate results. Now you can imagine what faced Greg Joly, first overall draft pick in 1974, and first player ever signed by the expansion Capitals. G.M. Milt Schmidt lifted expectations for his rookie to stratospheric heights. "He's the kind of defenseman everyone has been looking for since Bobby Orr." (*AP*) The same Bobby Orr who is among the top five NHL players *ever*?

Joly was flush with promise, plus a $400,000, five year contract. "This is a great opportunity to play for a new team," he said. "It's better than being with one of the older, established clubs." Ah, naïve optimism. That contract turned the number 3 on Joly's sweater into a dollar-sign shaped bulls-eye. When he tore an Achilles tendon at 1974 training camp, one Canadian newspaper headline bleated, "Rich Kid Hurt." The $400K deal caused physical abuse from jealous opponents to sometimes border on the vicious. Even Greg's own coach, Jimmy Anderson, piled on. "Joly is playing lousy. Maybe it's the big money, press notices, and trying too hard to live up to expectations. If I could take half his bonus money away, I would do it." (*San Mateo Times, Philadelphia Daily News, SI*)

THE LEGENDS OF LANDOVER

Neither coach nor some Caps cared that Joly was all of 20; one play summed up his season: "Joly corralled a loose puck and tried to backhand it around the boards. Instead, he picked the top corner past his own goalie. Teammates applauded. Best shot he made all year." *(Tor. Globe & Mail)*

What's worse, Joly could never outrun a black cloud of injuries. Following the training camp Achilles issue, "We found he had two impacted wisdom teeth," explained Schmidt. "The poison ran through his system. We had them removed and now he's playing better." Later, a knee injury limited him to 44 games. A broken ankle reduced Joly's second season to 54 games.

The weight of 126 team losses in two years also took a toll. Plus, new coach Tom McVie's system didn't cater to puck-rushing defensemen. "He has a lot of bad habits that are holding him back," said McVie. The Capitals exiled Joly to the minors to start '76-'77, until a trade to Detroit for veteran d-man Bryan Watson. Parting jabs at Joly could be read into praise for Watson. "Bryan is an excellent team player," said G.M. Max McNab, lauding his "experience and aggressiveness." *(UPI)*

Years later, Greg assessed his time in D.C. "Washington didn't have a team that should have played in the National Hockey League," Joly said to the *AP*. "In my case, I don't think it was fair or realistic to think that any one person was going to push the Caps into a competitive situation. But I'm not blaming them at all, because in all fairness to them I did not play very good. It's an honor to go number one, but there are no guarantees."

✪ Out Of Washington's Price Range

Would you believe the '74 Capitals pursued *another* "Next Bobby Orr"? Teenage sensation Pat Price, like Joly, was saddled with the Orr comparison. The two new expansion teams were exclusively allowed to sign underage juniors, so naturally Price was coveted by the Caps.

Unfortunately, they weren't alone, causing a surreal bidding war inside a Calgary hotel. In one room, Caps G.M. Milt Schmidt; in a second, G.M. Joe Crozier of the WHA's Vancouver Blazers; and in room three, the 19 year old defenseman and his family. Price's agent played the two general managers against each other, then informed the family as offers escalated. "It was crazy," Price recalled. "It was like, 'What kind of car do you want?' 'A Ferrari? We'll get you a Ferrari.' 'Clothes? Stereo? No problem.'"

Atypical for cash-strapped WHA clubs, Vancouver was owned by a multi-millionaire, car dealer Jimmy Pattison. When the bidding reached levels that would make a Sotheby's auctioneer blush, Schmidt bowed out. Price signed for the princely sum of $1.3 million over five years, plus a $250,000 bonus. Ogling the bonus check, Price's dad joked, "There's something wrong with this. There's too many zeros." As for the rich teen, "I wanted to take everyone out to dinner, but there was no place to cash the check."

THE LEGENDS OF LANDOVER

The expansion Caps could have used Price's presence on their blueline. The kicker is, he only played one season in Vancouver. (When the Blazers flopped at the box office, owner Pattison enlisted church volunteers to work the concession stands and play the organ!) While Pat pieced together a 13 year career with six NHL teams, he never fully recovered from the frenzy of sky-high expectations. Price admitted, "It was too much, too soon. I didn't have enough guidance." Somewhere, Greg Joly shouted, "Amen, brother."

(Pat Price quotes from the book, The Rebel League by Ed Willes)

✪ Custard's Last Stand

Abe and Irene Pollin's NBA squad, the Bullets, played almost as well as the Caps did poorly in 1974-75, winning 60 games and making it to the Finals. As Irene told *Sports Illustrated*, the hockey team didn't do their waistlines any favors. "It was a good night if both teams won. It was a bad night if both teams lost. It was a medium night if it was one and one. Then we would go get frozen custard on the way home to cheer us up. We ate a lot of frozen custard that year."

✪ John Adams (1974-75)

The Caps missed a patriotic marketing opportunity with goalie John Adams. He's known as the only Capital to share a name with our 2nd President. "We've looked everywhere for a goalie named Tom Jefferson," Assistant G.M. Lefty McFadden once joked to the *Washington Star*. "Adams was the best we could do." (Actually, Adams was *best* known for getting his name engraved on the Stanley Cup with the 1970 Bruins, although he didn't play his first NHL game until two years later!)

During the 1974-75 season, Adams played eight games when both Ron Low and Michel Belhumeur were injured, or needed a night off. Yet the Caps never took advantage when John stood between the pipes - perhaps holding a "Founding Fathers" night, and, say, handing out powdered wigs.

One of those games could have been December 3, 1974, when Adams faced sniper Rick Martin and his high-flying Sabres. John had precious little time to prepare; with Low (broken toe) and Belhumeur (flu) unavailable, Adams was told at noon to race up I-95 from his Richmond farm team. John's reaction: "Oh no. I know who they're playing tonight." Afterward, Adams said, "I had Martin's number for about 40 minutes – unfortunately, it's a 60 minute game."

Well, yeah. By the time Martin's number "was gotten," he had scored a hat trick in the game's first 15 minutes. That's not to imply that John played poorly. He made 41 saves in a 5-3 loss, and Martin said later, "Adams made some terrific saves." *(Quotes from AP, Hockey News)*

THE LEGENDS OF LANDOVER

✪ Michel Belhumeur (1974-75)

Whenever hockey fans bring up the name Michel Belhumeur, the talk naturally turns to the team that hung the goaltender out to dry. The name of that team, of course, is the... Philadelphia Flyers. Wait... what? The expansion Capitals of 1974-75 were the ones who left Belhumeur, sometimes literally, defenseless. His winless season - 24 losses, 3 ties, 8 no-decisions, zero victories - is by far the most games ever played in a season by a goalie without a "W".

The closest he came was early the second season in Oakland, leading 3-2 until the Golden Seals dribbled in a power play goal with 73 seconds left. Coach Milt Schmidt said the ref had called a "pantywaist" penalty that denied Michel his first Caps win.

Even on the night when Belhumeur stopped two penalty shots by the Blackhawks *in the same game*, and made 37 other saves, he still lost, 3-2. From the *UPI* story: "Chicago's Jim Pappin missed the first penalty shot in the first period after Murray Anderson gloved the puck in the crease. Stan Mikita missed the second penalty shot late in the third after Belhumeur threw his stick at a loose puck."

The stop on Pappin was especially noteworthy. A year earlier, Pappin won a shootout-style competition called "NHL Showdown" on Canadian TV, so he obviously was an expert at one-on-one confrontations. *The Hockey News* described admiration from the home dressing room. "A couple of the Black Hawks said they were willing to take Belhumeur out for an evening on Rush Street." Michel's postgame wish, as quoted by *The Sporting News*, was more modest. "I hope I never see another penalty shot."

Were Caps opponents allowed to shoot multiple pucks? Michel shares (with Olaf Kolzig in 2000) a positive single-game team record that no Caps goalie wants to top: 52 saves in a regulation 60 minutes against the Blues on Pearl Harbor Day. In a 1975 preseason game against Toronto, he faced 29 shots in the third period, and stopped them all! At his stall following a heroic 42-save effort in Atlanta – only three got past him – "Belhumeur kept mumbling numbers. '45, 42, 59, 43, 45, 60, 42.' He chanted the litany of the nightly barrage of shots. 'How long has this got to go on?'" *(Wash. Star)*

As the joke goes, he could have sued the Caps for lack of support. He actually did take legal action against the Flyers, and it was no joke. Belhumeur was a farmhand, called up during Philly's 1974 playoff run. Since he didn't play, the Cup champs didn't pay his $19,000 playoff share. Belhumeur sued for $1 million, and according to Jerry Lindquist of *richmond.com*, the matter was settled out of court. For the record, Michel won nine games in goal for the Flyers in the '72-'73 season, so he did taste the NHL thrill of victory there... if not the thrill of appreciation.

THE LEGENDS OF LANDOVER

✪ Ron Low (1974-77)

No netminder ever deserved the "warrior" label more than Ron Low, D.C.'s number one goalie for their first three seasons. Let's get past the ugly won-loss record, 30-94-9, because Ron deserved better. A truer guage of Low's ability is how his goals-against average, 5.45 in each of those first two woeful seasons, plunged to 3.87 backstopping a competitive Caps team in Year Three. A website came up with a formula to determine the goalies since 1955 with the hardest job. Ron Low topped the list. (*brodeurisafraud.blogspot.com*).

Picked by the Capitals in 1974's expansion draft, Low had told the *Toronto Globe & Mail* he would enjoy playing for Caps coach Jimmy Anderson. Said Ron, "Hockey players aren't worked hard enough these days." Hoo boy. This turned out to be the textbook definition of "Be careful what you wish for." The never-ending barrage of shots and lopsided scores took an emotional as well as physical toll. Anderson, quoted by *espn.com*: "I'd see Low with tears in his eyes after games."

"It was a pretty scary hockey club, not a whole lot you remember as great," Low recalled to *nhl.com*. "You look at things that took place, 13 goals at Buffalo against and four of them by your own defensemen. You could make a pretty good movie out of it." (Don't tell Ron it was actually 14 goals.) One night in Montreal, Low surrendered three first period scores - and drew nothing but raves from Canadiens' great Ken Dryden. "I felt real bad for Low," Ken told the *Montreal Gazette*. "He did everything a goalie can be asked to do. He made some great saves. He was always in position."

We wouldn't be surprised if Low laid out one set of street clothes for wearing to the rink, and a second, one size smaller, for after the game. In that first-ever regular season start in New York, Ron lost 14 pounds between puck drop and final horn. A blowout home loss to the Flyers in 1975 cost him 13 pounds. It's a wonder he didn't evaporate completely.

A *Sporting News* profile started this way: "He slumped at his locker, exhausted. There was an angry bruise on his forehead, another under his eye. Sweat trickled down his face onto his black mustache. Ron Low had twisted himself into a human pretzel preserving a tenuous one-goal shutout until, as expected, the Capitals had yielded to the Bruins."

Speaking of Boston, Low was reportedly headed there in a deal for winger Terry O'Reilly - except he wasn't. Longtime radio host Phil Wood knows how this one got started. One night, talk in the Capital Centre press room turned to which opposing players might help the home team, and what it would take to obtain them. Other media members overheard the names Low and O'Reilly, and casual speculation morphed into a legitimate trade rumor.

THE LEGENDS OF LANDOVER

Wood writes at *masnsports.com*, "It reached a point where O'Reilly pleaded with the Bruins not to send him to Washington, and Low's wife asked the Caps if she should prepare to move." Feeling financially unappreciated, Low did move in 1977, signing with Detroit. Not until 1980 did Ron, now a Nordique, play his first game as a visitor at Capital Centre. A triumphant return, stopping 39 shots to preserve a 1-1 tie. Afterward, he recalled Washington as "the three best years of my life." Not that his competitive fire didn't still burn; with the Oilers the following season, Low insisted on playing against the Caps despite a stomach flu. Why? Another ex-Cap, coach Bryan Watson, told the *Edmonton Journal*, "He hates Washington."

On nights that Ron backstopped a Caps victory, he was good for a memorable line. After the first win in team history: "I'm celebrating. I think I might drink a couple now. A couple of cases, that is." On recording the team's first-ever shutout: "It wasn't that I felt so good - I just felt like I do when I don't feel lousy." (*Quotes from the Washington Star*)

Ron had a stylistic triumph with Washington, too - his Bicentennial goalie mask is considered one of the fraternity's finest. The Hockey Hall of Fame in Toronto featured the mask in its goalie exhibit. Ron, if you can walk into a hall of fame and see your equipment behind glass, you're a success.

✪ First Road Win - March 28, 1975 at Oakland

This unforgettable night unfolded while most Washingtonians were fast asleep. The opening faceoff in Oakland didn't drop until after 11 p.m. D.C. time. and though the contest was televised, Caps fans had no reason to believe bleary-eyed viewing would be rewarded. The Capitals had lost all 37 of their previous road games, after all. But, as Tony and Maria sang in *West Side Story*, "Tonight, tonight, won't be just any night."

Defense carried the Caps, limiting California to nine shots over the first two periods, 20 shots in total. Washington's penalty kill erased all five Seals power plays, and winning goalie Ron Low noted to the *Washington Post*, "The defense covered and the wings came back, that was the difference." On offense, quick strikes by Doug Mohns and Ron Anderson in the first 4:12 built a 2-0 lead. Although the Seals battled back to tie at 3-3, Nelson Pyatt put Washington ahead for good at 6:31 of the 3rd period, and added an empty-netter at 19:44. The *Fremont Argus* described fans at Oakland Coliseum as "disgruntled, frustrated, booing."

The Capitals, after five months of futility, had finally won a road game! "It's like winning the Stanley Cup," coach and general manager Milt Schmidt told the *Oakland Tribune*. The win also snapped a 17-game Washington losing streak. "You started to feel like you might never win another hockey game," recalled goalie Low. "You started to think, 'Maybe it's just not possible.' It felt like forever. That's why there was so much jubilation in our room."

THE LEGENDS OF LANDOVER

The real fun started after the 5-3 victory, as Ron Lalonde described to *washingtoncaps.com*. "There weren't too many fans in Oakland," noted Lalonde. Indeed, only 3,933 witnessed history. "We came into the locker room, and there was a big green garbage can. We pretended that was our Stanley Cup. We signed it and skated back out onto the ice. All the fans had left for the night. That can with our signatures on it was there for years afterward. We had to have a little bit of fun that long season."

For once, the anguish was in the opponent's locker room. "It is a deep hurt feeling to lose to this team," said Seals coach Bill McCreary. "They don't have the personnel we have and they do not have a tough team." Reserve goalie Gary Simmons was shocked. "Can you really believe this? We're again in the history books. We are the first team to lose at home to them. It has to be one of the low points of the season for us."

Caps center Stan Gilbertson, a former Seal, looked forward to reminding his former mates all summer. "The team knew I lived in the area, so they came up with the win for me," he joked. "I'll see some of the (Seals) players every now and then. It sure is going to be nice to talk about this game."

✪ Tommy Williams (1974-76)

Tommy Williams, who won a gold medal with the 1960 U.S. Olympic team, knew how to celebrate. When a game ended, the party was just starting. While in flight, he was known to wield shaving cream to decorate the hair of sleeping teammates. Or take his nickname, "Bomber" – earned for telling a customs agent he was carrying a bomb (a remark that got him arrested). "He was a wild man off the ice," recalled a teammate.

Williams didn't need to be airborne to remind teammates of a stunt plane, with his less-than-disciplined routes on the ice. As Ron Lalonde told *Sports Illustrated*, "We used to joke about his flight patterns. Nobody knew what he was going to do. He was skating around, and hopefully someone found him with the puck." The winger did fly right enough times to lead the team in goals with 22 and points with 58.

On a 1974-75 Capitals team that lost 67 times, most of the celebrating took place away from the rink. "We drank better than we played," Williams told the *Washington Star*. "The more we played, the more we wanted to drink."

So when the Capitals beat the Seals in Oakland for their first road win – after 37 straight losses – naturally it was Bomber who led the cheers. Teammate Yvon Labre described the memory to *washingtoncaps.com*. "Tommy got hold of a trash can, and we paraded it around the locker room like the Stanley Cup," said Labre. All the players signed it, and it became known in lore as the "Stanley Can."

THE LEGENDS OF LANDOVER

The story of the Caps' 5-3 win gets even better. Tommy's younger brother, Butch, played for the Seals, and was upset at the result. "It's so (expletive) losing to a team like that." Later, he reflected on something more personal than the final score. "Our dad was listening to the game," Butch recalled. "I was the first star, with one goal and two assists. Tommy (two assists) was the second star. After that we called up our father. He was beside himself that his two sons were first and second star of an NHL game. That was something else." Truly a night for the Williams family worth celebrating.

(Quotes on pages 35-37 from *vintageminnesotahockey.com*, *Oakland Tribune*, *bleacherreport.com*, Brad Kurtzberg's book, *Shorthanded*.)

✪ Barbarians At The Gate

Think you know about Planes, Trains, and Automobiles? The fictional Steve Martin-John Candy comedy can't hold a candle to the real-life road travails of the '74-'75 Capitals. The real craziness during a season, as you'll discover, takes place away from the rink. The following follies are excerpted from Robert Fachet's reporting in the *Washington Post*.

• Recently-hired coach Red Sullivan returned from a road game to his Maryland hotel room. His phone messages weren't there; his clothes weren't there; in fact, the room wasn't there – the hotel had forgotten to extend his reservation. Adding to the you-can't-make-this-stuff-up, the visitor occupying Red's room was the coach of that night's opponent, the Kansas City Scouts. Red got the last laugh, as the Caps beat K.C., 3-0.

• Heading home from Canada during a losing streak, border guards almost denied Sullivan re-entry to the U.S. because he couldn't produce a green card. "'I see they let you go,' a reporter commented as Sullivan, coatless and snow-covered, returned to the bus. 'Yes, darn it,' Sullivan replied." No wonder ulcers forced Red to resign 19 games into his tenure.

With so much time to waste, players made airport terminals a frequent stage for goofiness and hijinks, although some of the jokes were on them.

• Jack Egers would pretend to walk a dog through the terminal.

• As travelers bent down to pick up a dollar bill, players would snatch it out of their grasp with a hidden string; one of their victims was a nun.

• Assistant G.M. Lefty McFadden accidentally entered a women's restroom, then wondered where the urinals were.

• As Bruce Cowick pushed a healthy teammate in a wheelchair to their departure gate, an agent remarked, "Your whole team needs help."

THE LEGENDS OF LANDOVER

- A wee-hours charter plane was ready and waiting steps away at the St. Louis airport, only the Caps couldn't reach it - the doors to the jetway were locked. Players convinced coach Sullivan not to forcibly crash through the doors. Instead, they waited 20 minutes for airport personnel to find a key.

- Trying to fly from Los Angeles to Oakland, the Caps were foiled by fog at LAX. Engaging Plan B, the team bused to Burbank, hoping to catch a flight from the airport there. Around 1:30 a.m., a realization set in - the airport was empty. The traveling party trudged back to their L.A. hotel, making it to Oakland the next morning. Par for the course, after the Seals' game, the bus to their departing flight was late arriving. A frustrated Pete Laframboise said, "The next itinerary will be multiple choice."

✪ Excedrin Headache Number 1974-75

William Barry Furlong in 1976 co-authored a book titled, "More Than Two Aspirin: Hope for Your Headache Problem." It cannot be a coincidence that a year earlier, the *Washington Post* assigned Furlong to join an ill-fated Capitals road trip.

The ill-fated part wasn't even the games, lopsided losses of 8-3 in Detroit and 10-2 in Montreal. I've culled a few of the juicy bits from Furlong's reporting; I heartily urge you to find and enjoy his full two-part series, in the April 6 and 7, 1975 sports sections of the *Post*.

Ominously, the road trip begins on April Fool's Day, and several players miss the bus from Capital Centre to National Airport. Bad luck boards the commercial flight to Detroit, as the airline misplaces Michel Belhumeur's bag containing his wallet and visa.

Having lost to the Wings, the Caps depart through a raging snowstorm. Detroit's airport is open, but a blizzard has shut the airport at their intended destination, Montreal. Time to juggle options. Wait for a flight out of Detroit the next morning? No, Motown might be snowed in by then. Travel closer, say Rochester, N.Y., and figure it out from there? No, won't work. G.M. Milt Schmidt decides to book 25 seats on a train from nearby Windsor, Ontario to Montreal – a 10 hour ride. To kill time, players stuff snow down teammates' pants.

Tommy Williams and Ace Bailey smuggle buckets of fried chicken aboard the train. They don't share. Later, they smoke cigars in the men's room, making entry difficult for other passengers. Williams playfully tells Schmidt, "I'm only going to play one more year. You're not going to get me for longer than that." Schmidt's mock terror: "I won't be able to sleep." When the train passes Yvon Labre's off-season home, he considers jumping off.

THE LEGENDS OF LANDOVER

The Capitals arrive in Montreal to a dispute between the city and snow plow operators. Ten inches of snow (and rising) clog the streets. With roads impassable, the Caps head for the subway, then finally arrive at their hotel. Once there, players rescue a woman trapped inside a hotel elevator. Other players, at midnight, are seen scampering down hallways, naked. Bob Gryp isn't one of them. Feeling sick, Gryp wanders the corridors wrapped in a gold bedspread. Next morning, Bailey and Ron Lalonde race to avoid a fine for oversleeping. Hitchhiking through the snowstorm, they catch a ride to practice in a police car, and barely arrive on time.

The game at the Forum ends; time to go home. But how? The scheduled late-night charter? No, a commercial flight would save $3,000. A player complains, "The next charter we get will be a balloon." But a flight the next morning is risky; if snow delays departure, the Caps will miss their home game that evening. Bus to Boston, fly home from there? No, the players would mutiny.

Fortunately, the morning commercial flight from Montreal takes off on time. The only delay is the departure of the bus from the hotel - Bill Lesuk has to return to his room to retrieve his teeth.

✪ First (Season) Impressions

At a team reunion in 1989, Greg Joly joked to owner Abe Pollin, "Don't worry. This isn't a nightmare." Back in '74, they *wished* it was only a bad dream. It's easy to forget that even spectacularly awful teams are made up of proud athletes and managers, who had achieved success in their careers. In that light, these collected quotes from the 1974-75 season are sad, funny, and especially, poignant.

G.M. Milt Schmidt, describing his roster:
"I thought it would be worthwhile to start a franchise. But just high school kids is all I had."

More Milt:
"I don't walk across water. I'm not Houdini."

Asst. G.M. Lefty McFadden on office decorum:
"We've become grouches. Me or Miltie walk in, someone asks, 'How are you?' and we say 'Terrible, just terrible.'"

Goalie Ron Low, defining success:
"Having a good game is a big challenge. And here, less than five goals is a good game."

Goalie Michel Belhumeur, after another loss:
"I don't know what we're doing wrong, but we're doing something wrong."

THE LEGENDS OF LANDOVER

Winger Mike Marson, on his slow start:
"I didn't give the fans in other cities any reason to even boo me."

Winger Dave Kryskow, preparing for the onslaught:
"We were happy to keep it down to a touchdown."

Defenseman Bill Mikkelson:
"It wasn't who was going to win, but by how much."

Washington Post, Feb. 24, 1975, on 3 losses in 3 nights:
"The Capitals wound up the most totally lost weekend in NHL history by dropping a 7-2 decision to St. Louis. The non-contest followed a 9-4 loss to Buffalo Friday and a 10-3 shellacking at Chicago Saturday."

Fan banner at Buffalo's Memorial Auditorium:
"The Tokyo Geishas could beat the Caps."

Defenseman Yvon Labre, distraught following a loss:
"Oh my God! How do I keep going?"

Defenseman Doug Mohns:
"Even though it was hopeless, we had to keep trying. But I'd be lying if I said it was easy to go to the games."

More Mohns, a 20-year NHL vet:
"I guess I played too long. This is it. I'm through."

Winger Denis Dupere, avoiding the Zamboni:
"If that thing had hit me, it would have been the best thing that happened to me all season."

Winger Mike Bloom, on Dupere's family attending a game in Montreal:
"Dupere says, 'I come into the dressing room, my mother's crying, my sister's crying, everybody's crying.'"

Coach Jimmy Anderson, after a hard-fought defeat:
"I went outside the arena and just screamed into the night."

Red Sullivan, who replaced Anderson as coach:
"I hope I can be behind the bench for 10 years." (Red lasted 19 games)

Goalie Ron Low, before the final game, asked about his best memory:
"Tomorrow night, when this damn thing ends."

Low, on retreating to his Manitoba farm in the off-season:
"The hogs didn't smell too great, but they didn't take any shots at me."
(Washington allowed a league-high 3,064 shots.)

THE LEGENDS OF LANDOVER

When Caps players routinely arrived late for morning practice, the team moved the starting time an hour later! The last quotes address this attitude.

G.M. Milt Schmidt, who replaced Sullivan as coach:
"I need the players more than they need me."

Winger Bill Lesuk:
"Some players would take the games a lot more seriously than others"

Center Ron Lalonde, observing the Capital Centre recreation room:
"There were more guys injured then playing. It was like a country club."

Defenseman Yvon Labre, echoing that sentiment:
"You wondered if all of them had their hearts in it."

Center Jim Hrycuik, wishing management had cracked down harder:
"We weren't a serious hockey team. We were a bit of a party team."

✪ The Legacy Of '74

The Capitals had two reasons to celebrate in Landover on April 6, 1975. They beat Pittsburgh 8-4, behind four goals by Stan Gilbertson. More importantly, their maiden season was finally over. "One player blended a liter of rum and a can of Coke soon after the final game," wrote Ken Denlinger in the *Washington Post*.

The carnage was numerically unmatched. "There have been 1,506 team seasons in the NHL over the past 100 years," *espn.com* calculated in 2017. The 1974-75 Capitals earned 13% of possible standings points, "which ranks them at No. 1,506." *UPI's* Milton Richman said if the first-year Caps had a number, it would be 179. "That's the total number of major league teams in operation now - baseball, football, basketball, hockey, soccer and tennis - and any way you stack them, the Capitals are the worst team in professional sports."

Reviews from sports media were merciless. Absorbing a late-season beatdown, outshot 43-19 and outscored 5-1 by the Kings, the *L.A. Times* described how "the Capitals kept falling down, losing their sticks." Columnist Jim Murray wisecracked, "The Capitals may be a good team when they learn how to skate."

Murray's ironically named *Times* colleague Don Merry smeared an entire region as well as a hockey team, calling the Capitals, "The National Hockey League's answer to Appalachia." The *Philadelphia Inquirer* went with, "(Caps) Defense could apply for federal aid as a disaster area." A Montreal paper grabbed low hanging fruit, "Washington's worst disgrace since Watergate." Also trying too hard, Dan Donovan of the *Pittsburgh Press*, who wrote, "Washington had as much punch as Goldie Hawn." (?)

THE LEGENDS OF LANDOVER

Cheap shots didn't really increase the hurt, because it wasn't possible for the organization to hurt any worse. "I used to keep very calm in front of the coaches and fans," admitted general manager Milt Schmidt. "But all the time inside I was eating my heart out."

Had the NHL made a colossal blunder? None other than the Capitals' first coach thought so. "We've expanded the league too fast," Jimmy Anderson told the *Lowell Sun*. "It will take at least three or four years for the kids on our team to even compete."

Defenseman Jack Lynch, traded to Washington midway through that first season, laid blame on the expansion draft. "A joke" was Lynch's description in the *Chicago Tribune*. "The players who were exposed for the draft back then, you were getting access to the 17th, 18th and 19th player on the existing teams' rosters." Legendary sportswriter Red Fisher, in the *Montreal Star*, validated Lynch's verdict. "I can't see where Washington and Kansas City came close to getting what the 1967 (expansion) teams received."

Don't accuse Jack Lynch of sour grapes, either; he said on the *Can't Win 4 Losing* podcast, "I really mean this. I was playing in the best league in the world. You know how many Canadians, how many Americans would love to have done what I did for eight years? Even the years of bad losing, there's not a person out there that's a hockey person that wouldn't have traded places with me in a minute."

✪ Winning Despite Losing

Late in the season, goalie Ron Low recalled, "We were in Buffalo, and it was a beautiful, warm spring day, like 54 outside. They've got the shot clock up beside the temperature gauge. Yvon Labre came by and said, 'Jesus Christ, Ronnie, if we give them one more it'll be higher than the temperature outside.'" Four decades later, Low and Labre, two of the true warriors from that first Capitals campaign, were able to look back through the perspective of time.

Low: "What did I learn from that season? Perseverance. You can feel sorry for yourself all you want, but really, it's not live and die. It's not like being a farmer and not have it rain for five months, and you know at the end of it all your crop is not going to be there. This is games. We're entertainers. We were piss poor entertainers that year. But that's where it ends.

"There were times I wanted to leave the building and drive home to Manitoba. But you always figured things would be better the next day. There was always that next game, that next chance. That's what got us through it, I think. In the end, people looked at you and said, 'If you could deal with that, you can probably deal with anything.'

THE LEGENDS OF LANDOVER

"There were a lot of really good people on the team. Otherwise we would've all gone insane. I'm not too sure we didn't anyway." Having retained his sanity, Low fulfilled a personal goal with Edmonton in 1981-82, by keeping a daily diary of the season. "I first thought about doing it when I was playing for Washington. Can you imagine the X-rated things I would have written about that team?"

Labre: "It's all in my memory in a dark place. My father's death, the bad years we had. Maybe that's what kept me going for so long. If you don't have a sense of humor, you're going to die. Losing is hard, but it does help you. In business, you get turned down nine out of 10 times, then all of a sudden it works. That's what I learned." He also learned two invaluable words for avoiding questions about '74-'75: "Total amnesia."

(Quotes on pages 39-41, 43 from *San Mateo Times, washingtoncaps.com, New York Times, Washington Post, Washington Star, Baltimore Sun, AP, McClatchy News, CJCL Radio, Montreal Gazette, Toronto Globe & Mail, Sporting News, Sports Illustrated, In The Crease by Dick Irvin, King Kaufman's podcast: Can't Win 4 Losing, Bill Speros and Adrian Dater at bleacherreport.com, Changing The Game by Stephen Laroche, The Hockey News, 20th Anniversary Program*)

THE LEGENDS OF LANDOVER

LOSS LEADERS

TERRIBLE TWOS

"Now you know how Custer felt." Coach Tom McVie, after the Caps were outshot 55-14 in a second-season loss at Chicago. With their car-wreck of a freshman season behind them, the Caps couldn't suffer a sophomore slump. But they tried.

✪ Beer League

The expansion Capitals drowned their frequent sorrows a six-pack at a time. "One player claimed the Caps had the five best beer drinkers in the league." Linemates Stan Gilbertson, Tommy Williams and Ace Bailey were dubbed the Brew Line, a moniker well deserved; "Bailey holds an unofficial record for breaking chairs at a watering hole near Capital Centre and was awarded a special chair of his own." As games became blowouts, the beer was known to flow "even between periods." A Canadian scribe observed multiple Caps ordering Bloody Marys before noon at an airport bar.
(*Items in quotes from New York Times, The Hockey News, Wash. Star*)

See a sudsy pattern? Coach-G.M. Milt Schmidt did, instituting a no-alcohol policy at the Caps' second-season training camp in 1975. Gilbertson and Jack Egers, however, instituted a disregard-Milt-Schmidt policy. The duo ran a nightly speakeasy in their hotel room after practice, featuring an ice-filled bathtub chilling bottles and cans of beer.

"When confronted by Schmidt," reported *AP*, "they made disparaging remarks in a shouting match." As a remorseful Egers recounted, "We had a few too many beers and we weren't using our heads. Stan and I went down to Milt's room. We forced his door open and that's when we started yelling at each other. We're very sorry about doing that." Schmidt suspended the pair of Prohibition violators. "They ran all over (former coach) Jimmy Anderson last year and one thing is for sure – they won't run all over Milt Schmidt," said Milt Schmidt. "I'm not afraid of these kids."

Schmidt's efforts to quickly unload the pair through trades failed, but their days in D.C. were numbered. Egers lasted 12 games before being released; Gilbertson was shipped to Pittsburgh in December. In 31 games, Stan was on a point-a-game pace (27), and a minus-a-game pace (-25).

✪ Beer League 2

Those who do not learn from Capitals history are doomed to... incur fines. A year after the Gilbertson-Egers incident, coach Tom McVie instituted a curfew at 1976 training camp. Despite that, Bob Sirois and Guy Charron decided to watch Friday turn into Saturday at a local watering hole. They weren't the only ones, just the only ones who got caught when the coach walked in - teammates fled to the kitchen or hid under tables. "It was like Mardi Gras," said McVie. "I was like a gunslinger in a western movie. When I walked into the place, the music stopped." (*Brandon Sun*)

THE LEGENDS OF LANDOVER

✪ Playing To Their Potential

Back to the '75-'76 season, the Caps' high hopes put ants and their rubber tree plants to shame. Coming off a 67-loss season, the team's media packets included Stanley Cup press passes. The *Annapolis Capital* called it "the height of optimism." The P.R. staff should have listened more closely to G.M. Milt Schmidt, who wryly predicted, "If we don't get too many injuries, if we play to our potential, we can finish last." *(Ottawa Journal)*

To secure immediate help, Schmidt exchanged 1975's 1st overall pick in the offseason for 4th-line Flyers center Bill Clement. Bill instantly became a first-liner in D.C., not to mention captain. The Caps also got Philly's first-round pick, 18th overall, which they used on a forward named Alex Forsyth. Red flags were raised when Forsyth announced at his first media session, "Skating is not one of my finer points." Uh-oh.

Sent to the Caps' AHL team in Richmond, Forsyth was buried on the Robins' bench, shattering his confidence. Signed by Schmidt to a multi-year contract, Forsyth would play just one NHL game. On November 12, 1976, Secretary of State Henry Kissinger showed up at Capital Centre, and so did Alex, for a 5-4 loss to Chicago. Two years later he hung up his skates, went home to Kingston, Ontario, and began a more successful career as a police officer. (*originalhockeyhalloffame.com, Washington Post*)

This trade sometimes gets brought up on amateur draft day, and how the Flyers got the sweet end of the deal - drafting Mel Bridgman, a center who amassed 701 points in a 14-year NHL career. At the time, Philly writer Bill Fleischman called it "a deal that left many hockey observers shaking their heads in disbelief." *Sports Illustrated*, though, pointed out the deal's x-factor: the WHA was always lurking with big-money offers. "Washington realized it probably would have been unable to sign the NHL's No. 1 amateur draft choice, so the Capitals wisely traded the pick."

Decades later, *nhl.com* weighed in with a far harsher review. "The trade set the Caps' franchise back several seasons and stands as one of the worst decisions in the team's early history." That's a wildly overblown hot take, especially in a diluted draft. Again, top prospects had been plucked as underage juniors in prior drafts. Consider also that Bridgman developed within the protective embrace of the Broad Street Bullies. Caps rookies received no such protection, making it unlikely Bridgman would have prospered as well in the Capitals' organization.

Bottom line: no one player, much less a rookie, was going to alter the Caps' trajectory. As proof, consider the player Washington would have drafted had it kept the pick. Not Bridgman, according to *The Hockey News*, but Don Ashby, a prolific scorer with the Calgary Centennials. What caught the Caps' attention was 52 goals in Ashby's just-completed 70-game season.

THE LEGENDS OF LANDOVER

Selected 6th overall by Toronto, Ashby was promoted directly to Maple Leaf Gardens. He wasn't ready, scoring a meager six goals as a rookie – though he did improve to 19 goals as a sophomore. The escalator only went down from there. Don spent four years bouncing between the minors and the NHL in Toronto, Colorado, and Edmonton. He'd only play 62 games total in the majors over that span, which included his temporary retirement.

The real tragedy for Don Ashby came while driving on May 30, 1981. He and his wife Terry were struck in a head-on collision. Ashby died hours later, at the age of 26.

✪ Bill Clement (1975-76)

As for Bill Clement, getting traded from the Stanley Cup Champions to the Capitals tore him up. "It was as if I was exiled from my family." Sandwiched between four seasons with the Flyers and seven years with the Flames, Clement spent 46 games as captain of the Capitals in 1975-76. He scored a respectable 10 goals and 17 assists - despite thinking of his new teammates as, quote, "dog meat."

"It was like Custer's last stand," Bill said. "That team (the Caps) had no firepower – nobody physical, no talent, no force. Now opponents who had been bullied by the Flyers came looking for you for revenge," Clement remembered. "It was imperative that I didn't show fear, because these were guys who had been gutless against the Flyers who now thought they were King Kong." And the chance to be a captain? "All it really did was grind me down. I'm afraid I was too sensitive, too emotional. I took everything that was happening to the team personally, and there was too much to take."

The night after Clement was the Caps' All-Star rep, "I stayed up late with the guys in Washington. They wanted to hear about the All-Star Game. I hardly had any sleep. (Coach) Tommy McVie killed us in practice the next day, and then said, 'Max McNab wants to see you.'" McVie had decided to jettison his captain because, "I was trying to get guys to be proud that they were Washington Capitals, and all I ever heard from Billy Clement was, 'That's the way it was done in Philadelphia.'"

The end came during an Unhappy Meal with the general manager. "McNab sits down with me and takes a big bite of this hamburger and mumbles, 'We had to make a trade.'" McNab handed Clement the phone, so he could talk to Atlanta G.M. Cliff Fletcher. "And you know what? As I talked to Fletcher, Max finished that hamburger!" After you eat, aren't you supposed to wait at least an hour before making a hockey trade?

(Quotes from *Washington Post, Philadelphia Inquirer,* and the books *Walking Together Forever* and *Hockey Card Stories*)

THE LEGENDS OF LANDOVER

✪ Gaining Pounds, Not Wins

The Capitals in '75-'76 endured a 25-game winless streak, causing McVie to quip, "We ought to take our goaltenders from one city to another in an ambulance." Broadcaster Ron Weber, in *The Hockey News,* wrote about a particularly frustrating mid-February section of the streak: "In the last five games, both Dale Tallon (Chicago) and Darryl Sittler (Toronto) got goals at 19:59 of the second period... They say the breaks even out. The Capitals are still waiting." An 11-2 mauling at Philadelphia, in which the Caps surrendered 62 shots, caused the normally indefatigable Weber to turn salty. "The Washington Pussycats had bedded down for the night."

Dick Schaap, one of the premiere sports journalists of the 20th century, penned a few guest columns for the *Washington Star* in 1975. He regretted not mingling with the local icemen. "As a youth I covered the New York Mets, and I wanted to meet the Capitals and tell them not to worry, that after a generation or two, they, too, might get better." Schaap followed that jab with his knockout punch. "I had a choice – I could work two months on the *Star*, or until the Caps won a game, and everyone warned me that if I picked the Caps, I'd be here longer..."

Drowning with a 5-41-5 record, owner Abe Pollin made a public apology. In a half-page newspaper ad, Pollin wrote, "There is no question who is responsible for the Capitals miserable record. I am." The ad went on to say the team wasn't broke, wasn't moving, was spending money, and, hey, would you like to buy some tickets?

Players showed up late for practice, according to *Sports Illustrated*, while others included cigarettes and coffee in their training regimen. Tobacco wasn't the only risk to the lungs. "The practice facility had gas-powered heaters," recalled Ron Lalonde. "The fumes almost made us pass out." Every player, without exception, somehow managed to gain weight during the season – as much as 17 pounds!

Bad habits may have contributed to losing, but losing certainly contributed to the bad habits. "You hate to come to practice, because it's a rotten feeling inside," Mike Lampman told *AP*. "Morale," G.M. Milt Schmidt lamented to the *Washington Star*, "has reached the lowest ebb that it has been in two years. There are players with their heads between their knees. There's no laughing, no joking, no one even talking."

One player spoke up to make this bleak and startling assessment at a team meeting: "No one else will admit it, but we're all thinking the same thing: We're going to lose every game we play, so what's the point." Those, the anti-motivational musings of ironically-named defenseman Bob Paradise, as quoted by *Sports Illustrated*.

THE LEGENDS OF LANDOVER

While Paradise spoke the dictionary definition of pessimism, on the Caps, even optimism sounded depressing. "We all feel things are going to get better," Chip Campbell, the Caps' publicist, told *UPI*. "You have to keep thinking that because if you didn't, losing the way we have been, you'd go batty. You'd go right over the wall."

Tommy Williams went right home. At the lowest point of the winless streak, a 14-2 slaughter in Buffalo, Williams ended his 16-year pro career. "I would like to be with them when they start winning," Tommy told the *Washington Star*, "but it looks like I can't wait that long."

✪ Columns Of Contempt From Bob Verdi, *Chicago Tribune*

- *Oct. 26, 1975*: "The Capitals win with the frequency of lunar eclipses."
- *Dec. 11, 1975*: "Washington is still awaiting major league hockey."
- *Feb. 8, 1976*: "The Caps, prefaced by lowly or inept, are usually both."

✪ Truth In Advertising

Out of necessity, the Capitals' marketing department in 1975 came up with a brilliant example of Brand Judo. That refers to twisting a product's negative attribute into a selling point. For instance, one foreign automobile company in the 1960's reacted slyly to complaints that its cars were too small. Their advertising response: "It'll make your house seem bigger."

No gimmicks could obscure that the Capitals won just seven of 40 home games in their first season. The answer, then, was to make the very novelty of possibly seeing a victory into a selling point. After all, fans in Boston and Philadelphia routinely got to see their team dominate; how mundane! In Washington, a full-page program ad proclaimed, "*When we win, it's like heaven.*" The lure resembled a pitch for lottery tickets rather than hockey tickets; sure, the chances of winning were small, but if you did, "*The most you'll feel is ecstatic, unadulterated, complete and total euphoria.*" Where else could you purchase a shot at nirvana, especially for "*as little as $4.*"

Unfortunately, the Capitals won only six home games - one fewer than their inaugural campaign. So it's possible that any euphoria realized in the upper reaches of Capital Centre may have been caused by a lack of oxygen climbing the stairs to Row ZZ.

✪ Everything's Relative - December 6, 1975 at Montreal

The Caps stunned fans at the Forum, jumping to a quick 2-0 lead. At 2:32 of the middle frame, Nelson Pyatt restored the lead, 3-2. Then the Habs woke up, outshot Washington 23-1 (!) in the third period, and cruised, 9-3. One cheery Capital in the locker room noted, "Well, it could have been worse. We lost to this club 10-0 last time." *(Chicago Tribune)* The rest of the '75-'76 meetings were Montreal waltzes, too: 6-0, 7-0, 3-2, 5-1 and 4-3.

THE LEGENDS OF LANDOVER

The Caps had company - Montreal ran roughshod over the NHL, including a sweep of the defending champion Flyers in the finals. Nine days later, *Montreal Star* readers opened their paper to a $400 ad purchased by the Caps. "Our warmest congratulations... on your magnificent Stanley Cup victory," the ad said in bold letters, concluding, "With admiration and envy, best wishes from the Washington Capitals."

✪ Studio 54 - December 19, 1975 vs. Philadelphia

"Goalie Bernie Wolfe might have been thinking about asking for political asylum." So began Chuck Newman's dispatch in the *Philadelphia Inquirer*, as the Flyers outscored the Caps, 7-5. "By the end, he had faced 54 shots. On one occasion, linesman Matt Pavelich appeared to help the goalie maintain his stance."

Wolfe admitted to fatigue on the final goal he surrendered. "I think I was a little too tired to do anything about it." Bernie kept perspective, saying, "I don't wish I was anywhere else, doing anything else." Gallows humor was left to Assistant G.M. Lefty McFadden: "Well, the Bullets lost, too. That keeps the pressure off."

✪ Milt Schmidt (General Manager & Coach, 1974-75)

Milt Schmidt won two Stanley Cups centering Boston's famous, if crudely named, "Kraut" line, and two more as general manager. As the first G.M. of the Capitals in 1974, "(He) embarks on perhaps the most difficult assignment in hockey," cautioned a *Pittsburgh Post-Gazette* profile. Undaunted, Schmidt boasted to *The Hockey News*, "I don't know the meaning of the word *can't*, and I don't want any of my players here to know it either." He gushed, "I feel like a kid with a new toy."

This Toy Story wasn't a comedy. By the late stages of that eight-win season, G.M. Milt appointed himself coach, too - he had fired his first coach, while the second resigned because of ulcers. He was quoted by the *Sporting News* saying, "I've tried to embarrass some of these guys, but they apparently can't be embarrassed." The *Washington Star* described one repeated display of poor manners: "Schmidt sneers when certain members of the team time after time fail to go to the goalie to either congratulate or solace him after a game. Only a handful visited (Bernie) Wolfe after Atlanta punished him with a 45-shot assault."

By the start of the 1975-76 season, Milt was general manager in title only. Former deputy Lefty McFadden now reported to new team president Peter O'Malley, that duo handling executive duties such as player contracts and trades. In the midst of an eight-game winless streak, Schmidt said to the *Star*, "My doctor told me that I'm strong as a horse. Then I started to think about it. They shoot horses, don't they?"

THE LEGENDS OF LANDOVER

And they fire coaches. Schmidt was relieved of the coaching reins – officially a resignation - when the team won three of its first 36 games in Season Two. *THN* reported, "Players commissioned their captain, (Bill) Clement, to make an 11th-hour plea that Schmidt reconsider." Milt declined, in the mother of all understatements, telling *UPI*, "All in all, perhaps a change is for the best." That, fans, is how the Caps created a Sour Kraut.

✪ Sentences Of Scorn From Don Ramsay, *Toronto Globe & Mail*

- *Feb. 5, 1976*: "Hapless, lowly, and pathetic are words that come to mind when dealing with Washington Capitals competence."

- *Feb. 5, 1976*: Leafs owner Harold Ballard: "If we lose to these guys... look up at the CN Tower. I will be standing there ready to jump."

- *Jan. 3, 1977*: "The Capitals, winners of 19 games in their first two years, erred in simple basics, performing in a manner that, if they were a group of eight-year-olds, their parents would have sent them to summer hockey school to rectify the problems."

✪ New Sheriff In Town

The Capitals were a lawless frontier town in late December, 1975. Tom McVie was Randolph Scott, hired initially not so much to coach, as to bring the townsfolk to heel. McVie remembered asking a player about the Caps' system. "They guy looked at me kind of crazy," the new boss said to the *Washington Star*. "He told me that all he had ever been instructed to do was to go out and play, not to worry about any system." After a poor effort, McVie addressed his team in the dressing room. "Guys, it wouldn't matter to me if the bridge collapsed with our team bus on it because you fellas floated so much, you'd never drown!" *(nhl.com)*

The new coach's debut was a 4-0 New Year's Eve shutout loss in Detroit. "Washington's most pathetic moments were during over a minute of a five-on-three power play in the first period," reported Russ White in the *Star*. "Not only did the Caps fail to score, they didn't get off a shot." If that represented the on-ice low point, the just-hired coach was more distressed by what he saw – or didn't see – when the period ended. "I walked into the dressing room and there was no one there," McVie recalled to *Canadian Press*. "I went into the trainer's room and there they were – 16 guys sprawled out on the trainer's tables. The rest were in the back smoking."

That was about to change. *The Hockey News* explained, "McVie introduced strenuous practice conditioning sessions, film studies, curfews and bed-checks." By February, the team had shed a combined 160 pounds. "That's like losing one whole man," the coach beamed.

THE LEGENDS OF LANDOVER

Players were given five new rules per day – each day for two weeks. "There was a definite change in the team's discipline, conditioning, and personality," McVie said. Although results didn't show right away, winger Hartland Monahan offered, "It's not each man for himself. With Tommy, we know where he wants us to be." (More McVie on pg. 86.)

✪ NHL President Talks Smack

Today's pro sports commissioners are loathe to chastise team executives for poor performance. Not only because they're employed by league owners; if the NHL's Gary Bettman and his NFL, NBA, and MLB brethren called out clubs for every bonehead move, they'd hardly have time for anything else. Only criminality or conduct detrimental to the sport usually compels a league boss to step in.

So Clarence Campbell's verbal barrage against the Caps in January, 1976 can accurately be called "jaw-dropping." Asked in a TV interview about Washington's 21-game winless streak, the NHL President unloaded both barrels. "There are better players available than those on the Caps roster," Campbell said. "The problem has been management." The Prez followed with his hot take on the Caps dealing the number one overall pick in 1975. "If you're willing to trade away your first draft choices, you have to take the consequences." Campbell conveniently overlooked NHL HQ's own culpability; the league ensured Capital failure by denying access to players.

In a separate *Washington Star* interview, the Prez said "people were laughing" at the Caps' front office, which he further labeled "a disgrace." Talk about kicking a guy when's he's down – Campbell's broadsides were aimed at former G.M. Milt Schmidt, fired barely two weeks earlier. Schmidt told *AP* he was surprised by the criticism, adding an offer. "Tell Mr. Campbell he can come down and be manager." Oh, Campbell didn't have time for that; he was attending to vital league matters, like demanding to know why Caps statisticians were crediting more assists on Caps goals than opponent scores. *The Horror!* (The *Post's* Bob Fachet answered simply that opponents' breakaways led to more unassisted goals.)

Campbell extended a tepid vote of confidence in Milt's replacement, Max McNab. "I don't know whether the new management is going to be good or bad. I just hope it's going to be better." McNab reacted about the way you'd expect. "We know there is much to do. We have not been able to make trades overnight or just for the sake of making trades."

A month later, McNab proposed an "equalization draft," in which frail franchises could select surplus players from top-echelon teams. "Players of that caliber could help a weaker club," said McNab, adding that established teams would benefit by shedding salary of players they couldn't use. Clarence Campbell gave the idea lip service, but not much more.

THE LEGENDS OF LANDOVER

✪ Stanley Can, The Sequel – January 28, 1976 at Oakland

Stanley Can Part 2 isn't as well known as the original – even though both premiered at the Oakland Coliseum. This sequel was also beginning-to-end wackier than its predecessor. Before the beginning, actually. In warmups, a wayward puck smacked Seals G.M. Bill McCreary above his left eye, opening a six-stitch cut. The Caps weren't the picture of health either, colds and fever gripping many players, including primary goalie Ron Low.

The crowd of 4,274 was roused by a first period fight between Yvon Labre and the Seals' top scorer, Wayne Merrick. Not a bad tradeoff; Merrick had eight goals in his previous five games. As Labre skated to the box, Merrick made what wire accounts termed an "obscene gesture" at Yvon. Referee Alf Lejeune assessed a game misconduct, ending his night. "I just lost my temper. I didn't know about that rule," said Merrick.

All other factors seemed to line up against Washington. They'd lost 16 in a row on the road, while the Seals were riding a four-game winning streak. Beat writer John Hickey wrote that California was "playing as well as at any time in the history of the franchise." Plus, the ailing Capitals had lost the night before in L.A., then had to travel up the coast.

Sure enough, the home side dominated the first 50 minutes. Only, no one told Caps starting goalie Bernie Wolfe. In a brilliant two-minute stretch of netminding in the third period, Wolfe stymied three scoring chances from a talented Seals rookie named Dennis Maruk. For the game, Wolfe would make 32 saves (California doubled Washington in shots, 34-17). Caps coach Tom McVie said, "Bernie Wolfe was the whole story for us."

Well, he was until a three-goal explosion out of nowhere in less than three minutes. 7:51 remained when Gerry Meehan scored to tie the game, 2-2. 1:34 later, Hartland Monahan's long drive eluded Gilles Meloche, to give D.C. the lead. 61 seconds after that, Harvey Bennett converted a 2-on-1 break to make the final score 4-2.

"We were very happy when we came into the dressing room," said Wolfe, the winning goalie. "In those days, garbage cans were galvanized steel, so we emptied one out, dumping all the orange peels and stuff on the floor, and hoisted this shiny can. We knew it was our Stanley Cup." The stirring comeback gave Washington its second win in the last four. Tom McVie, in his first month, said, "We're not going to conquer the world, but these guys now believe that they can win."

(*Sources: Oakland Tribune, Hayward Daily Review, AP, nhl.com*)

THE LEGENDS OF LANDOVER

✪ Oakland Feasts On D.C. Teams

The Seals better represented their hometown the prior Thanksgiving. On three consecutive days, in three different sports, visiting Oakland teams laid an epic combined smackdown on their D.C. hosts.

The first two came at Capital Centre. Friday, Nov. 21, 1975, Oakland's NHL team shut out the Caps 2-0, in Seals rookie Dennis Maruk's first-ever game in Landover. Saturday, Nov. 22, Oakland's NBA team, the Warriors, dealt the Bullets a 40-point home loss. The Bullets managed just 71 points, matching a franchise low. Sunday, Nov. 23 at RFK Stadium, 48-year-old George Blanda booted an overtime field goal for the Oakland Raiders, handing the Redskins their second straight O.T. defeat.

Thankfully, because it was November, and because Washington no longer had a baseball team, the A.L. West champion Athletics could inflict no punishment on the Nation's Capital. (Little could we imagine that Oakland would suffer the ultimate punishment, with the Seals, Warriors and Raiders all eventually abandoning the East Bay.)

✪ The Soda Truck Game – March 23, 1976 vs. Kansas City

As the Scouts built a 4-0 lead in Landover, new Caps coach Tom McVie had to be regretting his pregame bravado. "Lose to these guys and I'll quit," McVie was quoted by *AP*, adding, "and some of our players ought to consider going back to Canada to drive a soda truck." This provided the proverbial bulletin board material for Kansas City coach Eddie Bush, who told his players, "The guy (McVie) will be looking for a job."

Management was wincing, too. This game was promoted as a Guaranteed Win Night; a loss or tie by the Capitals would obligate the club to distribute free tickets to a future game. Even worse, the 11,235 at Capital Centre were joined by Japanese embassy officials, invited for an advance look at the Scouts and Caps. The two squads were headed to the Far East in a few weeks for a series of four exhibition games. Dignitaries could be forgiven for wondering if shame ever drove an NHL coach to Hara-kiri - ritual suicide.

"Here we were playing a team we thought we could skate away from," defenseman Jack Lynch explained to the *Washington Star*. "We were so sure that we would, that we tried to do things we had never done before." Thankfully for McVie and all involved - except the Scouts - the Caps mounted a furious 3rd period comeback. Bob Sirois, Blair Stewart, and Lynch all scored in a 2 minute, 18 second barrage to forge a 5-5 tie. The fans got a thrilling rally, and their free tickets.

THE LEGENDS OF LANDOVER

Now it was Kansas City's turn at masochism. This was K.C.'s 20th straight contest without a win, a prize seemingly in the bag when the Scouts led 4-0 and 5-2. "Jesus Christ and the disciples couldn't help this team," Steve Durbano spewed to the *K.C. Times*. "This team stinks." The Scouts lost their last seven games of the season too, extending their winless streak to 27. That erased a Capitals NHL record of 25 in a row, suffered earlier the same season.

About his pregame boasts and the rally that backed them up, McVie conceded he'd been "given a reprieve." More predictions were unlikely, with McVie musing, "Me and my big mouth."

Though he might have retired his crystal ball and Ouija board, there was this one other conversation the quick-witted McVie himself detailed to *nhl.com*. The occasion was an offseason Capitals pep rally. "The crowd was screaming, 'We love you, coach.' (Owner Abe) Pollin mouthed over to me, 'I love you also, coach.' Me being a clown, I said, 'Will you still love me, Mr. Pollin, when we don't make the playoffs again next year?' He said, "Sure. I'll miss you, too.'"

✪ Land Of The Rising Slapshot

The Capitals made their first postseason appearance in the spring of 1976 - in fact, they won the Cup. It's not in the record books; the appearance was in Japan, and the trophy was the Coca-Cola Bottlers Cup.

A week after the conclusion of the 1975-76 season, the Caps and Kansas City Scouts were invited to play a series of four exhibition games in Tokyo and Sapporo. To put it politely, K.C. and D.C. had the essential quality promoters wanted – no chance of a playoff scheduling conflict.

Facing the logistical nightmare of transporting a team halfway around the world, the two clubs almost declined - especially the Scouts, already an organizational and financial mess. Sensing this, Coca Cola Japan nearly walked away from its $400,000 sponsorship. A Japanese promotions company, a sports publisher, and even the U.S. Embassy helped overcome resistance on both sides of the Pacific. (*Toronto Globe & Mail*)

A Canadian columnist scoffed, "Sending these two clubs makes as much sense as having the Broad Street Bullies at a meeting of the Mothers For Clean Hockey Society." Sourpuss. Their won-loss totals certainly didn't dampen the heroes' welcome awaiting players and companions in Japan. Banners read, "Welcome great great fighters and sweet ladies." (*L.A. Times*) Caps goalie Bernie Wolfe recalled, "My wife laughed, because here she's almost seven months pregnant, and after 15 hours on a plane, she said she looked anything but beautiful."

THE LEGENDS OF LANDOVER

Tokyo's swanky Hotel New Otani - featured in a James Bond film, home to a 16th century garden, past host of Olympic dignitaries - opened its doors for the Caps and Scouts. Tokyo's American Club held a reception in their honor, as players and coaches from both teams donned Japanese robes provided by Japan Airlines. The royal welcome included $1,250 per player, all expenses paid, and prizes such as pearls, geisha dolls, wristwatches, and radio-cassette audio players for the winners of each game. The companions made out OK, too. Mike Lampman's wife, Robin, said, "Some girls never left the hotel, when they found they could get such bargains in facials, manicures, and getting their hair done." *(Winnipeg Free Press)*

The Scouts probably wished thuggish Steve Durbano had never left the hotel, either. During one of the games, Durbano fired the puck at an official, earning a three-game suspension to start the '76-'77 season. (Durbano led a disturbed, destructive, and tragic life. Look it up if you need a quick dose of depression.) More enlightened players, like Kansas City's Guy Charron, took in the sights, including sumo wrestling. "To have an opportunity to go this far and see a different culture, it was exciting," Guy told *nhl.com*.

The Capitals took the competition more seriously than their expansion twins, flying to L.A. a day early to practice before heading overseas. Once landed, coach McVie held another practice; one so demanding that some players, who had imbibed during an unexpected layover in Hawaii, threw up on the cameras of Japanese reporters hanging too near the boards. Soooooooo, you won't be at all surprised to learn the Caps skipped a beer factory tour on a game day. Scouts players made the visit.

Also not surprisingly, the Capitals won both matches held in Sapporo, home of the 1972 Winter Olympics. Two-goal performances led the Caps, by Bob Sirois (Game 1, 5-2 win), and Gerry Meehan (Game 2, 6-2 win). Hartland Monahan, more honest than diplomatic, compared the quiet Sapporo crowds to "a morgue." A fan explained to the *Washington Post*, "I expected more fighting and blood." Expectations could be traced to Japanese promoters, who breathlessly announced that Canadians, "Learn to fight on the ice before they fight on the street, when they are little."

The second set of games proved more festive. Near capacity crowds of 9,200 attended each of the Tokyo matches, and Yvon Labre told *Stars & Stripes*, "They seemed to be into the game. The cheering helped us to get going." Enlivening the atmosphere, "Cheerleaders at rinkside, and a U.S. Army brass band entertaining in the stands." In the third game, the teams obliged Tokyo fans with the spectacle that bridges all cultural divides: fights. D.C.'s Blair Stewart led the way with a pair of brawls. *Stars & Stripes* reported that spectators were mesmerized, "As gloves and sticks littered the ice in the wild opening stanza." Scouts' coach Eddie Bush sparred, too, "Riding referee Malcolm Ashford and his own players with a kind of purple prose rarely heard in this sedate country." (*The Hockey News*)

THE LEGENDS OF LANDOVER

Washington in game three again benefitted from a two-goal performance, this time by Mike Lampman. *UPI* also credited the 6-2 victory to "the acrobatic play of goaltender Bernie Wolfe." If Bernie was inspired to perform Back Somersaults with a Half-Twist in the Pike Position, we know why. The Tokyo games were held on a makeshift rink inside, of all places, the 1964 Olympic swimming stadium. Wolfe said, "Right above my net there were about two or three high-diving boards."

Why the swimming stadium? Because the Caps and Scouts weren't the only ones fighting. Off the ice, Japan's Hockey Federation was feuding with the consortium running the event. Frozen out from involvement with the tournament, the Federation refused use of its rinks or affiliated hotels. When Calgary visited the same Yoyogi Arena for their own NHL contest 22 years later, Flames star Theo Fleury got off the best line. "If you climb up on one of those things and jump," Theo inquired, "do you get two minutes for diving?" (*nhl.com*)

As for the playing conditions, better you shouldn't ask. The lighting wasn't bright, the boards were too short and poorly anchored, and warm April evenings created soft ice. Fishing nets behind the goals were, Wolfe said, "sort of like a boomerang. You had to be careful on a high shot that you didn't get hit in the back of the head on a rebound." The *Life is a Puck* blog noted that combining low boards and netting in place of plexiglass, "Players could easily tip over to the other side or get caught in the net during a body check."

Really, though, how much could be expected of a rink floor placed over a swimming pool? A jovial Yvon Labre said with a smile, "Thank God we didn't fall through. It was wet enough on the ice." Minor quibbles for squads used to rude treatment on and off the ice back in North America. "We've been treated extremely well," said Caps coach Tom McVie, a man used to dispensing praise with an eye-dropper. "The Japanese people have gone out of their way with gracious hospitality."

By winning the first three, Washington secured "The Cup." The fourth and final contest, won 4-2 by the Scouts, was televised by Tokyo Broadcasting System, right after *Let's Shop Sensibly* and *The Orchestra Is Here!* If the Capitals needed any consoling, crates of Coca-Cola were waiting to be consumed in their dressing room.

Apparently overcome by winning the series, Caps winger Blair Stewart told a reporter he planned to spend his off-season "drinking." (Probably not referring to soft drinks.) Stewart quickly revised his answer. "I mean, traveling and relaxing." Blair wasn't kidding about the traveling; between Tokyo and training camp, he made summer visits to Florida, San Francisco, Lake Tahoe, Winnipeg, and Montreal.

THE LEGENDS OF LANDOVER

Blair's first post-Tokyo destination was Hawaii. On their way home, all the players from both teams spent a five-day Hawaiian vacation as one final perk of the tour. For the Scouts, "home" was a relative term, as the franchise relocated from Kansas City to Denver over the summer.

We have proof the actual Coca-Cola Cup made it back to Landover. A 1976 photo inside the Capitals' offices shows that behind the posing staff members, on top of a filing cabinet, above the staples and whiteout, stands the trophy in all its less-than-glorious glory. From its placement, evidence suggests the Cup was regarded by the franchise with only slightly less reverence than the employee of the month plaque. But at least it's on display, right?

Actually, not for a long time. Mike Vogel, Caps' website senior writer, told Steve Currier of *goldensealshockey.com* that he "found that trophy in a storage closet years ago." (Currier wrote about the Japan Series at his great website, and was the source for some quotes in this essay.) "It's probably in an office or a closet somewhere," concluded Vogel, who's lost track. "Or maybe someone took it home to use as a flower pot."

Capitals management coveted a prize of greater value while in Japan - Kansas City center Guy Charron. The Caps wisely signed Guy to a free-agent contract over the summer. "Charron was one of the few Scout players who cared they lost," said coach McVie. "Right then, we decided we wanted him." *(Pittsburgh Press)* We discuss Charron's Capital contributions on page 66.

THE LEGENDS OF LANDOVER

LOSS LEADERS
3RD TIME'S A CHARM

The Capitals of 1976-77 represent one of the feel-good seasons in the team's 40+ year history. On the surface, that's an odd claim about a squad which lost more than half its games. Only from the perspective of where the Caps had been, could one truly appreciate the joys of Season Three.

Don't take my word for it. Fred Shero and Al Arbour combined to coach six Stanley Cup winners, so they qualify as hockey authorities. Arbour: "They're the hardest working team. They never stop." Was Al talking about his Islanders? Nope. Shero: "He's put character into them. I didn't think it was possible." Was Fred lauding his Flyer assistants? Not quite.

The two coaches were heaping praise on the 1976-77 Capitals, especially coach Tom McVie. The secret was conditioning, which throughout sports was primitive – sometimes non-existent – compared with today's training methods. That gave McVie an opportunity to compensate with fitness, for what his players lacked in talent. Until this year, said McVie, "Clubs came into Capital Center counting on two easy points. They didn't bother turning off the ignition on the team bus." This year, "We fought hard at home and won." (*Toronto Globe & Mail*)

McVie explained, with a straight face, "Washington will always play as if our lives depended on it. Guys that don't play like that don't play for me." P.R. Director Pierce Gardner told the *Frederick News-Post*, "He began two-a-day practice sessions, which was unheard of during the regular season. Two-hour practices that took place in full uniform. And strict discipline with a curfew, dress code and weight limits."

Ah, the dress code. When McVie took the job, "I thought I was traveling with the Hell's Angels." The coach instructed players that "if anyone asked who they were, they weren't to answer." Soon, coats and ties became mandatory road trip attire.

Professionalism carried over to on-ice performance, something opponents noticed. "They don't have the attitude they did before – kidding around, a defeated attitude," J.P. Parise of the Islanders told *UPI*. "They play with authority." A Pittsburgh standout delivered his praise personally, as McVie told the *Washington Star*. "Pierre Larouche in his broken French-English came over and told me, 'You crazy (expletive deleted), you change those guys, you really do.'"

Added Toronto assistant Johnny Bower, "They're a well coached, well disciplined team that doesn't get out of position too often." McVie concurred. "The minute we stray from positional hockey is the minute any success ends."

THE LEGENDS OF LANDOVER

✪ Guess Who's Coming To Landover – Oct. 5, 1976 vs. Atlanta

Fact or fiction: on the ice for the Capitals' third-season opener - besides the Caps and Atlanta Flames - were (A) Miss America, (B) a gorilla in a Capitals sweater, and (C) all the local weeknight sportscasters.

(A) Fact. Minnesota's Dorothy Benham, newly-crowned Miss America, sang the national anthem. In fact, she returned and sang at the next season's home opener, too. So we'll forgive her for marrying a Pittsburgh defenseman, Russ Anderson. (Anyway, Benham divorced Anderson - and her next two husbands, for that matter.)

(B) Fiction. OK, it wasn't a real gorilla posing by the glass (he didn't make it onto the ice.) The Caps' fan newspaper, *Good Times*, wrote, "This gentle simian promised to return." Maybe Douglas MacArthur was under that fur. More likely, marketing director Andy Dolich, who was known to show up in ape costume when hawking tickets to local businesses. In any case, too bad he wasn't a genuine gorilla. The Caps could have used a mobile 350-pound enforcer with a long reach who's tough to knock off his knuckles.

(C) Fact. Between periods, sports anchors Jim Karvellas (channel 5), Nick Charles (channel 4), Dan Lovett (channel 7), and Mike Wolfe (channel 9) grabbed hockey sticks to shoot pucks toward the net. It's remarkable that most of these guys even knew which end of the stick to hold, given how little attention they paid to hockey. Except for Charles, that is; best known as an anchor for CNN Sports and Showtime boxing, Nick also worked briefly as color analyst on Caps road telecasts.

Oh, and the game: beauties, beasts, broadcasters, and 13,152 regular folks were sent home happy. Hartland Monahan scored a power-play goal with 1:48 left for a thrilling 6-5 Washington victory. As *WTOP* radio's Ron Weber exclaimed at game's end, "The final shots on goal were 35-22 Atlanta, but the scoreboard, folks, is the only thing that counts. How many times have I said that in apology rather than glee?"

✪ The Eyes Have It – November 9, 1976 vs. Vancouver

By the middle of their game against the Canucks, the Capitals had received a heaping helping of rotten. Washington was about to go shorthanded for eight straight minutes. Meanwhile, center Ron Lalonde was headed to the hospital, wondering if he'd keep his eyesight.

The evening had begun so wonderfully. Doug Patey's first NHL goal was followed by tallies from Mike Lampman and Gerry Meehan, as Washington built a 3-0 lead 12 minutes into the game. The nightmare started when Lalonde intercepted a pass while killing a penalty. "I was two steps ahead of their defenseman, Dave Fortier," Lalonde told *AP*. "He slashed me twice on the arm. The third time, his stick caught me straight on the left eyeball."

THE LEGENDS OF LANDOVER

During a second period brawl, the Caps' Tony White threw his stick. When all the penalties were sorted out, the Capitals faced an eight minute penalty kill. White was ejected (he later served a five-game suspension), and the penalty wouldn't end no matter how many times Vancouver scored.

Well, Caps goalie Ron Low must have summoned the ghost of Georges Vezina, making one spectacular stop after another, and not allowing a goal during the eight minute kill. "I wasn't worried about the pressure on me," Low told the *Washington Star*. "I was more worried about the guys who kept pouring on the ice. They had to form a tight box and not allow the good shot on goal. In eight minutes there were really only two, maybe three, difficult chances." The Caps won 4-2, behind Low's 34 saves.

With hemorrhaging in his left eye, Lalonde faced an uncertain future. "Lying in bed and not able to see, I was really scared." A *Star* photo showed Ron, both eyes bandaged, being comforted by a nurse named Betsy Ross. Shouldn't she have been attending to a patient who needed stitches? Happily, Ron recovered to play in 76 of 80 games in the '76-'77 season.

✪ We'd Seen This Before

Three weeks before the Lalonde injury, Capital Centre fans witnessed a similarly gruesome scene. As Harvey Bennett and Montreal's Doug Risebrough battled for the puck, referee Ron Wicks sensed he was in a bad spot. "They told me later that I tried to get out of the way by reflex," said Wicks. Bennett explained, "My stick went up as Risebrough and I were moving together. Suddenly, Wicks was all crumpled up." Bennett's stick had speared Wicks, causing bleeding behind his right eye.

Repaired at a local hospital, his badly injured eye suffered no permanent damage. "I've been officiating 20 years, and that's the first time I've ever had a scratch," Wicks said. Caps' fans eased his recovery. Wicks received a fruit basket from the team's fan club at his hospital bed, and an ovation at his next Capital Centre assignment. "It lasted about five minutes," Wicks recalled. "I think I made one call they didn't like and they were all booing again. But it was nice while it lasted."
(Sources: AP, UPI, CP, Washington Post)

✪ Winning Streak

Consecutive November wins over the Stars and Canucks provided the Capitals with their first winning streak. It reached three in New York, thanks to a 7-5 knockout of the Rangers. The club ordered a large print ad featuring beaming players Hartland Monahan, Blair Stewart, Rick Bragnalo, and coach McVie. The copy promoted their unprecendented success. *"Nobody expected us to beat Minnesota... Vancouver... New York."*

THE LEGENDS OF LANDOVER

Reflecting on the win over the Rangers, goalie Ron Low couldn't believe the confidence his teammates displayed. "Our guys were so high in the dressing room," said Low, who had suffered through all the bad times. "They knew they were going to win before the game. I didn't, but they did."

Jack Lynch told *AP*, "We've been working so damn hard you wouldn't believe it. We had to come to training camp able to run a mile in 5:45, do 50 situps a day, pushups, you name it. We know that if we aren't together, we're not worth a darn. We've got 20 100-percent efforts; it may not be the best hockey, but it's paying off. We're getting what we deserve now."

✪ Goalie Shuttle – January 8, 1977 at Montreal

The 1976-77 Canadiens were named by *The Sporting News* as the best in NHL history. With 132 standings points, nine Hall-of-Famers on the roster, and a Cup Final sweep of the Bruins, few would argue. The Capitals saw way too much of this awesomeness up close, due to some sadist in the NHL offices placing the young franchise in Montreal's division. To face a 60-minute barrage by the Habs, Caps coach Tom McVie told the *Montreal Gazette*, "just takes too much out of a goaltender."

All of which is prelude to the remarkable happenings at the Forum. "I had seen Montreal on TV against the Flyers," McVie explained. "They drilled 55 shots against Bernie Parent. I don't think there's a goaltender around who can withstand that kind of attack. Even Parent was beaten six times." So McVie proposed a strategy even Montreal coach Scotty Bowman had never seen. At the morning skate, McVie told Bernie Wolfe and Ron Low that they would alternate every few minutes. "Right after he told us, I stopped thinking if I was going to be hot or cold," Wolfe said. "You just better be hot when you go in." Low added, "I can't really go against (McVie), because everything he does is for the best."

PER	TIME	IN GOAL	SCORE M	W
1st	Start	Wolfe	0	0
	5:48	Low	0	0
	9:43	Wolfe	0	1
	15:29	Low	0	1
2nd	Start	Wolfe	1	1
	3:32	Low	3	1
	11:00	Wolfe	4	1
3rd	Start	Low	5	1
	9:33	Wolfe	6	2
		FINAL	7	2

The chart at left lists the goalie rotation. Wolfe and Low each played two "shifts" in the first period, combining to stop 9 of 10 Montreal shots. The period ended 1-1. "Jim Roberts, an injured Montreal player who watched from the press box said, 'Never have I seen anything like this – I admire that coach and what he has his team doing. It is very good hockey." (*Washington Star*)

That concludes the good news in a 7-2 Montreal victory. Wolfe played 35 minutes, allowing four goals on 26 shots. Low played 25 minutes, allowing three goals on 14 shots.

THE LEGENDS OF LANDOVER

In the final analysis, said Wolfe, "It had no bearing on the outcome." Maybe if they'd played together, side-by-side... Incredibly, the alternating-goalie gambit was employed 36 years earlier - in the same building! On March 15, 1941 at the Forum, "Montreal rotates goaltenders Bert Gardiner and Paul Bibeault approximately every seven minutes for the NHL's first shared shutout, a 6-0 victory over the New York Americans." (*From nhl.com*)

When the Caps next visited Montreal two weeks later, McVie modified his strategy, with Wolfe playing the first two periods, and Low the third. The Habs won again, 5-2.

✪ Cold Building, Hot Goalie – January 10, 1977 at Detroit

Two nights following the goalie shuffle, the game in Detroit contained another Capitals first - and almost nobody was there to see it. Goalie Bernie Wolfe recorded the first road shutout in team history, 2-0.

Wolfe felt anything but confident before the game, as he said to *The Hockey News*: "I didn't have a good warmup. My left toe strap broke and you don't like having anything like that ruining your concentration." It wasn't fixed until the first intermission. That occasioned an immediate attitude upgrade, and Wolfe began thinking goose egg. "You're always aware of shutouts, but I knew there was 40 minutes to go," Bernie told *UPI*. Wolfe overcame a bad back to stop all 26 Detroit shots, getting goals from Billy Collins, shorthanded 2:38 into the game, and Yvon Labre in the 2nd period.

The game was pushed back from Sunday to Monday, so it wouldn't conflict with the Super Bowl. The 24-hour delay then conflicted with a massive snowstorm. Although paid attendance was given as 7,200, *AP* estimated only 2,500 fans were actually in the building. Of the empty arena, Wolfe would say, "I don't think anybody felt much like playing hockey, so I wasn't exactly overworked."

✪ If You Can't Beat 'Em, Fight 'Em – March 13, 1977 at Detroit

Fights! Unretirement! Fights! Rallies! Fights! Only a winner was lacking. Washington's Gerry Meehan made sure of that, his second goal with 1:22 left tying the Wings for good at 3-3.

A minute earlier, the Olympia – a snowbound morgue on the Caps' last visit two months ago – morphed into piranha tank. An amazing fight card erupted, featuring three bouts within 14 seconds of game time! First, Smith and LeBlanc dropped the gloves at 17:24. A mere five seconds after play resumed, Labre and Polonich brawled. When they were sent off, the teams managed to play another nine seconds before White and Bergeron tangled, with Bergeron adding a gross misconduct for good (bad?) measure.

THE LEGENDS OF LANDOVER

For the first two periods, the story was Caps goalie Roger Crozier, playing his first game in 15 months. "I hadn't been in the net since Christmas, 1975 with Buffalo," Crozier told *AP*. "My pancreatitis flared up and I wasn't sure I would ever play again." The Capitals somehow coaxed the Hall-of-Famer from his beachfront home in Florida. Before the game, "I prepared in my usual way, sitting around worrying," Crozier joked to the *Windsor Star*. "The game starts, and I don't think the Wings got a shot for nine minutes."

Oh, Roger, they were about to make up for lost time. Detroit tested Crozier 10 times before the 1st period ended, and forced Roger to make 20 saves, some spectacular, in the 2nd. No wonder he spent the 3rd period recuperating, while Bernie Wolfe finished up. "I felt good about the way things went," said Crozier. "I didn't expect to be as strong as I was. But I felt reasonably sharp."

Roger was a beloved member of the Red Wings for seven seasons in the 1960's, playing all 70 regular-season games in 1964-65. So 8,617 fans at the Olympia got to welcome back one of their heroes, along with a wild hockey game.

✪ "19 Guys All Pulling The Same Way"

Coach McVie set remarkably high expectations for a team which won just 19 of 160 games combined its first two seasons. Listen to him after a game vs. the Maple Leafs. "Everything we have been working on in practice, we were doing the opposite tonight," said McVie. "The wingers were not coming back and covering their men and the defense were backing in instead of standing their men up." Psst, Tommy, you *won the game*.

Center Gerry Meehan had a more philosophical outlook on the 7-4 victory over Toronto. "When you play a bad game and score seven goals, it shows you must be doing something right," said Gerry, who scored twice against the Leafs. A respected veteran who produced 28 goals and 36 assists for the '76-'77 Caps, Meehan would be welcomed on any roster. Yet he was fully committed to the company line in Landover. "We concede that on paper, we are not as good as almost any team in the league," Gerry said to the *Pittsburgh Press*. "We know we have to capitalize on a pattern of play based on hard work."

A March 30 game in Pittsburgh exemplified McVie's insistence on "19 guys all pulling the same way." The Caps fell behind Pittsburgh 3-1, then roared back with the next three goals. Veteran defenseman Bryan Watson knew why. "We're in great shape," said Bugsy. "That's why we took off in the 2nd period." An admiring Pittsburgh coach Ken Schinkel said, "They have a lot of heart. You think you have them down, but they come right back at you."

THE LEGENDS OF LANDOVER

At the tail end of a grueling season, eliminated from the playoffs, Washington had still rallied for a 4-3 victory. "It has taken a year to instill pride," McVie said to the *Chicago Tribune*. "We're not going to throw it away, regardless of whether we're in the playoff picture or not."

Powerhouse Montreal paid the Capitals an unprecedented tribute in the final game of the regular season. Moments after the final horn in a 2-1 Habs win, Caps players heading off the ice made u-turns. Canadiens players spontaneously lined up for a playoff-style line of handshakes. Each team deserved congratulations: Montreal won 60 of 80 games; Washington overachieved almost as much in fashioning a 24-42-14 record. It may be the only handshake line in a non-event, regular season NHL game.

Canadiens coach Scotty Bowman explained the motivation behind the handshakes. "We are proud of our record, and Washington should be just as proud of theirs. They have made a tremendous improvement. It will not be long until you see the Capitals as a playoff team." (*The Hockey News*) The Caps and Habs shared one other experience; players on both teams received rings after the season. Montreal got theirs by winning the Stanley Cup. Caps players earned their less traditional jewelry for bringing a sense of pride to the franchise for the first time.

The feared Flyers managed only 4-4 and 5-5 deadlocks in their two visits to Capital Centre, a fact not lost on Philadelphia captain Bobby Clarke. "They started working from the first day, and never quit. They were disciplined, organized, and gave you everything they had, every minute." *(Capitals Media Guide)*

The surest sign that all the hard work paid off? The Caps announced that next season's ticket prices were going up – by a dollar for the premium seats (to $9.50!), and 50 cents in the nosebleeds (to $4.50). I think $9.50 and $4.50 gets you a beer and a pretzel these days.

THE LEGENDS OF LANDOVER

2nd Shift: *Expansion Era*
Skaters

✪ Garnet "Ace" Bailey (1975-78)

Gregarious Ace Bailey and coach Tom McVie were friendly adversaries at training camp. Bailey, to the *Wash. Star*: "I have this recurring nightmare about the hot cement track, running that blasted mile for Tom McVie."

From *Sports.jrank.org*: "Bailey received a four-inch-manual from McVie, telling him how to get into condition. Bailey used the manual to prop up a beer keg in his home. On the first day of camp, Bailey beat several players in a footrace. McVie said approvingly, 'Ace, I can see you used your book this summer.' Bailey replied, 'Coach, I used it every day.'" Teammate Mike Lampman, to the *Seattle Times*: "Camp under Tommy was brutally hard. Every night, Ace would smuggle beer into the hotel room and hide it in the back of the toilet tank. When camp ended we had a huge blowout party."

Bailey-McVie 2: The ice at the Caps' Tokyo exhibition games in 1976 extended behind the benches. "To prove he wanted to get back into the game," Steve Currier writes at *goldensealshockey.com*, "Bailey started doing starts-and-stops. 'McVie was going crazy; he was so upset,' remembers the Scouts' Robin Burns. 'We yelled over to Ace and said, 'What are you doing?' and he said, 'I'm trying to work up a two-beer thirst!'"

Bailey-McVie 3: The morning after a poor game, the coach scheduled a practice for 6 a.m. As Mike Vogel of *washingtoncaps.com* tells it, groggy players in the hotel lobby didn't know that Bailey, pretending to be McVie, had called and cancelled the bus to the rink. Eventually, the players were granted a reprieve for some more shut-eye. Future player itineraries, by the way, would no longer include the phone number of the charter bus service!

At a practice, Bailey heard goalie Michel Belhumeur bet Stan Gilbertson - that Gilbertson couldn't score on Ron Low. The wager was for the princely sum of one quarter. In the next drill, Bailey fed Stan an intentionally terrible pass, one Gilbertson couldn't possibly convert into a shot. Bailey then skated back to Belhumeur and loudly announced, "I want half the action!"

Bailey stepped into the breach at a 1976 game in Denver. Ron Low started in goal despite a bruised heel, usual backup Bernie Wolfe was ill, and emergency callup Jim Bedard was in-flight from Dayton, Ohio. So as coach McVie said to the *Washington Star*, "I've never seen Ace so excited. The first thing the guy did was write his name on a batch of goalie sticks. He tried on masks and, even if they didn't fit, I know Ace would have played goal without one if he had to." Fortunately, Bedard arrived during warmups, and even better, Low was brilliant in backstopping a 2-1 Caps victory.

THE LEGENDS OF LANDOVER

Ace Bailey, at the time director of pro scouting for the Los Angeles Kings, was aboard one of the planes that crashed into the World Trade Center on 9/11. "It was a sad day for his family and hockey," said McVie. "Ace was one of hockey's all-time characters. He was the kind of guy that when someone would bring a kid into the dressing room, Ace would take the kid around, locker to locker and make the experieince memorable."

His family created the Ace Bailey Children's Foundation, funding projects to aid sick kids. As friend Dave Andrews told *espn.com*, "Ace loved children and Ace never really lost the child in him. He had a terrific sense of humor. This is a tough business and it can become a grind. But when you were around Ace, it was never a grind."

✪ Guy Charron (1976-81)

Before Ovechkin, before Bondra, before Gartner, the first player to make Capitals fans rise from their seats was Guy Charron. Sure, Montreal had the more famous, smooth-skating, high-scoring, French-Canadian Guy (Lafleur) - we liked ours just fine.

Like Montreal fans, we got lots of chances to shout "Ghee!" after a score. In his first three D.C. seasons, Charron tallied 102 goals, while serving as captain and never missing a game. In 1980, the *Washington Star's* Russ White called Charron "the classiest player the Caps have ever had." Coach Tom McVie said Guy also deserved praise for sparking whichever wingers were lucky enough to play on his line. "When we got Charron, we didn't get one player, we got three." *(Pittsburgh Press)*

Guy understood the first rule of Superstition Club. "Everyone must have had something along the way, but what it was you didn't share until you retired," Charron told *Kamloops This Week*. As for Guy's personal ritual, let's just say he tried to put his best foot forward. "I always put the left skate on before the right skate," he said. "I caught myself a couple of times putting the right skate on first, so I took it off and put the left skate on."

Guy could be less strict about other parts of his wardrobe. Reporters entered the dressing room on a night Charron scored a hat trick, to see him wearing one of the hats flung onto the ice – a red railroad cap with white polka dots. Questionable fashion choices couldn't obscure the good looks that added to his appeal: "With curly black hair and haunting eyes, he is movie star material," wrote Joan Ryan in the *Washington Post*.

Never drafted, Charron collected a first-round worthy 530 career points. Playing 700 NHL games for overmatched teams in Detroit, Kansas City and Washington, Guy's misfortune was to never appear in a Stanley Cup game. Our good fortune was to see #15 at his best, a member of the 30th anniversary All-Time Team named in 2004.

THE LEGENDS OF LANDOVER

✪ Bill Riley (1976-79)

Bill Riley earned his NHL chance with a bluff worthy of the World Poker Tour. Languishing in the Caps' farm system at age 26, Bill said, in effect, call me up by New Year's Day 1977 or I'll quit. On December 30, 1976, Riley got the callup.

Talk about pressure; league rules allowed a player to participate in 10 games before being offered a contract. "My first five games I felt decent," Riley said. "After that I wondered if they were going to sign me. For the last five games, I (couldn't) sleep either before the game or after."

On a Wednesday morning, as the rest of the team left for Buffalo, Riley met with general manager Max McNab. Offered a two year, $100,000 contract, Bill felt he came out second-best at the bargaining table. "The Capitals never gave me a decent contract," Riley recalled. "That contract was peanuts compared to what other guys were getting who weren't contributing anything near as much as I was."

The newly-inked Riley hustled to upstate New York. He arrived in time to record three assists, as the Caps beat the Sabres for the first time in team history, 4-2. "It didn't seem like I had any strength," Riley said. "I got in late and the rest of the team was taking the afternoon nap, and I didn't get anything to eat. Just because I signed, I didn't want to let up." Riley added that with the game behind him, "I feel a lot better tonight."

Bill never took for granted the opportunity to play in the NHL. Perspective was likely provided by his previous occupation as a welder in an aluminum plant. It also helped Riley keep a healthy sense of humor during endless hours spent on the road. Barry Lorge of the *Washington Post* had this case in point: "'Who are you guys? You all seem to be together,' asked a curious civilian as nine Caps piled into a van for the shuttle to the St. Louis airport. 'We're a band,' said Bill Riley. He motioned toward a sportswriter. 'This is our bass player.' 'What's the name of your group?' the man asked. Riley did not hesitate: 'We're the Tower of Power.' 'Have a good trip,' the man said. 'I'll look for your records.'"

Bill provided a consistent blend of scoring touch and teammate-supporting muscle in 1976-77 (43 games, 13 goals, 124 penalty minutes) and 1977-78 (57 games, 13 goals, 125 penalty minutes). As often happens, a new coach favors "his players," and under Danny Belisle in 1978-79, a confused Riley spent most of the year in the minors. Riley told the *Winnipeg Free Press*, "I was better than at least five" players on the Caps roster. "I say that and I'm not an overconfident person."

(Sources: AP, UPI, Breaking The Ice by Cecil Harris)

THE LEGENDS OF LANDOVER

✪ Pierre Bouchard (1979-1981)

Popular Montreal defenseman Pierre Bouchard didn't want to leave town. Of course he didn't – Pierre played on five championship teams in eight years. For that matter, the Canadiens didn't want to trade him. Even the Capitals never intended to acquire him. So how the heck did Bouchard end up finishing his career in Washington?

Consider it a backroom deal gone wrong. During the intra-league draft before the '78-'79 season, Montreal made a "wink-wink" deal with the Caps. To wit: we'll expose Bouchard, you select him, then trade him right back to us, and we'll send you a prospect. Except the NHL didn't look the other way, so the Habs lost Bouchard. The Caps did, too, because Pierre retired and the prospect couldn't stay.

"Everybody said I quit rather than play for Washington, but it wasn't like that at all," Pierre explained to Allen Abel of the *Toronto Globe & Mail*. Bouchard felt disrespected by a lack of communication from the Canadiens' front office. "I was dressing for practice... a reporter called and told me... I realized all the other guys knew; no one was talking to me. Everybody has to go sometime... but they wouldn't tell me to my face."

The Caps did everything they could to make Butch feel wanted. At his retirement press conference, the *Montreal Gazette* reported, "A surprise guest was Peter O'Malley, general counsel for the Capitals." Schmoozing continued all winter, culminating in Pierre's March workout in Washington. Returning was tough physically, and geographically. "I have got to get my legs back," Bouchard said. "They are somewhere between Montreal and Washington. Maybe they are on a train between here and San Diego."

More Bouchard *bon mots*: being one of four healthy Caps defensemen in a 3-3 tie at Boston, "The Bruins came at us so strongly, we had flat noses." Asked why he ultimately joined his new team, Pierre explained, "Jimmy Carter asked me to." Bouchard shared more political insight gleaned from his two full seasons on the Capitals blueline. "It's great for players in Washington," he told the *Gazette*. "We can stay here forever, but the crowd changes every four years when a new Administration comes in."

✪ Rick Green (1976-82)

Rick Green had fame as the first overall choice in the 1976 draft, riches from a $450,000 contract, and talent Capitals G.M. Max McNab predicted would only grow. "He hasn't met a situation yet where he couldn't handle himself." Plus, he was a handsome 6-foot-3. What more could a 20 year old rookie want? One thing. Green needed a cure for a condition fame, riches, and talent couldn't fix: loneliness.

THE LEGENDS OF LANDOVER

Alone for the first time in a new city, he spent $110 in a month on phone calls home. "Early in the season, I was going a little crazy," Green told the *Toronto Globe & Mail*. "I'd come home and look at the four walls. I'd put (a TV and stereo) on at the same time just because it was something to do."

Those jitters subsided, and as McNab foresaw, Green grew into a trusted, stay-at-home defenseman. Quintessential Green: In Minnesota, goalie Mike Palmateer wandered up ice, but lost the puck. Rick, backing up, stopped two shots to save a goal.

His quiet efficiency never won over Caps fans, who unfairly blamed him for the team's shortcomings. "Even when I hear my name announced on an assist or a goal, it's a boo," Green lamented. "When they flash the pictures on Telscreen and there are some boos, I know who it is." Flash may have been the one quality Rick lacked. "It's always been my appearance not to show emotion," Green conceded. "It's not like that deep down. There's a lot going on inside that's not apparent in my expression or style. People don't seem to realize I'm going as hard as I can go." Opposing scouts realized it; in 1978 alone, the Leafs, Hawks, Bruins and Kings all inquired about trading for the young blueliner.

Coach Danny Belisle also jumped to the d-man's defense. "Fans have been booing Green even before the National Anthem. It's not right. In my opinion, he's been the club's best defenseman." Rick welcomed the later hiring of a coach, first name Gary, with the same surname. "Now these people will have to listen carefully to which Green is being introduced. They won't be able to jump on me with just a mention of the name." (*Washington Post, Washington Star*)

✪ Alan Hangsleben (1980-81)

Midway through the 1979-80 season, the Caps were looking for a physical presence to protect Swedish forwards Rolf Edberg and Bengt Gustafsson. In Connecticut, Alan Hangsleben was about to be showcased. "I figured something was coming up because they moved me from defense to left wing," Hangsleben told *whalerssports.com*. Beloved in Hartford for his scrappy style, active with the team's fan clubs, Alan was moved to tears on learning he'd be leaving. "One of the Whalers' most unpopular trades ever," claimed the *Hartford Courant*. Hangsleben received more than 300 letters from Whalers fans mourning his departure.

He arrived in Landover just in time to face the Flyers. "I got into one fight in the first period and two fights in the second period," recalled Hangsleben. He contributed more than muscle, scoring a 3rd period goal to help forge a 4-4 tie. The converted d-man also scored in his 2nd game as a Cap, the next night in Quebec City. He finished with 10 goals in just 37 games after the trade. "He's been a stabilizing factor on defense and added aggressiveness," said coach Gary Green.

THE LEGENDS OF LANDOVER

Most satisfying was a 9-5 win over his old Hartford teammates. Alan and the player he was traded for, Tom Rowe, scuffled two minutes into the game. Rowe, perhaps trying too hard to make a point to his former employer, drew five penalties in all, including a fighting major. Fittingly, Hangsleben's 2nd period goal proved to be the game-winner.

Hangsleben's value to the Capitals continued even after his release early in the '81-'82 season. That story begins back when the draftee chose to sign with WHA Hartford rather than Montreal. How come? "I couldn't speak French and my middle name wasn't Pierre," Alan explained. The Minnesota native added, "And I'd seen enough snow." Hangsleben's rights reverted back to the Canadiens as part of the 1979 WHA-NHL merger. Montreal, though, left Alan in Connecticut. The quid pro quo? Hartford agreed to pass on a talented young defenseman Montreal left exposed in the expansion draft, named Rod Langway. Because Rod remained property of the Habs, he was available for trade to Washington three years later.

✪ Bob Sirois (1975-80)

Bob Sirois recorded a career high with 61 points in 1977-78. Another number confirmed Bob was a big plus for the Caps. At midseason, Sirois had been on-ice for 50% of Washington's even-strength goals, and 28% of opposition scores. The plus-22% led the league – better than superstars like Cournoyer and Bossy. By season's end, Bob's strong two-way play kept him in the top five in the NHL. Quite a feat on a Caps team that wound up the year outscored by 126, winning just 17 games. (*Canadian Press*)

An accomplished chef, Sirois got burned as part-owner of a Montreal eatery. "The restaurant failed and many of those involved disappeared," said the *Washington Star*, "leaving Sirois alone to face creditors." In July, 1980, the Capitals gave Bob permission to play the season in Switzerland, where he'd have time to sort out his finances. "I am very sorry to leave the Capitals," Sirois said. "This is the hardest thing I have ever had to do."

So hard, in fact, that within three months he asked for reinstatement to the Caps' roster. Back surgery made the request moot, but not the dream. Bob caught up with club officials when the team played the Canadiens in December, and again at the NHL draft at the Montreal Forum in June. Although Sirois wrangled an invitation to camp in September, 1981, his playing career ended after 13 games on the farm at AHL Hershey.

Sirois' most entertaining Capital Centre performance came at a 1989 alumni scrimmage. At various points he used "a gigantic stick, a two-bladed stick, an adjustable stick that suddenly grew to 10 feet, (and) late in the game he broke across the blue line, lost the blade to one of his skates and went sprawling into the boards." (*Washington Post*) "That's what people want to see," Sirois said. "It was a lot of fun."

THE LEGENDS OF LANDOVER

✪ Bob "Hound" Kelly (1980-82)

Sports team owners expect hate mail. Heck, Caps owner Abe Pollin once got an angry letter five pages long. This correspondence was noteworthy only because the author was one of his players. Bob "Hound" Kelly played 741 games and won two Stanley Cups in Philadelphia before being traded down I-95. In his first D.C. campaign, Kelly achieved personal offensive bests of 26 goals, 36 assists in 1980-81.

"At Philadelphia," captain Ryan Walter said to *AP*, "Bob was the 'designated hitter' and his job was to get the team motivated while on restricted shifts. Here, he plays on a regular line and on every shift, and he stands in front of the net." Playing on the "Roaring 20's" line with prolific scorers Dennis Maruk (#21) and Jean Pronovost (#22) didn't hurt Kelly (#24) either.

Early next season, new G.M. Roger Crozier decided this Hound could no longer hunt. "Who is going to help you more, a young kid with skills, or some old veteran?" explained coach Bryan Murray to the *Sporting News*. Little used, Kelly terminated his contract and picked up a pen. He called his former bosses "henchmen" and "back-stabbers." Kelly mused, "I scored on Crozier (then a Buffalo goalie) in the finals in 1975, and then he helps end my career six years later." *(From the book Walking Together Forever by Jim Jackson)*

✪ Dennis Maruk (1978-83)

Dennis Maruk, dubbed "Pee Wee" and deemed too small by many scouts, finished with an amazing 431 points in 343 games as a Cap. During his 60-goal campaign in 1981-82, Maruk earned a second nickname, reported by *The Hockey News*. Because Dennis favored dark suits and buried so many goals, teammates took to calling him "The Undertaker."

In '81-'82, he not only raced to a since-eclipsed franchise best for goals (60), but also club records for assists (76) and points (136) that stand to this day. Maruk holds an additional distinction, as the only Capital to be a hometown selection for the NHL All-Star Game.

If you think all athletes are blasé about all-star appearances, read what Maruk told *Hockey Digest* about being the fan favorite in 1982, the only time Capital Centre ever hosted the game. "I was the last guy introduced. The place erupted with applause, a standing ovation. It was great to see that we did have a lot of fans in Washington. It sent chills down my spine. I was so happy my mom and dad were there to see it. A lot of players are fortunate enough to play on a Stanley Cup winner. I wasn't one of them. But with the reception I got from the fans that day, I consider that my Stanley Cup. That's the game I'll never forget."

THE LEGENDS OF LANDOVER

"I encourage offense and a fairly aggressive style," said new coach Bryan Murray, behind the bench for most of Maruk's 60-goal campaign. "There had to be a change to more offense," Dennis approved. "The players had been too concerned about what the other team was doing, instead of doing the things they can do."

Maruk's opinion of Murray would change the following season. "Bryan put him on left wing," Rod Langway said to the *Philadelphia Daily News* in December, 1982. "A couple of nights Dennis was mouthing off and was really upset, but the majority of time he accepted it and worked his butt off."

Before the 1983-84 season, when Murray switched to a two-way defensive system, Maruk was shipped to Minnesota. It seems he failed the Rand McNally test. "The Capitals are going in different directions and Dennis was not a multi-directional player," general manager David Poile told *AP*. "Dennis did not do the job" last year as a left wing. Could that be because center was his natural position?

Despite being one of only 19 60-goal scorers in NHL history, fame never went to Maruk's head. Case in point: In 2008, Alexander Ovechkin broke his Caps record for goals in a season when he scored 65. The *Kingston Whig Standard* reported, "The pair talked several times during Ovechkin's big season." Maruk said of Alex, "He called and said, 'I'm sorry I broke your record.' I said, 'Don't be sorry, I was cheering you on.'" It turns out "Pee Wee" was, and is, a big man in the ways that really count.

✪ Bryan "Bugsy" Watson (1976-79)

For almost 40 years, the Capitals were never the subject of a *Sports Illustrated* cover. Which proves, I guess, that you don't need an *SI* cover jinx to be jinxed. One Cap did sneak his way onto the front of Volume 46, Issue 6, February 7, 1977. The cover photo clearly shows Bryan "Bugsy" Watson in his road red Caps sweater, marking Montreal's Guy Lafleur.

Pictures don't lie; Watson made a career of shadowing opposing stars - with trash talk, flying elbows, whatever it took. "Bugsy" got his nickname from an irritated Gordie Howe. Bobby Hull dubbed him "Superpest." Lafleur got the treatment too, from his fellow *SI* cover boy. "We were playing the Canadiens one day and we were up 3-0," recalled Watson's D.C. teammate, Guy Charron. "(Watson) ran Lafleur. That was the end of it. We lost the game, 6-3."

Legendsofhockey.net cited Watson's "tradition of hustle and crime," a nod to his 2,212 penalty minutes (at 5-9, 175!). With 17 goals in 878 games, Bryan's stick was for pestering, not scoring. One night, "Watson went in alone from center and missed the net by 40 feet." Watson explained, "I couldn't get my stick out of cross-check." (*NHL 75th Anniversary Book*)

THE LEGENDS OF LANDOVER

Watson's off-ice personality was polar opposite. Charron told Gregg Drinnan of the *Kamloops Daily News*, "He was caring, involved with charities. He was a quality, super type of individual." For his work with Special Olympics, Watson won the Charlie Conacher Humanitarian Award.

A less publicized example of Watson's quality: attending the memorial for Barry Ashbee, a Flyers defenseman who, like Watson, was known as a "gritty battler." An *AP* reporter asked why Bryan had come, since he didn't know Ashbee that well. "The reason I'm here is out of respect for the way he played the game," explained Watson. "I always had tremendous respect for an individual who played so long in the minors. He really stuck with it."

Washington was Watson's final stop of a six-team, 15 year NHL career. He played two stints each in Montreal and Detroit – and his rights were briefly owned by two additional NHL teams. To Bugsy's credit, address changes never dulled his enthusiasm. "Before Bryan Watson came, we had no character at all," coach Tom McVie joked. "Now we have more character than we'll ever need." *(Detroit Free Press)*

Evan Weiner of *nhl.com* tells how when McVie played motivational music, Bugsy "put a bandana around his head, marching back and forth through the locker room." Watson said, "The first time I heard it, I thought Tommy was stark raving mad. A month later, I was singing all the songs. It didn't make you play better, but it made you feel good." Like being a fan of the early Caps; they didn't win much, but rooting them on made us feel good.

✪ Walt McKechnie (1977)

The NHL, unlike the Catholic Church, doesn't permit annulments. If they did, the Caps would have applied to erase any record of Walt McKechnie.

Only miscalculations by two front offices compelled McKechnie to pack for Landover. In the summer of 1977, Caps goalie Ron Low thought he had agreed on a new contract with G.M. Max McNab. The first domino fell when club president Peter O'Malley vetoed that agreement. "What O'Malley offered was a $5,000 cut and the advice that Low would never get what he was asking for." (*Toronto Globe & Mail*)

O'Malley recinding McNab's contract offer was mistake one. Mistake two was made by Detroit, failing to double-check a claim by Ron Low's agent. On the promise that Washington wasn't due compensation, the Red Wings signed the free agent goalie. Too late, the Wings learned that in fact, they did owe the Caps a player in return, and that's why McKechnie got shipped to Washington. So you see, Walt and the Capitals were forced into an arranged marriage neither side bargained for, and it was destined for trouble.

THE LEGENDS OF LANDOVER

Sure enough, *The Hockey News* reported that "McKechnie's play was so uninspired he picked up the nickname, 'Sludge.'" As with many failed partnerships, coach Tom McVie cited lack of communication. "Walter is a troubled, troubled man. I tried to get him to tell me what was bothering him, but it didn't work." 16 games in, Walt was ordered to pack up and get out. "I love Walt McKechnie," McVie said, "but I love the Capitals even more. His trouble spread like a cancer and hurt the hockey team."

One anonymous Caps player disagreed, saying, "Walt's really getting the shaft." In a *Hockey Night In Canada* interview, McKechnie took the feud public, expressing anger that Detroit didn't try to keep him. "You would think he would have worked harder to prove to them it was a mistake," said a puzzled McVie. Could the relationship have been saved? Probably not. On his way out – suspended, then traded to Cleveland for Bob Girard – McKechnie said to *THN* that "he wasn't the only Capital who was in need of a psychologist."

As hockey's answer to Mickey Rooney, Walt was married to eight NHL partners: the North Stars, Golden Seals, Bruins, Red Wings, Capitals, Barons, Leafs, and Rockies, before finishing his career back in Detroit. Oh, he was also briefly property of the Rangers, though he never skated for them. Mickey Rooney had once quipped, "I'm the only man in the world with a marriage license made out 'to whom it may concern.'" (*irishtimes.com*) McKechnie could've used a hockey sweater like that.

✪ Gordie Lane (1975-79)

Gordie Lane scored a hockey goal and attempted a free throw in the same game. For the rugged Caps defenseman, the goal by itself was rare; he scored 10 in 235 games with Washington. No, his forte was standing up for himself and mates, to the tune of 614 penalty minutes with the Capitals. Besides courage, Gordie displayed tireless effort. "Lane worked overtime after practice and encouraged teammates to do the same." (*Wash. Post*)

His puck-throw though, in L.A. on October 24, 1979, may have been an NHL first. From the *Washington Star:* "Lane lost his stick and became so frustrated in his effort to freeze the puck at the rear of the goal cage that he picked up the puck and tossed it into the Forum crowd. Caps' general manager Max McNab said that he has been watching hockey all his life and never saw a player pick up a loose puck and toss it over the boards and into the seats."

Lane's frustrations ran far deeper than a momentary brain freeze, feeling under-utilized and underpaid. "They did not seem to feel I was important," he said. "It got to the point I wondered if I could play anywhere." A month after the Kings' game, Lane walked out on the Caps and got suspended. In December, Lane was traded to the Islanders for center Mike Kaszycki.

THE LEGENDS OF LANDOVER

How Gordie felt about the move depended on his audience. To D.C. reporters: "I'm sorry to leave the guys on the team." To N.Y. writers: "The Islanders work harder. In Washington, the players don't help each other. They just go around blaming each other." To a group of Caps fans at a restaurant: "You've got to be crazy to pay those prices to see this team."

Kaszycki lasted 28 games in Washington, while Lane blossomed on Long Island, playing on four Stanley Cup teams. Off the ice, Gordie became an inspiration to others who, like him, stuttered. He'd been more reluctant to go public while a Cap. "There are times when I can converse fluently," Lane said, "but when I get rattled or become tired, I wander off a bit."

Lane was a sharp guy, earning an accounting degree from the University of Maryland. As well as bookkeeping, Lane learned beekeeping, owning a commercial honey business. The *New York Times* asked him, "Which is more dangerous, keeping bees or playing hockey? 'Hockey,' Lane said, 'because you have to drive the Long Island parkways to get to the rink.'"

✪ Ryan Walter (1978-82)

Save time and just accept that Ryan Walter is better than the rest of us. Better at hockey, without question. In four seasons after Washington made him 1978's second overall draft pick, Walter racked up 114 goals and 163 assists, averaging almost a point-per-game. He accumulated 468 penalty minutes in defense of teammates. A pillar of responsibility, the Caps made him the league's youngest-ever captain.

Walter is also better, *period*. Whatever the opposite of wacky is, Ryan's that. He was once named "NHL Man of the Year." How did he spend his signing bonus? "I went straight out and bought an aluminum canoe." How did he spend his summer? "While driving across Canada, I squeezed my wrist, to make it stronger."

That came in handy when relatives came to visit; Walter would rise early to make fresh-squeezed orange juice. Ryan's off-ice pursuits included history classes at a community college. Post-hockey, along with motivational speaking, he created a hockey board game. Somebody stop this man – he's out of control!

✪ Chris Valentine (1981-84)

Chris Valentine did play one game for the Capitals on February 14. In Denver on Valentine's Day, 1982, Chris assisted Dennis Maruk's tying goal in the second period. Maruk told the *Hockey News*, "Chris had good hands, was not a fast skater, but real good with the puck." Colorado won the game with two late scores, 5-3 - a rare heartache for Valentine in '81-'82.

THE LEGENDS OF LANDOVER

When Bryan Murray was promoted from AHL Hershey, he summoned Chris to join him. Valentine paid off, scoring game-winners against Philly and Montreal. In fact, he scored three goals in his first four NHL games, at age 19. "I'm on cloud nine," Chris gushed to the *Sporting News*. Coach Murray didn't feel for his farm team's loss. "Too bad for the Hershey Bears."

Murray chewed out Valentine in a February game; his first-minute gaffe led to a Hartford goal. "I guess it got me mad, too," Chris said to the *Post*. He got even – a tying goal on his next shift. In the second period, he tallied three more, with all four goals on the power play, still a Caps single-game record. Late in the contest, Whalers goalie Greg Millen sacrificed his body on a wicked Valentine blast. "Millen was smiling as I went by. He was doing his darnedest not to let another one in."

Chris finished with a stunning 30 goals and 67 points in 60 games. But as the Caps' roster improved, Valentine cracked the lineup for only 45 more games. He went on to become an all-time great in German hockey.

Brian Kinsella (1975-77) lived the dream, even if his NHL career spanned only 10 games over two seasons. At first, Brian couldn't believe he was sharing an NHL rink with his heroes. A 1976 game at Chicago Stadium, for instance. "My first shift, I was about to take a face-off. I look up and here is Stan Mikita, a guy I idolized all my life. And he looked at me and said, 'How you doing kid?' The linesman dropped the puck and I just stood there. I mean, I didn't even move my stick. I was so star-struck. I thought, 'Oh, my God it's Stan Mikita.'"

Other brushes with greatness involved more contact. "I had my head down and Jim Schoenfeld of the Sabres nailed me. Flipped me right up and over." Kinsella doesn't wince at the memory. "That would be a great highlight on TV today." Kinsella only gets wistful considering the razor-thin margin for sticking in the NHL. "In Kansas City, I was standing in front, the puck came to me. I had the whole net, I mean the whole net. The puck was bouncing, I took a swing and missed it. If my stick had touched that puck, and I bounced it in, I might still be playing, instead of getting sent back down." (Kinsella quotes from *The Advance*, *The Toledo Blade*)

Eddy Godin (1977-79) scored his goals in bunches. Godin's NHL career lasted 27 games over two seasons, with three goals. Amazingly, two of those came on the same *shift*. Late in the 2nd period of a 1977 game on Broadway, Godin lit the lamp twice, 24 seconds apart. It helped the Caps secure a 5-5 tie with the Rangers.

Steve Self (1976), who played three Caps games early in the '76-'77 season, on being a non-regular: "I had to dress for some practices in the Bullets locker room. Sitting at my stall, I realized my feet were not touching the floor. Those guys were big."

THE LEGENDS OF LANDOVER

☕ **Brent Tremblay (1979-80)** won't ever forget his first NHL goal in ten games with the Capitals, not just because it was his only NHL goal. As Steve Winter described in *The Hockey News*, it came at home against the Whalers. "(Tremblay) slid his body along the boards, protecting the puck from a rapidly approaching Hartford checker. As the green-clad defender skated past, Tremblay drilled a rising slapshot into the net."

You'll notice that Winter coyly withheld the name of the Whaler. "Tremblay glanced over his shoulder to see which Hartford defender he left standing in his tracks... Tremblay had just beaten... Gordie Howe." Brent admitted, "I was almost unconscious by the time it went in the net. I mean, that's Mr. Hockey out there." Tremblay did have enough presence of mind to skate – with breakaway speed – to center ice, where he obtained the puck from the referee, and deposited it safely at the Capitals' bench.

☕ **Jay Johnston (1981-82)** was nicknamed "Jonah," so you'd figure he'd find employment with the Whalers. Instead, he played eight games with the Capitals over two seasons. In his first NHL contest, Johnston traded blows with an established tough guy, Calgary's Willi Plett. How'd he hold up? As Jay recalled later, "Well, I'm still breathing." (*musingsofahockeyenthusiast.com*)

Oh, about that nickname; Johnston says it refers to the newspaper boss of *Spider-Man's* Peter Parker. "Look up J. Jonah Jameson online, and you'll see that there is a striking resemblance between the two of us." And sure enough, "Jonah" years later did play with the Whalers, on their alumni team, because he ended up living in Hartford!

☕ **Greg Carroll (1978-79)** was released by the Capitals in January, 1979, when the center ice prospect's 24-game tryout proved disappointing. There'd been so much promise back in 1976; excited by Carroll's 60-goal junior season, the Caps selected Greg 15th overall in the draft.

Something unexplained had hastened his exit from Landover. In a cryptic, terse statement, G.M. Max McNab said, "It is best this way for Greg and for the Capitals." The *Washington Star* could only add, "McNab concluded that Carroll wasn't the type of athlete he wanted with the young Capitals." We can't share Carroll's thoughts, as he was "little more than a 'yep' and 'no' man in interviews."

The Red Wings picked Carroll up, only to release him, too. So the player nicknamed "Buzz" took an off-season job. Allegedly, as a drug dealer. The Whalers didn't know this when they signed Carroll for the 1979-80 season, but Hartford teammates soon sensed something amiss. "Immense talent but strange," observed Mike Rogers. "Really out there." Another described Buzz as "a bit adrift."

THE LEGENDS OF LANDOVER

Fast forward to April 4, 1980. Carroll scores with four seconds left in a Hartford victory over Quebec. The clock was expiring off the ice as well; weeks later, he'd be arrested in a drug raid. Along with his fiancée and several others, Carroll was charged in an Edmonton court with selling and distributing $500,000 worth of cocaine and MDA. Save for nine games with a semipro team in Montana, Greg's hockey career was over. Even though the most serious charges were later dismissed, it was a trip down the legal system rabbit hole that even Lewis Carroll wouldn't want to imagine.

(Sources: *Edmonton Journal*, *Canadian Press*, *Changing the Game* by Stephen Laroche)

Doug Gibson (1977-78) is the name I'd nominate, if they ever rename the Lady Byng trophy for gentlemanly conduct. In Doug's brief NHL career - 63 games, 11 with Washington - he was *never* whistled for a penalty. That, friends, is an NHL record for the most games with zero penalty minutes. Gibson also played one NHL playoff game with the Bruins, and no, he didn't get called for a penalty in that game, either. One other bit of Gibson trivia: when Gary Green was promoted from the farm team to coach in D.C., Doug was named player-coach in Hershey. Gibson's Bears won the 1980 AHL crown, and he scored 12 playoff goals!

Todd Bidner (1982) made his debut with stellar linemates. "I flew to New York to play the Islanders. They threw me on a line with Ryan Walter and Mike Gartner. It was my first shift in the NHL. I faced off against Wayne Merrick, who came from my neck of the woods. He asked, 'What are you doing here?' I said, 'I don't know.'" One of Bidner's two career Caps goals was a game-winner vs. Chicago. Todd apparently had worked on his flexibility since training camp, when a summer of weightlifting had left him too bulked up to shoot the puck.

Bidner's Big Weekend

This is mind-blowing. On one day, February 27, 1982, Bidner played two full pro hockey games, in two leagues, in two cities. And that's only half the story! "I'm in the American League, playing a game on Friday night in New Haven, Connecticut. I get the call I have to get right back to Hershey, drive to Washington, because there's a game at one o'clock on Saturday. I played every shift (in a Capitals victory over Hartford).

"(New G.M.) Roger Crozier came into the shower after the game and said, 'Bidner, they want you back in Hershey for tonight's game at seven o'clock. Get in your car, get back to Hershey and play.'" Todd completed his personal doubleheader Saturday night at Hersheypark Arena against Nova Scotia. Much as he deserved a sabbatical, Interstate 83 beckoned and Todd was on the road again. "They called me into the office and said, 'Bidner, you've got to go back to Washington, you've got another game on Sunday against Edmonton.' I played four games in 48 hours!"

THE LEGENDS OF LANDOVER

How did the Caps reward Bidner for his four-game ironman weekend? Two days later, they traded him to the Oilers. Apparently, G.M. Crozier was showcasing Bidner to Edmonton brass on the previous Sunday, hoping Todd wouldn't pass out from exhaustion before the trade was finalized. "I was just told to pick up my ticket at the Harrisburg airport, and thinking I was going to Edmonton, but the plane took me to Wichita, Kansas. Being 19 years old, I didn't even know there was a team in Wichita."

(Confusion also befell defenseman Doug Hicks, the player dealt to D.C. Hicks described to *The Hockey News* two contradictory conversations with Oilers G.M. Glen Sather. "He called me in Monday and said there would be no changes because he didn't want to screw up the chemistry. Then on Tuesday, he called me in and told me… he'd traded me to Washington.")

Todd Bidner's claim to fame is a dozen years starring in the British Hockey League, once he was done with the AHL. He has a book-full of stories about playing in the U.K., which we fervently hope he's writing right now.

(Bidner quotes from oldtimehockeyuk.com and slapshotdiaries.com)

✪ Bernie Wolfe (1975-79)

Acrobatics made Bernie Wolfe a '70's fan favorite. "Wolfe, only 5-foot-9, made saves while lying on his stomach, sitting on his pants, diving to the left, right and bearings in between. He was given a standing ovation after just seven minutes." So wrote Bob Fachet in the *Post* after one game.

If goalies had a guage for distance traveled around the crease, Wolfe's tank often would read "E" by game's end. Late in 1975, he started for the first time in his hometown of Montreal, facing 54 Canadiens shots with his mom and dad in the stands. "Driven by his parents to the Capitals' charter flight back to Washington, Wolfe was so dehydrated that his entire body cramped. His mother swore she'd never watch him play again." (*nhl.com*)

Early in the '76-'77 season, Wolfe faced a far graver health crisis. Bernie's fine reflexes disappeared when a mysterious illness attacked his nervous system. Even the name was scary: post-inflammatory polyneuritis. "I was worried I couldn't ever play hockey again," Wolfe told the *New York Times*. Actually, that was the least of Bernie's worries. "I couldn't stand up right. I couldn't walk a straight line. I had double vision and no reflexes."

Remarkably, Wolfe started a game against Buffalo during his month-long illness. *The Hockey News* explained, "(Coach Tom) McVie tried to get Wolfe scratched after the warmup, but was told that beginning with Ron Low in goal would cost a minor penalty."

THE LEGENDS OF LANDOVER

Even though Wolfe had been listed on the starting lineup card, enforcing that technicality was, in this instance, insane. "I had no feeling below the waist," Wolfe said to the *Washington Star*. "I didn't even know that I had on pads or skates." Today's rules are more humane; for instance, a substitution is allowed for an injured player, even after his team ices the puck. Bernie played for the initial 18 seconds, thankfully without incident, then was removed at the first whistle.

As mysteriously as its arrival, the virus disappeared. Wolfe recovered to have a fine season, never more so than a pair of weekend games against the Islanders. The Caps narrowly lost on Long Island, 2-1, then battled New York to a 2-2 tie at Landover, and Bernie played exceptionally well in both. Wolfe preserved the 2-2 deadlock in the 3rd period before 14,567 at Capital Centre, as Parton Keese described in the *Times*: "Drawing constant chants of 'Bernie! Bernie!', Wolfe was at his best during a 5-on-three... Arms flailing, legs kicking out in all directions, Wolfe stopped Bob Nystrom's drive through a covey of players, as well as Denis Potvin's shot through a heavy screen."

Islanders coach Al Arbour called Wolfe's performances, "As good an exhibition of goaltending as I've seen in a long time, and that goes for both of these back-to-back games." Told of the praise, Wolfe replied, "That's quite a compliment, considering all the fine goaltenders in the league. But it's easy to play well when the forwards are getting back and defensemen are standing." Arbour was less charitable in the Islanders' room, scolding his players, "You're putting that guy into the hall of fame." (*Wash. Star*)

Wolfe was also involved in a bizarre trade. Just don't look for it on any official transaction list, because it was a gruesome experiment in the trading card industry. For his 1977-78 hockey card, the Capitals netminder is pictured in a Cleveland Barons sweater. Meanwhile, Barons winger Al MacAdam is outfitted in a Caps sweater.

Wait, did they switch sweaters... or did they switch... heads? Holy Dr. Frankenstein! And why switch anything? Wolfe and MacAdam weren't *actually* traded for each other at any time in their careers. "I don't know what I should do when the kids give me a card to autograph," Wolfe said. "I try to explain that it's not my picture. I sign a few anyway." Noting to the *Washington Star* that mistakes on cards become collectors' items, Bernie joked, "I could be worth something in a few years."

Between bizarre illnesses and photo mix-ups, Bernie wisely prepared for other employment. Already a college graduate, he studied finance when not stopping pucks. In 1981, he opened a financial planning company. Buddy Yvon Labre ribbed Wolfe that if he'd hung out his shingle sooner, "The team would have done better and I would've had more money." *(Capitals Hockey Magazine)*

THE LEGENDS OF LANDOVER

P.S. When Wolfe and Chicago's Mike Veisor stood between the pipes for a 1977 game at Capital Centre, it was likely the first and only time both NHL starting goaltenders were Jewish. And now you know why Bernie's nickname was "Bagel." (Two years earlier, Wolfe made his home debut; the Centre organist celebrated each of Bernie's saves by belting out the refrain to "Jesus Christ, Superstar.") Fittingly, the Wolfe-Veisor showdown ended in a 2-2 tie. *Mazel Tov!*

✪ **Gary Inness (1978-81)**

"The Cup" is what it's all about in pro hockey. There's the Stanley Cup, of course; the AHL awards the Calder Cup; the old IHL played for the Turner Cup. Then there's Gary Inness, and the Dixie Cup. "Inness had to have a row of Dixie cups lined up on a table in his dressing room. There had to be the same number, in the same order, every time. Also, there had to be ice on the right side of the cups, water on the left side, a wet towel on the right side, and a dry towel on the left. He went berserk if anyone screwed it up." (*From Dick Irvin's book, In The Crease*)

It's no secret that the goaltender's union has more flakes than a ski slope. Yet Inness followed up his time on ice with a most sober profession: 25 years as a high school teacher in Barrie, Ontario. Gary also coached - not hockey, as you'd expect - football, his first love.

In D.C., Inness helped salvage a sinking 1978-79 season. First, the Caps rescued Gary, left jobless when the WHA's Indianapolis Racers ran out of gas. Signed in December, Inness rallied the Capitals to their finest moments of a sad year, with a 14-14-8 record and 3.70 GAA.

✪ **Jim Bedard (1977-79)**

Jim Bedard tended goal in the '70's, when penalty shot calls were almost as rare as playoff races in Landover. Some background: by 2010-11, more teams, a faster game, and new officiating standards led to 78 penalty shots - versus, for example, 15 being called in 1985-86. It's extraordinary that in just 73 games in goal spanning two seasons, Bedard saw referees whistle three of the one-on-one showdowns. Even better, Jim saved all three!

In a December, 1977 home loss to the Penguins, Bedard stoned Blair Chapman. Jim repeated the larceny in Pittsburgh six weeks later, making 41 saves, including Peter Mahovlich's penalty shot, in a 5-2 victory. In a November, 1978 loss at Montreal, Bedard again played well with 39 saves, one of them on Jacques Lemaire's penalty shot try.

During the '79-'80 season, Bedard played for teams in five minor league cities: Hershey (2 games), Cincinnati (8), Rochester (6), Tulsa (3), and Dayton (16). Making him a well-traveled kindred spirit to...

THE LEGENDS OF LANDOVER

✪ Gary Smith, Man Of Many Masks (1977-78)

Of his two nicknames, Gary Smith must have preferred "Axe," earned for intercepting a man rushing toward a teammate while, allegedly, holding an axe. With the Caps, Gary's second mask featured a medieval battle axe. Legendary mask-maker Greg Harrison, a former goalie, described his Axe design for Smith as both interesting and disappointing. "Unfortunately (it) looked like a bat from a distance," Harrison wrote to *gameusedmasks.com*.

Gary's frequent changes of address left him tagged with a less flattering nickname, "Suitcase." When Washington acquired Smith in September, 1977, they became his 6th NHL employer in 11 years. As Smith knew all too well, changing teams instantly invalidated his goalie mask artwork. Fortunately, upon joining the Caps, but before switching to the Axe mask, Smith got Harrison to rework the design Gary used in Minnesota.

The green and gold North Stars became red and blue patriotic stars. The horizontal gold stripe turned red, the horizontal green stripe became blue, and presto, Smith was ready to start the '77-'78 Caps season in style. Red, white, and blue suited the mask, inspired by the U.S. Air Force. As Harrison wrote, it was "based on the Thunderbird aerobatic team." Specifically, the paint scheme on tail section of a USAF stunt plane.

Speaking of stunts, Jack Lynch named Smith his most superstious teammate. "(Gary) strips down to his underwear and then puts back on all his clothes and equipment four times a game – before the warmup, after the warmup, and after each period." (*Washington Star*)

Caps coach Tom McVie trekked to Vancouver for a preseason pep talk with Smith and his wife. "I told him about how I felt at the end of my playing career, and how I wanted to hang on so badly." Motivated, Gary jogged his weight down from 230 to 206 pounds. Alas, new masks, new waistline, and new teammates couldn't help Smith make saves. He posted just two wins in 17 Caps games. "We lead the league in team meetings," said the quotable Smith, "and look where we are in the standings." By February, the Capitals unloaded the perpetually wandering netminder back to Minnesota.

(Quotes from *Minneapolis Star, Hockey Play By Play.*)

✪ Wayne Stephenson (1979-81)

Late in the 2nd period of a 1980 game at Capital Centre, Detroit was whistled for icing. The teams prepared for a faceoff in the Wings' zone, when players stopped and peered down to the other end of the ice. A pane of plexiglass had come loose. During the stoppage, Caps goalie and amateur handyman Wayne Stephenson, attempting to re-secure the glass, wedged the blade of his stick between the panes.

THE LEGENDS OF LANDOVER

It's not like Wayne had much else to do - the Wings had recorded just one shot in the first 18 minutes of the period. Except now the stick was stuck. With some mighty tugging and a little help from fans in the first row, Stephenson pulled the stick free. I'm pretty sure that Wayne christened the stick "Excalibur," and named himself "The True and Rightful King of the Goalies." Yup, I expect that's just what happened.

✪ Mike Palmateer (1980-82)

CBC's *Hockey Night In Canada* didn't know what they were foreshadowing when they paired Robert Picard and Mike Palmateer during the 1979-80 season. Caps defenseman Picard and Leafs goalie Palmateer took part in a taped shootout-style exhibition shown between periods. Little did Robert and Mike realize they would be swapping cities months later. At the time, Toronto was balking at Palmateer's demand for a big, multi-year contract without a buyout clause. Caps general manager Max McNab was looking for a franchise goalie who could help the team finally make the playoffs.

The trade, on June 11, 1980, was a blockbuster in Canada's largest city. The *Globe & Mail* featured a giant, above-the-fold, front page picture of Palmateer. The photo shows Mike, wearing a Capitals sweater and a wide grin, pouring a tall glass of champagne in his suburban Toronto home.

Palmateer arrived in Washington along with his colorful reputation - flashy in net, feisty with opponents, and funny with the media. Dubbed "The Popcorn Kid" for munching boxes of the stuff before games, Mike told *Goal* magazine, "The popcorn at Maple Leaf Gardens was okay, but Washington's is the best in the league. Nice and puffy."

He could be equally sanguine about a goal that ruined a shutout bid. "Yeah, it was a fast one. I clocked it at 119 mph." When Alan Iverson went on his famous rant about practice, bet you didn't know he was channeling Palmateer, who told *Sports Illustrated,* "I admit it. I don't kill myself in practice. To me a practice is four or six ouches. Over a season, those ouches add up. Games are another story. That's real hockey." And he blamed sharing his net with Wayne Stephenson for subpar results. "I'd rather be carrying the burden. I get my practice in by playing games. I have a feeling if I was playing more, I would be playing better." *(CBC)*

Some teammates bristled at his laissez-faire attitude. Mike spent part of one practice firing pucks over the glass, endangering people in the seats. At training camp, he took target practice directly into the glass until it broke. On a road trip, players were embarrassed by the discovery of scuba gear among Palmateer's belongings – a discovery made, with amusement, by another team. Privately, one Caps teammate called him "a jerk." A second labeled him "a lunatic." A third said, "That guy is a f***ing idiot." Now *that* hurts.

THE LEGENDS OF LANDOVER

In retrospect, neither player met expectations in their new locations. Toronto G.M. Punch Imlach, in his book, *Heaven and Hell in the NHL*, tracked Picard's downfall to his first game as a Leaf. Getting hammered in a fight shredded his confidence. Palmateer's two years in Washington were marred by hamstring, ankle, wrist, and knee injuries. Moreover, McNab noted that off the ice, "Mike was unhappy and missed the atmosphere in Toronto." Mike confirmed that diagnosis in a *Hockey Night In Canada* interview, lamenting the anonymity of the Maryland suburbs. "I go for dinner here and there and nobody knows you at all. It's certainly a different feeling than you get in Toronto." For good measure, his goalie mask was stolen!

The deal was equally rough on the men who made it. Wrote Imlach, "Not far into the 1981-82 season when Palmateer was not playing, McNab was fired, and the Palmateer contract was at least a contributing factor." The *N.Y. Times* reported on the last straw: "A 6-1 rout by Minnesota in which Capital Centre fans jeered the players, wore paper bags over their heads and displayed a sign that read 'Handi-Caps.'"

Imlach's punchline: "Max wrote me a note: 'That Palmateer-Picard trade didn't do us much good. You got a heart attack and I lost my job.'"

(Additional sources: *Washington Post*, mapleleafslegends.blogspot.com, *The Hockey News*,)

✪ Goalie Karoshi

Japanese has a word, *Karoshi*, meaning "death from overwork." *Karoshi* doesn't literally apply to expansion-era Capitals goalies, although it felt like it could. As Steve Winter wrote in *The Hockey News*, "Management has always found cause to press some poor unfortunate soul into extended duty between the pipes, which often resulted in the shellshocked destruction of a promising young star."

Also in *THN*, Robert Fachet listed the roll call of the fallen, veterans and youngsters alike. "Ron Low, who slipped off to Detroit; Michel Belhumeur, who played 42 games without ever winning one; Gary Smith, who played 17 and won two; Bernie Wolfe, who stayed in the area as a financial consultant; Wayne Stephenson, injured more often than he played; Gary Inness, shunted to the doghouse; Jim Bedard, who went to Finland; Mike Palmateer, back in Toronto after two years of grousing; Rollie Boutin, toiling in Minnesota's farm system; Dave Parro, troubled by a left shoulder first dislocated in a softball game."

As far as we call tell, the *Oxford English Dictionary* doesn't illustrate the definition of masochist with a picture of a 1970's Capitals goaltender. They could have.

THE LEGENDS OF LANDOVER

Coaches & G.M.

✪ Max McNab (General Manager, 1975-81)

"One of nature's noblest men," is the high praise NHL president Clarence Campbell ascribed to Capitals G.M. Max McNab. Added Canadiens' coach Scotty Bowman, "Max had to build (the Caps) virtually from scratch. He is a pretty thorough guy." Future Devils G.M. Lou Lamoriello's one word for McNab: "Integrity."

"The reputation is flawless," began one writeup. "The silver-haired McNab is 56 but looks older, and is often referred to as a father figure." NHL star Peter McNab confirmed same about his dad. "I've never heard anyone say anything bad about him. Absolutely no one badmouths my father." Not that the elder McNab was incapable of anger. "He said if he hears one more guy poke fun at the Capitals, he's going to punch the guy in the nose."

Max kept a gag gift called a "Tension Meter" on his Capital Centre desk. He should have packed it for road trips, too. During a 2-2 tie in St. Louis, "McNab downed a half-dozen cups of coffee and smoked a pack of cigarettes." In the Detroit press box, "He began pacing and entreating. Before the game was half over, his jacket had been shed and his ashtray was full." In the stands in Denver, "McNab encouraged and criticized the players, using first names in a voice too gentle for them to hear."

McNab would abandon the action when one of his fallen charges left for the dressing room. "The impression," wrote one observer, "was that he was hurrying to the man and not to the hockey player." Hurry wasn't otherwise a word associated with McNab. As Max himself said, "I don't like to see anyone make a decision in the heat of the moment." Least of all himself. "He really drags his heels sometimes," said one agent, in a poll which named McNab "Slowest to make a decision." A fellow executive joked, "I called Max to tell him I'd trade him my first round draft pick for a third round pick. He said he'd call me back."

McNab regretted a rare action in haste, when broadcaster Ron Weber made some mildly negative on-air comments. "McNab angrily confronted Weber. The result was ostracism by the team, although McNab insists he had no part in that decision." Regardless, Weber was soon accorded an apology, with McNab saying, "In retrospect, I don't say I handled it well." Six years of insanely bad luck and no playoff appearances would try anyone's patience. (We suspect Job would have only lasted five seasons.)

Second-guessing was a job hazard at home, too. "The guy my father was trading always would be someone with a nice family," said Peter McNab. "Do you really have to do this?" June McNab, Peter's mom would ask. "It's the move to make," husband and father Max would patiently reply.

THE LEGENDS OF LANDOVER

Then there's things they don't teach in general manager school. Like the time Max fielded an urgent call from goalie Rollie Boutin's mother. "Mr. McNab, Rollie's dad and I have just found his goalie's mask in the basement." Max conducted a quick investigation before returning the call to Rollie's mom in far-flung Dapp, Alberta. "Nothing to worry about. Rollie has a mask." Ruby Boutin had a last request. "Tell him to call home once in a while." "I will," said McNab. (*Quotes from Wash. Post, Wash. Star, Boston Globe, Toronto Globe & Mail*)

✪ **Father G.M. Knows Best (or, My Two Sons)**

David McNab was more than an NCAA champion goalie prospect at a Caps training camp; his dad was general manager. "Now he might realize how difficult my job really is," said Max McNab, "because I'm going to have to cut him." No hard feelings; Max hired David as a Caps scout. And David did learn from his father, becoming a Senior V.P. with Anaheim in 2008.

Another son, Peter, produced 813 points in 954 NHL games. Son could have signed with dad in 1978, but dad reluctantly advised against it. "He'd have helped us, and we sure need help," admitted G.M. Max. However, "I thought he might have a hard time in Washington, where I might be accused of playing favorites." Of course, the Capitals were having a hard time in Washington *without* Peter, who said, "I wish I could have helped Dad, but I took his advice."

Wise advice it turned out to be, as son later recalled. "I've had guys come up to me and start talking about 'your blankety-blank old man.' I've had friends, good friends, who have been cut by my father. I go up to them, want it to be the same, but it's different. The ice is there. I feel it." The younger McNab signed a contract in 1978 with Boston, reaching 35 goals in six straight seasons. (*Quotes from The Hockey News, Boston Globe*)

✪ **Tom McVie (Coach, 1975-78)**

By the middle of their second season, the Capitals were so far down, they couldn't see up. Enter Tom McVie, hired, in his words, to "rattle some cages," because a 25-game winless streak led players to expect, and accept, losing. Not Tommy, who famously explained, "I'd rather find out that my wife was cheating on me than to have to keep losing like this." How's that? "At least I could tell my wife to cut it out."

Seeing limited talent on the roster, McVie compensated with extreme conditioning. "During summer, I wouldn't let up," Tom recalled for *nhl.com*. "I kept calling the players every week. I had them on endurance training. Back then, people thought lifting weights would make you muscle bound. Now every team does it." So what if players squawked. "Hartland Monahan told me that running kills him. All I said was, 'Hartland, be prepared to die.'"

THE LEGENDS OF LANDOVER

In-season, the Caps could be found practicing at 6:30 a.m. or 10:30 at night, and sometimes twice in the same day. Players' (printable) nickname for the hard-driving coach was "Simon" - as in Simon Legree, the cruel slave dealer in *Uncle Tom's Cabin*. One player termed his exhausting workouts "sick." A reporter teased players by wearing a T-shirt which read, "McVie Can't Get Me." *(Minneapolis Star)*

Before selected games, McVie favored 22 minutes of military march music. "Bryan (Watson) asked how much the audio equipment cost," McVie recalled. "I asked him why and he said he was thinking of smashing it." McVie even alternated goalies every few minutes in one game to keep them fresh against the powerful Canadiens. To shame his forwards near the end of an 11-4 loss, he played four defensemen at one time, including Yvon Labre as a winger. On a non-game Saturday night in Minnesota, he treated the squad to an evening's entertainment – at a WHA game between the Fighting Saints and Nordiques.

The results were astounding. Largely on hustle and team unity, the '76-'77 Caps earned 24 wins and 14 ties – 62 standings points, exceeding their first two seasons *combined*. McVie finished second in coach of the year balloting to Montreal's Scotty Bowman. "It hasn't been any miracle," McVie protested. "Just hard work by the players." Owner Abe Pollin gave Tom a $10,000 bonus, mailed to McVie's wife because he refused to accept it. (*Winnipeg Free Press*)

✪ Fat Squad

"The Biggest Loser" sounds like an unkind description of the 1970's Capitals. Instead, it was a recent NBC reality show featuring obese contestants competing for prizes by losing weight. Also, re-confirming that there is no minimum qualification either for entertainment or self-respect. The concept wasn't even original. Thirty years earlier, Caps coach Tom McVie came up with the idea, by a different name. Fat Squad!

As Bill Riley explained, "McVie used to have a 'Fat Squad' for players he would make practice harder because they needed to lose weight." (*Breaking The Ice*) If you're not convinced this had all the elements of a game show, consider that failure at the scale would result in a player being fined $500. McVie was fanatical about fitness, boasting, "No team in the NHL is in better shape."

Forward Mike Marson was a frequent participant in Fat Squad, and in April, 1976, he played for the most fantastic of prizes. If contestant Marson could meet his target - less than 200 pounds - he and his wife would enjoy an all-expenses-paid trip to Japan. McVie dangled that carrot, as the Caps were about to jet to the Far East for four exhibition games against Kansas City.

THE LEGENDS OF LANDOVER

The catch: Mike tipped the scales at 212, and was given a measly three days to shed the extra weight. In place of food, Marson's week became consumed with saunas, stationary bikes, and sweat. Subsisting mainly on a diet of chewing gum, Mike somehow managed to drop 14 pounds in those three days! Marson won his spot on the Caps' Japan roster, although he admitted later, "I was dizzy like you wouldn't believe."

For a youngster three months shy of his 21st birthday, the sights of Tokyo soon left Marson feeling the good kind of dizzy. "It was an eye opener, like going to some other planet." The technology of the upscale Ginza district left a lasting impression. "They had all these big televisions outside, the way most cities now have TVs downtown." So Mike, no hard feelings toward your fitness-fanatic coach? "Tommy McVie was arguably the best hockey man I ever worked with." (Marson story from Ben Raby's book, *100 Things Capitals Fans Should Know And Do Before They Die*.)

✪ Don Cherry (Bruins Coach, 1974-79)

Depending on whom you ask in Canada, Don Cherry was a national treasure, an entertaining TV pundit, or a reactionary bigot. And as the Bruins' coach during the late '70's, a Caps antagonist.

During a Capitals game in Boston on January 19, 1978, Cherry originally vented his wrath on referee Ron Wicks. The furious B's coach believed the fix was in, because Mike Milbury received a double minor after a brawl. Cherry later claimed in his book, *Hockey Stories and Stuff*, "To keep the score down," referees would "give the winning team penalty after penalty." The implication being that the four minutes to Milbury were intended as a muffler to the Bruins' superior skill.

When Cherry shared his theory with Wicks, the ref hit the coach with a bench minor. At period's end, Cherry tried to hit Wicks back - literally. "Police officers were seen restraining Cherry," reported *AP*, though they couldn't contain his expletive-laden verbal assault. The feisty 4-1 Bruins victory featured another odd spectacle. Boston Garden's benches were on opposite sides of the ice, so players engaged in profane shouting matches across the width of the rink.

The acerbic Cherry quipped after the game, "Why don't they just put lead in our skates to make it even." (*AP*) And he ridiculed the Caps' offense. "Isn't that a beautiful team? I never heard of a team not getting a shot in the first period." (They did have one.) McVie thought slight of tongue was evident in Cherry's mocking words. "He was hiding the fact his boys lost every fight." Indeed, Russ White reported in *The Hockey News*, "Bob Picard got the best of Terry O'Reilly, Gordie Lane took John Wensink, and both Bill Riley and Bryan Watson roughed up Mike Milbury."

THE LEGENDS OF LANDOVER

McVie also noted Cherry's confrontations with Wicks. "We don't feel sorry for ourselves. We don't cry about officials." Told of Cherry's postgame insults, McVie fired back. If Cherry had to coach the undermanned Caps, "He'd be selling Cadillacs in Rochester."

Before the rematch eight days later in Landover, McVie penned a letter detailing the shortcomings of the Boston coach. Cherry not only read it to his Bruins before the game, he also read it in front of the Capitals' bench. At the time, he told *UPI*, "He doesn't have the guts to face me. He leaves letters." Even Don later wrote, "I'm not too proud of that."

This sparring brought 17,651 riled up fans to Capital Centre. *UPI* reported a switchblade was thrown toward the Bruins bench, and a soda doused Cherry's suit. Boston won, 5-2, causing McVie to lament his squad's lack of offense – three shots on goal to start the game, then 27 minutes without another one. "Without pressure, their wives could walk out of their own zone." Years later in his book, Cherry, with characteristic bombast, exaggerated his team's performance. "I think it was 6-0 in the first 10 minutes." Actually, the Capitals scored first and trailed just 3-1 after two periods. For that matter, *UPI* printed Cherry's claim that the game drew the largest crowd in Caps history; it wasn't.

McVie achieved a measure of satisfaction in the clubs' final meeting, a 4-4 tie powered by Guy Charron's hat trick. Moreover, the Caps fired 16 shots on goal in the first period. Still, Cherry couldn't let go. The Caps pulled their goalie in the final seconds with a faceoff in Bruins territory. Bold strategy? Nah. Cherry called it "bush league."

The man knew bush league - Cherry climbed into the Capital Centre stands between periods to confront a heckler. "I kept saying, 'Why don't you come up here?'" Caps fan Bill Cummings told the *Washington Post*. "Even the security people were surprised, he walked right past them. He said, 'Well, I'm here. What are you going to do about it?' I said, 'I'm not going to do anything. I'm just glad I was able to make an ass of you.'" Cherry was neither fined nor suspended.

✪ McVie, Cherry, And The Last Laugh

The Capitals took a backward step in their fourth season, as other clubs narrowed the conditioning gap. Former goalie Ron Low "hinted some of the players weren't working as hard as they had last year. Hartland Monahan, another ex-Capital, thought the Caps were worn out." (*The Hockey News*)

All McVie knew was that mounting losses weren't from lack of preparation. "We know exactly what the other team's going to do," he said to *AP's* Frank Brown. "I can pretty well tell you who's going to score for them and who the three stars are going to be. But the same things that worked last year aren't working this year."

THE LEGENDS OF LANDOVER

The toll extended to the coach's family. "I was so fired up this one night we got really smoked that I drove the 20 minutes home and I forgot my son, Dallas, at Capital Centre. He was the stick boy. I was so fired up it hadn't even crossed my mind." *(nhl.com)*

McVie was let go, in bizarre timing and with no public explanation, at the end of training camp in 1978. *The Hockey News* speculated that owner Abe Pollin wanted a fall guy for weak ticket sales. The *Washington Star* thought "Pollin and Max McNab felt McVie was too tough on players, especially first draft picks Rick Green and Robert Picard, who needed to be coddled instead of constantly scolded." Pollin might have been further angered by discouraging words overheard at a "Welcome Home" luncheon, or McVie's candid admission his roster wasn't good enough. (He was right.)

Anyone who's ever lost a job can relate to what happened next. "The first two days everyone in hockey called to sympathize. It was almost exciting," said McVie. "Then the calls stopped. I'd check my phone to make sure there was still a dial tone." (From *The Rebel League* by Ed Willes) During better times, Pollin gushed that Tom deserved a 20-year contract. "When he fired me, my comment was that I still had 19 years to go," McVie told *Sports Illustrated*. "I gave my soul to that team."

McVie turned down a job as a Bruins' minor-league coach, giving Cherry another opportunity for unsportsmanlike conduct. "I'd never work in the same organization as a man like that," Cherry sneered to *UPI*.

We're happy to report McVie earned the last laugh. In 1994, he joined - who else? - the Bruins, as a West Coast scout. Boston won the 2011 Stanley Cup in Vancouver and Tommy got to lift the trophy. "I've had 55 years in hockey and it's never happened before so it's great," said McVie. "I don't want it to happen right away, but I can die in peace now." *(bostonbruins.com)*

Speaking of making peace, McVie and Cherry found an unlikely place for a reacquaintance in 2016. The Bruins played host to that year's Winter Classic at the Patriots' NFL stadium, and Boston alumni were invited. Prior to the game in Foxboro, McVie and Cherry posed for a smiling picture together – with no evidence of knives hidden behind their backs.

Decades earlier, McVie made a wish. "My advice to Don Cherry is to see what it's like on the other side before assessing judgement. Let's see him walk a mile in my shoes." Cosmic justice granted that wish when the Bruins axed Cherry, and he hooked up in 1979-80 with a mediocre squad in Colorado. The man who boasted that he could have gotten more out of McVie's Caps won just 19 games, with 48 losses. As he wrote, "It was so bad on my nerves that I couldn't sleep at night." Not so easy without Orr and Espo, eh, Don?

THE LEGENDS OF LANDOVER

On March 18, 1980, 12,239 at Capital Centre saw a first; Washington beating a Don Cherry-coached team. The Caps outshot the Rockies 31-18, shut them out for the final 59 minutes, and used goals from Lofthouse, Gartner, Hangsleben and Maruk to win going away, 4-1. Cherry lasted nine more games, got fired for the second straight season, and never again coached in the NHL.

Cherry came a hair's breadth from another coaching job in 1981... with the Capitals! We know this because Don prematurely spilled the beans on TV in the middle of a Leafs-Rockies game broadcast. Cherry announced to viewers he was going to meet owner Abe Pollin to continue negotiations. Speaking like the job was already his, Cherry warned, "I hope they don't expect a miracle in one year." Pollin was set to hire Cherry, until Bryan Murray so impressed Pollin during his interview that Murray landed the job instead. All Don got was a meeting of egg and face. *(Toronto Globe & Mail)*

✪ Capitals Coaches Go Hollywood

Danny Belisle spent 13 undistinguished months as Capitals coach, winning 28 games, losing 51. His brush with greatness came three years earlier. In the climactic scene of the movie classic *Slapshot*, Reg Dunlop (Paul Newman) and his Chiefs are in a brawl. Evan Weiner of *nhl.com* points out, "You might recognize Belisle as the player absorbing Dunlop's blows." Belisle explained, "We weren't assigned fight partners. I knew if I could get to Paul Newman, I'd get in the movie." Belisle also got his son a brief on-camera role as a stick boy.

What Belisle didn't consider was that film shoots drag on longer than the final minute of an NBA game. "I was laying on the ice for six hours with Newman on my chest," Belisle told the *Washington Star*. "He was supposed to pull his punches, but you can't pull all of them." For his 10 seconds of celluloid immortality, Danny collected a sore shoulder and a purple arm, but also a more welcome memento. Above Belisle's Capital Centre office hung a 5x7 color photo of the coach with Newman, both men smiling for the camera while fake blood drips from Belisle's nose.

Bruce Boudreau coached more than 1,000 minor league games before the Caps called him up in 2007. Years earlier, he also landed a bit part in *Slapshot*, playing for Hyannisport; he's No. 7 of the "Presidents." Boudreau told the *Toronto Star*, "I'm the little hog that stays in front of the net because I knew where the camera was."

✪ Danny Belisle (Coach, 1978-79)

The Capitals put Dan Belisle in an impossible situation, naming him coach 48 hours before the start of the '78-'79 season. Fired a year later, even Dan wasn't sure he was right for the job. "Maybe I lost this one. I don't know," Belisle told *UPI* after a home loss to Edmonton. "I'm befuddled somewhat."

THE LEGENDS OF LANDOVER

The miniscule gathering of 5,214 piled on, singing, "Goodbye Danny" and waving handkerchiefs. The *Washington Star* described his face as "ashen." Mired in a 4-10-2 start to the season, Belisle was let go after the game.

A bad omen came the moment Dan took the call from Washington G.M. Max McNab offering him the job. "I was so stunned, I leaned back in my chair, hit my head on the filing cabinet, and had to get three stitches," Belisle told *The Hockey News*. (Danny might have been accident-prone. Dennis Maruk told thehockeynews.com about Belisle missing a team flight. "He must have had a few too many. When we saw him later his tie was crooked, he had a black eye. He said he fell in his room and hit a table.")

The biggest margin of defeat on Danny's watch came in L.A. on December 4, 1978. The Kings outshot the Caps 18-5 in a brutal 3rd period, scored five times, three in a 46-second span, and cruised to a 10-2 victory. What sticks out in the *L.A. Times* game story is Washington's utter lack of system or organization. "They arrived winless in their last six games, and it was easy to see why. Their defensemen were repeatedly caught out of position, their passes in their own territory bordered on ridiculous, and the forwards showed little inclination to backcheck." Belisle showed no mercy to his goalie Rollie Boutin, making his NHL debut; at no time given sanctuary on the Caps' bench, Rollie surrendered all 10 Kings goals.

The Caps once were assessed a penalty for icing a different starting lineup from the one Belisle submitted on his lineup card. In the same game, he tried to use seven players at one time, also not allowed. Of course, since his team beat the Rockies 9-3 in Denver that night, all was forgiven.

Coach Belisle bungled his relationship with respected veteran Guy Charron. For a crucial faceoff late in a tie game in Chicago, Charron was summoned to the bench, replaced by Ryan Walter, playing his first NHL game. Belisle would say later, "I lost Guy's confidence when I took him off the ice in such a critical situation." (From Walter's book, *Off The Bench And Into The Game*.) The move foreshadowed the following October, when Belisle stripped Charron of his captaincy, again in favor of Walter.

Let's detour, to hear from nutritionist Nancy Clark: "An analysis of elite hockey teams showed players with a high carbohydrate diet skated not only 30% more distance, but also faster." Got that? High Carbs *Good*; Low Carbs *Bad*. Yeah, so?

Here's what, reported by *AP*: "The team drifted into awful shape under Belisle, some say as a result of the *low-carbohydrate diet* he instituted." Granted, we know more now than we did then about sports nutrition. Still, shouldn't coaches have a version of the Hippocratic Oath? Like, "First do no harm with cockamamie eating rules."

THE LEGENDS OF LANDOVER

The preceding would be the prosecution's case against Dan Belisle. A defense also deserves to be on the record. Let's start with more details of McNab's job offer, as Belisle recounted to the *Detroit Free Press* "I asked if I could have a day to think about it, and he said, 'No, we need to know right away.' Hell, I knew more about the Russians than I did about the Capitals." Danny had recently purchased a home in Philadelphia, where he coached the AHL Firebirds. But he worried about declining. "Word would get around that maybe this guy didn't think he's qualified to coach in the NHL." Belisle met McNab for the first time when he signed his contract, then hopped a flight to Los Angeles for the season-opener - and to say hello to his players.

What a weird night that was. "I remember being behind the bench. I had to read their names on the back of their jerseys to tell them apart." Besides Bryan Watson, "The rest were all strangers." Despite somehow winning their first game together, 4-2 over the Kings, the new coach assessed his charges as "an unhappy crew."

The rug was pulled out from under Belisle at the home opener, too. "They introduced everybody but me. I thought that was a little weird." Only later did management explain that they thought he'd get booed. "I was the villain right off the bat because fans liked the other coach." (Fans at the opener chanted, "We want McVie. We want McVie.") "If they like McVie, was it my cross to bear? It was like I never had a chance." The Caps didn't hire an assistant for Belisle, either.

Ladies and gentlemen, does this sound like a man put in a position to succeed? Not even Max McNab, the man who hired him, thought so. "Think of what Danny was up against. Not even Winston Churchill could show any leadership under those circumstances."

Once the coach and players got to know each other (and grabbed goalie Gary Inness from the WHA), the team reeled off a 9-5-1 run in January. Dan was known to light up a foot-long victory cigar - sometimes after a tie, too. "Danny Belisle is a very likeable chap – understated, low key and witty in a gentle way," wrote Russ White in the *Star*.

But in February and March combined, the Caps managed a meager four victories. "It was a long, tough year," said Belisle, who knew about tough as a native of South Porcupine, Ontario, 440 miles north of Toronto. Danny was fond of saying there were only two seasons there, "A week of fall and 51 weeks of winter." Not unlike his memories of Landover, Md.

An assistant coach in Detroit in 1986, Dan was put in charge while coach Brad Park served a suspension. Who else could possibly have been his first opponent except the Capitals. At the time, Detroit had the league's worst record, while Washington had one of the best. In a turn of poetic justice, Danny's Wings won in a rout, 7-0. For his five other games as interim coach, Belisle joked, "I'll gather the players to watch a replay of it."

THE LEGENDS OF LANDOVER

✪ Dennis Hextall (Assistant Coach, Oct. 17-Nov. 14, 1979)

We said the Capitals never furnished Dan Belisle with an assistant. Well, he did have one, sort of, for his final four weeks. The Caps announced on October 17, 1979 that henceforth, when 36-year old center Dennis Hextall wasn't in the lineup, he'd serve as a part-time assistant coach. "I never contemplated coaching before," Dennis said to the *Washington Post*.

When Belisle was shown the door 12 games later, Dennis' nascent Caps coaching career came to an abrupt end. His playing career, too. No formal announcement was made, but by December, a rookie defenseman was assigned Hextall's number 22 sweater.

✪ Gary Green (Coach, 1979-81)

Gary Green, age 26, succeeded Belisle in November, 1979, the youngest coach in NHL history – a distinction Gary still holds. That seemed the plan from the moment the Caps lured him to minor-league Hershey with major league perks: $50,000 salary, car, apartment, and expense account.

Though his surname served to describe his limited resume, Green convinced Caps brass his youth was actually a plus. "Communications (with players) should be no barrier," he said. "I'm in their age bracket." *The Hockey News* declared on its cover, "Wunderkind At Work In Washington"

Green preached positivity. He needed every bit of it to untangle the mess left to him. The Caps "didn't have the legs for the third period," said Green. "They didn't have organization or discipline." *AP's* David Ginsburg recounted the blunt words of Green's first team meeting. "I can't walk in and expect respect," Gary told players, "because I haven't earned it. But give me the next month to show I'm capable of coaching in this league, and that I can teach. (If I can't) my butt will be out of this league anyway."

Captain Ryan Walter approved of the coach-as-one-of-the-guys approach. "He never points a finger at anyone," Walter said of Green, to the *Toronto Globe & Mail*. "It's 'We have to do this or that.' He's excellent one-on-one with you. It's always 'We.'"

Green embraced the unorthodox. Against Toronto, he noted that netminder Curt Ridley was "very big and been known to let low shots go by." Yet Green instructed sniper Dennis Maruk to shoot high. "That made him stand up a little more," explained the coach. "In the second period, we keyed on keeping the shots low, and overall, we put on good pressure." Indeed, Maruk scored one of Washington's three 2nd period goals, adding two more in the 3rd en route to a 6-2 victory.

THE LEGENDS OF LANDOVER

Their record stood at 5-20-5 on the fateful night of December 15, 1979. Entering the 3rd period against the Rangers, Washington trailed, 4-0, but mindful of a stirring message from their coach. "The question now is a matter of believing in yourselves," Green told them in the room. "If you don't do something, these people are going to boo all of us off the ice." Then the turnaround Green had promised for a month shockingly arrived over the course of 12 minutes. The Caps forged a stunning comeback on goals by Rick Green at 3:01, Wes Jarvis at 4:01, Mike Gartner at 10:29, Rolf Edberg at 12:22, and Paul Mulvey at 14:46. Washington won, 5-4, and from then until the end of the season, the Capitals posted a winning record, 22-20-8.

Unfortunately, that was exactly one win too few to make the playoffs. Doubly unfortunate, they also fell one win shy the following season. At the time he was hired, Gary laughed at the constant comments about his age. "Sooooo young," he mimiced to the *Washington Star*. "Every time I hear that, it sounds like I've been killed in a car accident." If back-to-back heartbreaks hadn't killed him, it had certainly aged him.

"I feel like I'm 48 years old," Green admitted to the *Globe & Mail*. "After two years with the Caps, I guess that can happen." From *Today* magazine: "His face is pale and drawn, eyes red. Hamburger wrappers lie on the floor; eating on the go has become a way of life." The profile continued, "The job pays well - more than $100,000 a season - but the hours are long and hard and he's paying the price: a hiatus hernia he treats with endless bottles of Rolaids and half a dozen stress vitamins every morning. A good sleep is a luxury he no longer remembers."

The Caps started the 1981-82 season 1-12. Typical was a 6-1 loss to Minnesota on November 4, where two Caps suffered injuries, and two Washington goals were disallowed. "Nothing seems to go our way," Green lamented.

The next thing to come Green's way was a pink slip. As he told the *Minneapolis Star*, "I had friends in the business who called me up and said, 'With the (tough early-season) schedule you've got, the team will be 1-8 after the first nine... but then the next coach should have an easier time ahead of him.' At the time, it was a joke - but I'm not laughing anymore."

In spite of the travails, Gary Green stayed true to his positive outlook. Reminiscing with John Feinstein of the *Post*, Green believed he actually could have reversed his dismissal. "Abe (Pollin) called me at 9:30 in the morning. I'm not a fighter in the morning. If he had called in the afternoon, I would have shook him by the shoulders and said, 'Abe, let's not panic. We're losing, but we're going in the right direction. You knew when you hired me this would take time. You have to give the Gartners, the Walters, the Carpenters time. They're going to be stars, and we'll get it done.'"

THE LEGENDS OF LANDOVER

The owner splashed cold water on that scenario, telling the *Washington Post* that Green had "lost control" of his team, and that they were playing "patsy hockey." Reading that, Green saw red. "When it comes to be considered by other hockey teams, those quotes go a long way in the media. General managers tend to take something like that and accept it as gospel. I think that's unfair." Gary never did coach again in the NHL.

Back when he was hired, Green believed he could outwork elder counterparts. "I don't need as much sleep at night. I've got more energy than I'm going to have at 45, if I'm alive at 45." Maybe Gary had a premonition; he suffered a heart attack when he was 33. But in 2014, at age 60, Gary was still a spry and cheerful network TV analyst.

✪ Suspending Disbelief

The real shame of the Capitals just missing the playoffs is that coach Green never got to use his lucky charm. *Today* magazine broke the news that Green owned a magical pair of white suspenders with gold buckles.

He first called on their powers while with the Peterborough Petes junior team. "I wore them at a game once under my suit and we won, so I wore them again, and we won again, so I kept on wearing them." When Gary reached the NHL, the suspenders got called up, too. "I tried them and we went on an instant winning streak. But then we lost a game, so I put them away because I figured they needed a rest, right? You know – recharge their supernatural powers kind of thing. I'll probably bring them out for the playoffs when we need them most."

Alas, they never made it back out from the bedroom dresser. Imagine how the white dress suspenders with gold buckles would have overpowered the opposition in the postseason. Then, as the legend grew, imagine the sensation as Washingtonians all over town began wearing white dress suspenders with gold buckles… All right, don't imagine that last part.

✪ A Team Divided

Gary Green's Caps didn't have a prayer. Or they had too many, depending on whom you ask. Either way, off-ice issues may have bled into the poor play that cost Green and G.M. Max McNab their jobs in November, 1981. *Minnesota Star* columnist Doug Grow wrote, "The team, according to the league grapevine, is split down the middle. Born-againers on one side, those with traditional beliefs, or perhaps no beliefs, on the other."

Grow cited the example of born-again Christian Jean Pronovost, who had converted teammate Jim McTaggart. "In hockey eyes, the change was not a good one. McTaggart was in the league because he was a hitter. Now he's in (minor league) Hershey, Pa., turning the other cheek."

THE LEGENDS OF LANDOVER

McTaggart himself had once told *The Hockey News*, "When they do come at you, either you stand up to them or you walk away. If you walk away, you're finished."

In the midst of a losing streak, coach Green called a team meeting to confront the religious rift. "There wasn't the closeness of players off the ice," Green said to the *Washington Post*. Regarding Christianity, "I know some guys are and some guys aren't. Some guys go to coffee shops, some guys go to bars. It's important that we compromise and sometimes go out together." Whether or not faith was the distraction impacting team play, Green and McNab were the ones directed out together shortly thereafter.

For the record, the religious divide didn't close under new management. Coach Bryan Murray signed off on Sunday services led by Ryan Walter and Mike Gartner, but cautioned them against being "a hard recruiter." In his eponymous autobiography, Dennis Maruk put it this way: "The Capitals of 1982-83 were made up of two distinct groups – sinners and saints. Or, as we called ourselves, 'Christians and Lions.'"

THE LEGENDS OF LANDOVER

3rd Shift: *The Stuff Legends Are Made Of*

✪ Doing The Time Warp

Einstein taught us that elapsed time is relative. His theory got an unexpected workout on November 29, 1979, in a 5-3 Caps loss in Pittsburgh. Distortions began as the Civic Arena scoreboard clock malfunctioned in the second period. "The poor guy keeping the time below didn't have a clue," said Pittsburgh's Tom Bladon. "I asked him once how much time was left and he said 6:13. A minute or so later I asked again and he said 6:19." Caps coach Dan Belisle confirmed, "The time was way off."

Washington's Pete Scamurra took a penalty at 18:32. Officially, 18:43 was the listed time of Rick Kehoe's power play goal, but those at the game were sure much more than 11 seconds had elapsed. And time should have expired before the score, or the penalty for that matter. "The Penguins conceded the period lasted anywhere from two to four minutes longer than the prescribed 20." (*Washington Star*)

✪ Scoring Points On A Hall-Of-Fame Goalie

Taking pity on a fellow goalie before a Caps-Canadiens game, Ken Dryden said to Bernie Wolfe, "It must be awful to play in Washington." Bernie gave Dryden – one of the brightest pro athletes ever – an education. "Ken, it's still the NHL, where I always wanted to be." Replied Dryden, "You're right." Bernie's pal Yvon Labre was known for grit, not goals (14 in 371 games). Yet, he once beat Dryden – when the Habs reacted like he was radioactive. The D backed in, forwards peeled off, and Dryden misplayed the shot. "His glove got there a half-hour before the puck," Yvon recalled, laughing.

✪ With Friends Like These...

Labre took friendly fire from Wolfe one night in Minnesota. Labre and Dennis Hextall were battling for position near Wolfe's net. Earlier, Yvon had urged Bernie to be more aggressive. As told in Dick Irvin's *In The Crease*, Wolfe chose this moment to make like Paul Bunyan. "I take my stick and I two-hand Hextall right across the ankle," Wolfe remembered. "He doesn't move. He doesn't budge, doesn't blink, doesn't even get mad." Yvon soon explained why, telling his goalie, "I'm proud of you for trying, but you missed him and you hit me."

A hit and a miss became a teachable moment for a second pair of Caps. In Atlanta, defenseman Gordie Lane charged at Randy Manery of the Flames. Manery sidestepped like a bullfighter, and Lane ended up goring teammate Tommy Williams. Sent sprawling 15 feet down the ice, Tommy rose with advice for his raging bull. "Listen, Gordie. We're in the red jerseys. Atlanta – they're in the white jerseys." (*Washington Star*)

THE LEGENDS OF LANDOVER

✪ There Goes The Neighborhood

Throughout the '70's, as the Flyers and Canadiens battled for hockey supremacy, Bob Kelly and Pierre Bouchard staged many a bruising battle.

(This next paragraph should be read while humming the tune from "The Odd Couple.") *"In 1980, Bob Kelly was asked by Philadelphia to remove himself from his place of residence. With nowhere else to go, he appeared at the home of the Washington Capitals. A year earlier, Montreal had thrown Pierre Bouchard out, requesting that he never return. Can two relocated men share an ice surface without driving each other crazy?"*

Kelly recalled the surreal arrangement in a chat with *thehockeynews.com*. "In 1980, I end up in Washington. Pierre Bouchard ends up in Washington. We end up in condos next to each other, three doors apart. One day he's playing with my kid." Kelly smiles at the memory. "Something is wrong with this picture - five years ago he was beating the s--- out of me."

✪ Bad Breaks

Seven years before the birth of the Capitals, Albert King recorded *Born Under a Bad Sign*. The blues standard could have served as the theme for the medical misfortunes of the expansion-era Caps, especially the signature line: "If it wasn't for bad luck, I wouldn't have no luck at all."

In Gordie Brooks' case, the bad luck came in 1975, out of thin air. From the *Orlando Sentinel*: "During warmups, Brooks skated in on Ron Low, and unleashed a routine shot. The puck caromed off Low's skate and into Brooks' face. Brooks would require reconstructive surgery." Gord played another decade in the minors, but never again in the NHL.

"We went through a lot of players" in 1974-75, said forward Ron Lalonde. "We had one injury after another that created an awkward atmosphere. Right beside our dressing room was a community room that had a pool table, a fridge, ping-pong table. We're trying to get ready for the game, and all you could hear were these guys laughing. It became an issue as the season wore on." (*Can't Win 4 Losing* podcast)

In 1976-77, Bob Sirois could have used his own clinic. And talk about a Bad Sign. "On the first day of training camp," reported *AP*, "he leaned back while watching teammates run - and cut his hand on a piece of glass." Bob never did stop singing the blues. In September, Sirois strained knee ligaments. In December, he broke his left thumb. In February, a violent check into the boards put his right arm in a sling. Oh, and did we mention his bout with food poisoning?

THE LEGENDS OF LANDOVER

Among those ringing in 1978 on the injured list were Blair Stewart, Bob Girard, Rick Green, Ace Bailey, Jack Lynch, and Yvon Labre. Six regulars out of action at the same time. Beleaguered general manager Max McNab told the *Washington Star*, "We don't like to even try to keep track of the injuries we've had, because if we ever started, we'd be sick."

20 games into the 1979-80 season, the shorter list was Capitals who *hadn't* been injured. Nearing Thanksgiving, four forwards (Dennis Maruk, Guy Charron, Rolf Edberg and Sirois) and four defensemen (Labre, Pete Scamurra, Pierre Bouchard, and Paul McKinnon) were all sidelined. Five other Caps had missed at least one game with an injury.

For sheer volume, nothing matched a 1981 Western Canadian road trip. Three goalies (Mike Palmateer, Wayne Stevenson, Dave Parro) were banged up. Two forwards (Charron, Edberg) and six defensemen (Pat Ribble, Rick Smith, Howard Walker, Bouchard, MacKinnon and Labre) were in various states of distress, from separated shoulders to dislocated jaws to damaged spleens to sprained ankles to bad knees. The only "healthy" D-man, Rick Green, played with stomach cramps!

Between 1976-77 and 1980-81, injuries to Capitals players were both staggering and unrelenting. Here's the number of man-games lost each of these seasons, with league rank in parentheses: 277 (1st), 265 (1st), 242 (2nd), 410 (1st), 347 (1st). A young franchise being chased, year after year, by an injury bug the size of Mothra hasn't got a chance. This nightmare, more than any other factor, kept the Capitals from being a successful franchise prior to 1982.

✪ Blackouts

Playing with that injury-decimated lineup, the Caps suffered their most total power blackout in Calgary on January 8, 1981. Washington failed to score on 13 – you read right, 13 – power plays, including a pair of two-man advantages lasting more than a minute each. *And* they allowed a shorthanded goal! Almost as lopsided, the Caps went 0-12 with the extra man in a home loss to St. Louis on November 9, 1975. The Blues were granted three power plays in the game - and scored on all three.

✪ What's My Line?

See if you can guess the professional athlete from these clues: a pro who played home games in Maryland in the '70's; was known for his good glove; and who, as his ball cap from a newspaper photo suggested, spent his summers playing baseball for the Orioles. Don't bother digging through your old Memorial Stadium programs for his name. The mystery man is... Caps goalie Ron Low.

THE LEGENDS OF LANDOVER

During the hockey off-season, Low played first and third base for the *Binscarth* Orioles of the Manitoba Senior Baseball League. "I like baseball," Low told the *Brandon Sun*. "It helps me to keep in shape and I just enjoy being with the other guys." He could play, too, hitting .381 during his first season. Couldn't a bad-hop grounder be hazardous to the Caps' number one netminder? "When asked if general manager Milt Schmidt thinks it's a good idea for him to play baseball in the summer, Low said, 'He doesn't know I'm playing.'" Low fessed up when he signed a new contract.

✪ Golden Jet Never Landed In D.C.

"Hull Destined For Capitals?" blared the *Winnipeg Free Press* headline on July 31, 1979. Yes, *that* Bobby Hull, Chicago's Golden Jet, of the curved stick, booming shot, blazing speed & five 50-goal seasons. Hull defected to the WHA Jets in 1972, then retired in 1978. By next summer, at age 40, Hull itched to return, but not with Winnipeg. The *Free Press* reported, "Capitals have made an offer interesting enough to have caught the attention of Jets general manager John Ferguson."

Ferguson even granted the Capitals "permission to negotiate salary terms with the Golden Jet." For his part, Caps President Peter O'Malley didn't play coy, sensing a chance to upgrade on the ice and at the ticket window. "We will do everything in our power to land Bobby Hull," O'Malley said. "It would be a great shot in the arm for the franchise."

The Caps indeed were on the ice when Hull made his NHL return - as the opposition; by October, Bobby had a change of heart. "Hull said personal problems had been resolved." *(UPI)* On November 3, 1979, Hull basked in a three-minute standing ovation, then skated 10 uneventful shifts as the host Jets and Caps tied, 1-1. "I was unfair to myself and the team, trying to force myself into the lineup as quickly as I did," Hull said. *(CP)*

Another Caps connection: a rare appearance by Hull and Gordie Howe as teammates. Hartford, where Gordie finished his career, acquired Bobby late in the '79-'80 season. The two aging immortals played nine regular season games together, including March 8, 1980 at Capital Centre. Gordie contributed one assist, while Hull didn't dent the scoresheet. The Caps sure did; two goals each from Mike Gartner, Bengt Gustafsson, and Bob Sirois keyed a 9-5 Capitals victory.

Hull went back into retirement following the season. When Hull attempted one more comeback in September of '81, his first NHL opponent again was Washington. Playing in pre-season in Sweden for the Rangers, Hull poked a rebound past Caps netminder Mike Palmateer. It would be Bobby's last goal, as he called it quits for good before the start of the season.

THE LEGENDS OF LANDOVER

✪ Two Teams, Two Contracts, One Player

"He likes to fight," said Gilles Picard about his newly-drafted son, Robert. Washington in 1977 made the offensively-gifted defenseman their first-round pick, third overall. For a while, the younger Picard took his fight, and his offense, to the Caps, famously vowing, "I'd rather deliver pizzas in Quebec than play for Washington." (*Washington Post*)

The friction traced to the absence of a standard player contract. At the same time the Caps and Picard were negotiating, the NHL and players' union were updating standard contract language. Lacking the usual template, Picard inked a "salary agreement," with a promise to sign the real thing when finalized. (*Toronto Globe & Mail*)

Picard signed with the Capitals for a $50,000 bonus and about $330,000 over five years – then changed his mind. A new agent convinced Robert the letter of intent wasn't binding, so he was free to accept a higher-paying deal with the Nordiques of the World Hockey Association. A Quebec native and Canadiens fan growing up, Picard liked the idea of playing in his home province (and the extra $25,000 per season).

Alarmed Caps G.M. Max McNab raced to Quebec City, locating Robert in the stands at a junior league game. Picard told *The Hockey News* what happened next. "Everyone around us was looking, and some of them wanted to have Max thrown out of the building. A security man asked, 'Is this man bothering you?' I told him no, we were talking. We talked for quite a while. I learned something that night."

McNab said his message was, "The first thing a young man has to learn in life is that he is no better than his word or handshake." He also told Picard, "It is easy to understand how a French-Canadian kid could get his head turned by talk about playing in French Canada, but I pointed out he'd get a better opportunity playing for our team against the best players in the best league."

In case Robert wasn't convinced, the Caps also filed a $1 million lawsuit, which proved unnecessary. Anxious not to jeopardize a future merger, the WHA nullified the Nordiques contract. In the end, Washington matched the deal Quebec originally offered. (Robert's highly-charged exhibition game in Quebec a few weeks later is a story in itself, which we tell on page 175.)

Picard in Landover was counted on to be a puck-rushing, offensive defenseman. The problem, as Robert saw it, was that the Capitals didn't have the personnel to rush with him. "The opposition would send in someone to take me out of the play. What other teams realized was that, if I couldn't get the puck out of Washington's end, we just didn't get it out."

THE LEGENDS OF LANDOVER

Picard never felt completely comfortable in a Caps uniform, going back to his double contract signing as a rookie. "I let the lawyers fight it out, but all of it still bothered me," he said to the *Globe & Mail*. That was just one of the reasons he welcomed the 1980 trade to the Maple Leafs. "It's going to be nice for a change to walk down the street and have somebody recognize me. In Toronto, they know hockey. In Washington, they don't."

✪ Home Away From Home

Caps fans have reserved a special loathing for the hockey teams from Pennsylvania. So you may be surprised to learn of the hospitality shown way back when by Capitals management. In April, 1976, Capital Centre offered Telscreen viewing of a Flyers playoff game. Then, on opening night in Landover in 1977, "In deference to the opponents, a giant Penguin will stroll the concourse, meeting children and fans." *(Annapolis Capitol)*

What in the name of Punxsutawney Phil were they thinking? And get this: one Keystone State team played a "home" game in Landover. In April, 1979, Hersheypark Arena became an evacuation center for people living near the crippled Three Mile Island nuclear plant. The Bears, Washington's AHL farm team, relocated a home game to Capital Centre. Hershey played a 1-1 tie with the Firebirds, the team from – where else – Philadelphia.

✪ Esposito Howls At Wolfe Signing

Phil Esposito was the first opposing superstar to be hazed at Capital Centre. First, because heckling is more fun when you're winning, and the early Capitals had uncommon success against the Rangers. Second, fans knew they could burrow underneath Phil's skin. He'd argue a referee's call, the fans would wave white hankerchiefs, and coming off the ice, Espo obliged them with a single-finger salute.

As Tampa's first G.M. in 1992, Esposito, preparing for the expansion draft, thought the Capitals were giving *him* a single-finger salute. Washington didn't want to expose a goaltender, so they exploited a rule "that each team make one goalie who has played at least one game in the NHL available." The Capitals complied – technically – by signing 40-year old ex-Caps netminder Bernie Wolfe, who had retired a mere 13 years earlier! When the NHL frowned, the Caps backed down. Esposito's funny line, referencing the team's expansion fee: "I didn't pay $50 million for Bernie Wolfe. He wasn't any good when I played against him."

Never let facts get in the way of a funny line, Phil. Esposito and his Rangers went head-to-head with Wolfe three times… and Bernie played brilliantly in two of them.

THE LEGENDS OF LANDOVER

On March 25, 1977, Wolfe stopped 31 of 33 shots in two periods of relief of Roger Crozier. The Caps won, 7-2, the white hankies made their first appearance, and Esposito was held without a point. On December 30, 1977, Wolfe made 29 saves in a 3-3 tie, and again, Esposito was held scoreless.

Espo broke through on March 24, 1978, scoring a hat trick as New York rolled, 11-4. So maybe Phil suffered from a selective memory. Perhaps residual anger at the Centre faithful. Or hard feelings because he didn't get the Capitals coaching job he applied for in 1981. Of course, Fred Shero and Don Cherry also missed out on the job that Bryan Murray got, so Esposito was in high-profile rejected company.

(*Baltimore Sun; AP; Washington Star; scottywazz.blogspot.com*)

✪ Drafty

At the 1981 NHL Draft, Caps G.M. Max McNab negotiated with New York, was enticed by Edmonton, and wound up hated in Hartford.

The previous April, on the regular season's last day, Rangers goalie Steve Baker pitched a 34-save shutout in Philadelphia. The irony was that New York desired to upgrade its netminding, but the two points from Baker's whitewash pushed New York (9th) behind Edmonton (8th) in the draft. That mattered because the Oilers and Rangers coveted the same prospect, goalie Grant Fuhr. The Rangers went to McNab, whose Caps held the 5th selection, and inquired what it would take to switch draft positions. Oilers G.M. Glen Sather got wind of this, so he too contacted McNab. "I told Max I would match or better the Rangers offer."

Neither club knew that McNab wasn't interested in moving *down*; he was maneuvering to move *up*. Max had his eye on Massachusetts teen phenom Bobby Carpenter. However, he'd have to leapfrog Hartford, picking 4th. "The Whalers made it clear they were going to use that pick on the home town boy to help their struggling team on the ice and provide a marketing boost off the ice," wrote Gord Stellick at *cbc.ca*.

Bob Carpenter Sr., a Peabody, Mass. police sergeant, got chummy with Whaler management, and was looking forward to the short drive to Hartford to see his son play. "Carpenter had been all but measured for his Whaler jersey when the Capitals negotiated a quick deal with the Colorado Rockies to secure the third pick," which McNab used to swipe Bobby Carpenter. "An angry and emotional Whalers entourage sat in stunned silence." Whalers assistant G.M. John Cunniff admitted, "I don't think we could have hid the fact that, yes, we wanted Bobby Carpenter." *(Items in quotes from UPI, N.Y. Times, Sporting News, Hockey News, and cbc.ca)*

THE LEGENDS OF LANDOVER

Carpenter Sr., sitting at the Whalers' draft table at the Montreal Forum, "reacted by storming out of the arena and threatening legal action against the league." In a voice loud enough for everyone to hear, the elder Carpenter phoned his wife. "Honey, we got f***ed."

All four teams in our drama made out fine. Edmonton got Fuhr, and five Stanley Cup rings. The Rangers "settled" for defenseman James Patrick, who played nine full seasons on Broadway. Hartford's "consolation" was center Ron Francis, who starred there for a decade. And wither the Carpenters? The Caps mollified the father, hired as a part-time scout, and the son delivered 172 goals in his first five seasons with Washington. Unfortunately, he then reached his expiration date, and his relationship with the Caps turned sour. (See page 232.)

✪ Ooh La La

"Jeans are sex." Calvin Klein said so in 1980, at the height of the designer denim craze. Attempting to prove the point, Klein infamously had 15 year old Brooke Shields declare in a commercial, "What gets between me and my Calvins? Nothing." (Right now, you're thinking this paragraph parachuted in from a completely different book. But stick with me.)

Rival jeans brand Sasson commissioned a TV spot featuring members of the New York Rangers. Adorned in the skin-tight pants, they skated, they twirled, they even sang the company slogan, "Ooh, la la, Sasson." Soon after, Sasson produced a similar TV commercial for the D.C. market, starring Ryan Walter, Mike Gartner, Pierre Bouchard, and Paul Mulvey of the Capitals. "We were all pretty hip," Mulvey recalled in an interview, stroking his now clean-shaven upper lip. "The longer hair, the mustache, that's what was sexy back in the day."

In the category of "One of these is not like the others," the ages of the players selected for the shoot. Gartner was 21, Walter and Mulvey 22... and Bouchard was 32. No problem for handsome Pierre, the former Canadien, a favorite of women on both sides of the border. A raconteur of the first order, Bouchard allowed that he found American females more assertive. "In Canada, they sit on the hood of your car for three days and hope you notice." When someone joked there are seven women for every man in Washington, Pierre deadpanned, "Then somebody must have 14."

But I digress. The 1980 TV ad featured players in Sasson jeans and Caps sweaters. As cheerleaders shake red pom-poms, the four skate up to a Sasson logo painted on Capital Centre ice. Walter, Gartner, Bouchard and Mulvey then glide Ice Capades-style, arm in arm, each with one leg raised behind them. Cut to Pierre and Paul playfully jostling as they skate toward the camera. The quartet finish by making the Sasson A-Ok hand gesture.

THE LEGENDS OF LANDOVER

The Fab Four performed as many starts and stops as a morning practice, at least 20 takes. The secret to keeping the "talent" peppy through all this repetition: a cooler of beer. "It's easier to sing and dance that way at 8 a.m.," explained a Sasson rep to Jane Leavy of the *Washington Post*. Where's that ad now? Mulvey told *washingtoncaps.com*, "I'm the only one who has a copy in Washington, D.C., and that's the way it should stay."

✪ What Was Sexy Back In The Day, Continued

Early in the 1975-76 season, coach Milt Schmidt encouraged his charges to "keep their heads up." The heads of two free-spirited players had undergone radical changes; Stan Gilbertson and Tommy Williams got perms. Williams said it was the bravest thing he'd done in 16 years as a pro. Buddy Ace Bailey resisted peer pressure to visit a stylist, so Williams warned, "He's the one who's going to look like a goof." (*Washington Star*)

✪ This Must Be Bill, Because It's Not Art

"Bad art is a great deal worse than no art at all." - Oscar Wilde
Back in the '70's, hockey cards were "enhanced" by paint jobs. For Bill Clement's 1975 monstrosity, we guess the assignment got outsourced to a 2nd grade art class, which left the watercolor in the rain. The source photo came from a Caps-Flyers game the prior season, before Clement was dealt to D.C. Topps artists airbrushed over Bill's Philly jersey... very poorly. On the painted Capitals logo across Clement's chest, the hockey stick "T" appears to be melting. The letters in the word "Washington" extend to Clement's armpit like ants on the march.

As *puckjunk.com* points out, "Clement was 'given' double-zeros (00) as his number. Strange that Topps would add a number – albeit an insulting one – but then ignore the legs." What about the legs? "What puts this over the top as one of the worst paint-overs ever is that there are actual Capitals players in the picture. Are we not supposed to notice that Clement's socks are (Flyers) orange, while his teammates' socks are white?"

In Ken Reid's book, *Hockey Card Stories,* Clement shared the teammate's identity. "I ask people after they finish laughing at the card, 'Okay, if you really want to be good at this, who's the guy in the picture with me?' That's Gordie Smith, Billy Smith's brother. Hardly anyone has ever gotten that." To his credit, Bill has embraced his place in sports on cardboard. "It's one of the ugliest hockey cards ever. And I'm proud to say that I was part of it."

✪ A Loss For Words

"Our city is filled with distraught and frustrated hockey fans." So began an angry fan letter to broadcaster Ron Weber. "We're tired of settling for a minor league operation." The correspondent might have been qualified in his assessment, based on his name: Ira Loss. (*The Hockey News*)

THE LEGENDS OF LANDOVER

✪ O'Malley's Closing Argument

Lawyer Peter O'Malley, power broker in Maryland politics, mastered the persuasive argument. O'Malley in the '70's also spent three seasons as Capitals president, finding that what worked in the courthouse and at the statehouse didn't always fly at Capital Centre.

"Flyers violations were being ignored, O'Malley concluded. So, he collared one of the officials – on the ice – as the first period ended. 'I told him he was a coward. I said our team deserved to have the rules enforced,'" O'Malley recalled. "At some moments in life, you have to be bold." (*Washington Star*)

✪ Baltimore Had The First Shot

Baltimore almost became the NHL's Maryland home in the first wave of expansion in 1967. A Maple Leafs spokesman gushed, "The Baltimore people are the sort we like for partners." One of those prospective Charm City partners, Jake Embry, said confidently, "How can they resist our bid?" Here's how. NHL Commissioner Clarence Campbell, seeing the permanent stage at one end of Baltimore's Civic Center, asked, "Who designed this place - Frank Lloyd Wrong?" (*Toronto Globe & Mail, Baltimore Sun*)

Spurned by the NHL, Baltimore in 1975 flirted with the World Hockey Association. The vagabond WHA Blades, kicked out of previous homes in Los Angeles and Detroit, debuted at the Baltimore Civic Center on February 2, 1975. A marquee match, too, with Gordie Howe, sons Mark and Marty, and the Houston Aeros providing the opposition. 9,023 showed up, about equal to a typical Caps crowd.

Using a well-worn publicity ploy of upstart leagues, the Blades tweaked their neighbors. "If people will pay to see the Capitals, they'll pay for anything," were the gauntlet down-throwing words of Blades G.M. Skip Feldman. (*The Hockey News*) Far from offended, Caps G.M. Milt Schmidt welcomed the increased hockey presence in the region. "Schmidt said that the Caps and the Blades would probably even play exhibition games in the pre-season." (*Washington Star*)

The Blades weren't sharp enough to last that long. By April, a different *Hockey News* story began, "Want to buy a major league hockey team? The Baltimore Blades are up for bids." The answer was No, no one did. A "Save the Blades" campaign went "mostly unnoticed," wrote *The Sun*, which described the team as "struggling and inept." And quickly, defunct. Skip Feldman was unavailable for comment.

THE LEGENDS OF LANDOVER

BRUSHES WITH GREATNESS

BwG Obeying The Boss

Coach Gary Green, to *slapshotdiaries.com*: "A lot of celebrities would drop by: Sinatra, Bruce Springsteen. When Springsteen showed up, I let him and Clarence Clemons into the dressing room. I went to my office for a while, and when I came back Bruce had dressed Clemens up in Mike Palmateer's mask, pads and goalie gear."

BwG Gong Shows

Connecting the expansion-era Caps with the phrase "Gong Show" is so trite, so clichéd, so unoriginal, that the mere act of writing it is shameful. Sadly, it's unavoidable. The *Washington Star* reported that in June, 1981, "Chuck Barris, known for his creation of 'The Gong Show' and other entertainment programs, came to Washington to discuss the Caps. Talks with Barris did not get past the early stages." For those too young to remember, "Gong Show" was a sendup of TV talent competitions. Today, they might call it "America's Got No Talent," or maybe "American I-dull."

Imagine for a moment, Chuck "Gong Show" Barris bringing the show's ethos to the Capitals. Game officials replaced by judges Jaye P. Morgan, Rip Taylor and Jamie Farr. Announcers saying, "We'll be back with more 'Stuff'." A player committing the "Most Outrageous Act of the Week" receiving a dirty tube sock and $516.32. Confetti and balloons falling from the rafters. As mascot, the guy with the bag over his head, "The Unknown Comic." Scratch that – a better choice would be "Gene-Gene, The Dancing Machine." We won't even speculate what the anthem singers would do.

Barris, who falsely claimed to be a CIA assassin, might still have been only runner-up as Capital Centre's most bats**t crazy owner. Also in 1981, L.A. divorce lawyer Donald Sterling negotiated to buy the Bullets. Yes, the same Donald Sterling who instead purchased the Clippers, mismanaging and penny-pinching the franchise to 28 losing seasons in his first 30 years as owner. Rampant racism and sexual harassment were his other trademarks; Donald Sterling in Landover would have been the real Gong Show.

BwG Only Room For One Ringmaster

Years prior to Barris and Sterling peeking inside Abe Pollin's Big Top, Irvin Feld became a Pollin ally, then adversary. Feld, at the time, owned Ringling Bros. and Barnum & Bailey Circus. *Regardie's* magazine revealed that Feld helped sway the NHL to choose Washington at 1972's Board of Governors meeting. The two men disagreed about the value of Irvin's influence. Feld claimed he'd been promised 24% ownership in the new team. Pollin offered a 3% stake, which Feld angrily refused. The Caps thus avoided corporate relation to a three-ring circus; ended up they were anyway, in spirit at least.

THE LEGENDS OF LANDOVER

BWG This Borg Would Not Be Assimilated

Swedish tennis superstar Bjorn Borg "used a two-handed backhand, adapted from the slap shot in hockey, a game he favored as a child." (*from atpworldtour.com*) When Borg took a five-month sabbatical at the end of 1981, he returned to his first love. "In Sweden," reported *Sports Illustrated*, "Bjorn Borg, right wing, scored four goals for the Malmo Vets against the Malmo Juniors."

The Caps, who had already imported a Rolf, a Leif, and a Bengt from Sweden, thought a Bjorn might look sharp in red and blue stars. "I have casual invitations from the Capitals and the Maple Leafs to go and practice with them," Borg told *Tennis Week* magazine. "It would be great fun to play in some of the practice games. I played ice hockey until I was 16." Unfortunately for the Caps, Borg harbored no illusions about pulling a Bo Jackson. "Obviously I'm not going to get into the big stuff. That would be crazy, and anyway I wouldn't be good enough."

BWG King Of The Cowboys Practices Hockey Shtick

Capitals All-Star center Guy Charron got together for a photo-op with movie cowboy Roy Rogers. Guy, in a suit, and Roy, in 10-gallon hat and bolo tie, smiled while each tugged on a sleeve of a Capitals sweater. Guess why.

A. Roy's burger chain was a major advertiser with the Caps.

B. Roy has agreed to let players know they're off the team by singing "Happy Trails To You."

C. Guy has just told Roy that his restaurant's Double-R-Bar Burger "Tastes like Trigger."

If you answered "A", you're correct. And if you answered "C", you should be ashamed of yourself.

SPIRITED EFFORTS   Monster Chiller Horror Hockey Theatre

Gather 'round, kids, for a spooky story about the scariest night of the year… Christmas Eve. Back in the late '70's, Gordie Lane, a Capitals defenseman, shared a house with goalie Jim Bedard and forward Tom Rowe. On this Xmas Eve night, though, Jim and Tom weren't home. Gordie tried to get to sleep, even though he was all alone. That's when the noises began. "He heard the toilet seat going up and down."

THE LEGENDS OF LANDOVER

Aahoooooooo! You've got to howl at something that scary. Gordie "was thankful for the dawn of the new day, because only then did he feel safe enough to doze off." Okay, kids, let me tell you, there's few things more terrifying than a toilet seat left up.

The teammates suffered other hauntings. "On more than one occasion, the three left their beds unmade prior to heading out for a morning practice. They made sure to lock the doors and switch on the burglar alarm. Upon their return, the beds were all neatly made." Whoa, that's super-scary, boy. Who was doing the haunting? The ghost of *Hazel*? She's one spooky maid, kids. *Aahoooooooo!*

"Really, I have never been in a haunted house and I don't believe in ghosts or anything," Bedard claimed. "But I'm just about certain this place is haunted." Not just inside, either. "There's this big open field right behind us, and sometimes the wind really whips up and makes some strange things happen. The noises in the night are enough to keep anyone up."

(Items in the above quotes are from actual newspaper stories in the *Brandon Sun* and *Washington Star*. And yes, for those of you old enough to remember, I was channeling SCTV's *Count Floyd* while writing.)

Doomed By Voodoo From Saskatoon

Owner Abe Pollin once speculated on the team's bad luck. "Maybe the Capitals were cursed by some voodoo doctor from Saskatoon." Coach Tom McVie described constant losing in mystical terms, too. "Worse than dying. When you do die, you're done. But when you lose, you have to live with it. It slaps you in the face and leaves a scar." (*L.A. Times, The Hockey News*)

 Harry The Hexer

Four years before Jason first donned his hockey mask for the movies, the Caps on a Friday the 13th in 1976 hosted the Blues on "Hex Night." As *UPI* reported, the promotion included "Black cats, paper four-leaf clovers, and a mystic named 'Harry the Hexer' who pronounced a pre-game incantation." St. Louis still won, 2-0, because who's going to be frightened of a hexer named Harry?

Harry didn't explain that his spell was a slow-acting, timed-release formula. The Blues finally succumbed in January, 1977, losing three times to the Capitals in a 27-day span. Caps wins came in Landover on the 2nd, 2-1, and on the 23rd, 6-3, thanks to four goals in the final four minutes. Then, in St. Louis on the 29th, the Caps scored three times on six shots in the first period and twice on five shots in the second period, en route to a 5-2 win, even though the Blues outshot them for the game, 38-13. Thanks, Harry!

THE LEGENDS OF LANDOVER

✈ Admit One

The early Caps often found transportation as baffling as a Montreal power play. For example, the time security officers at Denver's Stapleton Airport were suspicious. The gaggle of athletes passing through the gate were Capitals players. But who was the older gentleman at the rear of the group? A guard stopped the man and said, "Where are you going?" Tom McVie, Caps coach, replied, "I'm the coach of the team." The security guard said, "How do I know that?" McVie answered, "Would anyone else admit it?" (From King Kaufman's podcast, *Can't Win 4 Losing*)

✈ The Plane Truth

October 27, 1975 in Chicago, the Caps stun the Blackhawks, 7-5. We hope players savored the victory, because that was the only savoring they would enjoy on the plane ride to Los Angeles.

Cash-strapped management purchased no-frills tickets, forcing the Caps' traveling party into the very last rows of a commercial flight. As broadcaster Ron Weber remembered in his Hall of Fame induction speech, the indignity only grew. "We had been booked in the non-food section. As they were bringing the food up that we were not to get, Ace Bailey says to the flight attendant, 'Could you slow down please, so I can sniff it?' And then he goes up to Milt Schmidt, the general manager and says 'Milt, do you know a good shoe store? I might need to get a comfortable pair of shoes because we might be standing up on the next trip.'"

Predictably, the Caps got outshot 40-16 by the Kings in a 6-0 loss. "What could you expect? We're still starving," one player groused to the *Washington Star*. Ace Bailey wasn't sure the team still qualified for air travel. "The way we played against the Kings, we may be walking back."

Happily, airline seats were purchased for Washington to continue its road trip. Taking nothing for granted, players stocked up on cookies and candy bars in L.A. before boarding. "I promise you," said captain Bill Clement, "it's going to be better in Kansas City." Sure enough, the Caps won their game against the Scouts, 6-2, behind Bernie Wolfe's 30 stops in his NHL debut. Safe to say, the Caps were the hungrier team.

Two months after the no-frills adventure, the Caps scheduled a midnight excursion from BWI Airport to Montreal. Except you really should avoid an aircraft with an oil leak. The replacement plane had to fly all the way from the Canadian border north of Detroit. BWI clocks read 4 a.m. before the team was airborne. Another delay greeted them in Montreal; customs officials were asleep, and had to be awakened.

THE LEGENDS OF LANDOVER

✈ Penalty For Boarding (The Bus)

In a span of 27 hours in 1976, the Caps lost a tripleheader to the Bruins - once at Boston Garden, once at Capital Centre, and once at Logan Airport.

On the ice, the Bruins won 3-2 Nov. 18, and 4-1 Nov. 19. In between, the teams had to fly from Massachusetts to Maryland. The *Boston Globe* reported, "The Capitals were planning to leave on a 9:50 a.m. plane, but Boston had made reservations on the same flight." Before private charters, the NHL frowned on opposing teams sharing a commercial flight. (Wouldn't that have made for juicy stories, though? Talk about turbulence!) The groggy Caps were forced to depart almost three hours earlier.

Once off the plane, the Capitals suffered a glass-rattling hit - even before the rematch with the Bruins. As their team bus sped down the highway, a large-antlered deer started running alongside. The deer rammed the bus, shattering windows and ripping the fabric off an empty seat. (Perhaps a Milwaukee Buck, in town to play the Bullets.) Pete Scamurra narrowly avoided antler punctures, and Harvey Bennett sustained a nick to his neck.

Ron Lalonde told *McClatchy News*, "You didn't know what to expect. There was supposed to be a bus waiting for you at the hotel in Buffalo or somewhere, and there wouldn't be one. It was like a traveling circus." And that was even before a deer joined the act.

✈ Meet Me In St. Louis

A lazy afternoon for Michel Bergeron morphed into a crazy one. In a scoring drought – one goal and one assist in 11 Caps games – Michel got left home from a November, 1978 trip to St. Louis. At 1 p.m. on game day, though, the team phoned. Due to an injury, they'd need Bergeron after all.

So began Michel's solo version of The Amazing Race: drive to Baltimore, hop a flight, visit Indianapolis because no non-stops were available, take off again, land in St. Louis, wait for luggage, race to the Checkerdome, realize his favorite skates got left behind, get into uniform anyway, and join teammates for the end of warmups around 8 p.m. central time. "I was going crazy," Bergeron told the *Washington Star*. "Time was short and I really started to worry when I had to wait 25 minutes for my bag."

The Blues should have bribed the folks at Lambert Field to hide his bag. Bergeron not only played, he starred, doubling his point total with a goal and assist; Michel's late 2nd period tally was the decider in a 4-3 Caps victory.

THE LEGENDS OF LANDOVER

✈ Snow Job

The Capitals were on a road trip while the 1979 Presidents' Day blizzard, 19 inches worth, the region's worst in 50 years, blanketed the District. Landover, too, as players discovered returning to their cars in the Capital Centre parking lot. No pampered pro athletes here, just guys with shovels in the 3 a.m. chill, trying to dig out and drive home. "I didn't get to bed until 7 a.m.," said Dennis Maruk. Too soon, they were back at the rink, hosting Detroit, and losing, 4-3. Wee hours snow shoveling hadn't helped. "When the game started," Maruk said, "I just couldn't move." (*Washington Star*)

✈ One Puny Bun

Averaging 50 miles per hour on a trip is making good time – unless you're flying. In that case, the journey is torturous, as the Capitals experienced in October, 1979. Trying to jet from from Vancouver to Edmonton, Air Canada announced their 8 a.m. flight would be delayed. Seems the aircraft the Caps planned to board had been disabled by lightning. At 10:30 a.m. the team lifted off – briefly. Mechanical problems forced the replacement plane back to the gate in Vancouver 45 minutes later. In one of the more infuriating quirks of air travel, passengers weren't allowed off the increasingly hot, stuffy aircraft.

A working jet finally escaped Vancouver airspace for good at 2:30 p.m., touching down in Edmonton at 5:30 p.m., two hours before gametime. "We were tired and hungry," Ryan Walter said to the *Washington Star*. "All we had to eat for six hours was one puny bun on the second flight. We didn't even get a Coke." Walter took it out on the Oilers with a goal and two assists, and the weary Caps won the game, 6-4.

✈ In A Fog

In late December, 1981, the Caps cooled their heels at Buffalo Municipal Airport, anxious to return home from a 3-2 loss to the Sabres. Fog in Washington made that impossible and subsequent flights were packed, so back to the hotel they trudged. Gaetan Duchesne checked in without his skates, Ryan Walter without his coat – they'd been stolen at the airport.

The team eventually ditched the idea of going home, traveling instead to Pittsburgh, site of their next game. That flight was delayed too, the charter bus was late, and at gametime, the Caps didn't show up either, losing 6-2. Goalie Dave Parro smashed his stick on the crossbar, mad either at the lopsided score, or the lack of clean clothes he and his mates had packed for an unexpectedly lengthy trip. For some reason, the flight home stopped in Roanoke, Va., and while at the gate, a snowstorm briefly extinguished the plane's electrical system.

THE LEGENDS OF LANDOVER

One week later, back to back Caps wins over the Canucks and Rangers had 1982 off to flying start. Then the flying part got trickier. Heavy snow in Montreal caused the team to land there 2½ hours late. The same storm cancelled their connection to Quebec City, where the airport was closed, anyway. Ice on the Trans-Canada highway made the bus ride there an adventure. Ordering 30 fast-food dinners further delayed the trip, but not as much as when the bus broke down. G.M. Roger Crozier, looking for something, anything, positive to say, suggested if there had to be engine failure, better on the bus ride than the plane ride. Good try, Rog.

The Nordiques beat the Caps 3-0, but by this point, who really cared? Amazingly, the team was about to experience airport déjà vu with the Bruins. The Delta flight home from Montreal to D.C. was first making a stop in Boston, and guess what? Both teams were booked on that leg of the journey. The Bruins, losers the previous night to the Canadiens, were tired. The Capitals were understandably weary. The NHL looked the other way, letting both teams board the same aircraft. Perhaps one man deserves credit for the excursion being incident-free: NHL linesman Swede Knox, who coincidentally was booked on the same flight!

THE LEGENDS OF LANDOVER

4th Shift: *Games Of Note 1977-1982*

| OCT. 26, 1977 | WAS 6 ATL 2 | ATLANTA |

Historical trivia: In which city did the Capitals go the longest between victories? The answer is Atlanta, at 22 years, 1 month, and 19 days. It's a bit of a trick question, of course. The Capitals rolled into Phillips Arena on December 15, 1999, for their first road test against the expansion Atlanta Thrashers. It wasn't much of an exam. Washington scored four times in the first 17 minutes (Konowalchuk, Oates, Mironov, and Bulis), and Olaf Kolzig coasted to an 18-save, 4-0 shutout.

The Flames, Atlanta's original NHL team, had bolted for Calgary in 1980. Prior to that, the Capitals made 12 trips to the Peach State, winning just once, on October 26, 1977. Although Ace Bailey didn't appear on the scoresheet, he delivered the knockout shot, literally. Late in the first period, Bailey's blast bowled over Flames goalie Dan Bouchard. The cut under Bouchard's left eye would require 10 stitches.

Replacement netminder Phil Myre got out of the first frame unscathed, but a Caps barrage awaited him after intermission. Walt McKechnie broke a 1-1 tie at 31 seconds, Billy Collins scored at 1:12, and Gerry Meehan joined the assault at 3:58 - three tallies in just over three minutes.

Three was also the number of fights between Washington's veteran tough guy Bugsy Watson and Atlanta's 220-pound rookie Harold Phillipoff. Why all the bad blood? Depends who you asked. Watson: "He was coming after me all the time. He was just trying to stick with the team, I guess." Phillipoff had a somewhat different explanation: "Watson broke a stick over my head. There was a score to be settled."

Bob Sirois' second goal completed the 6-2 rout. Flames coach Fred Creighton wasn't impressed by the effort of his charges. "I would tell you what we did wrong," Creighton told *AP*, "But it would take until midnight."

| DEC. 7, 1977 | WAS 5 CLE 3 | RICHFIELD, OH |

So what if the Capitals hadn't won a game in their last 20 outings. Such trifles couldn't dampen the boundless enthusiasm of rookie defenseman Robert Picard, eager for his first NHL score. "Picard has been driving us crazy," winger Bob Sirois said with a laugh, "telling us, 'I should have had my goal tonight,' or 'I'm going to get that goal in this game,' or 'I had my goal if it wasn't for that post.'"

THE LEGENDS OF LANDOVER

Cleveland winger Ken Kuzyk tied the game late in the second period, to the delight of 3,842 at Richfield Coliseum – 14,702 below capacity, if you're wondering. (Ken Kuzyk trivia: 1. His two NHL seasons coincided with the only two seasons the Cleveland Barons existed. 2. If, as rumored in 2010, proper names ever become allowable in Scrabble, you could get 25 points just from Ken's five-letter surname.)

Kuzyk's tally caused spirits to sag on the visitors' bench. "When they tied it at 2-2, everybody thought it was all going to fall down around us again," Sirois told *AP*. Not to fear; Picard made good on his prediction with a go-ahead goal for the Caps 44 seconds later. "Robert went in and scored, and we knew we were going to get them," said Sirois, who scored twice himself.

Coach Tom McVie, how ya doin'? "This victory felt awful good. But we won't order the (championship) rings yet." Whoop it up, coach, you won for the first time after 20 failures! "It's like a guy mugging 20 women and then helping one old lady across the street. It's a step in the right direction, but it doesn't clear everything." Tommy, really, how tough was it? "Our players were like a bunch of coal miners after a cave in. They were buried for 40 days and all there was left was the hope of survival." (*The Hockey News*)

As for rookie Picard, he was overheard saying, "We won 5-3. It feels real good. And I scored a goal." This time he wasn't talking to teammates; he was on the phone with his mom in Montreal.

| DEC. 5, 1978 | WAS 4 COL 1 | DENVER |

Outside McNichols Arena, seven inches of wind-whipped snow was falling, the temperature plunging 20 degrees in a half-hour, not stopping until the thermometer read 14 degrees. Inside, 1,952 blizzard-mocking fans – likely the smallest regular-season gathering ever at a Capitals game – received a certificate reading, "I braved a blizzard to watch the Capitals play the Rockies." The certificate showed a skate sticking out of a snowdrift.

A midweek matchup of the NHL's two weakest team wasn't going to be a high-demand ticket regardless of the forecast. Washington came in on a seven game winless streak, while the Rockies sported the only worse record than the Caps.

True to the weather outside, the home team's league-leading power play unit turned frigid. Colorado was denied on all six advantages, including a 5-on-3 for 1:28. If defeat was painful for the home team, so was victory for the visitors: Rick Green, stick to the eye; Dennis Maruk, hyperextended elbow; Bob Sirois, bruised hip; Robert Picard, shoulder separation; Leif Svensson, bruised ribs. And their goalie wasn't shivering from the cold.

THE LEGENDS OF LANDOVER

Bernie Wolfe heroically overcame fever and headaches to make 36 saves. "It felt like a time bomb ticking away inside my head. It didn't help to have my helmet on," Wolfe said. The night before, shivering in his hotel room, Bernie was certain he'd be scratched. But coach Dan Belisle needed to shelter Rollie Boutin, victimized for 10 goals in his first NHL game.

"It was the way Danny asked me," Wolfe said. "Like he was telling me, please, you can play, can't you? I could only say 'Yes.' I would never pull the ripcord when the team needed me." Admiring teammate Guy Charron noted, "We all saw how sick he was at the airport. It was a remarkable night's work. Bernie wasn't out of position even once."

One year later the Capitals returned to Denver, along with 18 inches of snow, the city's biggest blizzard in 33 years. This time, 2,003 fans showed for "The Second Annual Blizzard Bowl" to see the Caps and Rockies deadlock 3-3. (*Quotes from The Hockey News, Washington Star*)

| DEC. 9, 1978 | WAS 7 VAN 5 | VANCOUVER, BC |

Mark Lofthouse grew up 10 miles from Pacific Coliseum, home of the Canucks. Ryan Walter grew up even closer. So lots of friends and family held tickets when Mark, Ryan, and their Capitals teammates came calling. Walter later told *Goal* magazine, "The first game I played in the Coliseum was the most nervous I've ever been before a game." No worries would be necessary – the hometown duo didn't disappoint.

The evening started painfully for Lofthouse, during a line change on the fly. "He suffered a finger cut near the end of the first period," the *Vancouver Express* reported, "when teammate Guy Charron's skate went through his glove." The skate cut caused pain, but didn't affect his aim. Mark scored at 2:35 of the 2nd period, and again at 13:50. Later, he said, "I didn't really play that well. I put pucks in the net, but all the work came from someone else." That someone was Walter, who assisted on both goals.

During the 2nd intermission, Lofthouse received five stitches to close his stinging wound. Then he went out and completed his hat trick at 8:18 of the 3rd period – with Walter picking up his third assist. Fame is fleeting; Mark was sent down a month later. He finished with 13 goals for the Capitals, adding 15 during the '79-'80 season.

On a side note, *Express* writer Tony Gallagher took Vancouver's loss hard. In his acerbic game story, Gallagher described the Canucks as "timid" and "agonizing," their deeds "folly," and a "lesson in humility," and something about a "weather balloon" (yup, weather balloon). For good measure, he ripped the Caps' "Central League defence." Bitter much, Tony?

THE LEGENDS OF LANDOVER

JAN. 19, 1979 | DET 1 WAS 5 | LANDOVER, MD

Bernie Wolfe drew 15 minutes in penalties, which is a big number for a goalie… and even bigger, when you consider Wolfe didn't play in the game! As the final horn sounded, trash talking continued between Washington's Gary Rissling and Detroit's Dennis Polonich. When words became punches, the two teams that had been headed to their locker rooms put on the brakes, did a 180, and joined in an ever-expanding brawl.

In the past, Wolfe and Detroit netminder Rogie Vachon had publicly praised one another; they first met when Bernie, as a youngster, had been gifted a hockey stick by Rogie. Said Wolfe, "I watched him when I was a kid in Montreal. He was good then. Now he's one of the best." Vachon, in turn, had admired Wolfe's performance: "The kid had been great, really great. He has to feel inside he can play, and that he can stop the good shooters." (*Washington Star*)

The growing postgame scrum wouldn't provide a similar opportunity for niceties. "I saw Bill Lochead jump Rissling," Wolfe said to *AP*. "I couldn't get to Lochead, so I went after Polonich." Enter Vachon. "Normally, a goalie takes a goalie in this kind of thing," explained Rogie. "I was closest to Bernie, so I had to go pick him up." Bernie, back to you: "Vachon started swinging, so I swung back." Vachon, who gave up five goals, also lost his jersey in the scuffle. Rogie didn't come away empty-handed, though; he and Wolfe both were assessed majors and misconduct penalties.

The NHL had started using data entry in 1979, but their computers threw a fit trying to figure how Wolfe could draw penalty minutes without playing. So the league decided, what the heck, we'll give Bernie credit for playing. In the words of former British Prime Minister Benjamin Disraeli, "There are three kinds of lies: lies, damned lies, and statistics."

JAN. 24, 1979 | NYR 1 WAS 5 | LANDOVER, MD

The Rangers got rid of Greg Polis, according to *legendsofhockey.net*, because he made "too many single-man rushes that were halted at the blueline." Polis got sweet revenge just nine days later, after being claimed off waivers by Washington. Late in the 2nd period against his former club, Greg began a rink-length rush that would've made Bobby Orr proud.

With puck in tow, Polis revved up in his own end, accelerated through the neutral zone, raced over the blue line, and as Russ White poetically described in the *Star*, split the defense "like a Concorde slicing through the morning fog at Dulles." He deked goalie John Davidson, parked a backhander, collided with the post, and spun into the boards.

THE LEGENDS OF LANDOVER

"It's one of the greatest feelings I've ever had," said Polis. "Before I had time to think what I was going to do, I had already done it... and it was in the net." The 180-foot dash received boffo reviews. Teammate Tom Rowe: "Unbelieveable." Coach Dan Belisle: "Sheer determination." G.M. Max McNab: "The perfect goal." Even some of Greg's former Rangers pals told him it was "a hell of a goal."

Polis' effort was a clue - this wasn't your typical midseason game. How about coach Belisle deploying three defensemen at one time during a Rangers power play. Or referee Bruce Hood missing the first period because of travel delays. Most significant of all, the Rangers came in with the 4th best record in the league, and left 5-1 losers. The Capitals recorded their 7th win in January, most in the NHL to that point.

| MAR. 4, 1979 | MIN 4 WAS 5 | LANDOVER, MD |

In the final minute of this game, both benches emptied. No, not for a brawl - for scoring celebrations. It's a little-remembered fact that after a crucial goal, players on the bench used to join teammates celebrating on the ice. Still, having it happen twice a few seconds apart, with just a few seconds left, qualifies as unusual. First, the North Stars spilled over the boards to congratulate Mike Fidler, who tied the game 4-4 with 0:35 remaining.

Bob Sirois restored Washington's lead at 19:47. Undecided about whether to shoot or find Ryan Walter at the side of the net, Sirois ended up banking a crossing pass off a Minnesota defender and into the net. "It all happened so fast," Caps coach Danny Belisle told the *Minneapolis Star*. "I was looking for something to kick (in anger) when we scored." Joy replaced disgust as Caps players held their own 20-man on-ice hug, and did so again, more traditionally, when the final horn sounded 13 seconds later. The NHL soon banned this time-wasting tradition.

| JAN. 27, 1980 | NYI 1 WAS 7 | LANDOVER, MD |

Hot sports debate #867: How much do coaches or managers really affect a team's won-loss record over the course of a season? Whatever the answer, bench bosses don't stop looking for new ways to reinvent the sports wheel. The Caps-Islanders tilt provides a case study. One night earlier, Capitals coach Gary Green had watched his team tie Quebec, 1-1, despite outshooting the Nordiques, 40-16.

Green sensed his team – unrewarded for their dominance – might suffer a letdown against the Islanders. So he made an unorthodox decision. "We played so well (against Quebec), I cancelled a pre-game skate," Green told the *Canadian Press*. "I tried to psychologically keep them going from the third period into the first."

THE LEGENDS OF LANDOVER

The strategy didn't pay immediate dividends. At the first intermission, the Caps had taken 11 more shots without a goal, and trailed, 1-0. Then, in the 2nd, the dam burst; Mike Gartner scoring eight seconds in, and Bengt Gustafsson at 30 seconds – at the time, the fastest two goals at the start of a period in NHL history. At 58 seconds, Washington's third shot of the period was also the third to elude Billy Smith, as Paul Mulvey's rebound goal made it 3-1. By period's end, the Capitals had tallied a club record six times. Ryan Walter, who finished with two goals and three assists, said, "You start to wonder when the shots are going to go in. But in the second period, we broke the bubble." *(Washington Post)*

The rout was all the more unexpected because illness forced Washington to rotate four healthy defensemen. And this wasn't just any team the Caps were steamrolling; the Islanders were riding a seven game winning streak. Chalk one up for psychology, and the coach who made it work.

| FEB. 15, 1980 | WAS 2 EDM 8 | EDMONTON, AB |

Shaking his head, Capitals coach Gary Green said, "It was one of those games that you want to forget as fast as you can." Well, yeah, giving up eight straight goals and all. So why are we choosing to remember this rout? A good reason would be Wayne Gretzky's eye-popping seven assists. Gretzky accomplished this feat by double-shifting, centering the Oilers first and fourth lines. "Some people have questioned my endurance," Gretzky said, "But I think I've got as much endurance as anyone in the league."

The seven assists tied a 33-year-old NHL record, and Wayne would repeat the seven-helpers mark twice more in his unparalleled career. This first time was most impressive, though, because Gretzky was all of 19 years old! Coach Green didn't blame his netminder nearly as much as the stumbling skaters in front of him. "Wayne (Stephenson) had no chance with 10 guys against him – five of their guys and five of ours."

What stands out equally to the Great One was the Oilers' goaltender. This victory was one of only eight he would record in his lone NHL season. See if the name of this obscure netminder rings a bell: Jim Corsi. The "Corsi Number" is one of the pioneering advanced metrics to judge puck possession. Is it somehow related to Jim Corsi? Yes and no. And yes.

The first "Yes" is because the metric is named for him. The "No" is because he didn't develop it, exactly. Tim Barnes, a financial analyst by trade, came up with the formula. As Bob McKenzie relayed in a *tsn.com* column, Barnes was perusing the Buffalo Sabres website when he happened upon their goalie coach. "Corsi became Corsi because he liked the look of Jim Corsi's picture, especially his moustache, on the Sabre website and the sound of his surname."

THE LEGENDS OF LANDOVER

The second "Yes" was remarkable coincidence. Barnes, who used the pseudonym "Vic Ferrari," got his brainstorm for the analytic after listening to an interview with Sabres G.M. Darcy Regier. From McKenzie's column: "Jim Corsi was actually the individual responsible for measuring a goalie's workload by counting shots on goal + missed shots + blocked shots and, therefore, Ferrari's random naming of Corsi turned out to be fortuitous, that Regier wouldn't have been talking about it if not for Corsi."

So here's to Jim Corsi, who on a long-ago night at Northlands Coliseum surrendered goals to Alan Hangsleben and Paul Mulvey, on the way to authoring a 16-save victory.

(Game quotes from *Canadian Press*)

`FEB. 19, 1980` `MON 1 WAS 3` `LANDOVER, MD`

The Caps hadn't beaten Montreal in all 34 previous tries. No one informed the marketing department, which designated the game a "Guaranteed Win Night." In other words, free tickets for all 13,551 customers if the Habs didn't fall on this 35th attempt. Let's hope owner Abe Pollin wasn't told; he was already weakened from the effects of recent heart surgery.

Speaking of woozy, Caps defenseman Robert Picard's evening started wobbly, and ended up shaky. But boy, did the middle make it worthwhile! In warmups, a wayward puck struck Picard in the face. Despite a dozen stitches above his right eye, the Montreal native wasn't about to miss playing against his hometown team. Dizzyness made Picard's first shifts feel like a tilt-a-whirl. He regained his equilibrium by the 2nd period, sending a blast through a maze of players for a 1-0 Caps lead.

Bengt Gustafsson's superior solo effort re-established the D.C. lead with seven minutes left. Remarkably, up until that point, Washington hadn't registered a 3rd period shot. Gus breaking the 1-1 deadlock "produced the loudest sounds since The Who performed in the same arena," wrote columnist Morris Seigel. Outshot 32-16, the Capitals hung on to beat the Canadiens for the first time, after six years, 31 losses and three ties.

The enormity of the achievement overwhelmed Picard. "I was shaking," the 4th year d-man said in a gleeful dressing room. "I just stood there. I couldn't do anything." G.M. Max McNab knew someone else who was "absolutely overcome" – Pollin. The ailing owner, recuperating in the Caribbean, got the shocking score when he called the Capital Centre switchboard. He spent several minutes congratulating players, and running up his long-distance bill. "It's the greatest therapy in the world for me," Abe told each player he spoke with.

THE LEGENDS OF LANDOVER

Picard joked that when the teams next met in Montreal, "Maybe they will have a Guaranteed Win Night for their fans." It might not have seemed as big a deal to rookie coach Gary Green, winning his very first meeting with the Canadiens. "The guys played a very disciplined game," Green observed. "We stood them up in the neutral zone and didn't give them the blue line." (*Free Lance-Star, Washington Star*)

| MAR. 19, 1980 | NYI 1 WAS 3 | LANDOVER, MD |

For 10,716 fans at Capital Center, they went to a hockey game and a soccer match broke out. Nine minutes into the contest, the Caps led, 1-0. Not in goals – in *shots on goal*. Unimpressed *N.Y. Times* writer Parton Keese said the Islanders "treated the blue line like a barrier that made their sticks act like lead bars pushing a bucket of cement." Now that's entertainment!

The defensive, not so much slugfest as slogfest, was tied 1-1 in the 3rd period; the two teams combined to kill all seven power plays in the game. Swedish linemates sent the crowd home happy, when Rolf Edberg converted Bengt Gustafsson's pass for the winning score with seven minutes left. New York, which didn't register a shot for half the 1st period, managed only a measly two ~~cement buckets~~ pucks on net during the entire 3rd stanza. In other words, they never had a shot.

| APR. 1, 1980 | PGH 2 WAS 6 | LANDOVER, MD |

One Alan Hangsleben move triggered two remarkable events at 12:17 of the 3rd period. When Alan scored on a wraparound, it marked the Capitals' third power play goal in a 71-second span! A couple of minutes earlier, Pittsburgh's Ron Stackhouse had slashed Hangsleben, while teammate Gary McAdam was already in the penalty box. Rod Schutt argued so forcefully, he drew a third penalty.

Gifted a 5-on-3-palooza, the Caps cashed in. First, Ryan Walter on a 30-foot wrister at 11:06. At 11:29, Mike Gartner connected from almost the same spot. Hangsleben completed the power play goal parade 48 seconds later. Washington now led 6-1, on a trio of extra-man scores in 1:11. The shift of a lifetime for Robert Picard, who assisted on all three goals!

So at 12:17, a goalie change was no surprise. Except it was the Caps' Wayne Stephenson heading to the bench. Stephenson had started 20 consecutive games in the Capitals' late-season playoff push. With a sizable lead, Wayne summoned his understudy, Rollie Boutin, to finish between the pipes. Speaking from a postgame whirlpool bath, the 35-year-old Stephenson said, "I felt that we had the game won when I went out, and I needed a little break. Besides, Rollie is quite capable."

THE LEGENDS OF LANDOVER

One more goalie note: we hope Pittsburgh's Greg Millen never took up the javelin. Trying to dispose of a broken stick while play continued, Millen's no-look toss cleared the glass, and wound up in Capital Centre's end zone seats. Later, he provided unnecessary confirmation that "I really didn't mean to do that." He was assessed a 10-minute misconduct. *(Pgh. Press)*

| OCT. 19, 1980 | WAS 4 CHI 8 | CHICAGO |

Sure, it sounds heartwarming. Brothers Grant and Paul Mulvey scored two minutes apart for the Blackhawks. If only Paul wasn't playing for the Capitals at the time. When we say Paul inadvertently scored against his own team, we're not talking about a pinball bounce from in close, the kind of "own goal" that happens all the time. No, Paul Mulvey, behind the Chicago net, sent the puck crisply out to the point on a Caps power play. "I just tried to get it to Greenie (Rick Green)," Paul said. "To tell the truth, I just put my head down after the pass and started back to the bench."

The disc skipped past the blue line, skidding 175 feet down the ice. Still, why worry? Washington goalie Mike Palmateer would cover it. "It was going to come right to my pads," Mike lamented later. "All of a sudden it bounced up a foot-and-a-half, hit me on my right hip, and deflected in." Mike wore a sheepish grin for the next 10 minutes. "A game of bounces," said Palmateer. "The weirdest game I've played in, in a long time."

One that defenseman Pat Ribble wished to forget. "I had three tip-ins for them. Three; that's awful. You expect to get maybe three like that all year." Said Caps coach Gary Green, "There were so many strange happenings that it boggled the mind."

Apparently the Hawks didn't save any favorable bounces for the Capital Centre rematch two nights later. The team that scorched Washington eight times at Chicago Stadium couldn't pierce Wayne Stephenson even once in a 2-0 Caps win. Guess who scored the winning goal? Pat Ribble, on a deflection no less! "I just went out hoping any chances I'd have would deflect into their net this time." *(Chicago Daily Herald, Brandon Sun, Washington Star)*

| NOV. 2, 1980 | WAS 4 WPG 4 | WINNIPEG, MB |

In the dying moments, the Caps trailed 4-2; goalie Wayne Stephenson was summoned to the bench. "We had nothing to lose when I left the first time, with 1:36 to go," said Wayne. The 6-skaters-to-5 maneuver paid off, as Rick Green scored to halve the deficit. Soon, Stephenson scampered again from his crease to the bench. Winnipeg's Norm Dupont barely missed the vacated cage, which would have been his fourth goal of the game.

THE LEGENDS OF LANDOVER

With six Caps attackers on the ice, a mad scramble formed at the Winnipeg net. In pinball slang, a "Lazarus Ball" comes magically back into play when, by all appearances, it's headed down the drain. Finding the Lazarus puck was Jean Pronovost, who had played 908 NHL games and was a four-time All Star when he came to Washington at the twilight of his career.

"I cannot possibly describe how the puck came to me," Pronovost said. "It hit one leg here, another leg, a stick and another leg and more sticks and legs. I thought I was trapped in a real-life pinball machine." Pinball Wizard Jean used his flipper to backhand the tying goal with five seconds left.

Magnifique! Well, for the visitors. A hometown sportswriter called the Jets "pansies under pressure." If the Arena had a "Tilt" sign, Jets' G.M. John Ferguson would have made it light up. "The press box nearly collapsed," the *Washington Star* said, "as Ferguson slammed a door and pounded his fists at a couple of walls." The Capitals had performed a hockey Houdini - escaping defeat by scoring twice with their netminder pulled. Stephenson commented to *AP*, "I can never remember that happening before."

| NOV. 26, 1980 | WAS 7 DET 7 | DETROIT |

If a tie is like kissing your sister, the Capitals started the 1980-81 season with more sisters than a convent. And more stress than waiting for test results, as Caps coach Gary Green admitted to the *Washington Star*. "These tie games don't do much for my stomach." The wackiest of these draws saw the Caps trailing the Red Wings 4-1 after two periods. By mutual consent, the final 20 minutes were defense-optional.

The visitors erupted for six 3rd period goals, including two by Dennis Ververgaert in a 13-second span. Since they also surrendered three more scores to the Wings, Washington had to settle for the 9th tie in its first 21 games. The dizziest man at Joe Louis Arena had to be Wayne Maxner, in his first game as Detroit coach. Green joked, "I got a stiff neck from watching the red light go on at each end."

| DEC. 26, 1980 | NYR 3 WAS 7 | LANDOVER, MD |

Mike Palmateer the goalie made 29 saves. Mike Palmateer the enforcer threw body blocks, fought, and drew a double-minor for mixing in a 3rd-period melee. "I've never seen anything like it," marveled Caps coach Gary Green. "Palmy had as many hits as anyone."

"Maybe I should use my head a little more and stay in the net," said Mike. "This is the first time since I've been here I had to play this kind of game. I just had the chances to come out and help and I did."

THE LEGENDS OF LANDOVER

Near the end of the game, the 15,771 in the stands must have felt like they missed a fire drill. Save for the two goalies, all that remained on the Capital Centre ice were sticks and gloves. Referee Greg Madill enforced a new NHL rule - misconduct penalties for any skaters who engage in a brawl, so all 10 combatants were banished to their locker rooms. "Whatever it takes to win, we'll do it," said Green. "No use losing and being nice guys. We've tried that before."

FEB. 3, 1981	WAS 3 VAN 3	VANCOUVER, BC

What a whirlwind first month in the NHL for goalie Dave Parro. In the rookie's first big-league game on January 8, 1981, he stopped Wayne Gretzky on a breakaway (#99 did score twice, though). One week later, Parro was bombarded by another Hall-of-Famer; the Kings' Marcel Dionne fired 12 shots on net. "At least eight were the kind I usually score on," Dionne said to the *L.A. Times*. Not on this night: Dave repelled them all in a 3-0 shutout. Asked how his style differed from netminding partner and popcorn connoisseur Mike Palmateer, Parro explained, "I eat popcorn only when I go to the movies."

Now, 19 days later, a memorable encounter with a very different sort of opponent, Vancouver's Dave "Tiger" Williams. Tiger had built an eight-year reputation as a feared enforcer (goon?). When Parro replaced an injured Palmateer late the 2nd period, Williams wasted no time acquainting himself with the youngster.

"There was a faceoff deep in our end," Parro told the *Saskatoon Star Phoenix*. "Tiger doesn't line up. He skates right up to me, puts his nose against my facemask, and asks, 'Hey, where's your weakness?'" The goalie laughed that one off. Relations got more testy in the final minutes, when Tiger crowded Parro's crease. "I tapped him on the ankle. He came back for more and I really gave it to him," Parro recalled. "He turned around and pitch-forked me. If I hadn't moved, it would have been my throat."

Instead, the Tiger and the 'Minder were assessed matching penalties. Parro stood tall against a Canucks barrage – 19 saves in 26 minutes of relief, allowing just one goal – to earn the 3-3 tie.

FEB. 22, 1981	QUE 11 WAS 7	LANDOVER, MD

Not only is 18 goals a Capitals single-game record, the teams combined for 172 penalty minutes – and one case of writer's cramp for the official scorer. The Nordiques were supreme killjoys, scoring 88 seconds after the Caps' first goal, 41 seconds after the Caps' second goal, and 19 seconds after the Caps' third goal.

THE LEGENDS OF LANDOVER

The outcome was still in doubt, Quebec leading 5-4, when a brawl erupted late in the 2nd period. Paul Mulvey was skating past the Nordiques penalty box, when Kim Clackson apparently shared un-neighborly thoughts. Mulvey adopted his Hank Aaron stance, then threw his stick at Clackson. Cue chaos, as benches emptied. Eventually, referee Ron Wicks looked up at the scoreboard, saw it was near intermission, and thought, the heck with it. Both teams were banished to their locker rooms, with the final 1:34 of the middle frame to be played just prior to the full 3rd period.

The Nordiques returned to the ice with a vengeance, scoring power play goals at 18:51 and 19:41. The teams switched ends, and Quebec scored another power play tally at 0:34. At this point, shell-shocked Mike Palmateer was relieved by Wayne Stephenson… and Jacques Richard scored twice on Wayne in under a minute. Both goalies saw the Stastny brothers in their nightmares: Peter scored four goals + four assists; three goals + five assists for Anton. 16 points for the Stastnys in one game!

As Washington's Jean Pronovost asked rhetorically, "How can you explain it?" Coach Gary Green took a stab, telling *AP*, "That's why they're getting paid a half-million dollars a year. They're fantastic hockey players."

APR. 5, 1981 | DET 2 WAS 7 | LANDOVER, MD

The postseason chase had fallen just short on the last day of the 1979-80 season. One year later, some sick cosmic cruelty left the Caps in the exact same situation.

On the final night of the '80-'81 season, Washington needed a win, plus a loss by the Leafs, to make the playoffs. Coach Gary Green "invoked a news blackout on the arena's scoreboard of the Toronto-Quebec game," reported *AP*. "I apologize to the fans for not giving them that convenience," Green said, "but I didn't want our players even thinking about that game. I thought it might throw them off one way or another."

Green also couldn't afford to be a gentleman. Detroit goalie Larry Lozinski wasn't able to start the game because of an equipment issue. The Wings asked for a delay, which Green refused, explaining, "If we go into anyone else's building and Ryan Walter has something wrong with his skate, they're not going to allow us the convenience of waiting until it's fixed."

In what turned out to be a disastrous mistake, Wings rookie backup Claude Legris hadn't even taken shots in warmups. So he didn't appear ready when Glen Currie and Tim Tookey scored for the Caps in the first 3:21 of the game, before Lozinski could replace him in net. The Caps beat Detroit 7-2, then awaited the finish of the Maple Leafs-Nordiques game.

THE LEGENDS OF LANDOVER

As a piped-in radio broadcast announced that Toronto had won to grab the last playoff spot, players in their misery couldn't even retreat to the privacy of the dressing room. "Players, thanks to an advance promotion, were forced to skate onto the ice for a photo session with fans." *(The Hockey News)* Aggrieved coach Green asked the question on many fans' lips, "Where's the damn justice in this league?" And about the wait for the out-of-town result, "It was like a death watch. Agony."

| NOV. 7, 1981 | NYR 3 WAS 1 | LANDOVER, MD |

Fast forward seven months from that painful April day. With the Caps on an 11-game losing streak, coach Green and G.M. Max McNab were fired. The only member of the staff to keep his job? Assistant coach Yvon Labre. Management could hardly kick Labre to the curb - they were holding "Yvon Labre Night" at the next home game! Besides, in the absence of a coach, Yvon had to run the morning practice.

Against the Rangers two nights later, Roger Crozier made his one and only appearance as coach of the Capitals - and lost, 3-1. AHL Hershey coach Bryan Murray, who served as Crozier's helper behind the bench, would be named as permanent replacement before the next game. Assistant G.M. Crozier moved up to the top job on an interim basis.

Injuries had forced retirement on Labre. With characteristic self-depreciation, he explained to *The Hockey News* why he declined a comeback. "I would have had to fool myself. Before, I was fooling everybody else."

The commemorative program begged to differ: "If Labre's statistics are average, the man himself isn't... They haven't come up with numbers to measure his real strong points: guts, pride, and determination... Yvon's carrying of the Capitals cause transcends a line of type." The program was bankrolled by a Maryland Caps fan who organized "Yvon Labre Night" because the team had failed to do so. *(THN)*

| NOV. 21, 1981 | PHI 4 WAS 10 | LANDOVER, MD |

Belying his status as a blueliner and a rookie, Greg Theberge scored two goals in the first nine minutes of the game. He added two assists early in the 2nd period, then found himself with the puck on an odd-man rush. "I had a chance for a hat trick," Theberge told *nugget.ca*. "I had the goalie out, but I passed off to Dennis Maruk and he put it in. I've always felt I was a good team player, but maybe I should have kept that puck and got my NHL hat trick."

THE LEGENDS OF LANDOVER

Greg's unselfish play helped Maruk to a hat trick of his own. The helper was also Theberge's fifth point, itself a team rookie record. Perhaps his bloodline was shining through. Theberge's grandfather was a Bruins Hall of Famer who played from 1927 to 1947, "Dit" Clapper. (Old athlete names are the best.) Greg spent his childhood in the company of Clapper's teammates. "I had never been in the Boston Garden until I played with the Capitals and it was unbelievable," Theberge said. "I walked in and tried to picture all these Bruins I'd met."

Tim Tookey scored a hat trick as well - the only time two Capitals have scored three goals in the same game. For a sweet bonus, this marked the first time the Caps had beaten the Flyers in Landover. "Philadelphia's Brad Marsh skated up to Capital Rick Green, an old junior teammate, and asked, 'What are you guys on, bennies?'" (*The Hockey News*)

FEB. 25, 1982 — STL 1 WAS 9 — LANDOVER, MD

You're familiar with the "Gordie Howe hat trick," a goal, assist, and fight in the same game. Against St. Louis, Bobby Carpenter introduced his own variation - four goals, a fight, and a black eye.

Carpenter's first appearance on the scoresheet was a surprise, even to him; a 2nd period fight with Jim Nill. "I don't really know what happened," Carpenter said to the *St. Louis Post-Dispatch*. "All of a sudden, we were just throwing punches." He received a shiner and a fighting major, but the Blues would've preferred letting sleeping Carpenters lie.

Less than two minutes after exiting the box, Bobby scored to give the Capitals a 4-1 lead. The 18-year-old rookie was just getting started. Bobby scored twice in the first minute of the third period to complete his official hat trick, then added a fourth goal with 2:22 to play.

Except for one breakaway tally, Carpenter deflected the praise to linemates Mike Gartner and Lou Franceschetti. "The other (goals), my 15-year-old brother could have scored." So why not go for five? "The four pucks are enough to hold (for photographers)," Carpenter joked. "Look how small my hands are. I couldn't hold more than four." As a team, Washington scored nine consecutive goals - four in the 2nd, five in the 3rd - after trailing, 1-0, and outshot the Blues, 46-27.

Dennis Maruk celebrated his first goal as a Capital by tossing his stick over the glass. An opposing scout wryly noted, "Maruk is dangerous after scoring." And he only grew more lethal; the final five entries in this chapter highlight Dennis' 60-goal season in 1981-82.

THE LEGENDS OF LANDOVER

NOV. 22, 1981 | WAS 3 PHI 2 | PHILADELPHIA

60 Scoring 60 goals in the NHL requires more than skill. A dose of unexpected luck arrived as Caps defenseman Timo Blomqvist was sent to the penalty box late in the first period. Maruk told *thehockeynews.com* what happened next. "I was changing shifts and I shot the puck in about two feet to the side of the net. Pete Peeters came out but the puck deflected off the boards, hit his stick, and caromed right into the net. I came to the bench - I was just trying to put the puck in the zone - and they said, 'You just scored.' That was strange."

DEC. 4, 1981 | WPG 3 WAS 7 | LANDOVER, MD

60 Before the game, Dennis Maruk's hair wasn't apparent – he walked into the locker room wearing a curly blonde wig. Not that he needed to; Dennis sported naturally curly locks Shirley Temple could appreciate. "I like to clown around," Maruk told the *Canadian Press*. "It helps keep me loose." This blonde certainly had more fun once the game started, as Maruk scored four goals and added two assists!

DEC. 11, 1981 | TOR 2 WAS 11 | LANDOVER, MD

60 The Capitals absorbed a 9-4 beatdown in Toronto six days earlier. "The last game was in the backs of our minds," Maruk admitted to the *Canadian Press*. With two goals and three assists, Maruk led an epic night of revenge. Ryan Walter and Bobby Carpenter scored twice, Chris Valentine had one goal + three helpers, and defensemen Greg Theberge and Darrin Veitch each recorded three assists.

Remarkably, Washington scored all 11 goals (four on the power play) in the first 37 minutes of the game – five in the 1st, six in the 2nd. The Caps fired 41 shots on goal in the first two periods. In the category of massive understatement, coach Bryan Murray said, "We wanted to be aggressive."

JAN. 13, 1982 | EDM 6 WAS 6 | LANDOVER, MD

60 On this date, one of the worst blizzards in Washington history caused the fatal crash of an Air Florida jet into the 14th St. Bridge. More than 15 thousand had been expected for that night's game against Wayne Gretzky and the Oilers. 3,284 hearty fans made it to Capital Centre, and were rewarded twice; first, with free coffee and hot chocolate, and in the final 10 seconds, when Maruk scored to lift the Capitals into a 6-6 tie.

THE LEGENDS OF LANDOVER

It was a spectacular individual effort, as Maruk won a faceoff from Gretzky, then shook off The Great One to score the equalizer. In the timeout before the draw, Maruk swayed coach Bryan Murray. "He wanted me to go backhanded," Maruk said, "but I have better success forehanded." Murray agreed, on one condition: "OK, but make sure it works." Maruk's strategy paid off, leading Murray to note, "We got a point on a great call, and Maruk made it." In the more somber visitors' locker room, a visibly upset Gretzky said, "It's all my fault." (*Canadian Press*)

What Wayne deserved was anything but blame. Earlier in the day, he generously performed the promotional duties asked of him in every visiting city. As reported by *The Hockey News*, Gretzky signed autographs for the deaf hockey players at Gallaudet University. Then he was whisked to four different TV stations for sit-down interviews. After scoring his 55th goal, he handed the puck to a Gallaudet player in attendance. So when Gretzky was named the game's number one star, in a way he didn't deserve it... but in a way, he did.

| APR. 3, 1982 | WAS 6 TOR 4 | TORONTO |

60 "Whenever my team would fly into Toronto," Maruk revealed in his autobiography, *Dennis Maruk*, "I'd head right to my mom and dad's place... We'd have a big family dinner... then I'd try to put on a little show on the ice." Home cooking and family in the Maple Leaf Gardens stands did the trick, as Dennis scored his 59th and 60th goals against netminder Vince Tremblay. Just don't ask for details. "It's kind of weird," Maruk wrote, "but I don't remember a lot of my goals... I wish I did."

Don't sweat it, Dennis! All of our memories of the '80's are as fuzzy as UHF reception. So here's the particulars: On his milestone 60th goal, Maruk shot across his body while skating through the left wing circle. His drive eluded Tremblay's grasping glove, snapping the twine inside the far right post at 17:59 of the second period.

Maruk's two-goal performance was all the more remarkable because he was playing with stretched ligaments in his right knee. Dennis estimated he was limited to 70 percent of full strength. "I didn't play my type of game," Maruk said to the *Washington Post*. "The knee gets sore when I shoot a lot, because it puts pressure on that leg." The real pain was missing the postseason for the seventh time in his pro career. "I'd give a few of those goals back to make the playoffs one of these years," he said. "I'd like to see what it's like."

SECOND PERIOD:
Capi-Pedia

Stories of...

- ✪ **The Name**
- ✪ **Uniform**
- ✪ **Prejudice**
- ✪ **Punches**
- ✪ **Pranks**
- ✪ **Politics**
- ✪ **Exhibitions**
- ✪ **Media**
- ✪ **Home Rink**
- ✪ **And a near-fatal financial crisis**

THE LEGENDS OF LANDOVER

5th Shift: *They Could've Been Pandas*
Logos, Uniforms, Names and Numbers

The Washington Pandas? The Pink Violins? The Slapsticks? Those were among 12,000 submissions in a team-naming contest for the expansion NHL franchise awarded to the Nation's Capital.

Starting January 2nd, 1974, more than 700 unique names were submitted. One devoted participant suggested 102 by himself, each mailed on its own postcard. Pollin attended the NBA All-Star game in Seattle on January 15th and, the *Washington Star* reported, spent the cross-country flight sorting through entries. According to a 20th Anniversary team publication, *Comets* was the most popular with 250 entries; 88 wrote in *Caps* or *Capitals*.

Late into the night before the January 22nd announcement, Abe and wife Irene decided none of the four most-submitted names would work. Shaune Lee, at the *weta.org Boundary Stones* blog, explained why. "*Comets* sounded too much like the cleaning brand, and neither liked *Pandas*. The (NFL) *Eagles* were at a low point, making the Pollins wary of letting their hockey team share the name, while choosing the *Metros* would be too close to the New York Mets. Moreover, the Pollins both thought *Capitals* had a good, solid ring to it."

Lee shared that oddly, "Abe Pollin vehemently disliked the name *Caps*, saying he found *Capitals* to be more appropriate for the area, and because it tied in neatly to the Capital Centre." That's the one Pollin settled on, explaining, "The names were novel, clever and original. I felt 'Washington Capitals' best described our entry. It took me eight to 10 hours," Abe added, "but I looked at every one." Now you can, too: Puck-Ups, Caputs, Belters, Goal Diggers, Tri-Stars, Largo Lizards and Beltway Bandits, Domes, Cyclones, Streaks, Blades, Cheetahs, Turtles, Koo-Koos, Ice Skins, Snowflakes, Mosquitoes, Dum Dums, Chimney Sweeps, Watergate Bugs, Wing Pings, Cold Cuts, Catfish, Isms, Apes, Delegates, Whips, Lizards, Troopers, Whippers and Colonials.

Political humorist Mark Russell found the winning nickname a wee bit lacking in imagination. "The Washington Capitals. Where else outside the tax-writing committees of Congress could we find such unparalleled invention? With the naming of the Capitals came the assumption that Pollin probably had a dog named Spot." *(N.Y. Times)*

Back to the "Pandas," think of it. The mascots could have been Ling-Ling and Hsing-Hsing, famously gifted by China to the National Zoo in 1972. Early on, the pair met with about as much success as the '70's Caps. "Hsing-Hsing attempted to mate with Ling-Ling's ear, wrist and foot." *(animalplanet.com)*

THE LEGENDS OF LANDOVER

✪ Caps, Capitals, and Capitols

Trivia doesn't get more trivial than this: Four previous D.C. franchises have briefly been Caps, Capitols, or Capitals. The *Washington Capitols* disbanded in 1951 after five seasons, the final two in the fledgling NBA. That beat the one season (1969-70) for the ABA's *Washington Caps*.

When the World Football League awarded D.C. a franchise in 1974, its corporate name was "Washington Capitals, Inc." The WFL entry held its first press conference the same day Abe Pollin announced he'd chosen Capitals as the name for his hockey team. The WFL ownership "was forced to drop the 'Capitals' nickname under legal threats from Pollin," wrote Dave McKenna at *deadspin.com*. "The team had two owners, four home cities, and five names before it held one practice," ultimately playing its only season in Orlando.

Finally, there's Washington's N.L. baseball team - of the 19th century. Kerry Keane's book, *1951*, references the early playing career of manager Connie Mack "As a catcher with the Washington Capitals in 1888."

✪ Hand-Me-Down Logo Design

The Capitals in 1974 adopted a "crew cut" mentality for their debut logo. No style, flair, or even originality. Two years earlier, the WHA's Philadelphia Blazers introduced one quite similar.

Any opportunity to create a dynamic logo was sacrificed on the altar of corporate branding. Remember, the Landover arena and its two sports tenants shared the same owner. The NBA Bullets already used a text-based logo, all lower case, in a custom font colored blue. The Capital Centre logo copied all four design elements. So the new hockey design was predestined to look like its siblings.

Yet the wordmark also sported a crew cut's positives: clean, crisp, neat, the words and art fitting together like jigsaw pieces. Stylistic heavy lifting on the uniform was carried by the stars, stripes, and shoulder color, so maybe the no-nonsense logo made sense. In any case, the logo on the '70's Caps sweaters was superior to the alterations made for the 1980's through 1995.

It's relevant to remember that in the early '70's, the Orioles removed "Baltimore" from their jerseys – a play for the hearts (and dollars) of the baseball-starved D.C. metropolitan area. The Capitals apparently felt that what worked for one Maryland-based sports franchise would surely work for another. So, hoping to tap into – oh, I don't know, hockey-crazy Towson and Ellicott City? – the Caps used a shrink ray to minimize the word "Washington" on their sweaters.

THE LEGENDS OF LANDOVER

Beginning in 1980-81, the city name became microscopic. It would have made more aesthetic sense to remove it – no one could read it anyway. What's worse, the miniscule "Washington" lettering wouldn't stay put. On some Capitals uniforms, it hugged close, just above the c-a-p. On others, it floated all the way up near the stars – almost collarbone level – even higher than the top of the hockey stick "T". Yuck.

The original 1970's Capitals sweaters had their own issue. Namely, names. The first season started without names on either home or road sweaters. Home whites finally got nameplates on January 7, 1975. The personal touch must have helped; surnamed Caps broke a nine-game losing streak by surprising the Bruins with a 3-3 tie. Another uniform change did the trick on January 24, 1976. The Caps switched from red to blue pants, and broke a 25-game winless streak by toppling the Rangers, 7-5.

Road unis still lacked names in Season Two. (The intentional omission supposedly spurred scorecard sales.) Strangely, home uniforms again lacked names until November. The sewing department wasn't ready for 1976-77, either. Even though the NHL mandated names on road uniforms, the Caps red sweaters didn't comply until well after the season started. *(capsjerseys.com)*

The Caps summoned the uniform gimmick again on December 15, 1989. Having won just four of their first dozen home games, the team donned red road sweaters at Capital Centre against the Islanders. What made this truly unusual was that New York played in their blue road uniforms, too. In a pre-NFL "Color Rush" game, the Caps failed to rock the red, losing 5-3.

✪ Irregulars

Say, if you're the kind of collector who's on the lookout for mistakes - if you get all tingly when you see the famous old stamp with the upside down biplane - then have we got a couple of authentic hockey sweaters for you!

Classicauctions.net showcased a sweater worn (we hope briefly) by Ron Lalonde, a center with the Caps from 1974-79. Notice we wrote "Lalonde," minus the extra "N" on the misspelled "Lalonnde" nameplate. As if the Caps of the '70's didn't suffer enough indignities. Happily, Lalonde is a rare positive trivia answer from the Capitals' debut season. In a March, 1975 game against Detroit, he scored the team's first hat trick.

Our next item, a pristine number 4 All-Star jersey made for Capitals defenseman Robert Picard. We can guarantee that his 1978 NHL All-Star sweater has no game-worn marks or tears. We confidently make this claim because Picard *wasn't named as an All-Star in 1978*. The Capitals' rep for the game in Buffalo that year was Bob Sirois.

THE LEGENDS OF LANDOVER

Classicauctions.net offered this explanation: "The NHL would do up jerseys for players who were on 'standby' because of injuries to players selected to play in the All-Star game." For the record, Picard would legitimately be a Caps All-Star, named to the team for the 1980 game.

✪ Roger Crozier Owns A Number Of Sweaters

#1. #31. #35. The Caps customized three authentic sweaters for goalie Roger Crozier. That's a lot of uniform numbers for a goalie who only played *three games*! In the curtain call of a 14-year career, Roger allowed just two goals in 103 minutes as a Capital late in the '76-'77 season. He even shared in a shutout victory. Still, three different numbers?

While all sweaters were authentic and custom-made, Crozier only wore #31 in battle. The following season, Roger posed for a team photo wearing #35, although he never played again. In '78-'79, Crozier joined the front office, and was gifted with a ceremonial #1 sweater. (To this day, he's the only man to serve the Capitals in three capacities, albeit fleeting ones: as a player, 3 games; as coach, 1 game; as G.M., 9 months.)

Roger learned to love numbers roulette during the course of seven seasons in Detroit. The Wings issued him three different sweaters, with numbers 1, 22, and 30. Despite recurring illnesses throughout his career, Crozier kept a sense of humor. "All goaltenders are going to heaven," he once said, "because we know all about hell."

Which seems an appropriate segue to Ron Low's hellish 1974-75 season. As a bonus indignity, his No. 1 sweater got stolen. So, according to *The Hockey News*, Low switched to No. 30 for the second half of that inaugural season. He switched back to No. 1 for the following two campaigns, but it's lost to history why in half a season the team couldn't replace his No. 1.

✪ Four Of A Kind

Three Capitals stand above all the rest in popularity with stadium scorecard vendors. The common thread among Rick Bragnalo, Doug Patey, and Mark Lofthouse, is that their threads were constantly changing. Time and again, they'd be recalled from the minors, invariably to find another player had been issued their former digits. Each wore four different numbers during their time with the Caps in the 1970's. (Not at the same time, smart guy.)

For Patey (#10, 23, 12 and 16), his finest moments came in 1976-77. Doug played 37 games, and scored three of his four NHL goals. Patey made his debut at age 19, the youngest player in the league. Speaking of being a "player," the *Annapolis Capital* reported, "Off the ice, Patey is frequently seen zipping around Landover in his blue Corvette. Not bad for a Toronto boy who used to spend his summers working in a sawmill."

THE LEGENDS OF LANDOVER

Bragnalo (#18, 27, 12 and 8) shined brightest during that same '76-'77 campaign, playing all 80 games and scoring 11 goals, two shorthanded.

Lofthouse (#11, 27, 20 and 8) shared a funny anecdote with *Hockey Card Stories* author Ken Reid about one of his numbers. "My claim to fame is I wore No. 8 with Washington. I told (Alex) Ovechkin, 'When they retire our number, I'd like to be there.'" An online search revealed a *fifth* number worn by Lofthouse, a photo of a supposedly game-worn number 28 sweater. But it's not listed by the official Capitals website, so that's mysterious.

No Cap beats Nelson Burton for speediest sweater switches. Playing just eight NHL games over two seasons, Nelson wore three numbers: 12, 27 and 8. His most cherished number is 1 – the lone goal of his career, scored against Tony Esposito, no less, in a 2-2 tie with Chicago in 1977.

These four spent the bulk of their careers out of the NHL, working for a shot at The Show. Patey spoke for all of them, in fact all players who have endured the grind of the minors, quoted by *greatesthockeylegends.com*: "I've been up and down. Up is better."

✪ Everything Old Is New Again

For their first two seasons, the Capitals sometimes wore red pants during home games (when the blue ones were in the wash?). 35 years after last donning them, the Caps dusted off the retro look red shells for use at the 2011 Winter Classic. The team has returned to various combos of their original uniforms ever since. Cue lyrics from the 1979 film, *All That Jazz*. "Don't throw the past away. You might need it some rainy day. Dreams can come true again. When everything old is new again."

✪ Four Will Get You Seven

Yvon Labre's 1974 press photo was a head-scratcher. An original Capital, Labre wore #7 from preseason in '74 through his retirement in 1981. The jersey was then retired - no one wore it in Washington after Yvon. So why did he slip on a #4 sweater at the very first class picture day? We only know that another blueliner, Joe Lundrigan, got to wear #7. A savvy career move by Labre? If he later made a bad play, Yvon could say, "Hey, that was number 7. I'm number 4!"

Labre got his #7 back by the start of the regular season, but sat out the first two Capitals games with an injury. Lundrigan, now wearing the #5 that would later be retired in Rod Langway's honor, skated on defense in the first three contests of the season. Then Lundrigan became the first ex-Cap, never again playing in the NHL. Of his 52-game NHL career (the previous 49 with Toronto), Joe said, "I enjoyed every minute I was there and I will always remember it for the rest of my life." (*sportnl.ca*)

THE LEGENDS OF LANDOVER

✪ Needing A Second Opinion

For years, sports sections routinely misspelled "Capitals" with an "o" instead of an "a". Even so, it's surprising the U.S. Capitol building wasn't a symbol for Washington's hockey team until the 1995 redesign. Admittedly, some nicknames - Lions, Rockets, Pirates - lend themselves to images. Franchises without a natural logo created stylized lettering - the Packers' G, Phillies' P, Canadiens' CH... in their own backyard, the Senators' and Nationals' W. The Caps neglected that work-around.

An aesthetics oversight, since the Capitals word logo didn't show up well in newspapers and magazines, or on television; to fit the stick "T" in a square box, the rest of the letters had to be shrunk to a tiny size. As for a secondary logo, the Capitals didn't have one. Creating an alternate design isn't that tough; the one at left took me 15 minutes, and people paid for this sort of thing surely could do better.

✪ It Must Be The Uniform

Somewhere in the dusty recesses of a wardrobe designer's closet hangs a rack full of knockoff Capitals sweaters. An early '90's TV commercial for Rold Gold pretzels, starring *Seinfeld's* Jason Alexander, looked like it had been staged at a Caps home game.

The pretzel-eating Alexander is summoned out of the stands by the coach when the home team goalie is injured. The goalie and his teammates are wearing re-created Capitals uniforms - though not completely. Presumably to avoid a licensing fee, the sweater is always partly altered or obscured. One player's sweater reads "apitals", the logo is completely missing from another, and on a third, the hockey-stick "T" in Capitals is backward.

Anyway, Jason makes a series of remarkable saves against the (Russian?) opponent, including one with his teeth, to win the game. The Russians seem content with this, as they've snagged their own bag of pretzels. Frito-Lay announced, "Since the launch of the 'Hockey' spot, Rold Gold sales have increased more than 25 percent." The ad's tagline is, "It must be the pretzels," but we can't help wondering if it wasn't really the uniforms.

✪ 2,500,000 Smiths In The U.S. & Canada; Here Are 2 Of Them

Among the infinite subsets of sports fans are those who focus on NOB - names on back. For a game in Toronto, the Caps' defenseman fending off an attacker near the crease was Gord Smith; his goalie a few feet away was Gary Smith. The rarity is that both have full names sewn on their sweaters... although since one wore a mask and pads, it couldn't have been too tough telling them apart.

THE LEGENDS OF LANDOVER

✪ The Uniform That Wasn't

The Capitals almost joined the long-pants fad of the early '80's, the so-called "Cooperalls" worn for two seasons by the Flyers and Whalers. The Caps' version had a blue shell, and within a vertical white stripe down each pants leg, one row of alternating blue and red stars. This information came from an *ebay.com* seller (and if you can't trust an *ebay* seller, who can you trust?). The seller wrote, "These were one of a few designs the Capitals were considering for the 1982-83 season." Naturally, the NHL banned all long Cooperalls shortly after the Caps began experimenting with them.

✪ Card-Jacked

Mistaken identity wasn't uncommon in 1970's trading cards, as Capitals defenseman Jack Lynch can attest. Lynch earned a card for the '77-'78 season; he even autographed some of them. Only thing is, the picture wasn't Jack. Someone must have looked at the photo, saw #2 for the Capitals, and assumed it was Lynch. The pictured skater is actually Bill Collins, #26, with part of his uniform number obscured. Truly odd is that Lynch would autograph the card, though it isn't him!

The Caps' own website put Lynch in the middle of another identity crisis. Traded to D.C. late in 1974-75, Jack briefly wore #19. In the photo chosen to accompany an article, only the "9" shows, and the website mislabeled him as the actual owner of #9, Ace Bailey. The lesson, in both cases: beware of hidden digits.

We presume Jack was more careful with facts during his own budding media career. "I wrote for a network of community newspapers around the D.C. area on what was happening in the National Hockey League," he told the *Owen Sound Sun Times*. Lynch also served as analyst on Caps TV games in the 1980-81 season. "I was able to build a resume around some really good practical TV and newspaper experience."

✪ When White Was Wrong

No discussion of Capitals' uniforms can be complete without one more mention of those white pants. As the road losing streak to start the 1974 season reached nine, Russ White noted in *The Hockey News* that the record for Washington was "0-4 in red pants, 0-4 in white pants, 0-1 in blue. Teams are simply beating the pants off them."

Okay, *now* the chapter can be over.

THE LEGENDS OF LANDOVER

6th Shift: *Pride & Prejudice & Pucks*
Tough Times for Black, European, French-Canadian Caps

Today's NHL includes players from two dozen countries; only about half hail from Canada. Longtime Caps goaltender Olaf Kolzig knows that better than most. Olie was born in South Africa, raised in Canada, played in the U.S. Capital, and with two German parents, Kolzig represented that country in the Olympics!

Quite a different landscape from when the Caps entered the NHL. The league was just opening its doors to an expanded universe of players. Metaphorically, it was the service entrance, because bigotry in hockey still took many forms. Here's one: in the late 1970's, Canadian magazine *The Actualite* noted that while 30% of the country's population was French-speaking, only 15% of NHL players were French-Canadian.

Montreal-born Bob Sirois, a Capital from 1975-1980, found that suspicious. What Gary Green did upon becoming coach in 1980, Bob found offensive. "One day when Bernie Wolfe and I were chatting in French in the locker room, he came out of his office to say, "No more speaking f***ing French in this room!"

Sirois protested that the English-only standard wasn't applied to Swedish players on the team. "When I went to ask him for an explanation, he told me that English-speaking players thought they were being talked about in the back when French-speaking players spoke French to each other. Bouchard, Girard and Jean Pronovost, who joined the team the following year, were sent to the minors. Picard was traded. Charron went to play in Europe." (*journaldemontreal.com*)

Sirois' curiosity resulted in his 2009 book, *Discrimination in the NHL: Quebec Hockey Players Sidelined*. "At equal or comparable talent," Sirois concluded, "a Quebecer, a European or an American will not be chosen. Only the very best athletes from those nations will make it to what is in fact the English-Canadian NHL."

Sirois, to Toronto's *CJCL* radio: "When you see 10 NHL teams don't even have a scout in the Quebec (junior) league, you begin to wonder. There's clichés and stereotypes. NHL analysts say about Americans, 'They don't play enough games in college to be ready for the NHL.' It's always something on the negative side."

Many insiders and fans found flaws in those conclusions. However, it's fair to wonder whether their reviews of Bob's analysis were scientific criticisms. Or, did they to some extent reflect their own biases? The debate rages on, much as the larger question of Quebec's place within Canada.

THE LEGENDS OF LANDOVER

✪ Skating While Black

No such debate exists about the treatment of blacks on the Caps in the '70's. For the audacity of playing what bigots regarded as "the white man's game," Mike Marson and Bill Riley were subjected to blatant racism. "It was a culture shock," Marson recalled. "Nobody should have to hear 'We don't have people like him stay at our hotel' and nobody should go for breakfast and they won't feed you. This is before you even get to the rink, before you have to deal with your opposition. It was non-stop."

Only a counter-threat ensured Marson received a room key. "They're asking the coaching staff, 'Who is this kid? Is he with you?' 'Well, we don't have people like him stay at our hotel.' I remember the coaching staff saying, 'If he's not going to stay here, the team won't stay here, and we'll be calling New York and nobody will stay here.' It didn't make sense to me. It still doesn't make sense to me."

As William Douglas wrote at *colorofhockey.com*, Marson "exuded unabashed blackness - an Afro, Fu Manchu mustache and mutton chop sideburns." More than a few whites exuded venom. Marson received death threats pasted from words cut out of magazines. One read: "You're on thin ice black boy... The n****r is going to die."

Marson explained to *washingtoncaps.com* senior writer Mike Vogel, "The hate mail was so cowardly. When you're going on a 10-day road trip and you have a wife at home, you have to be wondering if they're safe. I used to have a Jaguar, and I used to have people loosen the lug nuts. I got so tired, so tired."

Marson knew every time he skated onto an opponent's rink, some fans would be salivating for the inevitable cheap shots. "That's a whole different game, 'cause now you're not just playing to win. Now you've got to watch your back. You've gotta know to get your head up, 'cause so-and-so is going to be running you, somebody else is trash-talking you."

Racial slurs from opponents were just the beginning. According to Cecil Harris' book *Breaking The Ice*, teams would offer a cash prize to a player who injured Marson. A black teammate, Bill Riley, recalls the pair "getting high-sticked and slashed. Those things cut Michael's heart out."

In one typically ugly incident in a preseason game, Detroit's Dennis Hextall speared Marson so violently in the chest, the blade of Hextall's stick broke. In another preseason assault, Toronto's Dave Dunn speared Mike in the face. When Mike retaliated by swinging his stick, a benches-clearing brawl ensued. "I'm prepared to close my ears to anything stupid," Marson said as a rookie. "I anticipate the odd man mouthing off. But he might finally find himself skating with blood on his face." *(Hayward Daily Review, nhl.com)*

THE LEGENDS OF LANDOVER

Marson found no refuge with many of his so-called teammates. "Uncle Ben" was one of the printable slurs. Some pretended not to know him as they boarded planes. When a death threat was phoned to the Philadelphia Spectrum, linemates joked about sitting far from him on the bench. While Marson filmed a TV commercial, Dave Kryskow cracked that he could be chosen instead, "if I get my face painted."

Team members who had Marson's back included road roommate Yvon Labre, a pair nicknamed "Chico and the Man" after a 1970's sitcom about odd-couple coworkers. Another was coach Tom McVie, who, before a game, had to inform Marson about the sudden death of his teen brother. "Michael is one of our family, and therefore his brother was, too." Asked by a dull-witted reporter if Marson and Bill Riley were given roster spots to gin up interest among Washington's large black population, McVie shot back, "If Chinese could do the job they would be here."
(*Toronto Globe & Mail, Washington Post, nhl.com*)

G.M. Milt Schmidt, who drafted Marson to the Caps, had already proven his color-blindness. Willie O'Ree, the NHL's first black player, wrote at *theplayerstribune.com* about his debut game in 1958. "Bruins' coach Milt Schmidt and general manager Lynn Patrick took me aside. They said, 'Willie, we brought you in because we knew you could add something to the team. The Bruins organization is behind you 100 percent.'" Marson's father never forgot a *CBC* radio interview later that season, when "Schmidt made it clear O'Ree was a Bruin, not a black Bruin." (*Hockey News*)

At the time, Bill Riley worried about going public with the "terrible, terrible" invectives hurled his way. "We had to live with that," Riley told the *Toronto Star*. "We figured if we said anything, we would be deemed troublemakers." Bill cited an example in which the team bus driver dropped the n-word, and a Caps coach inexplicably reacted with laughter. "Nothing was said about it. Nothing was done about it," Riley said of the coach's reaction.

Compared to the explosion of nationalities, "Minority players in the National Hockey League only number in the dozens," estimated *NPR* in 2015, which still represented "an improvement on just a handful (of minority players) 30 years ago." Indeed, a record 28 black players skated in at least one NHL game in 2017-18. (*espn.com*)

Talent increasingly is the attribute which matters most to teams and fans; progress has been made. Just as clearly, not enough progress has been made. Even members of groups which have been targets themselves exhibited prejudice. Francophiles directed abuse at Reggie Savage, a #1 draft choice of the Caps in 1988, when Savage played as a junior in Quebec. "People threw bananas at me," said Savage, who is black. "They used the 'N-word' all over the place." *(Toledo Blade)* To this day, ugly incidents like those faced by Marson, Riley and Savage still aren't a thing of the past. Xenophobia remains alive and toxic in both sports and society.

THE LEGENDS OF LANDOVER

✪ Patty's Question Was (Pea)Nuts

Mike Marson's re-integrating the NHL in 1974 made waves beyond the sports section. Way out in California, he *drew* the attention of hockey fan Charles Schulz, better known as creator of the iconic *Peanuts* comic strip.

Now, there are many ways to describe Peppermint Patty and pals - topical and cutting-edge wouldn't be on that list. Schulz took a rare departure into social relevance in the funny papers of November 6, 1974, one month after Marson's first NHL game. This particular strip, featuring Patty and a black character named Franklin, was, to say the least, open to interpretation.

When Franklin explains he wants to be a pro hockey player, Patty's response is, "How many Black players in the NHL?" *Peanuts* fans saw this as commentary against the NHL's racial insensitivity. Some readers thought it was Schulz showing the intolerance, by implying that a black youngster shouldn't harbor NHL dreams. For his part, Marson posted the full strip on his website, without offering an opinion on its merits.

A *Peanuts* reader went to the source, writing to Schulz that the strip could be perceived as racist. Schulz responded, "I can't believe you are so ready to leap in with your criticism. When the strip was drawn... there was only one black in the National Hockey League. Does pointing out this fact make the strip racist?" (Letters posted at *thesneeze.com*)

✪ Life Of Riley

Enforcer Bob Gassoff led St. Louis in penalty minutes each year from 1974-1977, usually letting his fists do his talking. Which was fortunate in a sense, because facing Bill Riley, Gassoff's mouth proved even more primitive.

In the first period of a January, 1977 game at Capital Centre, "Riley was slashed by Gassoff. If it didn't necessarily start as a racial incident, it ended that way with the white Gassoff making nasty comments to blacks Riley and (Mike) Marson." (*Washington Star*) Bill answered by assisting on the third period go-ahead goal in a 2-1 Caps victory. About Gassoff, Riley said, "He showed me no class. You expect stuff like that in the bushes."

The rematch in Landover three weeks later allowed Riley an even sweeter response. Sadly and predictably, "Gassoff bloodied Riley with his stick after being checked hard into the boards by Riley." Bill pounded Gassoff in their subsequent fight. "I swear I didn't know it was him when I checked him into the boards," Riley said. "I was glad when I realized it. Yeah, real glad." The joy multiplied when Bill tied the game with 3:18 left, triggering a late burst of goals and a 6-3 Capitals victory.

THE LEGENDS OF LANDOVER

✪ Swede And Sour

Europeans were also targeted. *The Hockey News* cited Bengt Gustafsson's skating clinic goal vs. Toronto. "Instead of congratulating him, coach Danny Belisle warned him he would pay a price for showing up the opposition." Caps trainer Gump Embro rhetorically asked, "Why should I go to college to study anatomy? Treating Gus I've learned every bone and muscle in the body." Gustafsson once said, only half joking, "I think I'll get a goalie mask."

"A Swede has to be murdered before you give another guy two minutes," lamented Rangers coach Fred Shero to the *New York Times*. Capitals G.M. Max McNab, who recruited three Swedes to D.C., suggested culture played a role. "When a North American player is fouled, he retaliates and that calls attention to the infraction. The test of manhood for a Swedish player is how much they can take without retaliating. All Europeans go by the book."

Coach Belisle lauded defenseman Leif Svensson. "He moves the puck well and plays the body much better than we expected." Still, Leif told *Hockey Illustrated*, "It's harder than I thought it would be. Everything happens so fast. There's no time for passing and they play the body much more than in Europe. They tell me the games here are going to get more high-pitched. Well, I can't imagine that happening."

Countryman Rolf Edberg first faced Canadians during World Championship matches in the late '70's. "The Canadians were honestly real pigs during this tournament, and the funny thing was that when I later met the same guys in the NHL they said not a word, even on the ice." The Swedish Caps center iceman also marveled at the ferocity of North American training camps: "It was a culture shock. Here at home we were accustomed to train and have some fun. This was, especially youngsters, like madmen against each other to take a place on the squad." *(svenskbaskettelevision.se)*

A contrary word on mirth came from Caps goalie Gary Inness, who defended Canadian conviviality to the *Washington Star*. "Look at how determined players from other countries are compared to Canadians. Even guys like Rolf Edberg and Leif Svensson on our team rarely smile and never joke around." Hmmm. Until arenas add a laugh counter to the scoreboard, the international hockey comedy debate may never be settled.

✪ The Sport Where Men Celebrate In Group Hugs

By any standard, Philadelphia's Bob Kelly and Washington's Gary Rissling behaved deplorably. The one thing more disgraceful was how Kelly described it afterwards. First the particulars, from April 3, 1980. Rissling smashed Kelly into the Spectrum boards. Legally, contended Gary and his coach. With his stick up, claimed Bob and the referee.

THE LEGENDS OF LANDOVER

The Broad Street Bullies didn't tolerate hard checks, even legal ones. Kelly rose throwing punches, with possibly dirty tactics in the clinches. The scrap would be just Round 1; Round 2 took place in the penalty boxes, where Kelly threw a water bottle at Rissling. Sent to the showers, Bob and Gary confronted each other under the stands for Round 3. "It took both bars and a policeman armed with a nightstick to keep them separated," reported the *Washington Post*. "They screeched at each other through a locked and guarded fence, rather like baboons," was the *Washington Star* account.

Such pro wrestling-style theatrics were all too commonplace in the '70's and '80's NHL – especially by the Flyers. Kelly raised the stakes to casual bigotry with his postgame comments. "I'll take a punch and stitches any day," said the man nicknamed The Hound. "But scratches and bites? Rissling is not a man. He's a queer. Drop your gloves and fight like a man; don't be a queer." This from the player who added, in the same interview, "Would I rather play hockey? No, I play to win, whatever I got to do."

Today's social media has exposed the shocking number of athletes who still engage in anti-LGBTQ hatred. It's wrong today, and Kelly was wrong then. Happily, today's Caps are at the forefront of the NHL's "You Can Play" initiative. At a 2018 home game, Caps players wrapped rainbow-colored "Pride Tape" on their sticks used in warmups, then autographed and auctioned the sticks. Goalie Braden Holtby has marched in the D.C. Pride Parade, and spoke on behalf of the Capitals at the Human Rights Campaign's annual event. "Supporting LGBTQ equality is a winning decision, and we're honored to stand with you in the fight."

Four months after the Kelly-Rissling dustup, the Capitals traded for the former Flyer. Would the agitator who had bedeviled Washington since it entered the league now be embraced? You better believe it, because selective amnesia is an expected, if unsavory, pro sports skill. At a pre-training camp workout, Rissling said of Kelly, "We're friends now – got to be, we're teammates." (Only temporarily; Rissling apprenticed at AHL Hershey until the Caps dealt him to Pittsburgh in January, 1981.)

Management also found new appreciation for The Hound. At a team dinner, Kelly and his wife were introduced as part of the "Caps' family" by owner Abe Pollin. Fans greeted him with applause and banners. G.M. Max McNab called Bob "Tough, aggressive, but not dirty. The man is a classy veteran." (*Washington Star*)

When Dennis Maruk scored an early-season hat trick, he credited his new veteran linemates. "(Jean) Pronovost and Kelly both have a lot of experience with contending teams. They know what they're doing and they've helped me mature." Because of their uniform numbers (Maruk 21, Pronovost 22, Kelly 24), they were dubbed the "Roaring '20's" line. If they'd worn higher numbers, would they have been called the "Gay '90's" line?

THE LEGENDS OF LANDOVER

✪ Collyard v. Washington Capitals, 477 F. Supp. 1247

To find the link between Bob Collyard and the Washington Capitals, don't look in the record books - look in the law books. Minnesota-born Collyard, a stellar forward at Colorado College, apprenticed 10 NHL games with St. Louis. Invited to Washington's first-ever training camp in 1974, Collyard couldn't crack the squad, and played the next decade in the minors.

In March, 1979, Collyard sued the Capitals and NHL in U.S. District Court. For good measure, he also sued the U.S. Attorney General, Secretary of State, and Secretary of Labor. From *clearinghouse.net*: "Plaintiffs allege that they have been denied employment on account of their national origin.

"They contend that the Defendant teams are composed predominantly of Canadian-born players... notwithstanding the fact that there are many qualified Americans who could play hockey as well as - if not better than - some inferior Canadians." The suit maintained that the practice violated federal immigration law. A judge disagreed, dismissing Collyard's claim and a similar suit for a variety of reasons - among them, that you couldn't sue a Maryland-based hockey team in a Minnesota court.

Dan David of *hockeydraftcentral.com* suggests that while Collyard lost the case, he had a point. "Taking this issue to court was a bit much, but the mere existence of these cases is a reminder of what the NHL was like in the 1970s and reflect a very real sense within these players that they were not being given a chance because they came from south of the U.S.-Canadian border."

Although Bob didn't make it back to the NHL, he twice represened the U.S. at international tournaments. By 1981-82, the 32-year-old Collyard was elder statesman for the AHL's Milwaukee Admirals. "I'm the oldest, so I keep an eye on the rest of them," Collyard said. "Sometimes they're hard to keep up with. But it keeps me young." After Collyard scored a hat trick, teammates were heard teasing him, "Way to go, Dad." (*Milwaukee Journal*)

✪ The Promotion Was A Turkey

At the intersection of hockey and sexism, consider the "Turkey Shoot" promotion of the '70's and early '80's. Only female Capitals fans could participate; why will become clear once the rules are explained. A shopping cart was placed on the ice – in case any of the ladies had forgotten that grocery shopping is women's work, natch. Members of the fairer sex would try to shoot a puck through the cart's wheels – presumably after a man explained what a stick and puck were. Winners would take home a gobbler, which the lucky housewife – they're all housewives, right? – undoubtedly would cook for her hard-working, bread-winning, head of household hubby.

THE LEGENDS OF LANDOVER

The Caps held a few of these. Before one, a Virginia sportswriter cautioned, "A turkey shoot… does not necessarily mean the Capitals' players will face a firing squad." At some minor league rinks, women-only turkey shoots are *still a thing*. The Hershey Bears have one, for instance, but thankfully their contest is open to all genders.

✪ Many Cultures, One Team

Back to Bob Sirois, at least he could feel at home on the '77-'78 Caps, with French-Canadian teammates Guy Charron, Robert Picard, Bob Girard, and Jean Lemieux. Heck, the Caps also had two black players (Marson, Riley), a Jewish player (Bernie Wolfe), and two Yanks (Tom Rowe, Craig Patrick). For good measure, the team hired a European scout, which led to the summer 1978 signing of two Swedish players (Rolf Edberg and Leif Svensson). So whatever their talent level, the 1970's Capitals can be proud of being way ahead of the curve on workplace diversity!

THE LEGENDS OF LANDOVER

7th Shift: *Comedy Club, Fight Club, Health Club*

Every hockey team in every era forms its culture around pranks, punches and pain. These are the Culture Clubs of the '70's and '80's Capitals.

COMEDY CLUB

✪ Billy The Kidder

Billy "The Kid" Taylor played 323 NHL games in the 1930's and '40's, then became a real-life hockey outlaw. In 1948, according to Stan Fischler's *Handy Hockey Answer Book*, "A Detroit bookmaker mentioned Taylor's name during a police wiretap." A lifetime ban was issued to Billy and his one-time roommate by the league's Board of Governors, "who concluded that the two had placed bets on games."

The ban was lifted in 1970. By 1974, Taylor had joined the expansion Capitals as a scout, where his new nickname should have been "Billy The Kidder." Why? One example came in a crowded hotel elevator, relayed by Russ White of the *Washington Star*. "Taylor's room was on the ninth floor, (chief scout Red) Sullivan's on the 18th. Taylor thought he'd get under Sullivan's skin by kissing his pal and saying 'Goodnight, sweetie,' just as he got off on the ninth floor and the elevator door closed."

Archie Henderson and Bugsy Watson became prank victims of Taylor at training camp. Billy took each of the camp roommates aside individually, and confided that the other player had trouble hearing. Taylor told each to speak up loudly, maybe shout, especially when they were together in their motel room. "Needless to say there was noise from the Henderson-Watson suite at the Spinners Inn in Hershey," White reported. Billy The Kidder had struck again.

✪ Bananas

"It's a series of big, foolish but entertaining spectacle scenes." This could have been a review of the Capitals; instead, Vincent Canby in the December 18, 1976 *New York Times* was reviewing the big-budget Hollywood remake of *King Kong*.

More mysterious than Skull Island was the Capitals' decision to hold a "King Kong" promotion at Capital Centre. But they did, on December 14, in conjunction with a game against, of course, the L.A. *Kings*. Between periods, a group wearing ape costumes and Caps sweaters played broom hockey against a team of aspiring Fay Wrays. "I wondered what was going on," confessed one bewildered player, "when a bunch of apes came out of nowhere with broomsticks in their hands." Fan prizes distributed during timeouts included King Kong posters and crates of bananas. By the way, the Caps lost, 4-2. As Jessica Lange lamented in the film, "God it's scary. It's like there's a curse on all of us."

THE LEGENDS OF LANDOVER

✪ Bob Calls Buddha

You can't guess all hockey pranksters from their on-ice demeanor. Take Bob Girard, a responsible defense-first winger for the Caps from 1977-79, often assigned to the opposition's top scorers. Off the ice, Bob was, let's say, a "cutup." As in sneaking up during plane rides to snip the neckties of dozing teammates. "If a rookie was running late, he'd cut your skate laces," Greg Theberge told *thehockeynews.com*. "Or Vaseline on the phone - 'the phone's for you.'"

Girard could also be, to quote the Caps' *Media Guide*, "a turbaned figure in the locker room, throwing baby powder in the air, appealing to Buddha for goals." The incantations didn't often work; Girard scored 18 goals total in his two seasons in Landover.

✪ Tricks Of The Trade

Coveted Caps defenseman Robert Picard received a shocking greeting at practice in October, 1978. "The guys on the team told me that they heard I had been traded," Robert told the *Washington Star*. It took assurances from both his coach and general manager to convince Picard it wasn't true.

A prankster posing as a Canadiens team official had called Montreal radio stations to "report" the trade. In addition to Picard, the Capitals were purportedly surrendering their number one draft choice. Supposedly on the way to Washington were goalie Bunny Larocque, center Pierre Larouche, and defenseman Brian Engblom. Engblom did make it here four years later.

If the ficticious trade was lightning, media outlets spread it with the speed of dry tinder set aflame. Montreal radio blindly aired the hoax, wire service *UPI* repeated what the stations said, Montreal newspapers repeated what the wire service said, and fans poured gallons of fuel on the fire. Caps G.M. Max McNab, accustomed to taking heat for moves he did make, said, "We were getting ripped for a deal we knew nothing about."

✪ Self-Depreciating Pete

Pete Laframboise's 1972-73 Seals finished next-to-last with 16 victories. In '73-'74, his Seals fell to a league-worst 13 wins, in front of home crowds rarely exceeding 5,000. That preceeded the Caps claiming Laframboise in the '74-'75 expansion draft. Washington, riding an 0-13-1 streak, mercifully dealt Pete to Pittsburgh 45 games into the season. Given Pete's previous employers, "When friends congratulated him on moving to a contender, he replied, 'Give me two weeks, and I'll mess them up.'" Pete flashed his wit again, earning a star with three assists against the Caps. "They didn't tell me when I came off. They probably didn't know who I was." *(Pgh. Press)*

THE LEGENDS OF LANDOVER

✪ One-Liners

▷ Ryan Walter, too relaxed on a team flight: "We were en route to L.A., so I stretched out, took off my shoes and fell asleep. We got to California, my shoes were gone. I had to walk through the airport in my socks. When I got to the carousel, my shoes came down with my luggage!" (*L.A. Times*)

▷ "Once we were beaten so badly in Los Angeles," coach Tom McVie recalled, "when I got to my hotel, I told my equipment guy I was thinking of jumping out of a window. He said, 'The way you're going, Tom, you'll land in the swimming pool and ruin your new suit!'" (*nhl.com*)

▷ As a Bruin, Dave Forbes "was known as a practical joker, 'pieing' people" with shaving cream. The Caps claimed Forbes on waivers in Oct., 1977, and a month later visited Boston. During a live interview between periods of the on Bruins TV, a Boston trainer shoved a shaving cream pie into Dave's face. "Forbes laughed as he wiped the mess from his cheeks and eyelids, and kept chatting with interviewer John Peirson." (*AP*)

▷ Sometimes it's simply better to laugh than cry. During that interminable first season, Mike Bloom told the *Post*, "After we had lost 15 in a row, Tommy (Williams) called a team meeting and said, 'Guys, let's not get down. We're a good team. We're just in the wrong league.'"

▷ After a fight-filled contest in Montreal, coach Gary Green and assistant Bill Mahoney wandered into the hotel bar. Green recalls Mahoney "fuming, banging his fist and demanding: 'I'll have two beers immediately and make sure they're cold!' The waiter replied: 'Should I bring an intravenous kit for you, sir?'" (*Montreal Gazette*)

▷ Dennis Maruk, Bob Kelly and Jean Pronovost not only played on the same line in 1980, they were auctioned off together. At a charity event benefitting Ronald McDonald House, $1,300 was bid for Maruk to cook dinner at the winner's home, assisted by Kelly and Pronovost. When Dennis described his linemates as "butlers," Bob corrected him. "With Jean, you're getting a dumbwaiter, not a butler." (*WTOP Radio*)

▷ Yvon Labre auditioned some on-ice comedy material during a power failure at Nassau Coliseum on Long Island. "I was yelling, 'Alex!' in the dark. The referee said, 'Alex who? What are you saying?' I said, 'Alex-trician. We need an electrician.'" (*thehockeynews.com*)

▷ An anonymous teammate pulled what ranks among the world's most gentle pranks. All during the 1979-80 season, Swedish Caps Rolf Edberg and Bengt Gustafsson passed time on the road playing backgammon. At the Toronto airport, Bengt noticed non-regulation dice. "Look here, Rolf," Gustafsson said. "This is not right. This one has two number fives and no number twos." Edberg laughed.

THE LEGENDS OF LANDOVER

▷ An athlete who can make light of his own injury certainly qualifies as having a healthy sense of humor. Caps defenseman Rick Green, riffing about his own pulled groin: "If it's like this tomorrow I won't be playing unless the new leg I ordered has come in."

▷ Ace Bailey, on the mischief that confirmed Bryan Watson's nickname, "Bugsy": "He does things like putting Vaseline on the doorknobs so our trainer can't get out of the training room. Or, he and (Billy) Collins squirt shaving cream in Gump Embro's back pocket, all over his bandages and scissors." Ace could hardly claim innocent-bystander status. "Sometimes Gump gets so angry, he even suspects I'm doing some of those things." (*Final three items from the Washington Star*)

✪ Putting the Laugh in Laughlin*

*I know Craig's surname is pronounced Lock-lin. Leave me alone.

One thing we've learned listening to Craig Laughlin: he's a funny guy. The Capitals winger-turned-broadcaster created his own vocabulary - "Kabong" for a hard hit, "Coconatta" for forehead. As a player, Craig was witness and participant in a never-ending series of frat house antics. Any place, any time, as Laughlin related for Dan Steinberg's *washingtonpost.com* blog.

On Plane Trips: Players would ask flight attendants for sodas they knew weren't stocked on the plane. "I'd ask for a Mountain Dew. 'Sorry sir, we don't have Mountain Dew.' Rod (Langway) would be next, 'Give me a Pibb Cola' or whatever. We'd be driving people crazy."

At The Airport: "Davey Christian would light everybody's newspaper on fire. It was called Hot News - hey guys, what's the hot news - and he'd have this cigarette lighter under a guy's paper, and all of the sudden the paper would catch flames in the middle of the airport."

In The Hotel: Bobby Carpenter would steal teammates' room keys, "rip stuff off your bed, put everything in the shower, and turn on the water."

On one hotel visit, Rod Langway got locked out of his room... naked. Laughlin was his roomie. "I let him stand there for a while. Then we worked it out and he got in." Maybe that's how he really got the nickname "Locker."

In Meetings: "When (coach) Murray would leave the room, Larry Murphy would get up and act like Bryan Murray."

After Morning Practice: Returning to the hotel in frigid Winnipeg, "We'd walk through buildings because if we walked outside our wet hair would freeze immediately. We finally just said 'Ah, who cares?' And our hair was just frozen." (Laughlin, to *washingtoncaps.com*)

THE LEGENDS OF LANDOVER

✪ The Prankmaster

Pranking teammates is as much a part of hockey as slapshots and faceoffs. Dale Hunter, wrote David Sell in the *Washington Post*, was an impresario. "Teammates and others love (Hunter) for a hundred reasons... practical jokes among them." Even civilians weren't safe, as Hunter would "tape clear fishing line to a $1 bill and leave the bait on the floor of an airport terminal."

In the *Baltimore Sun*, Sandra McKee profiled Hunter's victims. "Yvon Corriveau never saw the scissors that snipped his tie while he was sleeping on a team flight. Garry Galley never saw the screwdriver used to remove the doors of his Jeep." Galley had reportedly escalated a prank war by dousing Dale with a bucket of water. Think about poor Gary, who had to ride down the highway in a blizzard, with no doors. That's one cold prank.

Speaking of vehicles, Hunter's ride, befitting his off-season farming life, was a big Ford pickup. Returning from a road trip, teammates used that truck to gain a measure of revenge. As Dale told *washingtoncaps.com*, the Hunter became the Hunted: "I jump in my truck, turn it on, put it into reverse to back out, put the gas to it, it wouldn't go. Tires just kept going around and around, it wouldn't go. I get out, thinking the transmission must be gone. They had jacked up my tires on the back. And I go, 'They got me back!'" To the impish captain's credit, he tells this story on himself with a hearty laugh.

On road trips, defenseman Calle Johansson learned to pack for two – the unfortunate consequence of being Hunter's roommate. "He'd take clothes for half a trip," Johansson told the *Post*. "Then he'd be in my bag, taking my clothes. Then he'd forget to return them. He's still wearing them."

Sometimes, Hunter didn't even need his classic ribs - shaving cream in pants pockets, tied skate laces, or Vaseline in helmets - to get the best of teammates. "Listen, Locker," he once explained to Craig Laughlin, "If I pass it to you, it's a mistake, give it right back."

✪ Larry The Quotable Guy

High-scoring Larry Murphy spent six seasons patrolling the backline in Landover. But his funniest Caps-related quote came while playing against them, as a member of the L.A. Kings. In a January, 1982 game, Dennis Maruk scored on a power play deflection off Murphy's skate. Then Jim McTaggart scored shorthanded, off Murphy's stick. Larry later set up one of his own Kings' teammates for the final tally in a 3-3 tie. "Two goals and an assist," Murphy said with a smile. "Not a bad night." *(L.A. Times)*

THE LEGENDS OF LANDOVER

✪ Hockey Broadcaster Deserved Hazard Pay

Play-by-play man Ron Weber loved the Capitals; experience taught him not to trust them on road trips. Like the morning in 1976 he arrived at Capital Centre with 45 minues to spare. "He visited the team's offices with coach Tom McVie and trainer Gump Embro, whom were aware Weber would be taking the bus with the players (to Philadelphia). Much to Weber's surprise, the bus left from another entrance and the announcer was left without a ride." G.M. Max McNab apologized to Weber, while claiming it wasn't a prank – though it was April Fools' Day. The real joke was on the players, who surrendered 62 shots and 11 goals to the Flyers.

Air travel wasn't a safe haven, either. On a 1979 charter to Quebec, "The lads snipped off all the buttons on broadcaster Ron Weber's smartest blazer. Weber blew the whistle and McNab scolded the troops. McNab was not impressed that the buttons were safely stashed in an air sickness bag." (Quotes above from the *Washington Star*)

Speaking of Weber's attire, "Outrageously loud" was how Robert Fachet of the *Washington Post* described it in print. As a sportscaster, "Weber needs little added color with his favorite ensemble of red jacket, red shirt, white tie, white pants, red socks, and white shoes." Weber got the last word, though, saying on-air that Fachet, "has been to too many somber affairs." Sitting nearby, Fachet roared with laughter that could be heard on the broadcast.

Ron's prank-wariness only grew once the team would reach its hotel. One day, Yvon Labre hopped from his balcony onto Weber's, clad in nothing but a towel. Seems Labre's roommate, Ron Lalonde, had locked Yvon out of their hotel room. Weber, not wanting a similar prank to befall him, made a pre-emptive maneuver: sleeping in a bathing suit.

Maybe Weber's swim trunks were prompted by a sinister-sounding comment from expansion G.M. Milt Schmidt. Back then, in the name of journalistic integrity, broadcast outlets claimed they alone hired and paid team broadcasters. That ruse has gone the way of the leisure suit, and local announcers these days are openly identified as team employees.

Schmidt, of course, knew better, even in 1974. If he wanted a play-by-play guy gone, he'd soon be gone. Referencing Weber's affinity for airport pinball machines, Milt explained, in his best mob-boss persona, "There are no pinball machines at the bottom of the sea." From then on, Weber no doubt dreaded the day the team would become displeased with his commentary, bust into his room, lift him into cement shoes, and dump him unceremoniously into Boston Harbor to sleep with the fishes.

(Ron recalled the G.M.'s words in a *washingtoncaps.com* interview.).

THE LEGENDS OF LANDOVER

✪ More Hockey Hilarity

▷ Kevin Hatcher can be found in the Capitals' official 1987-88 team photo. Well, his face can. Hatcher missed the team flight from New York, so was absent on picture day. "John Millsback, the Capital Centre's Zamboni operator, wore Hatcher's pads and sweater for the picture, with Hatcher's face to be superimposed later."

▷ Coach Bryan Murray, on bad dreams following a bad game: "You don't have to worry about nightmares when you can't sleep at all."

▷ Pat Riggin, in a *Washington Post* photo, was identified as fellow Caps goalie Al Jensen. "On the bus to Philadelphia, Riggin endured predictable taunts from teammates, who wondered when Riggin had suddenly become so good looking."

▷ General manager David Poile and coach Bryan Murray chose a particular New York restaurant for their postgame meal. "Although closed for a private party, the owner invited them inside and seated them in the group. It turned out to be a brokerage firm honoring the Rangers. Poile and Murray ate quickly."

▷ Out with a minor injury, Bengt Gustafsson made himself useful behind the bench. He communicated with coaches upstairs via walkie-talkie, for a game the Caps lost, 5-1. Gustafsson said, "I like the job, but with my record I've got a feeling I'm going to be fired."

▷ Utilizing his gift of gab, Craig Laughlin described a goal he scored: "I faked the defenseman one way and then I pulled the goalie down and lifted it over him." Actually, Craig was down on the ice, and the puck deflected off his leg, so Laughlin was asked to defend his embellishment. "I'm rehearsing what I'm going to tell my wife. She couldn't come tonight and the game wasn't on TV."

▷ The above quotes were supplied by Bob Fachet for *The Hockey News*. Occasionally, like a 1989 column, Fachet saved the best line for himself. "General Manager David Poile celebrated his 40th birthday Feb. 14. Poile has had gray hair for years. So has 46-year-old coach Bryan Murray. Trying to figure out the Washington Capitals can do that to you."

▷ Along The Dusty Trail, this mischief comes courtesy of goalie and equestrian expert Clint Malarchuk. On a team horseback ride at training camp in 1988, Malarchuk pranked the trail guide by claiming he was "Joey," a none-too-bright stick boy who'd never before been on a horse. Clint then prodded his mount to charge off the trail, as the horrified guide gave chase. (From Malarchuk's book, *A Matter Of Inches*).

THE LEGENDS OF LANDOVER

FIGHT CLUB

○ **Dwight Schofield (1985-86) – The Boxer**

Protection. Muscle. Hired Guns. Goons. No, we're not talking about The Mob. These affectionate terms refer to the fighters NHL teams employed so top players wouldn't get picked on. For the Capitals during the 1985-86 season, Dwight Schofield was that guy. In 50 games, he recorded one goal and 127 penalty minutes – in other words, doing his job.

Schofield took his role as an NHL enforcer seriously - to keep sharp on road trips, he traveled with boxing gloves. Dwight held his own against the league's heavyweights, and even protected his turf among teammates. Enter Kevin Hatcher. The young defenseman had trained at Detroit's legendary Kronk Gym, whose members included boxing champ Tommy "Hit Man" Hearns. Naturally, Schofield was intrigued.

As reported in *Sports Illustrated*, "Schofield challenged Hatcher to some on-ice sparring after practice. As teammates roared in approval, Hatcher quickly decked Schofield with a right. 'I took him too lightly,' said an embarrassed Schofield. 'Experienced veteran, young kid with no book on him, happens all the time.'"

Dwight didn't learn from his mistake. At training camp in 1986, G.M. David Poile invited a welterweight boxer from Toronto, David Poole. "We weren't teaching fighting, not at all," said Poile. "We thought it would help players with their confidence." Poole showed the Caps how to defend themselves, how to maintain balance in the clinches, how to effectively hold and grab.

Schofield, 6-3, 195, didn't want his alpha male status challenged by Poole, 5-5, 150. "I wasn't there to fight him, but to teach him," David said, but Dwight didn't care. "He really wanted to kick my butt. And finally I agreed to fight him. He had headgear, boots and a cup. I had nothing."

Poole made only one request – avoid his jaw, because Poole didn't bring a mouthpiece. "So the first punch he throws is right at my mouth," Poole recalled, smiling. "I slipped it, then came up with a left hook and knocked him cold." Not coincidentally, Schofield never played for the Caps again.

(Source for Poole story: Tony Kornheiser, Washington Post)

○ **Alan May (1989-94) – Punches, Then Polite Conversation**

For the undercard bout to the Schofield fights, consider this story first shared by Dave Fay of the *Washington Times*. It concerns tough guy Alan May. His 339 penalty minutes in the 1989-90 season is still a team record. He hardly slacked off after that, with 264, 221, and 268 minutes in his three other full seasons in D.C.

THE LEGENDS OF LANDOVER

One night, his dance partner was Jim Agnew of the Canucks. As often happens, the combatants continued jabbering once they were done jabbing. This particular conversation, though, raised eyebrows. After their fight, May said to Agnew across the penalty boxes, "How's your sister?"

May and Agnew became close as teammates in junior hockey, and May had attended the wedding of Agnew's sister. "You never let those things carry over," Agnew said of the fight. "We had a nice little talk."

✪ Tom Rowe (1976-80) – To Live And Die In L.A.

"Stanley" was the nickname bestowed on Tom Rowe. "He was shy, somewhat awkward and sometimes whimsical, and reminded his teammates of old-time comedian Stanley Laurel." (*Washington Star*)

Tom got the Capitals into another fine mess in Los Angeles on December 4, 1978, when he was neither shy nor whimsical, though definitely awkward. As the Kings scored their 7th goal, Rowe snapped. Penalties included a major for fighting Darryl Edestrand, a gross misconduct for biting Edestrand, a game misconduct for resisting and almost punching linesman Bob Luther, and unsportsmanlike conduct for kicking a stick on the ice. Rowe's sanity returned after the game. "I am embarrassed for the way I behaved. I've never flipped out like that before, not in this life." Suspended for two games, Rowe added, "I was wrong and I deserve to be punished."

Happier memories from the 1977-78 season for Tom included a four goal, two assist game in a 7-5 March victory over the Blues. Coach Dan Belisle produced a new nickname, "Gordie Rowe." He tallied again the next day in Detroit and made history. Rowe, from Lynn, Mass., became the first American-born player in NHL history to score 30 goals in a season.

✪ Ed Kastelic (1985-88) – Tiger Tale

Only in hockey could you find yourself in the position of exchanging blows with your boyhood idol. Ed Kastelic of the Caps didn't have much time to ponder the oddity in an October, 1987 game, since he was occupied receiving a facewash from Hartford's Dave "Tiger" Williams.

As a youngster, Ed once got to meet Williams under more pleasant circumstances. Tiger, who fought his way to an NHL-record 3,966 penalty minutes, now was mushing a sweaty glove in Kastelic's face. As Ed told *hockeyindependent.com*, "We ended up going at it. In something of a surreal moment, I recall sitting on him, and looking face-to-face with 'Tiger' Williams." Ed's bottom half was sitting – his fists were occupied battering Tiger's mug, for which Kastelic received a double game misconduct. Another surreal moment: When Williams retired after the season, guess who Hartford got to be their tough guy? Ed Kastelic.

THE LEGENDS OF LANDOVER

✪ Randy Holt (1981-83) – Tiger Tale II

Randy Holt had a way of drawing an official's attention - even when he was on the receiving end of goonery. As he told Caps teammates, "Trouble finds me." Like the opening minutes of a March, 1983 game vs. Vancouver.

"My litmus test was two words," recalled referee Kerry Fraser. "If I saw a play and I went, 'Holy F%#&!', that was a match penalty. When Tiger Williams charged at Randy Holt and snapped his stick on the back of Randy's helmetless head, that's a 'Holy F%#&!' play." (From Adam Proteau's book, *Fighting The Good Fight*.) As Fraser related in his own book, *The Final Call*, Williams was retaliating for a crushing hit Holt laid on a fellow Canuck. "To both Tiger's and my amazement, Randy remained on his feet (and) started trading punches."

Randy attracted official notice in a March, 1982 game against Philadelphia by knocking a linesman to the ice. Hits and slashes between Holt and Ron Flockhart devolved into a stick-swinging duel. As Randy worked free to rescue a teammate, linesman Paul Flaherty put up a roadblock, which Holt promptly ran over. Flaherty reported the number of that truck - #4 in white - and Randy was assessed 30 minutes in misconduct penalties, plus a double-minor for the Flockhart altercation. The 34 PIMs is one shy of the Capitals record for a period & game – achieved, oddly enough, without a single fighting major. For "physically abusing" the linesman, the NHL also socked Holt with a two game suspension. (*Canadian Press*)

Mayhem swirled around Holt in a 10-year, seven-team NHL career. He holds the league mark for single-game PIMs with 67, while playing in 1979 for L.A. In his two D.C. seasons, he racked up 575 penalty minutes. Still, Dennis Maruk wrote in his autobiography, "Randy Holt always had your back. He'd say, 'If someone comes after you, I'll fight them.'"

Randy honored that promise during a 1983 showdown with the Flyers. Seeing Maruk giving away six inches and 35 pounds in a scuffle with Philly roughneck Glen Cochrane, Holt came to the rescue. A noble deed, for two reasons: Randy knew his ejection would cost a one-game suspension; and he risked further injuring his chest, impaled by his own stick two nights earlier. It's no coincidence that Maruk scored his 30th goal and added an assist in Washington's 4-3 victory. Wrote Dennis, "I never would have put up the numbers I did if Randy didn't rack up the numbers he did."

Mayhem even followed Holt into retirement. Dropping the gloves in a pick-up match in 1989, "Holt knocked two teeth out of one player's mouth and broke another player's nose." (*Calgary Herald*) The kicker: Randy was playing in a *non-contact* league! "He turned a recreational game into an ugly event," said another type of official, Alberta Justice Mel Shannon. Found guilty of assault, Holt spent a day in jail and was fined $2,000. By the way, the name of Randy's team - The Flying Failures.

THE LEGENDS OF LANDOVER

✪ Scott Stevens (1982-90) – The Gladiator

Flyers defenseman Daryl Stanley, who twice fought Scott Stevens, on why Scott deserves his own wing in *Fight Club* – or at least his own page: "Stevens was a gladiator who loved to play the body. He was one of the hardest hitters, and a leader." (*Warriors on the Ice by Brian D'Ambrosio*)

Mark Pare knows hockey fights; he officiated more than 2,000 NHL games as a linesman. So believe him when he called a tilt between Stevens and the Islanders' Bob Nystrom "amazing." Pare described his front-row view in fellow linesman Ray Scapinello's book, *Between The Lines*. "It was like watching two cartoon characters. Both of their heads would snap back from a punch, and then come forward and they'd just keep whaling. They traded punches for 45 seconds continuously. Eventually, the two of them were leaning forehead to forehead out of exhaustion. When (linesman Ray) Foyt asked, 'Are you done?', they started laughing." Nystrom rejected Pare's escort to the penalty box, saying, "I'm not going there, forget that," and headed straight for the locker room instead.

Stevens delivered devastating, game-changing, career-threatening (and in today's NHL, possibly suspendable) hits. Fellow Caps defenseman Greg Theberge remembered one of the collisions Scott built his reputation on. "Pierre Larouche is skating in with the puck. Scott is backing up with him, completely telegraphing the hit. Scotty gets down in almost a three-point stance like a football player, steps up and just explodes into Pierre. I mean, just destroys him." (*musingsofahockeyenthusiast.com*)

Coach Bryan Murray made sure to keep his volatile young defenseman close. Kevin Dupont wrote in the *Boston Globe*, "Hardrock Stevens often fought, something Murray didn't discourage, yet he did urge (Stevens) to fight at the right time. More than once, Murray would plant himself behind Stevens on the bench and then wrap both arms around him to prevent him from vaulting over the boards to engage in a fight. It's the only time I've ever seen it in the NHL, a coach literally wrapping up his player."

Rangers' trainer Jocko Cayer wishes Murray's grip had been tighter during an October, 1986 game. "Stevens barreled over the boards and wiped out Cayer, who was taken to the hospital with a bruised hip." *(Sporting News)*

Stevens' intensity wasn't exclusive to gametime. As he told *The Hockey News*, "I'm serious in games and I'm serious in practice." Serious enough to break his stick when he failed to score. Serious enough to threaten a teammate who got in his way. Serious enough to kick his helmet and hurl a water bottle when he was beaten on a rush. Coach Bryan Murray pointed out, "Scott doesn't like to be outplayed in any situation." Coaches had to restrict Stevens' access to the weight room, because they felt he was actually pumping *too much* iron!

THE LEGENDS OF LANDOVER

✪ Tim Coulis (1979-80), Paul Mulvey (1978-81)

Two of 1978's Caps draftees are linked by aggression - or lack of same.

Owner Abe Pollin and G.M. Max McNab chartered a Lear jet to make sure Tim Coulis, chosen #18, didn't sign with the rival WHA. First stop was Sault Ste. Marie, to pick up Coulis' agent. "Next stop was Toronto, where Coulis was welcomed aboard. From there it was off to Washington, where the parties emerged all smiles." (*The Hockey News*) For all that, Coulis played only 19 games in D.C. In the minors three years later, Tim lost his mind. Enraged by a penalty, Coulis rammed the butt end of his stick into the referee's head. He was barred from hockey for one year.

Picked at #20, Paul Mulvey, at 6-4, 220, was no shrinking violet. Jack Mann wrote Paul served as "the Caps' designated tough guy" in his *Washington Star* column. "Mulvey is afraid of nobody. Well, almost nobody. There may have been an impression (in some recent games) that Mulvey was going soft. He was wearing a helmet. 'That was because my parents were in town,' Paul explained. 'I was afraid of what my mom would say if I didn't.'"

Well acquainted with the penalty box, Mulvey rated NHL refs for *The Hockey News*. "Ron Wicks is good. He keeps us in line. Andy van Hellemond is strict. No bull. The rest are tied for the worst." No humor would be found in a game Paul played as a member of the L.A. Kings. Mulvey declined a coach's order to leave the bench, join a brawl, "and don't dance." For perceived disregard of teammates, he was demoted; seeing no path back to the NHL, he retired. The silver lining was a whole lot of silver. Paul sued the Kings, and in the settlement, "I wound up with a good piece of change," said Mulvey. (*Washington Post*)

Something's backward when a player with skills, like Mulvey, is essentially blacklisted for *not* being a goon, while Coulis, who committed assault, gets forgiven - Minnesota called him up briefly in 1983, '84, and '85.

✪ Riot On Ice – March 25, 1978 vs. Detroit

What started as a Caps-Wings hockey game devolved into a Battle Royale. The *Washington Star* called it a "15-minute, name-calling, hair-pulling, fist-fighting, jersey-pulling fracas." The *Washington Post* described it as "a 38-man tag team match, with half-dressed warriors punching and pushing until they were too tired to continue."

"When they'd stop one (brawl)," recalled Yvon Labre, "another one would break out. When they stopped that one, another would break out." Referee Ron Wicks wondered if music might soothe the savage breasts; he called for the National Anthem to be replayed. "I didn't know what else to do to stop guys from killing each other."

THE LEGENDS OF LANDOVER

The fuse was lit, said Labre, "when Gordie Lane skated right down the bench and hit all the Detroit sticks. And then the benches emptied." Lane's supplemental punishment was unexpectedly delayed, because film of the free-for-all got held up at Canadian customs. Gordie put the temporary reprieve to good use, scoring a goal in a 4-3 win at Colorado. For Lane's throwing punches at the opposition bench, the NHL eventually socked him back with a one-game suspension.

The melee was all good fun for Wings goalie Ron Low. He sought out his goaltending buddy, former Capitals teammate Bernie Wolfe. Low later explained why Wolfe could be seen pulling on his sweater. "I grabbed Bernie and told him I had waited two years to punch him silly. Of course I was kidding, but you should have seen his eyes light up."

Newer fans might wonder whatever happened to this sort of benches-clearing brawl, the kind you can see in retro videos all over YouTube. The NHL created "Rule 72" before the 1987-88 season. It mandates a 10-game suspension - without pay - for the first player leaving the bench during a fight. Coaches also face suspension and a maximum fine of $10,000. There haven't been any full-team fights since.

✪ 344 Combined Penalty Minutes – Dec. 21, 1980 at Philadelphia

By their seventh year, the Caps had beaten the Bruins. They'd even beaten the Canadiens. The Flyers remained the final powerhouse opponent never vanquished. Perhaps the Caps were serving penance for ill-advised words from their first coach, Jimmy Anderson. "The Flyers aren't much better than the Capitals, take away Clarke and MacLeish. They've got too many guys thick between the ears." Bruce Cowick, one of Anderson's wingers, winced at the time, "Wish he'd stop that. It's our necks they're going to break."

In 1974-75, the Flyers won more games in the playoffs – 12, and the Stanley Cup – than the Caps did in the 80 games they played. It was the same old story on December 20, 1980 at Capital Centre – a building Philly writers dubbed "Spectrum South" because so many Flyers fans always made the trip. The Caps fell yet again to the Broad Street Bullies, 5-2, with Rick Green conceding, "I guess we were intimidated by them."

As both teams bused north up I-95 for the rematch, only one hockey observer believed a different outcome was possible. (More about him later.) The evidence said otherwise - the Caps had lost six of seven, the Flyers were unbeaten in 16 straight home games, and, not least of all, held a 19-0-6 lifetime chokehold in the series. Plus, injuries had decimated the Washington roster, with seven regulars out: goalie Wayne Stephenson, defensemen Paul McKinnon, Rick Smith, Pierre Bouchard, Pat Ribble, and forwards Bengt Gustafsson and Rolf Edberg were unavailable.

THE LEGENDS OF LANDOVER

All reasons why the outcome on December 21, 1980 in Philadelphia remains, decades later, one of the most stunning regular-season victories in Capitals history.

Bob Kelly admitted to nerves returning to the Spectrum for the first time as an opponent. "I was here at 2 o'clock walking around. Play in a place 10 years, you're bound to feel like that." Kelly had told teammates, "To beat the Flyers, you have to play like the Flyers, stand up for each other and not get flustered." Rick Green agreed. "Five years I've been here, this is the first time I've ever felt confident. We have guys who can stand up to them."

Both teams thought the mental game was decided along the Interstate. Caps defenseman Green: "From the time we got on the bus after the game to come up here, we were determined." Flyers Coach Pat Quinn: "We probably lost the game on the bus coming home last night. We must have thought this would be easy."

Final Score: Capitals 6, Flyers 0. Al Morganti described the magnitude of the upset in the *Philadelphia Inquirer*: "The coyote caught the roadrunner. The rabbit got the Trix." Caps coach Gary Green noted, "It had to end sooner or later, but you have to make it end." Jean Pronovost, who scored twice, saw the significance. "Beating the Flyers is a big thing, because the Flyers are the best team, the first place team."

When it was over - it took 3 hours, 20 minutes to be over, almost time for a fourth period in a normal game - 61 penalties, totaling 344 minutes, made the scoresheet the size of a booklet. (Was: 177 PIMs, Phi: 167 PIMs; all single-game Capitals records) Referee Dave Newell assessed the first 94 penalty minutes, initiated by a Jim McTaggart-Ken Linseman fight, 19 seconds into the game. A mere four minutes later, the two teams combined to have 15 skaters in the penalty boxes!

On a night chock full of Flyer goonery borne of frustration, Behn Wilson stood out, first for a pair of fights with Caps callup Archie Henderson. (Details on page 161.) Later in the game, the *Philadelphia Daily News* reported, "Wilson viciously drove Guy Charron's head into the boards. Charron rose after a few minutes, escaping with only a cut on the ear." Wilson cared not that Charron didn't even have the puck at the time. (All the bad blood was nothing new; in an October pre-season game, half the players on each roster were ejected.)

Caps netminder Mike Palmateer welcomed the shenanigans. "Sometimes all those fights break your concentration, but tonight, I enjoyed the rest." No wonder; Palmateer stopped 14 shots in the first seven minutes, six on a single Philadelphia power play, not counting five more which missed the net. At the horn, Palmateer had rejected all 44 Flyers shots, saying, "Right now, I'm too tired to be excited."

THE LEGENDS OF LANDOVER

Who was the one sage who believed the Capitals could pull off this most audacious of victories? Capitals general manager Max McNab, who explained, "One of the greatest motivators for any athlete or team is embarrassment, and I think they were embarrassed" at their play the night before in Landover.

The victory was sweetest for defenseman Yvon Labre, the last remaining Original Capital. "We beat them, we finally beat them. God, how we had to work. Look at the stitches. Look at the bruises. We played their game and we did it," Labre said in the trainer's room while holding an icepack. The cherry on the sundae was Yvon's first goal in what had been an injury-shortened last two years. Bob Kelly shot, shot again, then a third time, before Labre deposited the puck for the second Washington goal. "It was only right that I scored tonight. This will make for a shorter ride home and a good Christmas."

(*Washington Post, Philadelphia Daily News, Philadelphia Inquirer, The Hockey News*)

✪ Archie Henderson (1980)

Archie Henderson, in his first minor league season as a Caps' 10th round draft choice, racked up 419 penalty minutes! When you're 6-6, 220 pounds, and not a scorer, brawling is how to stay employed. "I don't think hockey is violence," Archie suggested to the *Washington Star*. "On the ice it's business. If I hit a guy some good shots and then met him on the street, I guess I'd say hi. There's nothing personal, you know?"

The Caps needed an extra "businessman" for that December, 1980 tussle in Philly, so they called up Henderson – and handed him number 31, because a spare goalie sweater was the only one big enough. (*washingtoncaps.com*) Archie stepped onto the ice for his first NHL shift – and immediately fought Flyer goon Behn Wilson. Ten minutes later, Archie took his second NHL shift – and fought Wilson again. Henderson would tell *hockeynews.com* that Wilson was "unbelievably mean. He didn't stop until he hurt you." The Caps won, 6-0, a sweet first ever victory over the Flyers after seven years, and teammates lauded Archie for standing up for them.

By the way, Archie's brother Don pursued a career breaking up fights, rather than participating... as an NHL linesman. We assume that as kids, when Archie was punished, Don would escort him to his room for a timeout.

Archie Henderson scored his first and only NHL goal a couple of weeks after his call-up, also against the Flyers. It would be his last of seven games in that #31 sweater; he was sent back to the minors after the 8-1 loss. "I guess my job wasn't to score goals," Henderson mused.

THE LEGENDS OF LANDOVER

✪ Jim Thomson (1986-87, 1988-89) – Pugilist To Pacifist

Even though Jim Thomson was a fighter, it was brains, not just brawn, which got him a shot with the Capitals. "I studied hours of tape," Jim explained in Adam Proteau's book, *Fighting The Good Fight*. "I studied everybody I fought, and everybody who was a fighter." As a result, Jim knew when to go toe-to-toe, and when it was safer in the clinches.

Yet he admitted to "drinking and drugging to kill the fear of fighting." Sometimes, Jim used dirty tactics learned from his older brothers. "Former bikers, tough guys. They made it clear to me that you fight to intimidate, you fight to win."

Fatherhood later gave Jim a new perspective. "There was some really stupid behavior on my part. When I watch what I did on TV with my three kids sitting beside me, it makes me sick." Post-NHL, Thompson chose a path all hockey-playing youngsters could admire. Jim got clean, became a motivational speaker and life coach, and advocates for the banishment of fighting.

Here's one story he's not ashamed to repeat: "My first game, Bryan Murray had me cover Mario Lemieux. I did really good. Until I screwed up an assignment and he got a breakaway. He didn't score but I was benched. It was a learning experience." (*thehockeynews.com*)

✪ Andre Hidi (1983-85) – Fighting The Good Non-Fight

Like Jim Thompson, winger Andre Hidi came to his own moral crossroad. Following seven games with the Capitals and two seasons in the minors, Hidi decided he'd rather switch than fight. "My decision not to fight regularly and with premeditation was not without cost," Andre said to the *Toronto Star*. "Had I gone along with management's wishes, stayed healthy and been relatively successful at fighting, I could almost certainly have played much more in the NHL."

Hidi called hockey fights "so obviously wrong," and suggested, "The men who run pro hockey... might find that running a succesful business is more rewarding if you can do so with a clear conscience."

Good luck in fantasyland with that business philosophy, Andre! Hang on, we've gotten word that Hidi earned a Bachelor of Arts and a Masters of Arts from the University of Toronto and an M.B.A. from Stanford University. He became President and Chief Executive Officer of Smith Barney Canada, and later Managing Director and Head of Global Mergers & Acquisitions at Bank of Montreal. A powerful argument for using your noggin for numbers, rather than as a repository for concussions.

THE LEGENDS OF LANDOVER

Pucks. Sticks. Goalposts. Boards. Skates. Ice. And large men flying into and on top of each other. Everything about hockey carries the potential for, and frequently does, cause pain. Whatever fault today's teams might have regarding player injuries, it was worse in the "old-school" NHL. As Original Capital Jack Egers, feeling he was rushed back from an injury, told *Sports Illustrated*, "You were treated like a piece of meat."

✚ Pain In The Neck

A long overdue NHL rule change implemented hybrid icing in 2013, eliminating kamikaze full-speed collisions into the end boards. A player-safety move that came 37 years too late for promising Caps winger Mike Lampman. Described as a natural goal-scorer (and with a perfect name to conjure the goal light), Lampman's career was permanently extinguished at a 1976 home game against the Flyers.

"Icing rules were different then and we were racing after the puck to try to touch it and Moose Dupont sent me flying into the boards," Lampman told the *Seattle Times*. "My neck was very sore. I knew it was bad. It's funny, but the way the game was back then, the team doctor was going to clear me to play against Boston two nights later. But my chiropractor said 'No way!' until he had a look."

Further examination revealed the wisdom of the second opinion. Lampman had suffered what's medically known as an abnormal slippage of the vertebrae – in lay terms, a broken neck. Happily, the injury did heal. But what tragedy might have befallen Mike if he'd listened to the team physician, and took a paralyzing hit inside Boston Garden?

✚ Improperly Treated

Moving to Washington reinvigorated Greg Polis' career. In 18 games as a waiver pickup in 1979, the forward exploded for 12 goals, adding six assists. Then disaster struck in Vancouver, where Greg fractured his right leg. His comeback attempt the next season failed, as Polis scored one goal in the final 29 games of his NHL career.

From *hockeydraftcentral.com:* "Polis complained about lingering pain in the leg to training staff, but they suggested he needed to 'play himself back into shape.' Polis continued to experience pain until January 1980, when an X-ray showed the knee had never properly healed. Following that discovery, Polis said the Capitals put him on waivers." Polis in 1981 filed a $5 million lawsuit against the Capitals, claiming team doctors improperly treated his injury. "No further reporting was done on the suit, likely settled out of court."

THE LEGENDS OF LANDOVER

✚ Bidner's Big Break

Todd Bidner's 12-game NHL career was cruelly interrupted by a broken leg suffered against Minnesota at Capital Centre. For just such an emergency, arenas today have advanced medical equipment, and games can't even start without an ambulance on-site. As Bidner painfully learned, treatment procedures back in 1981 were shockingly crude.

"They took me to the hospital in a taxi, with half my equipment on. They X-ray it, put my leg in a cast, call another taxi, drive back to the arena. Nobody's in the dressing room. I find out that everybody got fired after the game. Gary Green, the coach, Max McNab, the general manager, scouting staff, everybody got fired. I pile into my old beater car, because I hadn't even received a paycheck yet, and drive back to my hotel."

The ordeal of Todd's broken leg was just beginning. "Back in the early 80's, they didn't care for you when you were hurt," said Todd. "My roommate, Terry Murray, grabbed me a six-pack because I was in so much pain."

If you're a career minor-leaguer and have to suffer a serious injury, better to do it on a major league callup. Better for the player, not for the team. "I remember them (Capitals management) calling me, saying 'We've got to get that cast off, get you back on the ice.' I was getting paid an NHL salary while I was out. I think they were looking at that, 'We've got to get him down to the minors, pay him a minor league salary.'"

✚ Strained Relationship

Roger Crozier probably agreed a coma qualified as a legitimate injury. Probably. As interim Caps general manager during the 1981-82 season, Crozier valued old-school toughness. Or maybe he was a medieval jailer in a previous life. Either way, he certainly had no sympathy for a grade-2 medial-collateral strain.

Defenseman Greg Theberge found this out the hard way, as he told blogger Nate Oliver. "I'm hobbling up the stairs to get my paycheck, and Roger pokes his head out of his office and says, 'Hey Theberge, you know what happens to guys who get injured? They get sent down to the minors!'" We can't confirm Roger added, "And get off my lawn!"

Goaltenders have always been part contortionist, part masochist – the target in a shooting gallery with frozen vulcanized rubber as the projectile. A good night is escaping with only strains and bruises, but Caps goalies didn't always get the velvet pillow & bubble wrap treatment they deserved.

THE LEGENDS OF LANDOVER

✚ Palmateer's Ambulance

No player ever arrived at a Capitals game the way Mike Palmateer did once in 1981.

Legendsofhockey.net tells an incredible story about the day Palmateer was scheduled for arthroscopic surgery: "He was in hospital linen, on his way to the operating room when an urgent call came from the Caps. Their other goalie, Wayne Stephenson, had been injured. They needed Palmateer, bad knee and all, for the evening's game. He was packed into an ambulance and delivered to the stadium." We hope the driver didn't turn on his red lights, knowing how triggering that could be for a goaltender.

To *tenderslounge.wordpress.com*, Palmateer added this: "I had already been given some drugs" at the hospital. "The drugs hadn't worn off when the game started, but I guess they figured I was still a better option than the guy they called up from the minors. I had the surgery the next day. Probably didn't help prolong my career."

How could the team be so reckless with its franchise netminder? The answer might lie in a tidbit buried in a *Calgary Herald* article, citing unnamed members of Caps management who questioned how hurt Mike really was. Team captain Ryan Walter, meanwhile, wondered how Palmateer ever stayed healthy. "You look at him, flipping and flopping and doing those rollovers and crazy things," Walter observed to *Sports Illustrated*. "You say, 'How can he do that? He'll hurt himself.'" Indeed, injuries kept Mike from fulfilling his promise with the Caps. The goalie divided his career, half between the pipes, half under the knife - a numbing 20 knee surgeries.

✚ Shot Down

Pete Peeters needed a stretcher to get off the ice during a 1988 playoff game. A rising, end-over-end shot by New Jersey's John MacLean caught Peeters right above the eyes. Like a tree felled by a lumberjack, Peeters crashed onto his back, lying motionless for several minutes with a concussion. Later, Pete explained what had flown into his birdcage mask, describing his headache as "a big woodpecker up there."

Amazingly, Pete would have company in the hockey concussion wing of Hackensack Medical Center. A third-period puck struck defenseman Garry Galley on the temple. Galley also needed a stretcher escort, and later said he didn't remember anything after the national anthem. Because they're hockey players, and because no one stopped them, both Peeters and Galley returned to play in the series.

(Sources: New York Times, Pittsburgh Post-Gazette)

THE LEGENDS OF LANDOVER

✚ The Reluctant Backup

Management promised Wayne Stephenson up, down, and sideways that he wouldn't have to play goal, just sit on the bench as a spectator for a February, 1981 game against the Canadiens. So Wayne, 36 years old and with a seriously injured back, agreed to fly to Montreal and serve as backup to starter Dave Parro. The Caps' netminding situation was so precarious – Parro, Stephenson and Mike Palmateer were all banged up – the team at its morning practice didn't shoot against a goalie.

You already see what's coming – but Parro didn't. Scrambling back on his skates after foiling a Guy Lafleur shot, Dave reinjured an already dislocated shoulder, forcing him from the game. According to the *Montreal Gazette*, coach Gary Green looked at Stephenson, "Who's just telling me over and over, 'I'm not going in. I'm not going in.' There's a delay in the game because I can't get my goaltender to go in, our players are yelling at him to get out there, and the fans behind the bench at the Forum are hearing all this, thinking our backup goalie doesn't want to play. But the fact was, Steph couldn't play."

Reluctantly, the hobbled Stephenson agreed to take the ice – on the condition he wouldn't have to bend over! Talk about your stand-up style of goaltending. Somehow, Wayne managed to stop 13 of the 15 shots Montreal fired his way. A free-for-all brawl early in the 3rd period resulted in 20 penalties being called, including a misconduct on Stephenson. Too bad goalies get substitutes to serve their time, so Wayne still had to remain in net.

Lest anyone doubt the severity of Stephenson's injuries, he explained to a Montreal newspaper after the game, "My back is still pretty bad," and that he was contemplating retirement. Wayne would make one more relief appearance, calling it a career at season's end.

What if Stephenson really couldn't have finished the game at the Forum? That's why coach Green's first reaction to Parro's injury was, "Oh my God, no, this can't be true." Green considered defenseman Pat Ribble, who sometimes grabbed the goalie stick and mask to take shots in practice. The thought evaporated when the coach saw Ribble on the bench, "Shivering, his head buried between his knees, terrified I'd tell him to get into the equipment."

Not to fear, because Dennis Maruk began displaying his inner John Fogerty (you know, "Put me in coach, I'm ready to play"). The high-scoring centerman started to plead with Green, "I'll go in! I'll go in!" Green gave that offer even less consideration than the Ribble option. He summed up the memory in four words: "What a comedy act."

THE LEGENDS OF LANDOVER

Science still has much to learn about the brain, especially the long-term effects of having it repeatedly scrambled like an omelet. Head trauma may be a defining issue of modern-day contact sports, but when the Capitals were new, innovations like the concussion protocol were decades away.

✚ Ace Gets Clubbed

Halloween night, 1976 at Chicago Stadium, a violent check along the boards by the Blackhawks' Grant Mulvey spins Ace Bailey around. The back of Ace's head smashes like a pumpkin against the glass. Shattered bits of glass lay all over the ice, and so did Ace, briefly out cold. It took Bailey a full 30 seconds to regain consciousness, and another 10 minutes for the ice crew to sweep up all the debris. Despite the wealth of incriminating evidence, Mulvey isn't even assessed a penalty.

Today, Bailey would have been examined for his likely concussion. But this was the '70's, and after intermission, he was taking his next shift when he was pulverized again. Bailey collided with Dennis Hull, banged his head against the boards, and was rendered unconscious for a second time (although he skated off under his own power). According to *The Hockey News*, "Ace tried headgear in practice the next day, but his forehead was too swollen for it to fit properly."

✚ A Reason To Stop Streaking

Admirable qualities are built into Doug Jarvis' 964 consecutive-games record; skill, work ethic, toughness, pain tolerance, and a dash of good fortune. The hidden factor in Jarvis' streak - really, for any 20th century "ironman" - is that he played B.C.A. - Before Concussion Awareness.

Consider January 8, 1985 in Detroit. Jarvis, in his 761st consecutive game, puts a bow on a Caps 4-2 victory with an empty-net goal. A faceoff expert, Jarvis is back on the ice in the final minute, wins a draw, and skates straight into a collision with the Wings' Randy Ladouceur. Unconscious, Doug is carried from the ice on a stretcher. "I didn't remember anything until I woke up in the medical room," Jarvis said later. Wire reports that night say he "was sitting up in the dressing room, but needed 11 stitches in his head." What's more, he's diagnosed with a concussion, and spends the night under observation in the hospital.

The next day, Jarvis is cleared to play – "I must be okay," he reasons, "because the doctor's wife drove me out to the airport." He arrives in St. Louis, declines Bryan Murray's offer to join the coach in street clothes behind the bench, and continues his streak against the Blues. Doug records an assist on the Caps' first goal, and Washington wins again, 4-2. "What can I say," Jarvis shrugs. "I wanted to play." (Jarvis quotes from *The Sporting News, The Hockey News*)

Therein lies one of the problems; athletes then and now are reluctant to confirm concussion symptoms. To this day, answers remain elusive: What do leagues know about the long-term consequences of brain trauma? When did they learn it? What should they do about it? Will players put careers in jeopardy by admitting to headaches and blurred vision? (Not to mention the risks of *not* reporting symptoms.)

It's hard to argue with Joe McDonald of *espn.com*, who concluded, "The only injury that threatened Jarvis' streak was a concussion he suffered in Detroit. Had that occurred in today's game, his streak would have ended."

THE LEGENDS OF LANDOVER

8th Shift: *Hockey Sticks and Politics*

✪ From Capitol Hill To Capital Centre

The Lion of the Senate made a first-season visit into the Capitals' den. Meeting Ted Kennedy (D-Mass.) was the highlight of Tommy Williams' season. "He came into the dressing room," Williams said to the *Washington Post*, "Walked up and said 'Hi, Tommy,'" and we talked for five or 10 minutes. He told me he'd seen me with the Bruins."

Sen. William Proxmire (D-Wis.) would take his teenage son, who was also a Cubs fan, to see the expansion Caps. "I guess he has an affinity for losers," said the elder Proxmire. Rep. Dick Durbin (D-Ill.), viewing his first game, commented, "It looks a lot like Congress, except they wear helmets." Some politicos were more than casual fans. Sen. Lowell Weicker (D-Conn.) owned season tickets in the '70's. In fact, Weicker attended the first home game at Capital Centre. Hartford joined the NHL in 1979, so the senator had to change allegiance – at least officially – to the home-state Whalers.

Ken Duberstein, chief of staff late in Ronald Reagan's second term, also held season tickets. "In the sense that hockey is a rousing, enthusiastic sport, it's a good metaphor for Ken," said Marlin Fitzwater, White House spokesman. Duberstein received a presidential memento related to his favorite team. Seems there was a picture taken of the champion Islanders presenting Reagan with a goalie stick. As Duberstein explained in a *New York Times* piece he penned, "Reagan autographed a photograph of that incident in 1982 to me with the inscription, 'next year, the Caps.'"

V.P. George Bush picked a dandy game to attend – a 9-2 humbling of the Edmonton Oilers in 1984. Bush had to depart before it was over, though – something about a deteriorating situation in Lebanon.

Sen. Arlen Specter (R-Penn.) lived the hockey lifestyle when he was smashed in the eye during a squash game with fellow senator Robert Packwood. Like any hard-nosed competitor, Specter received stitches and was eager to return to action. So he contacted the Capitals. Using a special visor-covered hockey mask created for him by Caps trainers, Specter was back on the squash court within days. Going to all this trouble for a senator who represents Philadelphia *and* Pittsburgh? Sheesh. They should have put itching powder on the inside of the mask before delivering it.

Putting aside partisan differences, the Minnesota Congressional delegation attended a 1983 Caps-North Stars game. "I wouldn't miss this," said Rep. Gerry Sikorski, a freshman Democrat. "We take hockey very seriously in Minnesota, more seriously than Washingtonians take politics. After all, hockey is more important to the future of the nation."

THE LEGENDS OF LANDOVER

✪ Were Hockey Mask Posters In The Federal Budget?

When former Caps goalie Bernie Wolfe picked up the phone one day in 1988, he never could have imagined it was the White House calling. "President Reagan had seen a poster with my mask at the Calgary Olympics, and had been impressed," Wolfe told *lapresse.ca*.

Though a Montreal native, Bernie's design was All-American; a top half of white stars on a blue field, a bottom half of red and white horizontal stripes. Wolfe's headgear was one of 25 on a poster titled, "Mask," promoting an Olympic hockey exhibit at the Saddledome. The masks of fellow Caps goalies Ron Low and Wayne Stephenson were also featured on the poster.

Bernie delivered a copy to 1600 Pennsylvania Ave. "The chief of staff wanted the poster for the White House. They invited me for a meal, but the president wasn't there." Wolfe received presidential cufflinks, pens, and a personalized autographed photo. "I was sitting at the chief of staff's table in the White House with all these phones on it, being served lunch by people wearing tuxedos, and no one knew who the heck I was." (*nhl.com*)

✪ A Mask For Losers

The mask of a fellow Caps goalie should have been a political liability. Mike Palmateer's offensive Confederate Battle Flag motif was nonsensical, too, worn while playing in the *Union* capital. Even goalies of the Atlanta Flames, whose nickname derived from the torching of the city during the Civil War, never used a stars & bars design. Off-topic thought: Why would Atlanta choose a name from such an ignominious chapter of its history? Imagine if other cities copied the idea, like the Boston *Massacres*, or the Chicago *Capones*, or the L.A. *Riots*. If those names suit you, seek help immediately.

✪ There He Goes Again

Before the 1982 All-Star game at Capital Centre, players ate lunch at the White House with President Reagan. "I understand Washington has been trying to trade for Gretzky," Reagan said. "When I asked what could we possibly give Edmonton for such a great player, they said, 'Two first-round draft choices and the state of Texas.'"

In September, 1983, Capitals players and the '84 U.S. Olympic hockey team promoted their upcoming exhibition game with a visit to the Rose Garden. Rod Langway, attired in a Caps road sweater, was joined by teammates (in suits) including Bob Carpenter, Dave Christian, Mike Gartner, and Ken Houston. After shooting a puck into a net, Reagan declared, "You will never see me hit another puck again." Like all politicians, he was lying. To the surprise of the press corps, Reagan shot a foam puck at reporters.

THE LEGENDS OF LANDOVER

In September, 1987, the scene was repeated on the White House lawn, with the Caps and the '88 U.S. Olympians. This time, Langway smartly positioned himself safely behind the stick-wielding President. Less smartly, goalie and prankster Clint Malarchuk twice flicked the cord out of the ear of a Secret Service agent. Then Malarchuk asked Reagan if he'd ever "taken a run" at Barbara Stanwyck, his movie co-star in *Cattle Queen of Montana*.

Later, Reagan took aim at goalie Pete Peeters, dressed in his Caps sweater. As reported in the *Hutchinson News*, "Twice, Peeters easily batted the President's shots away. Then, as the goalie focused on a puck lined up ahead of him, Reagan reached in his pocket and dropped a second puck in front of the goal and fired it in." Congress later held ethics hearings on "Hidden Puck-Gate." Or maybe it was Iran-Contra, it's hard to remember.

✪ Line Forms On The Right

For a short time in the '86-'87 season, the Caps formed a makeshift trio of Jim Thompson, Bob Gould, and Dave Christian. Since all three were natural right wingers, they became known as the "Reagan" Line. Speaking of the Gipper, the Caps' early woes inspired a zinger from *Toronto Globe & Mail* columnist Trent Frayne, presented here without comment: "The Capitals were to hockey what Ronald Reagan is to the presidency; that is to say, they spent a lot of time wandering around saying, 'Huh?'"

✪ A Taste Of Home In Washington

The night before their first-ever home game, the Capitals were feted at the residence of the Canadian Embassy Minister. The minister's young son, in bathrobe and bare feet, padded around collecting autographs. Several players admitted they attended the tame affair only because the team ordered them to. They confided to preferring noisier parties - ones with alcohol, pot, and women.

The team was welcomed back to the Canadian Embassy for a December, 1976 soiree. "Hockey is our game," Ambassador Jack Warren said to the assembled players and club officials. "Each one of you connected with the Capitals are Canadian ambassadors of sorts – even those of you who spent time in the penalty box." Presumably, even the six American-born players who skated at least a portion of the '76-'77 season for the Capitals. (*Washington Star*)

Over the years, Capitals players would hook up Canadian Embassy staff with tickets – the basis of a sudsy friendship, said Ron Lalonde. "They had us down (to the embassy) two or three times. They'd have Molson Canadian, a trainload, shipped down. It was a bit of a taste of home in Washington."

THE LEGENDS OF LANDOVER

✪ Icy Reception

The early Capitals made use of celebrity connections, such as they were. For a 1975 home game against Toronto, the ceremonial puck drop was jointly handled by reasonable facsimilies of Benjamin Franklin and Prince George of Denmark (the Capital Centre being located in Prince George's County, Md.). Betsy Ross held the American flag during the Anthem.

Another 1975 game versus Chicago was designated Congressional Night. Between periods, owner Abe Pollin was joined on the ice by members of Congress, including Rep. Gladys Spellman (D-Md.), Senators "Mac" Mathias (R-Md.), Richard Schweiker (R-Pa.), Bill Brock (R-Tn.), and Bill Hathaway (D-Me.), and former Senator J. Glenn Beall (R-Md.). Some took a whack at a puck; two actually found the net. The *Washington Star* reported, "To judge from boos that showered down from the rafters, a man with the fruit and vegetable concession would have earned a tidy sum."

✪ Just Say "Goal"

The worst promotions in sports history – Disco Demolition Night in Chicago, 10-Cent Beer Night in Cleveland – belong on the "epic fail" list because of their unintended consequences.

No one's claiming Just Say No To Drugs Night at Capital Centre caused a spike in narcotics use. It's just that it's hard to imagine fans elbowing each other in a mad crush at the ticket window when they heard the promotion. Anyway, between periods of a 1988 Caps-Flyers game, First Lady Nancy Reagan appeared on the ice to champion her anti-drug campaign. Kept upright by Rod Langway, she shot a puck into the net past an obliging Pete Peeters. Her next shot missed, although Peeters helpfully tried to kick it in.

Mrs. Reagan was ready to call it a night, but Peeters invited her to try once more. "Your husband scored one, you have to score two." Nancy, a former high school field hockey player, scored on her third and final shot. Later, she popped into the Caps dressing room. Elsewhere in that same room, forward Greg Adams needled his goalie. "The Reagans own you, Peeters." (*Washington Post*)

✪ American Capitalism

The Capitals led the way putting Americans on NHL ice. Bobby Carpenter, third overall draft pick in 1981 and a Peabody, Mass. native, was an early example. Carpenter, Dave Christian and Rod Langway held flags tied to hockey sticks in front of the U.S. Capitol for a 1985 *Sporting News* cover story titled, "American Capitalism." The Caps' 1986-87 roster included Christian, Langway, Bob Mason, Kevin Hatcher, Kelly Miller, John Blum, Steve Leach and David Jensen – eight U.S. Caps in all.

THE LEGENDS OF LANDOVER

✪ Men's Room And Governor's Mansion: Abe Had Connections

Most folks needing bathroom repairs call a plumber. Abe Pollin called a governor. Pollin's influential friends included Maryland governor Marvin Mandel; In fact, Marvin was Abe's guest at the first Capitals home game on October 15, 1974. A few months earlier, Pollin needed help, as Capital Centre's grand opening, hours away, was in jeopardy. "At 3:30, I get a call from him," Mandel said. "They won't give him an occupancy permit because a couple of the men's toilets were not connected.

"I called the head of the health department in Maryland and I said to him, 'How would you like to go to the opening of the Cap Centre tonight?' He said, 'Oh, I'd love it. Can I bring my son?' I said, 'Sure, bring your son, absolutely!' I said, 'Meet me at the governor's house, we'll drive over together. And by the way,' I said, 'Bring an occupancy permit with you.' He did, and that's how we opened the Cap Centre." In politics, as in bathrooms, one hand washes the other.

✪ Nixon's The One – Or Was He?

Sports fandom was one of President Nixon's more benign obsessions. Hunter S. Thompson wrote, "He is a stone fanatic on every facet of pro football." Nixon biographer Evan Thomas shared, "On the White House tapes, you can hear him yelling at ball games on the TV." When D.C. angled for an NHL team in 1972, however, NBC's Mike Emrick said, "Nixon lobbied for another city to get a franchise. History does not record who the President got involved for. The Caps were discouraged that the guy who lived in town wasn't going to help them."

✪ The Russians Are Coming

As East-West relations warmed in the late '80's, *L.A. Times* columnist Mike Downey made this absurd-at-the-time prediction: "Maybe some Soviet hockey player will play for the Washington Capitals." As if! Americans in the federal city wildly cheering for a proud son of Mother Russia? The very thought was ludicrous!

Downey wanted to stretch the sporting imagination about a changing planet. The Ovechkin, Kuznetsov, Semin, and Varlamov jerseys worn by fans confirm that the once absurd has become reality. What's more amazing is that it almost happened years earlier. Owner Abe Pollin hoped to bring back some souvenirs for the Capitals on a 1974 trip to Moscow – a pair of hockey players. Irene Pollin, who accompanied her husband on the trip, recounted the story in her memoir. "Abe attended the meeting with the two heads of the Russian Hockey League." Pollin felt the conversation had gone so well, Irene described him as "jubilant, almost hyper."

THE LEGENDS OF LANDOVER

The next day, *da* turned into *nyet*. Abe held a second meeting, telling his hosts "how impressed he was with the Russian players and what a coup it would be to have two play in the capital of the United States." Pollin offered $1 million for the rights to the players, in vain as it turned out. "They were unwilling to send any players to the U.S., regardless of the amount of money… they were afraid the players would defect."

(Sources *for Political Items: Washington Post, N.Y. Times, AP, Syracuse Herald, A Matter Of Inches, Sports Illustrated, All About Abe* documentary)

9th Shift: *Exhibitions Of Note*

✪ Picard Tries To Make Extra Dough

Anyone who thinks pre-season games never matter should have been in Quebec City on October 10, 1977. As we detailed on page 102, top amateur defenseman Robert Picard first inked a deal with the Capitals, then a more lucrative one with the WHA Nordiques. When the Caps objected, Picard announced, "I'd rather deliver pizzas in Quebec than play for Washington." Words he'd have to eat, because the Capitals eventually won the legal wrangling for Picard's services.

His new team sensed a publicity bonanza. Caps G.M. Max McNab sent a letter to the Nordiques and media. "As an expansion team in the NHL, we are anxious to meet last year's WHA champion," the letter said. "The game would have great interest to hockey fans everywhere." McNab offered to play the game in Quebec, officiated by a WHA referee and linesmen.

Picard faced the nightmare of appearing at Le Colisee in Quebec as a Capital. Knowing how surly the crowd would be, Caps teammates teased Robert by avoiding him on the team bus. Sure enough, during warmups, fans greeted him by throwing pizzas on the ice. (The Capital Picard was traded for in 1980 would have welcomed an on-ice pizza delivery. Jim McTaggart, to the *Washington Post:* "Mike Palmateer told the staff he needed pizza before each game. They kept a stack in the equipment room and before the game put one in the sauna, then served it to Mike.")

As for the game, Quebec won 4-3 in overtime, before a standing-room only crowd of 12,480. What stood out, besides the pizza Frisbees, was new Caps goalie Gary Smith. A slash to the ribs of a Nordiques player by Washington's Gord Lane was judged deliberate. As if 10 consecutive minutes shorthanded wasn't bad enough, Picard was subsequently fingered for delay of game – meaning for two of those 10 minutes, the Caps skated three against five!

"I don't know what was going on in Gary's mind," admitted G.M. McNab, who might have regretted his offer regarding WHA officials. Goalie Smith rose to the occasion, though, shutting out Quebec during the marathon penalty kill. McNab gushed, "I'd have to say it was the best job of goaltending I ever saw." (*Washington Star*)

The Caps played eight preseason games in total from 1976-1978 against the rival World Hockey Association. Washington went 1-1 with Quebec and Cincinnati, won their only meeting with Indianapolis, and lost all three to New England. Some games were played by WHA rules, which included 10-minute overtimes. The Caps' 5-4 loss to the Whalers in 1977 was the first overtime game in team history.

THE LEGENDS OF LANDOVER

✪ A Sport Of Their Own?

Line from an actual game program: "The Capitals, led by captain and hard-hitting shortstop Rod Langway." An alternate athletic universe? No, a summer softball tournament called the Molson Slo-Pitch Challenge.

Starting in 1981, squads of NHL teams competed annually in the charity event, held in and around Niagara Falls, Ontario. Big names, too; the '84 rosters included Ray Bourque, Mark Messier, Marcel Dionne, and Larry Robinson. Only the Rangers, Hawks and Nordiques failed to field a team in '84 - but NHL on-ice officials did! The Caps' lineup boasted three Hall of Fame defensemen in Langway, Scott Stevens, and Larry Murphy. Goalies Pat Riggin and Al Jensen participated, as did Craig Laughlin. Former Caps Jim Bedard and Gerry Meehan played for the old-timers team.

✪ A League Of Their Own?

Original Capital Tommy Williams might have been wrong when he joked that the expansion Caps were playing in the wrong league. Maybe they were just playing on the wrong continent. Four years after their victorious romp through Japan, Washington and Minnesota participated in a 1980 pre-season tournament in Sweden. While it was an honor to be invited, the Caps' presence in Sweden was also borne out of necessity. "We can't get good exhibition games," G.M. Max McNab confided to the *Toronto Globe & Mail*. "Upper echelon teams mingle among themselves. Philadelphia, Montreal, Toronto, New York and Boston set up home-and-home games. At least the Swedes want us."

They sure did; one of the matches was televised nationwide on *Hockey Night In Sweden*. Absolutely true, though we couldn't confirm if they employed a big-mouth ex-coach commentator wearing an equally loud folkdräkt who went by the name Don Körsbär* (*Cherry).

NHL history was made on that trip - the first game between NHL teams held in Sweden. Prior to puck drop, the Caps won over the Stockholm crowd using a tip from McNab. "Just before a game," explained coach Gary Green, "Swedish teams always huddle around their goalie and give out with a loud 'Hey!', while lifting their sticks. We did this around our goalie, Mike Palmateer. The North Stars didn't. The crowd immediately liked us and got behind us." (*Washington Star*)

Those fans, some who paid $20 a ticket (about $65 today) got their money's worth. Jean Pronovost's third period hat trick erased a 3-0 Minnesota lead, forcing a fourth period, and then a fifth. Dennis Maruk scored on a mad dash five minutes into double O.T., giving the Capitals a 4-3 victory over the North Stars. The Caps also beat both of the Swedish host teams to capture the "DN Hockey Cup."

THE LEGENDS OF LANDOVER

✪ Playing By The Rules

Invited back to Scandinavia in 1981, Caps' management made a strategic change. Player sightseeing and down time would be limited compared to their previous visit. Increased workouts didn't increase results; the Caps went 2-3 when they and the Rangers played in Finland and Sweden.

In the 1980 tournament, coach Gary Green had been perplexed by disproportionate penalty calls against his team. Green wrote in the *Washington Star* about one egregious example vs. a Swedish team. "A.I.K.'s goalie, miffed that Bob Kelly had done an excellent job screening, came rushing out at Kelly and took a swing at him. Kelly did not retaliate. Still, the officials sent Kelly off while the A.I.K. goalie was not penalized."

In 1981, facing Kärpät, the visitors' penalty box was again getting a workout. Washington was shorthanded 12 times, their opponents two. Even the Kärpät coach called the disparity "embarrassing." Late in a contest in Stockholm, Green discovered a clue: the Finnish referee had been using the wrong rulebook. The tourney contract, which Green kept in a briefcase behind the bench, stated the games would be played by NHL rules. When Green protested to the referee, "He said he didn't know NHL rules. I told him I was taking my team off the ice and he just shrugged and said, 'OK.' The fans were booing us. They thought we wanted to leave because we were getting beat." Green said when tournament officials "explained to the fans that the ref was at fault," he agreed to finish the game.

In Goteborg, Washington's "stickboy" was a guy in his 60's with poor eyesight, wearing a three-piece suit. Green recalled, "He kept turning around to the crowd, like he was showing off that he was down there." Such complications weren't restricted to the games. A pregame skate got cancelled; towels, soap, even electricity proved hard to come by. *(Green quotes and game notes from The Hockey News)*

✪ That's The Ticket

As their '81 Scandinavian sojourn wrapped up, Jim McTaggart got his own bad news; he was being sent to the minors. Just before starting the 4,058 mile trip between Oulu, Finland and Hershey, Pennsylvania, McTaggart studied his airline ticket - and discovered how agonizingly close he'd come to making the team.

During the exhibition in Oulu against Oulun Kärpät, fellow defenseman Greg Theberge scored an impressive goal. Just how impressive, Theberge related to hockey blogger Nate Oliver. "Jim called me after he got home, and said, 'You're lucky you scored that goal, Bergie - *your* name was the one on the ticket!'. The Capitals had been planning to send *me* back, but after I scored they sent McTaggart back instead."

THE LEGENDS OF LANDOVER

✪ Team USA vs. Nation's Capital Team

The Capitals accomplished a feat in Lake Placid that no team could match during the Olympics – beating the 1980 U.S. hockey team. The squads met on the upstate New York ice surface on October 7, 1979. Dennis Maruk scored the winner with 34 seconds left as the Caps prevailed, 5-4.

One coach was impressed with the Olympians, and it wasn't USA coach Herb Brooks, who "was furious... tongue-lashing his players." (*Washington Star*) Caps coach Dan Belisle, meanwhile, had a prescient prediction about his opposition. "Those kids were sky high, really flying. They're going to blow some minds this winter, and by the time they play the Russians, watch out." Four months later, the Olympic team pulled off the "Miracle on Ice."

The 1984 U.S. Olympians didn't repeat the miracle, but did manage to beat the Caps 2-1 in their exhibition at Capital Centre on September 30, 1983. From a historical perspective, one encounter on the ice stands out. '80 Olympian and current Capital Dave Christian watched his scoring chance denied by '84 Olympian and future Capital goalie Bob Mason. Bob made 24 saves to lead Team USA to victory.

The Caps took two periods to wake up when the '88 U.S. team skated into Landover on September 25, 1987. Entering the 3rd, Washington generated just 11 shots. They cranked up 14 in the final frame, including Mike Ridley's tiebreaker with 4:37 left for a 3-2 victory.

✪ When Canada Abandoned Hockey

Here's a historical shocker: Canada did not field an Olympic hockey team in 1972 or 1976. According to *hockeycanada.ca*, "Canada withdrew (in 1970) from all international hockey competitions, in response to the International Ice Hockey Federation's opposition to allowing professional players to take part."

Hockey Canada and the IIHF patched things up in time for the 1980 games in Lake Placid. Like their USA counterparts, the Canadian Olympic team scheduled the Capitals during the 1979 preseason. In Regina on the first of back-to-back nights, the Caps fell behind 6-4 in the third period. Dennis Maruk scored his second goal with six minutes left, and completed his hat trick to tie the game on a disputed goal at 19:39.

Both teams traveled 470 miles west to Calgary, and again the Olympians put Washington in a two goal, third period hole. This time the Caps dug all the way out. Late scores by Gary Rissling, Maruk, and the game-winner by Mike Gartner in the final five minutes produced a 4-3 Washington victory.

THE LEGENDS OF LANDOVER

✪ Red Squared

ROCKING THE RED The first time Russians played at Capital Centre, the Caps were in the stands, not on the ice. The NHL didn't think it fair to subject the stumbling 2nd year franchise to either of two touring Soviet squads. "It's a good thing the Caps don't have to play the Russians," Tommy Williams observed. "Those guys would score 20 goals, maybe 30 against the Caps, and I'm not trying to be funny." (*AP*)

So on January 12, 1976, the Soviet Wings and Red Army played a 7-7 tie in front of 8,213 spectators, including Capitals coach Tom McVie and his players. Some whispered that the tie was pre-arranged. The only defense was played by the FBI, which thoroughly searched the Centre two hours before gametime. Plainclothed and uniformed officers were then deployed throughout the arena; anti-Soviet protests had interrupted games in Philadelphia and Long Island. (*Canadian Press, UPI*)

✪ From Dynamo With Love

ROCKING THE RED Just two weeks after the Soviet Union invaded Afghanistan, Moscow Dynamo invaded Capital Centre on January 9, 1980, for the only U.S. game of their North American exhibition tour. "Many waved U.S. flags, and, at times, the Caps received rousing ovations for elbowing and tripping." When the Caps outhustled Dynamo to cause an icing, that was cause for another "incredible roar." (*Toronto Globe & Mail*)

As Bob Sirois led Washington with two goals and two assists, the *Canadian Press* noted a warming of relations in the stands. "Some of the 7,369 fans booed the Soviet anthem. But cheers prevailed as the Capitals and Dynamo exchanged handshakes following a 5-5 tie." The crowd included 100 members of the Soviet embassy, who paid to get in like everyone else. "They had the nerve to invade Afghanistan," said Caps P.R. man Pierce Gardner. "I guess we can't be surprised they asked for freebies."

"This team could easily play in the NHL," coach Gary Green said of Dynamo. "They have good skating and passing. They're talented, especially fundamentally. They don't have the North American system, but they know where they're going." Knowing where Dynamo wanted to get to, the Caps adjusted their style, clogging the middle, preventing the give-and-go-pass. Captain Ryan Walter explained to *The Hockey News*, "We kept a centerman high in the slot when we forechecked, which is a derivation from the normal system. This made it a little tougher for them to get going."

Green referenced the political subplot in the locker room. "We didn't want to treat this like an exhibition game. I knew that to the fans, especially, it was more than just a hockey game."

THE LEGENDS OF LANDOVER

✪ The Original "Rocking The Red"

ROCKING THE RED Before the 1989-90 season, the Caps opened training camp once more in Sweden, winning two exhibition games. Then on to the U.S.S.R. along with the Calgary Flames for the "Friendship Tour" – September, 1989 games against teams in Riga, Leningrad, Moscow, and Kiev. The spirit of the trip extended to the United Nations, as a U.S. diplomat presented a Capitals sweater to his Soviet counterpart.

Packing for a hockey trip halfway around the world is daunting. Naturally, the team took skates, sticks, uniforms – and lunch. Tal Pinchevsky wrote in his book, *Breakaway*, "Upon hearing that there was no pasta in Russia, the team ordered thousands of pounds of pasta and hundreds of jars of sauce for the trip. If the Capitals were going to lose their games in the Soviet Union, it wouldn't be due to a lack of pregame carbohydrates."

Evidently, the edge in Italian food was too much for the Russians to overcome. Again the Caps were kings of Eurasia, winning three of four games vs. their Soviet competition. Most notable, the sensation around the Capitals' 2-1 O.T. win at Riga's Sports Palace; 5,000 fans secured tickets, while 40,000 more were turned away.

Overall, the Caps won five of their six games overseas. In two of the games, Washington rallied from three-goal deficits to win. Impressive, considering the six games were compressed into just 10 nights, in five different cities and two countries. Washington had also participated in less than a week of stateside practices prior to the 5-1 road trip. Поздравляю! (Pronounced Pazdra-vilya-yoo!, by the way, which means "Congratulations!")

"There's a lot of pride on the line just going in there. You don't want to lose. You are playing for the National Hockey League and you're hoping that you show well," Caps coach Bryan Murray explained to *UPI*. "We feel very good about the fact that we went over and represented the league and did very well. No one can say to us that we didn't carry our weight."

As *UPI* pointed out, "Players, coaches and front office officials got the chance to tour Soviet cities, sampling the local culture, as well as the local cuisine." The food sampling came at a price – flu and stomach pains for coach Murray and several of the traveling party. Back home, the players had to shake one other bug acquired overseas. "Playing on the bigger ice, you have more room to make passes," Doug Wickenheiser said to the *Washington Post*. "It's good over there, but sometimes here you've got to shoot the puck and hope you get a few lucky bounces."

THE LEGENDS OF LANDOVER

Hope faded when Washington stumbled to a 6-10-4 start, with players and coaches alike feeling the team didn't hit its stride until after Thanksgiving. Mike Ridley explained to *The Hockey News*, "So much intense play and travel burned some guys out. When the season started, it was tough in a lot of cases to get ready as a team." Of course, they won two playoff rounds in the spring for the first time, so who knows.

Over the course of the season, four Soviet teams toured all 21 NHL cities. On December 12, 1989, an impressive Capital Centre crowd of 15,918 watched the Caps skate past Chimik Voskresensk, 5-2.

✪ **Sequels: Dynamo II, III and IV**

As mentioned, the Caps and Moscow Dynamo first met at Capital Centre in 1980, battling to a 5-5 draw. In Russia during the '89 "Friendship Tour," Dynamo won, 7-2. Their third match took place at Landover in January, 1991. Jeff Greenlaw scored with 1:05 to play for a 3-2 win. The game featured a shootout exhibition of five skaters per side – held between the 2nd the 3rd periods! The teams met one last time, with the Capitals besting Dynamo in 2006… in U.S. District Court. Dynamo had filed suit, claiming contractual rights to a young Russian forward named Alex Ovechkin.

✪✪✪✪✪✪

THE LEGENDS OF LANDOVER

10th Shift: *Media*

✪ Robert Fachet (*Washington Post* Caps Beat Writer, 1974-88)

On mornings after a Caps victory, I would rush to retrieve the *Washington Post* from our doorstep, so I could enjoy Robert Fachet's game story. Here's a 1974 sample: "Cancel the plane to Buffalo. The Capitals were flying so high they could make the trip without one. After 14 winless games and 33 days without a victory, they whipped the California Seals, 6-4."

As you can infer, wins weren't always plentiful in the 14 seasons Fachet covered the Caps. And there's no more miserable assignment in sports journalism than being the beat writer for a bad team. Bob deserved an award of valor (purple typewriter ribbon?) for having to come up with new ways to report that the Caps had lost a game.

Fortunately, Bob was up to the task - never more so than the opening paragraph to his story for March 20, 1975: "Greek mythology records the plight of Sisyphus, who pushed a huge stone to a mountain summit. Watched it roll down and has to repeat his task for eternity. It does not record whether he wears a Washington Capitals' uniform." Another great line: "The Capitals endured a breech birth in 1974 and they have had difficulty trying to get turned around ever since."

Like long-time fans, Bob never shook his addiction to the Capitals. He often attended games even after he was no longer the team's beat writer. When Fachet died in 1998, his *Post* obituary included glowing praise from Rod Langway. "You talk about respect; he got it around the league. He did a lot for hockey in the Washington area."

✪ Russ White (*Washington Star* Caps Beat Writer, 1974-81)

For an afternoon paper, the prior night's score was unavoidably old news. Russ White used the delay to his advantage, procuring quotes & anecdotes for his recaps. Following a 4-4 tie with the mighty Canadiens in 1978, White eavesdropped on the Habs coach. "As the arena cleared, (Scotty) Bowman was on a pay telephone down in the bowels of the Centre. 'Hello, Montreal. You won't believe what happened here tonight.'"

Russ "qualified" for the Caps beat by spending the 1960's covering the expansion Senators baseball team, who in 11 seasons finished a combined 378.5 games out of first place. The extended two-sport misery entitled White to a certain amount of snark; besides, he was good at it: "Unless you read the newspaper upside down, the Washington Capitals are last in the National Hockey League standings."

THE LEGENDS OF LANDOVER

On the NHL president announcing the Caps and K.C. Scouts would play exhibitions in Japan: "Campbell did not say whether the two teams would return to the mainland." Or this, from their expansion season: "One day National Hockey League play will come to Capital Centre. Until then, there are the Washington Capitals."

White's paper once placed a large ad promoting his hockey coverage, but like the early Capitals, failed to check (its writing). "He knows having the Caps for a home team isn't just one big haberdashery of hat tricks," the promo read. Surprisingly, that stilted turn of phrase wasn't the problem; the next sentence was. "But he also knows." Knows what? We'll never find out. The promo copy ended in mid-thought.

Russ wasn't able to cover the Caps' resurgent fortunes, leaving the *Star* a few months before the paper folded in August, 1981.

✪ Larry King (Landover, Maryland, Hello!)

Many decades and several hundred pairs of suspenders ago, Larry King became enamored with the Capitals. King adopted the team soon after moving to Washington in 1978, to host a national all-night radio program. In 1980, the first hockey guest ever on Mutual Radio's *Larry King Show* was Capitals coach Gary Green. A trading card even anointed him as the team's "Celebrity Captain." (Sample pep talk: "Win tonight, and tomorrow we go to Duke Zeibert's and the corned beef sandwiches are on me!")

Larry fed his Caps fix by sitting in with Ron Weber on radio broadcasts, and appearances on *Home Team Sports*, the new regional sports cable channel. Oh, and if Larry had ever written one of his *USA Today* columns about the Capitals, it might have read something like this: *"That Langway fellow is a keeper... At Capital Centre, try the soft-serve ice cream by portal 9. Delicious!... Call me crazy, but I like the red line... Whatever happened to Pete Laframboise?... Gotta love a player whose surname means "The Raspberry" in French..."*

✪ Marv Brooks (P.A. Announcer, 1974-95)

Marv Brooks got the job as Voice of Capital Centre by pretending he already was. Brooks' booming voice was well-known as a DJ at *WPGC* radio. He also built a home recording studio for freelance voice work.

"Word came out that Abe Pollin was building the Cap Centre in 1973," recalled Marv's wife, Lynn. "Marv made an audition tape, complete with echo, crowd noises and cheers." (*amandfmmorningside.com*) "Marvelous Marv" won courtside & rinkside seats as P.A. announcer at the new arena. Brooks also did player interviews shown on the Telscreen.

THE LEGENDS OF LANDOVER

The gig was temporarily yanked in 1980 for the oddest of reasons. "Brooks said he was fired because he refused to wear a tuxedo at each home game as directed by the team's marketing director," reported the *Washington Star*. Meddling by the same marketers had infected the TV booth a few months earlier. "Analyst Jack Doniger was fired by the team for refusing to ask scout Roger Crozier a list of puff questions during an intermission."

At the 1980 home opener, Caps fans protested the loss of their favorite P.A. guy with chants of "We Want Marv." It took two years for the club to concede its mistake and rehire Brooks. Through the 1994-95 season, Marv resumed the happy task of trumpeting over cheering fans, *"Capitals Goal, Scored By…"*

✪ Guy Le Guy

When channel 9 gave up Caps telecasts in 1977, only one hockey guest got significant air time – Guy Le Guy. You know him better as Gordon Peterson, legendary TV-9 news anchor. One night, the station's weekly sports program, *Sidelines*, was actually going to focus on the Capitals, except a blizzard delayed the arrival of players.

Since the show aired live, the impish Peterson volunteered his alter-ego - French-Canadian accent and all - to fill time. "I said I was playing in Guatemala, where the rusting of skates was a big problem because the ice was constantly melting. But we speeded up the game by using a clear puck. When the Caps finally arrived, I refused to get off. I told them, 'I have all the time in the world for you.'" (From a *washingtonpost.com* chat)

✪ Media Guide Hat Trick

Hartland Monahan in 1977 spent preseason with the Capitals, was traded to Pittsburgh on opening night, and moved again seven games later to Los Angeles. Due to differing publication deadlines, Hartland appeared in the media guides of all three teams!

✪ Ron Weber (Radio Broadcaster, 1974-97)

For a generation of Washington hockey listeners, winter nights were warmed by Ron Weber's folksy radio play-by-play. Check his brilliant on-the-fly description of a Caps' shot barely trickling over the goal line before the goalie could sweep it away: *"One-handed, Mike Lampman tipped it in; the puck wasn't going real fast, and Davidson reached back and picked himself a peach off a tree, but the truant officer caught him."*

At Capital Centre, Weber broadcast from a desk built into the stands - fitting, because Weber was a fan's announcer. He conveyed the feel of the game, rather than every meaningless neutral-zone pass.

THE LEGENDS OF LANDOVER

When the Caps were born in 1974, Jimmy Anderson was behind the bench and Weber was in the booth. Anderson was gone after 54 games, while Weber lasted 23 years without missing a match. That kind of statistical note would no doubt please Weber, who peppered his broadcasts with arcane numbers and obscure facts. Weber said because he didn't play the game, he felt unqualified to give analysis, substituting voluminous research. Listeners knew that wasn't so; Weber showed plenty of hockey smarts.

His nickname among the team was "Stats." The reason why is revealed in his call of a Capitals goal in 1976 vs. Montreal: *"That's the first power play goal for the Capitals in 6 games. It's only their 2nd in their last 9, the 5th in the last 15. At one point, the Capitals were only 3 under the opponents in power play goals this year, 48 to 51. They've now fallen behind 10, 63-53."*

Certainly, no one knew the team better, or cared about their fortunes more deeply. During that awful 1974-75 season, the Caps were in Toronto, on the verge of their long-awaited first road win. The Leafs tied the score with two minutes to play, then scored the game-winner in the final 10 seconds. That cannonball to the gut was too much. After dutifully announcing the goal, Weber didn't say another word for more than a minute.

Winnipeg was almost his Waterloo, twice. One time, he walked a mile to the arena in minus-70 degree wind chill. Another time there, he suffered a torn retina. Neither time did he miss the puck drop. Ron's consecutive-games streak also once survived this nightmare flight itinerary:
San Jose - Las Vegas - San Jose - Calgary - Edmonton!

On happier occasions, Weber trotted out his catch-phrases, such as calling the puck the "little black biscuit." Or after a timely goal, "Way to go, Miss Twiddell." Ron revealed her (non) identity in a 1985 *Hockey News* article. "When I broadcast high school football, I'd often say, 'Way to go.' I don't know why I started to add Miss Twiddell. It just came out one night. There's no Miss Twiddell, although my wife, Mary Jane, was curious about that, too." Regardless of any momentary marital discord, the phrase represented an unassuming, folksy style that wore well year after year.

That is, until the team moved from suburban U.S. Airways Arena to downtown MCI Center, and Weber wasn't asked to come along. Years earlier, he'd said only half-jokingly to the *Washington Star*, "I've been around this business long enough to be paranoid." It should have mattered that Weber was the only person to have seen all 1,939 Capitals games up to that time. In the early years, when a road game wasn't scheduled to air, Ron would pay his own way to attend. But 23 years of dedication didn't count. With a move to a hip new arena, management apparently felt Weber would be brown shoes to their new tuxedo.

THE LEGENDS OF LANDOVER

All those years after describing Jim Hrychuk's backhander for the first goal in Caps history, Weber called Jaroslav Svejkovsky's power play tally at 16:14 of the third period in Buffalo on April 13, 1997. Yogi's fourth goal of the game would be the last of Weber's career. Here's his final signoff:

"It's not so long this time, it's goodbye. After 23 seasons, the Capitals have decided to continue without me. But I'm not bitter, not after a sweet sendoff to a long, beautiful ride. Sing no sad songs for me. My terrific wife Mary Jane and I have good health, three wonderful children all doing well, and three grandchildren. Whether I find and accept play by play with another team or another sport or not, life is good. I've known and accepted this moment for two years, and leave with good thoughts about an owner whose teams I have broadcast for the past 30 years. From the first, it's been a wonderful run."

What a tone-deaf management blunder. Hometown announcers don't become legendary because of their technical skills or "attitude." Fans appreciate how they've been there through thick and thin, and their quirks become embraceable "signatures." In the '70's and '80's, most local stations didn't televise many games, and cable was still something of a novelty. So by necessity, fans built an intimate relationship with their team's radio broadcasters. Weber *was* the Caps, and I missed hearing him.

✪ Good Things Come To Those Who Wait Dep't.:

For 13 years after his final signoff, Ron Weber received an outpouring of affection from fans who ran into him at MCI/Verizon Center. Then, that adoration was confirmed by no less than the Hockey Hall of Fame. Weber was named 2010 winner of the Foster Hewitt Memorial Award, presented by the NHL Broadcasters' Association

✪ Mike Fornes (Television Broadcaster, 1984-90)

"A house of horrors." Capitals TV voice Mike Fornes, describing the Philadelphia Spectrum of the '80's - and not just for visiting players. "You had to climb several flights of stairs and go through the stands. You were always at risk a little bit because Flyers fans knew who you were and they didn't mind sharing their opinion about the team or the broadcast." Fornes mentioned the trek during a telecast. "Al Koken is headed downstairs. The interview area, I think, is located somewhere in New Jersey."

Fornes had a unique employment history with the Capitals; no interview before being hired, no notice when he was fired. First, the hiring. *Home Team Sports*, a new regional cable channel, had a problem. Mere hours after launch on April 4, 1984, their first live telecast would be a Caps-Flyers playoff game. With no hockey voice on staff, *HTS* borrowed Fornes from the Hartford Whalers.

THE LEGENDS OF LANDOVER

One more note about that first-ever *HTS* Caps cablecast. Fornes' guest analyst was none other than Gordie Howe. Mr. Hockey wanted a good seat to watch his son Mark, a Flyers defenseman. However, Gordie gave due respect to the home team. Describing the replay of a Craig Laughlin goal, Howe called him "an alert young man."

Acing his on-air audition, Fornes earned the full-time Capitals TV job starting with the 1984-85 season. For home games on *HTS* and road contests on channel 20, fans got familiar with Mike's signature line, "A shot and a goal!" Fornes told *capsdegenerate.blogspot.com* that the call was actually borrowed from Blackhawks broadcaster Lloyd Pettit. Noman Chad favorably reviewed the Fornes-Al Koken pairing in a *Washington Post* review. "While these two gentlemen often look unsure on how to style their hair, they are cocksure on how to call a hockey game. They generally bring intelligence and insight to a broadcast."

The 1989-90 season would be Mike's last in Landover, a classless episode for the organization. "I got a phone call from the *Washington Times*," Fornes recalled. "That's how I was notified." What happened? "I think my focus was more hockey oriented and I think the team wanted to go in a direction that was more marketing oriented."

✪ Al Koken (Swiss Army Knife, 1974-Present)

Al Koken proudly admits, "I can trace myself literally back to the very first days of this franchise in 1974." The Swiss Army Knife of Capitals media, Koken is unmatched in both versatility and durability. He's covered the team into a fifth decade as a print reporter, radio talk show host, TV game analyst, play-by-play man, rinkside interviewer, and studio host.

Koken's Caps' connection began with a $35 assignment on September 28, 1974, in the players' lounge at Capital Centre. "Just graduated American University, got the hair down to the shoulders. I was working for this bi-monthly newspaper called *Sportscene*, and there was an expansion team in the Nation's Capital. Jimmy Anderson was the coach, and he had a pool cue in his hand when I walked in with Russ White and Bob Fachet.

"Here was the very first preseason (home) game in the history of the Capitals, playing the defending Stanley Cup champion Montreal. The Capitals tied that Canadien team, and everbody thought, 'Well, this'll be great. They're going to be fine.' Of course, eight wins later, we all know what happened." In Koken's view, the Caps in 1974 recruited too heavily from G.M. Milt Schmidt's former organization. "They drafted a lot of former 'Big Bad Bruins,' a guy like Mike Bloom, and you go, 'Wow,' 6-4, 210. Well, he couldn't skate. Milt wanted to have a Bruin-like team; the problem was, the 'good' Bruins who could play they kept, and the 'bad' Bruins ended up getting drafted."

THE LEGENDS OF LANDOVER

Koken, as TV game analyst, paired with Mike Fornes from 1984-1990. "Mike could not have been nicer. He was great on teaching me certain aspects of the broadcast. One time, a Capitals goaltender was working on a shutout, I said the word 'shutout.' You would have thought I dropped an F-bomb the way he looked at me." And broadcast booths, like locker rooms, had a pecking order. "Mike did every game with a hand-held microphone, and a beer. He never got drunk at all, it was only one beer. And as a rookie broadcaster, I was the guy to go the concession stand and get him his beer."

In tuxedos for an opening-night telecast, Koken's zinger: "We look like a bad lounge act at a Motel 6." More self-directed humor, hawking a Caps ball cap: "If you can put it on a fat head like mine, it'll definitely fit anybody."

Fan feedback was easy to come by. "At the Capital Centre, we had a (broadcast location) that today would be $150 a seat. We were right there on the concourse. People would literally be walking up the aisle." At one game, Al recalled a man shouting as he walked past, "'You're a (bleeping) homer!' 30 seconds later, a woman walks down the aisle, looks me in the face, says, 'Are you ever going to say anything nice about the Capitals?' I must be doing something right, because nobody's happy." Apparently so, because Koken is still part of Caps telecasts, 45 years and counting.
(Quotes from WNST Radio, Andy Pollin's DC Podcast)

✪ 20-20 Vision

Even when standard definition was the only definition, passionate Caps viewers made like Dr. Seuss' Whoville, yelling *We Are Here!* "Hockey fans are very vocal," Dave Reid of channel 20 told the *Post* in 1978. "It would be nice if the ratings services could hear from them as much as we hear from them. Hockey generated more telephone calls than all other sports put together."

Cable TV in 1979 was still in its Wild West infancy, creating a programming oddity during the '79-'80 NHL season. In addition to 15 Capitals road game telecasts on channel 20, some hockey fans in suburban Virginia had an alternative. "Arlington's Metrocable will carry all (Atlanta) Flame games, home and away. It would have carried 29 Ranger and 20 Islander games, but Capitals owner Abe Pollin objected," the *Washington Star* reported.

✪ Flourish Over Facts

As a young *Washington Star* sports reporter, Lynn Rosellini garnered a Pulitzer Prize nomination for a series on gays in sports. She'd later write a bombshell profile of *Washington Post* publisher Katherine Graham. So it's shocking how sloppy was her feature on the hardships of the '70's Capitals.

THE LEGENDS OF LANDOVER

Prizing flourish rather than facts, Rosellini wrote of winger Bill Riley, "This Riley was supposed to be the fiercest, meanest man in the minor leagues." The rookie was called up for his first NHL game in December, 1974 as muscle against the Flyers. "Riley proceeded to skate up and down his wing like Dorothy Hamill out for some exercise," the column continued. "He didn't throw a body check all night. Riley was back on the plane to Dayton before the rest of the Capitals were even out of the locker room."

Rosellini apparently neglected to confer with the NHL expert in her own newsroom. Compare her damning account with that written by *Star* hockey scribe Russ White, about the same player in the same game. "The first time Riley came to town, he lasted one night. The old management of the Capitals cruelly shipped him back to the minors after he failed to break up the Stanley Cup champion Philadelphia Flyers single-handedly in a sellout game here. Riley admitted he was nervous. 'We didn't have that many people (18,000) in the town where I came from.'" White was giving context to his story praising Riley's 1977 return to the NHL as the physical "catalyst" in a Capitals victory.

Media Rant One book claimed that, "During the '70's and '80's, newspaper columnists and local TV sports anchors were criminally negligent about reporting on the Caps." Oh, right, it was the introduction to *this* book.

I know, I know, lack of coverage is a complaint issued by fans of many teams in many cities. The 800-pound pro football gorilla has always sucked up most of Washington's sports oxygen, from the Capitals' inception into the new millenium. In the expansion era especially, the hockey product was poor and interest in the team was relatively small. But... did lack of fan interest lead to minimal coverage, or was it the other way around?

✪ **"Very Little Interest In Hockey"**

Rant For an insider view of hockey's standing with D.C. media, we turn to *Washington Post* columnist and author John Feinstein, writing at *cbssports.com*. "I worked on a sports staff at the *Post* that, collectively, had very little interest in hockey. Robert Fachet, the Capitals beat writer beginning their first season, covered the sport superbly. But he was pretty much the list of people who liked hockey when I joined the staff in 1979.

"The two columnists were Ken Denlinger and Dave Kindred, whose feelings about hockey were best summed up one winter when Denlinger grudgingly wrote a Caps column and declared the next day, 'I've built an insurmountable 1-0 lead on Kindred in hockey columns.' He wasn't kidding and he wasn't wrong." Feinstein revealed in the *Post*, "Whenever the two played golf, the bet was the same: loser writes the next hockey column."

THE LEGENDS OF LANDOVER

Denlinger, especially, seemed to revel in his gleeful ignorance of the sport, once writing, "My hockey style is more Ted Baxter than Ted Koppel." With perverse pleasure in column after column, Ken described his NHL interest level as "Wildly indifferent" and "Terminal apathy" and "Feverish apathy." His dream? "Haul in a rink-sized heating pad and when the ice melts, whoosh hockey off the jock map with the world's largest handi-wipe." He said "crease" made him think of trousers, not a goalie's outpost. Still too subtle? "If they held the Stanley Cup in my backyard, I'd close the blinds."

Late in the 1981-82 season, Denlinger contended metro D.C. shared his disinterest, writing, "In mid-March... came pivotal home games; came almost nobody." Denlinger was referencing a March 10 contest against Pittsburgh, which Pollin claimed was "our most important game of the year." The Caps lost, and many of the 12,000 who saw it – 6,000 below capacity – used free tickets. But the columnist needed to dig deeper. A *Post* headline the next morning – before "mid-March" – announced that losing to the Pens "Effectively Knock Capitals From Playoff Race." Yet, fans did continue to come, anyway; attendance averaged more than 11,500 over the final 10 games. That's a whole lot of nobodies, Ken.

To be clear, colleagues lauded Denlinger as a tough but fair reporter, gentle mentor, and family man. During 38 years at the *Post*, he even earned praise from coaches and executives. But hockey to him was a nerdy classmate who he felt free to bully, when he acknowledged it at all.

✪ **"Never Interested Me"**

Rant Foolish of us Caps fans to expect sports columnists to write about *all* the local teams, right? Still, they weren't alone. The 2015 book, *DC Sports: The Nation's Capital At Play*, falls prey to the same indifference. Each chapter of *DC Sports* is a well-researched academic essay by a different author. In his turn, professor John Soares offers a credible review of the Caps' political and social impact on the region.

The same can't be said about the wrap-up chapter by Daniel Nathan, "Washington Sports Memories." It covers the same time period as this book, the '70's and '80's. As you'd expect, there's reminiscences about Joe Gibbs, John Thompson, Len Bias, and Wes Unseld. In a 14-page essay, Nathan allots the local hockey team part - just part - of one, dismissive sentence: "...and the Washington Capitals (who never interested me) won exactly one division title until 2000." Despite claiming space limitations, Nathan found room to discuss a Romanian tennis coach.

Not all the fault is Nathan's; you can't write about memories you didn't have. The book's editors should have found a writer whose fondness extended to every pro team. Why? Because as Nathan himself concludes, "Inside and outside the beltway, DC sports have provided a lingua franca."

THE LEGENDS OF LANDOVER

Lingua franca means a common language among speakers whose native tongues are different. For many thousands of us, that adopted common language refers to pucks, goalies, and most passionately, Capitals.

✪ We Noticed The Pecking Order, Too

Rant On a Sunday afternoon in 1988, the Capitals provided all the elements of front-page sports news – a raucous home sellout crowd, a late-season showdown with the hated Flyers, and a nail-biting 1-0 victory, vanquishing the division leaders, in overtime no less. Later on this particular Sunday, the Redskins won the Super Bowl, so the Caps game story was squeezed into the *Washington Post* sports section on page 10. We know this because the Caps' beat writer for the *Post*, a presumably miffed Bob Fachet, mentioned the snub in his *Hockey News* column.

Did Caps players notice the discrepancy in coverage? Oh, yeah they did. Goalie Mike Palmateer, a recent arrival from Toronto, noted in 1980 about the Redskins, "They're 3-10 and they still get on the front page." One night in Pittsburgh, Dave Christian scored the game winner, as the Caps rallied for a 3-2 victory. Christian was on his way to a stellar 29 goal, 58 assist season in 1983-84. Afterward, Dave lamented to the *Pittsburgh Press*, "It's tough to get on the front page right now. It's all Redskins down there now."

Comparing his Nation's Capital to ours, the *Ottawa Journal's* Eddie MacCabe observed, "The fortunes of the Redskins are followed with uncommon fervor" by D.C. fans and media alike. "One kneels to football, as at the feet of a towering idol. One pats hockey affectionately on the head... nice little fellow... stay around but don't butt in... there's a good boy."

Another Canadian scribe pointed out that even the Capitals' blockbuster 1982 trade with Montreal hadn't distracted D.C. media from their usual obsessions. "Habs have been cast into exile," wrote longtime *Toronto Star* columnist Milt Dunnell. "Rod Langway and Doug Jarvis, a pair of refugees from the bleu, blanc and rouge, now sharing whatever Washington attention is left over after R. Reagan and (Redskins quarterback) J. Theismann have wallowed in it. And not necessarily in that order."

Veteran Caps saw different sides of the celebrity coin. Bryan Watson said of teammates, "They're trying to be modest when they say they don't need the recognition and enjoy not having it. Having a town turned on helps you play better." To Pierre Bouchard, anonymity had its benefits. "In Montreal, I couldn't go shopping. I had salesmen breathing down my neck. Here, I try it on and return it if it doesn't fit. In Montreal, they say, 'Who does he think he is?'" Craig Laughlin pointed out a low profile's advantage at times of bad news. "(Caps defenseman) Lee Norwood got into a fight outside a bar," he said. "But there was only a tiny blurb in the paper and that only came out when there was talk of lawsuits."

THE LEGENDS OF LANDOVER

Bobby Carpenter, as a teenage American star in the NHL, drew more than his share of media attention, and grew to loathe it. "At times after a bad game, I wanted to be by myself and think about it," Carpenter said. "There'd be five different guys and they'd all as the same questions. Then the next city there'd be 10 more, asking the same thing. Usually, it had nothing to do with the game. It was... how my father felt about me going to Washington, or whether my mother thought I should have gone to college. Questions about the game, okay. But about my family, I didn't like that."

(Quote sources: Watson/Bouchard, Washington Post; Laughlin, Toronto Globe & Mail; Palmateer, Washington Star; Carpenter, The Hockey News.)

✪ Gimme A Break!

Rant Local TV types usually showed little enthusiasm for hockey. For example, the time Lou Franceschetti scored a crucial goal for the Caps. One TV sportscaster wouldn't show the highlight, to avoid having to pronounce "Franceschetti." (No need to source this story, because I was there when it happened.)

Then there's channel 9 sportscaster Warner Wolf, beloved in the '70's for his pet phrases, such as "Boo of the week." Two others, "Gimme a break," and "Let's go to the videotape," Wolf later used as book titles. In one of the books, and without apparent shame, Wolf wrote these contradictory statements in the same paragraph: "I was never a huge hockey fan" and "I did the TV color the Caps' first year." He hints that he took the gig only to pocket extra cash, since channel 9 aired the games. Warner, that's a Boo!

Reviewing Wolf's hockey acumen, Daniel McCoubrey of the *Post* damned with the faintest of praise. "Wolf was smart enough to keep his mouth shut most of the time." The headline piled on: "TV fans find Wolf scoreless." In his first book, Warner claimed to work 20 Caps road telecasts in 1974-75. By his second book, the number jumps to 40. Both claims are bloated; *WTOP-TV* aired 15 Caps games that first season. Let's review, Warner. You're not into hockey, wedge yourself into the broadcasts anyway, then say you attended more games than you actually did. Boo, man, Boo.

In two books full of reminiscences, Wolf's only Caps anecdote doesn't even involve hockey. He spends a page describing difficulty finding his rental car in Detroit, because it had snowed during Warner's game broadcast. Worst of all, Wolf suggested to the *Washington Star* in 1979, "I don't know if the Caps will catch on here."

Warner, that's a Boo so big it would startle Frankenstein.

11th Shift: *Capital Centre*

The birth of the Capitals was inexorably bound to the place they would call home. To understand the story of Washington's first NHL rink in Landover, it's first essential to know the events which created the Capitals at a 1972 meeting of the NHL Board of Governors.

✪ Things Will Be Great When You're Downtown

Before the Caps, and Capital Centre, were even gleams in Abe Pollin's eye, fitful starts and stops were made at securing a downtown stadium. The dream originated during President Eisenhower's first term with House Bill H.R. 8138, introduced in January, 1956, "For the construction of a civic auditorium." The same month, Senate Bill 3053 was submitted, "To provide that the D.C. Auditorium Commission shall continue in existence until... such auditorium has been completed." Yeah, right. (*dchistorymatters.org*)

The name of the 34th President figured in D.C.'s next attempt at a sports venue downtown. Congress in 1972 authorized a convention center and sports arena complex near Mt. Vernon Square. Planners envisioned a 17,500-seat home for winter sports and events, part of a 25-acre, $82 million campus. One drawback; by the time sportscasters welcomed listeners to the projected "Dwight D. Eisenhower Memorial Bicentennial Civic Center in Washington," the first period might be half over.

Pollin preferred to have his new NHL team and the NBA Bullets play in a stadium he'd construct in suburban Maryland. That's why he pursued the NHL in the first place; without it, his arena wouldn't be economically viable. "The numbers dictated we have two major franchises," Pollin said. "We had to have a hockey team." However, as the *Post* reported, "An equal number (of political voices) were telling hockey fathers that a vote for Pollin would kill whatever chance there was for an arena in downtown Washington."

✪ From Deadlines To Just Dead

Pollin removed those concerns, and assured votes for his franchise, by agreeing to play at the Eisenhower Center. "Hockey Has Nixon's Backing," was the headline of a subsequent *Post* story, which said, "A telegram was sent from the White House to the NHL, welcoming the hockey team as the first tenant of the Eisenhower Center."

What Nixon refused was federal funding for the arena portion. Despite what mob movies tell you, it's not always business – with this President, it was about the likelihood of personal prestige. "Nixon's support for the project evaporated after he learned the Center probably wouldn't be finished until he was out of office."

THE LEGENDS OF LANDOVER

Flyers owner and Abe's ally Ed Snider challenged, "It's time for those pushing the (Eisenhower) Center to put up or shut up." Pollin confided, "I have evidence from Congress that there is no way that will be built." Abe further warned, "If we don't get assurances within a maximum of 90 days, we would start work on the site in Prince George's County."

The *Post* reported, "This deadline has accelerated to a frantic pace... memos, calls, statements and meetings at the White House, District Building, Capitol Hill, and community centers." Mayor Walter Washington heralded alternate sites such as Union Station, because he believed the NHL had obligated Pollin to locate within the District. NHL President Clarence Campbell dismissed that notion, saying, "It's just not true."

In the end, the downtown dream was an arena too far. The deadline passed, Pollin broke ground in Largo, the arena portion of the complex was abandoned, and in 1974, the rest of the Eisenhower proposal collapsed under political pressure. Now you know why Washington's pro hockey team grew up outside the Beltway, underneath the saddleback roof.

✪ Pollin's Palace On The Prairie

Maybe Capital Centre, like an aging and broken-down athlete who fails to hear the whispers, should have retired sooner. But like the flashy ballplayer in his twilight – oh, you should have seen the Centre in its strapping youth. Even for D.C. sports fans who came of age, like me, in the 1970's, it's getting harder to remember that Capital Centre was once a jewel in the crown of sports venues. Or, as a cheesy marketing campaign once described it, "That's Centre-Tainment."

"Abe Pollin's Palace on the Prairie," was the reverent description by broadcaster Ron Weber. "The magnificent arena in the county" was the less lyrical, though equally admiring review by *Washington Star* sports columnist Morris Siegel in 1977. "I always felt, having lived in this area all my life, that there was a gap, a hole, a need for a facility of this type," owner Abe Pollin explained in a *WTOP-TV* interview. "I mean, this is the Nation's Capital. There were talks about a facility in Columbia, Maryland, there was one considered in downtown Washington, hopeful groups in Virginia." Pollin's first choice, according to *Regardie's*, was "near what is now Grosvenor Metrorail station in Rockville, but Montgomery County officials feared a sports complex would 'ruin' their affluent community."

Pollin said, "My original intent was just to bring the Bullets over (from Baltimore) and really be a tenant. But after a year of frustration of seeing all the other ideas go down the drain and none of them come to fruition, I realized the only way it was going to get done is if I did it myself. Once we decided to build it, we tried to build the finest facility of its kind in the world."

THE LEGENDS OF LANDOVER

As Paul Schwartzman wrote in a *Post* retrospective, "Pollin ventured east to Landover, and, despite opposition from environmentalists, settled on 75 acres of parkland just outside the Capital Beltway. For 15 months, crews worked feverishly to erect the arena, which got its name when Pollin's wife, Irene, blurted out, 'How 'bout the Capital Centre?'" No one put in more time than Pollin. From the *Regardie's* article: "Working 18-hour days, he was a fixture at the site, sloshing through mud and exhorting workmen to meet his deadline. Obsessed with his pledge to finish a two-year job in 15 months, he kept driving himself, often going without sleep for days at a time."

The $18 million Capital Centre buzzed with innovation at its inaugural event, a Bullets' last-second victory over Seattle on December 2, 1973. As noted by the *Post*, "The new arena boasted state-of-the-art features including computerized ticketing, skyboxes and a four-sided Telscreen that flashed replays and video."

✪ Hockey, Playing On Four Screens

Capitals fans were the first hockey spectators anywhere to enjoy breakthrough video technology - live action, replays, taped segments and more, on those four 12-by-18-foot "Telscreens" suspended above center ice. No sports facility before had figured out how to shoot a beam onto a screen from far away, while making the moving images large enough and bright enough to be viewed clearly.

The Pentagon had been tinkering with such a device. So Abe Pollin contacted an engineering friend who happened to work at a U.S. Navy lab. The friend collaborated with a Swiss firm to develop a $250,000 video device for Pollin's new arena. The gizmo's name was Eidophor Projector. Purchasing four of them represented a $1 million investment.

The Eidophors' genius was in producing bright video at extreme distance and size. I can't explain how, except *earlytelevision.org* says it involved electron beams, light diffraction, oil layers, and wave deformation. It's just that simple! Like any cutting-edge device, the Telscreens could be wonky. Occasionally the picture would lose color, or disappear entirely, which was inconvenient because penalty time was shown on-screen. Fans on occasion were subject to ear-splitting feedback.

The displays, according to *bostonglobe.com*, were "built with lips above and below to shield the sensitive screens from the bright arena lights." With that attention to detail, it's surprising that the Centre was designed without dedicated camera positions. They did build a TV control room to coordinate the video feeds. In a brilliant stroke of media savvy, the feed was delivered live by microwave into local TV sports departments. Stations didn't have to devote a camera crew to record the action, and Pollin ensured highlights were available of every home hockey and basketball game.

THE LEGENDS OF LANDOVER

✪ Stripes In The Spotlight

Capital Centre requested, and was granted, permission from the NBA and NHL to show replays. "You can't shut out progress," said NHL President Clarence Campbell, who had previously opposed in-arena replays. "The officials still don't like the idea, but it's something we're going to have to learn to live with." For his part, Abe Pollin promised, "Our goal is to show exciting plays and not to embarrass the officials." *(AP)*

Like the first-year Caps, Telscreen operators suffered growing pains. At a 1974 game against Atlanta, referee Bruce Hood missed an obvious Flames penalty. The increasingly incensed fans couldn't miss it - the blown call was replayed five times! "Each time, the noise grew louder and louder," P.R. man Chip Campbell recalled to the *Boston Globe*. "After the game, we apologized to Hood. We were wrong. We haven't done that since."

G.M. Max McNab wanted Capital Centre to rival Disney as the happiest place on Earth, at least as presented on Telscreen. McNab produced a no-no list of seven deadly sins, never to be replayed. They included major penalties which involved stickwork; fights and what led up to them; offside and icing calls; controversial calls; controversial non-calls; altercations in the stands; and negative banners. Obvious minor penalties were okay. (*Washington Star*)

Max's commandments had vanished from the control room by New Year's Day in 1988. A Capital Centre sellout and players from both Pittsburgh and Washington found common ground; that inexperienced referee Mike Noeth was mismanaging the game. Noeth called 29 penalties, resulting in 20 power plays. Sensitive to mounting criticism, Noeth dished out multiple unsportsmanlike conduct minors. Worse, "He ordered Capital Centre officials to stop showing replays of controversial calls." *(Pittsburgh Press)*

✪ Feeling Full

The sporting potential of Capital Centre was fully realized for the first time on April 4, 1976. That afternoon, a basketball capacity crowd of 19,035 watched the Bullets battle New Orleans. Mere hours after the end of the game – which of course went to overtime – an evening hockey sellout of 18,130 saw the Capitals host Montreal. More than 37,000 hometown fans taking in the two-sport, day-night doubleheader provided validation to Abe Pollin's vision.

✪ Bonus Capital Centre Architecture Fact

To eliminate interior pillars and provide unobstructed views for fans, the roof was designed as a saddleback; a sloping middle between two gabled ends. Technically, it's known as a reverse hyperbolic paraboloid. Really!

THE LEGENDS OF LANDOVER

✪ Low Regard

Regardie's magazine published a largely scathing - too scathing, it says here - profile of Pollin in 1990. Writer Edward Kiersh asked, "Humanitarian or double-crosser? Shifty businessman or Honest Abe?" Concerning Capital Centre:

- Local and national D.C. politicians "pressured the NHL to award Washington a franchise" because they "believed that they had an agreement with (Pollin)... to locate his arena near Chinatown."

- Some felt Pollin received unfairly generous terms to build Capital Centre in Landover. Leonard Wiser, a Maryland state delegate, termed it "a giveaway in pure disregard of the public interest."

- Some felt Pollin *again* received unfair generosity during 1982's "Save The Caps" campaign. P.G. County councilmember Sue Mills called Abe "a spoiled child. There was no way he could've moved, since he had a lease, but Abe gets what he wants because of his connections."

Kiersh amassed evidence that Pollin "masked self-interest as public service." Those two, however, aren't mutually exclusive. Abe, like every titan of industry, wasn't above twisting arms, exerting influence, and protecting his empire. Despite 8,700 words, the profile said little about Pollin's accomplishments, or his legion of admirers. The imbalance, along with Kiersh's foray into amateur psychology – unsupported analyses of Pollin's motivations – impaired the credibility of his conclusions.

✪ Just Another Caps Fan In Landover

Abe Pollin was easy to spot at home Capitals games, because he never hid out in an unapproachable Skybox. Juan Williams' *Washington Post* profile observed that many fans actually walked right past the building and team owner without recognizing him. "He sits about 20 rows up, on the aisle, slightly to the left of center ice and across from the Capitals' bench. It's the only seat he's ever had for watching the Capitals."

Abe's body language was known to mimic the typical Capitals fan. "Pollin's knee jerks up and down as he watches. The knee goes into rapid movement whenever the Caps are on offense." He also experienced the same mood swings as the ticket buyers. "During intermission, a friend of a friend comes over to introduce his little boy. Pollin offers to take the youngster to the Capitals' locker room after the game – but only if the Capitals win. 'If they lose, they don't want to see me and I don't want to see them,' he says."

THE LEGENDS OF LANDOVER

✪ Ice Ice Baby

Hockey Ice is particular. It fancies expensive machines to keep it cold. Hockey Ice hates when basketball, horse shows and circuses perform on top of it. So Hockey Ice had a frosty (actually slushy) relationship with Capital Centre. Scott Stevens said, "The ice was terrible. It's hot, you sweat more and lose more fluid. It's cooler in other rinks and easier to play."

Goalie Bernie Wolfe's palms weren't damp from anxiety. "It hit the pocket of my glove," Wolfe said about a misplayed shot from Montreal's Mario Tremblay. "My hand was sweaty from the humidity. I mean it was really hot in the place tonight. If my hand isn't so sweaty, I catch the thing. Instead, I had no grip. My hand rolled and the puck went by (into the net)."

On a 1975 visit, the Flyers cooled their heels while the ice was resurfaced. "We should have had bathing suits," said Ted Harris. Bernie Parent chimed in, "It was a good game for frogs." In 1979, Toronto coach Roger Nielson worried the thin ice "might go right down to the cement." Leafs goalie Mike Palmateer added, "I probably ruined my skates on a big patch of cement in my crease." In 1985, "Officials used ice shavings and carbon dioxide to fill a big hole in front of the Caps' bench." In 1987, "The building was hot and the ice, newly made when the Caps returned from a road trip, was covered with pools of water."

Dan Steinberg's *washingtonpost.com* "Sports Bog" got the scoop from Rod Langway. "You get the heat down here and the humidity, the ice just turns to slush," said the Hall of Famer. "We didn't have the technology and air-conditioning units that they have now. And also, how many millions did Abe (Pollin) lose before he started making money? He wasn't gonna put a new air-conditioning unit in just for ice."

(Philadelphia Daily News, Washington Post, Toronto Globe & Mail)

✪ The Cop And The Cola

Bill Brooks occupied the same ice-level seat for every Capitals home game between 1974 and 2007 – as a penalty box official. Like players, Bill worked his way up; he'd served as sin bin keeper with the AHL's Baltimore Clippers. Supervising "lockup" dovetailed nicely with Brooks' day job, as a Maryland State Trooper. He rose to the rank of captain, retiring in 1992.

A *Baltimore Sun* profile listed some of Brooks' more memorable moments. "He's had things thrown at him by players, been called names, has had to separate players and officials, and one one time had to stop (G.M. Milt) Schmidt from kicking down the officials' room door." Seeing players at their surliest didn't change Brooks' opinion that "Hockey players are some of the finest individuals you can meet."

THE LEGENDS OF LANDOVER

Some took a little time to warm up to. Bill pulled no punches when Dale Hunter became a Cap in 1987, telling him, "I don't like you." The relationship improved – after all, they shared a lot of time together – so one time, when Brooks was drinking a can of Diet Coke, Hunter asked for a swig. Soon, Brooks was stocking six-packs for Dale's frequent visits. It was private stock, too. Kevin Hatcher requested a can once, and Bill turned him down. That's not to say Brooks was immune to the needs of fellow Capitals. He once helped Michal Pivonka get out of a speeding ticket. (*Washington Post, Baltimore Sun, Legacy.com*)

✪ Road Team Broadcasters

Many sports arenas built in the 60's and '70's neglected to include hockey broadcast booths. In his book, *Hockey Play-By-Play*, Vancouver's Jim Robson described the bare-bones Capital Centre setup: "The location was a makeshift table constructed in the stands." For extra fail, Robson was forced to hold a pencil microphone for the three hours of his broadcast. Perhaps that explains Robson's snarky punchline, "Back then, fan noise in Washington was never a problem."

✪ The Guard Needed Shin Guards

As security guard for the home team locker rooms at Capital Centre, the greatest danger Joe Gensor faced was from Capitals players. "They always come up and hit me with their sticks before going on the ice," Joe related to an in-house publication. "By the time the game is over, my legs are all bruised up." More from Joe: "When the Caps would be down on their luck, Bengt (Gustafsson) would come up to me and talk for a minute or two. He'd tell me who was going to score the big goals." Joe's heartfelt reply: "I'd tell him he was crazy."

✪ Hot Seats

Figuratively, the goalies occupied the hot seats at a wild October, 1979 home victory, 8-6 over the Kings. The literal hot seats were in the center-ice rows of section 107, "where sparks flew from malfunctioning electrical equipment." (*Washington Star*) Fortunately, 13,000 alternate seats were available, with 5,386 well spread-out fans seeing rookies Mike Gartner and Bengt Gustafsson score their first NHL goals.

The hot seat isn't stationary, of course; it fairly glowed underneath goal judge Ed Pantalone with the Sabres in town on March 21, 1977. The final seconds were ticking down as Washington's Hartland Monahan fired toward the Buffalo net. Pantalone squeezed the button activating the goal light, except it was pre-empted by the green end-of-game light. Believing Pantalone had been slow on the draw, Monahan charged the goal judge's enclosure behind the net and angrily hammered the glass with his stick.

THE LEGENDS OF LANDOVER

Nearby fans shared Monahan's rage. "I had to sneak upstairs by taking a different route," Pantalone said. "There was no way that I could go up through that crowd." What made the scene more absurd was that Buffalo led by four as Hartland took his final-second shot. Had the Monahan goal counted, the Sabres would still have coasted, winning 6-3 instead of 6-2.

✪ Landover, The Final Frontier

Popular culture is filled with opposites which detract, not attract. Superman had his Bizarro world. *Star Trek* had its Mirror Universe. And for one home game in 1985, the Capitals had Reverse Benches. In their first decade, as you looked across the Capital Centre rink, the Caps occupied the bench on the left. They also entered and exited the ice through the near left corner.

By that design, they and the visiting team were forced to weave amongst each other at the start and end of periods. As benches emptied at the first intermission on March 8, 1985, it became too much to expect warring combatants from the Flyers and Capitals to politely say, "pardon me," "excuse me," "you first," on their way to the dressing rooms. Flyers broadcaster Gene Hart warned, "We have a tinderbox here." By the time the 10-minute, 40-man mosh pit dispersed, referee Andy van Hellemond had issued five game misconducts and 94 minutes in penalties.

To prevent a repeat, the Caps switched benches, penalty boxes, and offensive zones. (Players did not, however, adopt goatees like the Mirror Universe *Mr. Spock*.) This created a new complication. Fans expecting to sit at the end of the rink where Washington shot twice, suddenly weren't. So the original configurations were reinstated after one game, with the switches made permanent in future seasons.

✪ Dark Days

By the late 1990's, as the renamed US Airways Arena prepared to lose its hockey and basketball tenants, there were few kind words. One Canadian journalist wrote, "No one will miss it. It's the darkest rink in the league and located in the middle of nowhere." 21st century pro sports wisdom, including for the Capitals, is to embrace downtowns for home stadiums. Way back when, Capital Centre's isolated, rural locale was considered a feature, not a bug. "You don't have to drive downtown and that is appealing," Centre president Jerry Sachs told the *Baltimore Sun* in 1974.

Defenseman Doug Hicks, traded from Edmonton in 1982, asked of his new home, "Washington? Where's that? We had been there to play, of course, but we got off the plane and got on a bus, and I didn't even know where we were." In 1995, as ground was broken for MCI Center downtown, '70's goalie Bernie Wolfe recalled, "We've always been called the 'Washington' Capitals. But friends would call and say, 'Where's Landover?'"
(Washington Post, Toronto Globe & Mail)

THE LEGENDS OF LANDOVER

Athletes surely agreed with *Post* columnist Tony Kornheiser, who called the place a "dungeon." Kings goalie Doug Keans once said he never saw a backhand shot by Bobby Carpenter until it was in the net. "The seats here are dark blue. My defenseman played it perfectly, but I just lost it." Islanders netminder Kelly Hrudy suffered the same fate, when Michal Pivonka whacked a popup that became an E-Goalie. "I was looking in the stands and it's so black there, I couldn't see a single thing." The puck flew over Hrudy's head and into the cage. *(L.A. Times, The Hockey News)*

I read once the black interior and dim lighting was an attempt to mimic a theatre-like setting. Even Pollin eventually admitted the shroud-like atmosphere was a strategic mistake. "You almost needed a headlamp to see the puck," joked defenseman Calle Johansson. "The ice wasn't quite white. It was bluish. And the boards were slow. You wouldn't get much bounce, which meant you always had to play the puck in the corners. You had to really think at Cap Centre." (*washington.cbslocal.com*)

Famed hockey pundit Stan Fischler lamented, "The Never-Never-Land of Landover, where getting a post-game cab was tougher than flying to the moon." Mass transit wasn't available, either. The *Post's* William Gildea explained, "Pollin originally expected Metro to build a line to the arena. 'There were these dotted lines that would bring it out there,' he said." Metrorail finally made it within walking distance of Arena Drive in Landover in 2004. Too bad the Capitals - and the Arena - weren't there anymore.

✪ Big League Memories

Kornheiser came to the arena's defense at its closing. "For 24 years that building made this area big league." Exactly. I got to cheer when Dennis Maruk scored his 50th goal. I saw Wes Unseld's tip-in with 12 seconds left for the Bullets, beating the 76ers in an Eastern Conference Final. I saw Billy Joel in concert, Ringling Brothers, and even a Sci-Fi convention. The Capital Centre's existence made these events, and more, possible.

Ironically, back in 1977, the *Star's* Morris Siegel prophetically wrote, "The vision of a sports complex downtown is still bogged down by red tape. If they are really serious about getting it built, they ought to turn it over to Pollin." 20 years later, that's just what happened. Abe's new sports palace, the MCI Center, opened in 1997 at 7th and F Streets in Chinatown, signaling the end for the Centre. It was imploded in 2002.

The replacement "Capital Centre" – a shopping mall – declined and fell by 2017. To me, the name will always mean the arena with the red and blue seats. Contrary to what was said and written as it closed, *that* Capital Centre is missed for the memories contained inside, and even for the structure, affectionately referred to by my sister as "The Potato Chip."

THE LEGENDS OF LANDOVER

12th Shift: *Save The Caps!*

By 1982, owner Abe Pollin announced if monetary relief wasn't forthcoming, the Capitals would be folded, merged or moved. This is the story of events leading to a near-fatal financial crisis, and the Summer of (Hockey) Love that "Saved The Caps."

No matter how many on-ice losses the young Capitals suffered, at least the counter reset with each new season. Financial losses, of course, don't work that way. The franchise was almost killed by eight years of bleeding red ink, from wounds both self-inflicted and the result of plain lousy circumstances.

The Capitals' front office overplayed its hand before the team ever played a game. (A marketing brochure touted watching the expansion Capitals as "Group Therapy." Feel free to create your own joke.) The 30,000 who made season ticket inquiries in 1974 were given a hard sell: payment due in full, six months in advance, right at tax time.

Fewer than 25% actually followed through on purchasing season seats. Capital Centre president Jerry Sachs promised, "We didn't lie about the 30,000 requests. They were very real." Centre P.R. director Bob Zurfluh wasn't so sure, saying to the *Baltimore Sun*, "Those were not season ticket requests, but merely an expression of interest in the package. A lot of people still think we're sold out. It's been difficult to get out from that misunderstanding." Ah, the Yogi Berra excuse – "Nobody goes to Caps games anymore. It's too crowded." *The Hockey News* pointed out, "For an outfit that was generously promising that it would hold back day of game ducats for those who couldn't afford season tickets, there are some red faces."

In 1975, to counteract fan apathy, "The Washington Board of Trade organized 'Operation Support,' designed to promote season-ticket purchases by local businesses." It didn't work. The Caps' season-ticket base of 6,800 in 1974-75 shrank to 4,200 in 1975-76. *(From John Soares' essay in DC Sports: The Nation's Capital At Play.)*

✪ No Guarantees

Previewing a 1974 cellar-dweller matchup with the visiting Oakland Seals, Robert Fachet of the *Washington Post* asked this withering question: "Who in his right mind would pay $2 to park and $8.50 for a ticket to see this Tuesday night game?" Fans were asking, too. On many home dates in their first eight seasons, the Capitals played before more empty seats than paying customers. Owner Abe Pollin, the proud papa who gave birth to the Capitals, was learning how painfully expensive it is to raise a child.

THE LEGENDS OF LANDOVER

Pollin tried almost anything to goose ticket sales at his half-filled arena, including "Guaranteed Win Nights." The home game itself vs. L.A. on Nov. 5, 1975 wasn't special – just the promotion that preceded it. "Believed to be a sports first," wrote the *Pittsburgh Post Gazette*, "The Caps opened their doors for Guaranteed Win Night. It turned out to be a gamble."

The Caps fell 3-1, despite a Tommy Williams goal and a competitive effort. Someone calculated the cost of free tickets at about $69K. But the crowd of 12,527 was about 3,000 above average, so the gimmick was less of a gamble than it seemed at first glance. A week later vs. Pittsburgh, "Fans producing a stub from last Wednesday's game were admitted for free." And were rewarded. Hartland Monahan scored a hat trick plus one assist (all in the 3rd period!), and the Caps rallied from down 3-0 to earn a 6-6 tie.

Before the 1978-79 season, Pollin generated the original "Cash for Clunkers" promotion. From *AP*: "Abe Pollin offered to rebate 20 percent of the purchase price of any season ticket holder who was dissatisfied with the team's performance." Pollin, with big money riding on a winning season, inexplicably proceeded to sabotage his team. The owner caused chaos by ordering a coaching change two days before the season started. The team predictably stumbled through a 24-41-15 campaign, and didn't come close to a playoff berth.

Surprisingly, only about half of the 4,200 season ticket holders requested those refunds. With an average rebate of $56, Pollin had to return more than $100,000. The gimmick also failed to spur sales - the number of season tickets sold actually dropped by 500 from the previous year.

✪ Hard Sell, In More Ways Than One

Financial losses haunted the Capitals from the beginning. Pollin agreed to pay $6 million to join the NHL; building Capital Centre cost another $18 million. Neither the Bullets nor the Capitals packed the house – the Caps actually lowered ticket prices after their second season.

"Washington is cutting back on expenses at almost every turn," wrote Clem Kealey in a 1975 *Ottawa Journal* column. "It used to be a league rule that a team had to arrive in a city the night prior to a game whenever possible. But that's been waved as the Capitals and other NHL franchises try to put a hammerlock on galloping operating costs." As Kealey correctly noted, other teams in the '70's - Oakland, St. Louis and Pittsburgh among them - were in the same leaky boat, drowning in The Sea Of Red Ink.

The Capitals appealed to the NHL's Board of Governors, who agreed to consider deferring and reducing payments on their $6 million entry fee. In March, 1977, the league, finalized a deal to accept $2.85 million as Washington's payment in full.

THE LEGENDS OF LANDOVER

The *Canadian Press* reported that similar relief was granted to the Flames and Islanders, as well as the former Kansas City Scouts and Oakland Seals (who became the Colorado Rockies and Cleveland Barons). The NHL's economic short-sightedness was thus exposed; so weak had they rendered expansion teams by withholding players, established clubs were eventually forced to forfeit millions of dollars in fees.

✪ "Inflated Salaries And General Mismanagement"

Reviewing the NHL's widespread financial straits in the 1970's, Capitals general manager Max McNab placed the blame, well, *everywhere*. "Inflated salaries, scheduling problems and general mismanagement have all contributed to the financial trouble," McNab candidly told *Associated Press* - in remarks that ring just as true today.

About mismanagement – Washington was saddled with dead-weight multi-year contracts signed before McNab's arrival. *The Hockey News* estimated that between 1975 and 1977, the Caps paid out $2 million in salary to a dozen players who never suited up for a regular-season game.

About revenue – Capital Centre averaged 8,000 empty seats per Caps game in 1974-75. Figuring a $5 average ticket price, that's $1.6 million in potentially lost revenue, not to mention fees for parking, concessions, etc. Now, multiply all that by eight years; it goes a long way in explaining why the pocketbook often stayed closed on badly needed roster upgrades.

About salaries – the *Toronto Globe & Mail* published salaries in 1977-78 for players on all 18 teams. (Some numbers were disputed by clubs and players.) Every team except the Capitals - even financially troubled franchises in Cleveland and Colorado - had at least two players making $100,000 or more. Heck, Montreal had ten in the six-figure club, while the Bruins and Rangers had nine each. The highest paid Capital? Guy Charron, at $85,000. Lower payroll begat weaker teams in Landover, further depressing ticket sales, and perpetuating the cycle.

"Ticket prices in entertainment are a problem, whether it's the Ford Theater, Kennedy Center or Capital Centre," said Caps president Peter O'Malley to the *Mansfield News Journal*. "When you have excessive talent costs, whether the talent is Rex Harrison or the Beach Boys or Gerry Meehan, ticket prices are going to reflect it." In fairness, Rex threw a poor hip check, and Gerry wasn't exactly sure where the *Rain in Spain* falls.

Sometimes, you just have to pay up, as Dave Stubbs wrote at *nhl.com*. Goalie Bernie Wolfe "signed with the Capitals (in 1974) for $40,000 a year for two years." A $15,000 signing bonus helped fend off the WHA Houston Aeros. Named the Caps' 1976 MVP, Wolfe was "rewarded with a contract that paid him $70,000 and a new Lincoln Continental every 6,000 miles."

THE LEGENDS OF LANDOVER

✪ Barren Barons

In retrospect, the California Seals should have asked if northern Ohio cared about NHL hockey, before the Seals moved there in 1976. Not until 1978, midway through their second season, did the relocated Cleveland Barons finally commission a survey to gauge fan interest. The result was a deafening yawn. Poor on-ice play combined with Richfield Coliseum's awful location, halfway to Akron, depressed average attendance below 5,700, lowest in the league. Financial losses exceeded $3 million, and the team almost didn't finish the season.

Here's where the Capitals came in. As D'Arcy Jenish writes in *The NHL: A Centennial History*, Cleveland owners George and Gordon Gund devised a unique escape plan. "Gordon Gund called John Ziegler one day in the spring of 1978 and suggested a union of the Barons and Capitals, since the Caps had never assembled a winning or even competitive team." Gund huddled in March at Capital Centre with owner Abe Pollin, who ultimately rebuffed the overture. "I told him what we intended to do for ourselves in Washington, to build a championship hockey team," Pollin told the *Washington Star*. "And no, we would not consider any kind of merger."

Ziegler, the NHL President, instead steered the Gund brothers to the North Stars. Later that spring, Minnesota president Walter Bush huddled with George Gund at a Czechoslovakian hotel. "We signed a deal on a napkin in the beer hall of the hotel," Bush recalled. Bet they don't teach *that* in business school.

The demise of the Barons left the Capitals with an existential question: When a franchise goes *Poof*, can its draft picks live on? After all, when a public company goes out of business, stockholders don't get to cash in their shares. The NHL decided to be more charitable than Wall Street, as explained by *prosportstransactions.com*. "The league moved the Barons' first round pick to the end of the first round (#18), and then packaged in the Barons-North Stars dispersal draft. The Capitals had the #1 pick in the dispersal draft, and were given the option of selecting the first two former Barons players or exercising the Barons' first round pick. They chose the pick." The Capitals selected Tim Coulis, discussed on page 158.

But wait, there's more! Back in 1977, as part of trading Walt McKechnie to Cleveland for Bob Girard, the Capitals received the Barons' 2nd round pick. So the last business before the Barons ceased to be, was Washington using the 23rd overall selection on defenseman Paul MacKinnon. Naturally, one more disappearing act would be necessary before MacKinnon joined the Caps. Paul chose to sign and play in '78-'79 for Winnipeg of the World Hockey Association. When the year ended, the WHA itself went *Poof*, with the Jets and three other clubs absorbed by the NHL. MacKinnon's rights reverted to Washington, where he skated for parts of the next five seasons.

THE LEGENDS OF LANDOVER

✪ Disability As A Benefit

The money-conscious Caps tapped unlikely sources to recoup expenses. For instance, a serious knee injury repeatedly sidelined top draft choice Greg Joly. Player injuries like Joly's eat up a lot of cash. So in 1976, the team applied for disability benefits from the Maryland Workmen's Compensation Commission. "We pay premiums as a Maryland employer," Peter O'Malley contended. "If our employees are unable to work, we feel we should get the benefits."

According to *UPI*, the Commission rejected the claim, "On grounds that Joly received his full salary while injured." If the Caps had prevailed, they would have been entitled to $102.30 for every week of Joly's injury.

✪ The Interest Didn't Add Up

In the final weeks of the 1980 season, the Capitals began accepting deposits on a 14-game playoff ticket package. It's smart business - the interest on those deposits was welcome cash when the Caps missed the postseason. Yes, smart business; just questionable math. The Capitals couldn't have hosted more than 11 playoff games.

✪ Summer, 1982: Merge, Move Or Fold

SAVE THE CAPS The financially troubled Capitals "sought permission from the NHL in June (1982) to move the franchise," said a *Canadian Press* report, "but were turned down because they lacked a destination." So they set out to find one, in, of all places, Saskatchewan. In fact, the fate of the Capitals might have changed dramatically, except a key figure in the Canadian province left town unexpectedly. Pollin had scheduled a meeting in Saskatoon for June 30 with Canadian investors, cabinet members, and Edmonton owner Peter Pocklington. But when Premier Grant Devine was summoned to Ottawa, the meeting was postponed, and never happened.

Indifference already doomed the Caps' 1974 expansion twins from Kansas City. When K.C.'s Scouts relocated to Denver after two years, the misery went with them; the new Colorado Rockies went through three ownership groups in six years. With bills piling up a Mile High, "The Rockies are exploring a merger with the Capitals." So reported *The New York Times* on New Year's Day in 1982. However, nomadic Rockies never reached Landover. The team was sold once again and moved to New Jersey.

Amazingly, this didn't end the mating dance between the franchises. Just months after the Rockies offered to dissolve into the Capitals, Washington owner Abe Pollin announced his own team had suffered a $3.5 million loss the prior season – and more than $20 million since their 1974 inception.

THE LEGENDS OF LANDOVER

By August, the *Times* indicated, "If the Capitals fail to win tax relief, the alternative would likely be a merger in which they would be absorbed by the Devils. Negotiations for such a merger... have been under way for several weeks." *The Hockey News* later revealed that Pollin himself had leaked the story. P.G. county council member Sue Mills, herself a former Caps season seat holder, opposed tax givebacks. "The hockey team is like any other failing business," she said to the *Baltimore Sun*. "What are we supposed to say to other county businesses that are struggling to survive?"

John McMullen, the Devils' principal owner, said, "We will definitely make the deal if Abe Pollin doesn't get what he needs." More from the *Times*: "McMullen met with Pollin in Toronto at a meeting of National Hockey League owners and several times since then." In lieu of a merger, Pollin announced the team might still be sold and moved, or folded.

Mere months earlier, the owner had promised his hockey team was staying put at least through the new millennia. Pollin's about-face remained a mystery, since – and this was an oft-repeated criticism of Pollin at times of bad news – he turned silent. As Bob Fachet deduced in *The Hockey News*, "Pollin was fooled by announced attendance figures, because of freebies and discount plans." Averaging 11,000+ at Caps games in '81-'82, ticket sales should have exceeded $4 million, when in reality, the gross failed to reach $3 million.

✪ Lights, Camera, Beg

SAVE THE CAPS Approaching August, 1982, 2,152 renewed Caps season tickets; 523 new subscribers had signed on. Evel Knievel couldn't jump the gaping chasm between those numbers and the 7,500 target Pollin was demanding. So they put on a show.

A stage was set up at Capital Centre for the "Save The Caps" broadcast, with WRC-TV sports anchor George Michael doing the Jerry Lewis bit, tuxedo and all. George was flanked by rows of volunteers waiting to take season ticket orders. If you imagine all the spine-tingling action of a PBS pledge drive, you're not far off. Shirtsleeved owner Abe Pollin pitched viewers, "We have a bank of 20 phones. So call 441-CAPS."

Redskins coach George Allen redeemed himself for his earlier sabotage of the team, showing up to support the ticket drive. "I was telling Abe," Allen shared, "Wouldn't it be something, one way to motivate this city, is to say that Dallas is interested in getting the Washington Capitals." Bullets great Wes Unseld and several Caps players also made live appearances. Taped hockey segments played throughout the show, including a *Do Not Adjust Your Set* moment: Flyer tough guy Paul Holmgren taking a stand for his Patrick Division rival. "Ice hockey belongs in the Nation's Capital. So pick up your phone and call." Behind a mischievous smile, Holmgren added, "And you thought I wasn't a nice guy."

THE LEGENDS OF LANDOVER

✪ Owner vs. Columnists

SAVE THE CAPS Up until "Save The Caps," *Washington Post* sports columnists Dave Kindred and Ken Denlinger waged a war of *No* words with the Capitals (detailed on page 189). When owner Abe Pollin claimed empty pockets, though, the pair churned out multiple columns written with acid pens.

Kindred objected, "It's hard to work up sympathy for a multi-millionaire banging on a tin cup to save a business selling a miserable product." He dubbed the ticket drive, "Save The Caps From Themselves," adding, "I don't agree with our editorialists, who believe hockey is vital to the dynamics of life in this city." Denlinger proclaimed, "If ever a gang merited burial, it's the Capitals," declaring them Pollin's "Eight year folly."

Bob Fachet, writing for *The Hockey News*, summarized the stance of his *Post* colleagues. "They did speculate, as did others, that Pollin had no intention other than to operate this season, and was using the four-point campaign to fill seats that would otherwise be vacant." Fachet also made note of the *Post's* business page, which described the campaign as a "boondoggle," vs. its editorial page, which championed the franchise as a community asset.

Pollin responded with a full page ad in the *Post*, blasting Kindred and Denlinger. "I have spent a lifetime in this community building a reputation for honesty and fair play that I will not allow you to attempt to destroy with your inaccuracies, your half-truths, and your slanted brand of journalism."

✪ Save Situation

SAVE THE CAPS Washington was all too familiar with fleeing franchises. The baseball Senators bolted for Minnesota in 1960, and the expansion Senators escaped to Texas in 1971. A fan-based grassroots effort, "Save The Caps," used those heartbreaks to expand their outreach. "One of our most successful tactics," explained organizer Steve Mehlman, "was to remind baseball fans that their hopes of getting another baseball team in D.C. would be dashed if the city were to lose yet another major league sports team. As a result, even non-hockey fans joined our campaign." (*sacbee.com*)

Abe Pollin lauded the Save The Caps Committee. "These people have worked tirelessly, giving of their time and money to prove to me that they want to keep the team in Washington." Pollin had come close to giving up, he revealed to the *Baltimore Sun*, until "all the feverish activity gave me new hope." Hope became results – Prince George's County granted the tax reduction, businesses & individuals shelled out for tickets, and the Capitals stayed put. In baseball parlance, Mehlman and friends had earned the save. Though from then on, Abe had a *Rockie* relationship with fans.

THE LEGENDS OF LANDOVER

✪ Facts & Figures Behind "Save The Caps"

SAVE THE CAPS Compiled in part by Dave McKenna of the *Washington City Paper.*

• Three of Pollin's demands for keeping the Caps in Landover - 10 sellouts, tax breaks, lower rent - were met. The 4th threshold, a season-ticket base of 7,500, fell two or three thousand short, but was judged "close enough." The bottom line: four new investors were sufficiently impressed to commit an infusion of badly-needed cash.

• One of those four, Dick Patrick of hockey's famous Patrick clan, was installed as executive V.P. Three years later he was bumped up to team president, a title he holds to this day. In 2018 he became the sixth Patrick family member to have his name inscribed on the Stanley Cup.

• As noted, channel 4 aired a ticket-selling telethon.

• The local Special Olympics chapter used contributions to buy tickets.

• Area businesses guaranteed sellouts for the first dozen Capitals home games, by agreeing to buy all unsold tickets.

• One of the businesses that signed up to guarantee a sellout, over Dave Kindred's objection, was the *Washington Post*.

• Organizer Steve Mehlman and "a volunteer posse worked phone banks at the Capital Centre from 9 a.m. to 10 p.m. every day to sell tickets."

• Pollin was willing to sell the team for $7.5 million. Put another way, just a smidge more than winger Alexander Semin's 2011 contract.

• If sold, they could have remained the "Washington" Capitals, because potential landing spots included Seattle Center and the Tacoma Dome.

✪ Abe Pollin (Owner, 1974-99)

Abe Pollin will be remembered as a giant in all the ways that matter: devoted husband and father, successful businessman, tireless charitable giver, and force behind two privately financed arenas, at times and in places they were desperately needed.

His legacy as a sports owner, especially in hockey, is less pristine. A kernel of truth – sometimes more – exists in criticism of Pollin as owner of the Capitals from 1974-1999. The gripes: that the Caps were a neglected stepchild to their basketball and arena siblings; Pollin didn't spend enough; Capital Centre's bad ice and bad location hamstrung the team and turned off free agents; threatening to move the team in 1982 was a power play.

THE LEGENDS OF LANDOVER

Pollin didn't pretend to have deep roots in the sport. As Robert Fachet revealed in the *Post*, "The Capitals owner never has been on skates." Up until 1974, he'd never even seen a hockey game, according to author David Smale.

Claiming Pollin shorted his hockey team ignored the disperate financial needs of NHL and NBA franchises. "You have to plan for the injury factor in hockey," Capitals G.M. Max McNab explained. "We have 40 players under contract." NHL farm systems add a seven-figure expense not incurred by the NBA. "Basketball gets players from college. Teams in our league budget $1.5 million to $3 million for player development." A 1981 *Washington Star* analysis showed, "The Caps' payroll is almost twice as much as the Bullets. Travel costs are double, and equipment expenses almost triple." Hockey TV revenue for U.S.-based teams was virtually nil.

The NBA was Abe's first and enduring sports passion. But he clearly grew to love his hockey team, too. While on vacation, he'd call home long-distance to get the hockey scores. And there's this basic truth: without Pollin, there'd be no NHL team in town to begin with. He had the players' backs, like a 1987 locker room visit following a tough road trip. "Mr. Pollin told us he's been an owner for a long time and seen a lot of ups and downs," said goalie Pete Peeters. "He told us to be proud of our uniforms, and to play our best for the organization and fans. It was inspirational." Apparently so; the Caps fired the first 12 shots in a 4-2 win over Toronto.

Don't blame him for building Capital Centre in Landover. The NHL awarded him a franchise on the condition he'd provide a place to play. The District couldn't, so Pollin deferred his dream of a downtown arena. You *can* blame Abe for claiming the Centre was still a "premier" building as late as 1993.

Capitals President Dick Patrick admitted to the *Washington Post* that front-office mistakes, such as declining to re-sign free agent defenseman Scott Stevens in 1990, "Made some fans think we're not committed to winning." Stevens would be enshrined in the Hall of Fame, leading the N.J. Devils to three Stanley Cups. That's the ultimate sports metric: championships. Pollin's Caps didn't win any. Given their regular-season success during the 1980's, though, blame for the Cup drought seems to belong more with the players and hockey management.

Owners have one other "ultimate" metric: profitability. Pollin acknowledged to the *Post* that the Caps represented "the major failure of my business career." Sports accounting is so tangled, it's impossible to know for sure how much pain the Caps actually caused Abe's sports empire. Documents from a lawsuit revealed that through June, 1984, Capital Centre had gross profits of $21.7 million, while the hockey team incurred losses of $22.8 million. The same suit showed the Centre repeatedly "loaned" money to keep the Caps from falling into default.

THE LEGENDS OF LANDOVER

If so, how much more should he have sunk into the team? Pollin didn't have the deep pockets of corporate-owned competitors. Even after the Capitals became a winner on the ice, revenue from gate receipts lagged. The *Toronto Globe & Mail* reported that the Caps ranked 19th of 21 NHL teams in gate revenue for the '83-'84 season.

1983-84 Gate Receipts (In Millions)

#	Team	$	#	Team	$	#	Team	$
1	CGY	$11.0	8	MON	$ 7.5	15	HAR	$ 6.0
2	EDM	$10.4	9	QUE	$ 7.4	16	BUF	$ 5.2
3	NYI	$ 9.0	10	NJD	$ 7.4	17	DET	$ 5.1
4	NYR	$ 8.9	11	MIN	$ 6.9	18	STL	$ 4.8
5	VAN	$ 7.7	12	BOS	$ 6.7	19	WAS	$ 4.4
6	CHI	$ 7.6	13	PHI	$ 6.6	20	LAK	$ 4.2
7	TOR	$ 7.6	14	WPG	$ 6.4	21	PGH	$ 2.1

When Pollin threatened to sell or move the team in 1982 due to financial hardship, the "Save the Caps" campaign felt unseemly, bush league, even a bald example of corporate welfare. Still, the landscape is littered with teams that pulled up stakes without giving fans and businesses a shot to keep them. Plus, the Caps' payroll did escalate into the league's top 10.

One almost-sale was in 1994. A deal between Pollin and a partner in baseball's Texas Rangers all but crossed the financial goal line. Five years later, when Pollin did sell to Ted Leonsis, he again almost backed out at the last minute. Pollin had many previous chances to sell, and didn't - probably the best indication the team was more than a business property to him.

Washington Star columnist Morris Siegel cut to the chase, writing in 1980: "Without Pollin's guts, money and faith in Washington, the nation's capital would occupy the same importance on a sports map as Green Bay, Wis. and Foxboro, Mass. They also have professional football but nothing else in the world of pro sports."

✪ "This Is No Bluff"

The Capitals balance sheet improved by $2.3 million in the 1983 fiscal year; which is to say, the team only *lost* $1.2 million. That autumn, the prospect of moving vans in Landover re-emerged.

The P.G. County Council made noises about repealing Pollin's tax break made 17 months earlier, so the owner threatened a relocation to Northern Virginia. Pollin went so far as to meet with Virginia investors about building a new arena. The threat seemed hollow – Abe still owned Capital Centre, and without the Caps and Bullets, how could the building turn a profit? But Pollin explained, "At this point it's a matter of honor. This is no bluff."

THE LEGENDS OF LANDOVER

The issue was finally laid to rest once and for all at a November 30, 1983 council meeting. By a 5-4 vote, the bill to restore a 10 percent amusement tax was "postponed indefinitely." *AP* reported that after leaving the session, "Capitals owner Abe Pollin smiled and headed back to his office to work on winning hockey and basketball games."

✪ Marooned Maruk

According to the *City Paper*, the fan-inspired "Save The Caps" campaign was hatched inside "Maruk's," an Alexandria, Virginia restaurant named for high-scoring Caps center Dennis Maruk. That the Capitals ultimately stayed put had to be a relief to Maruk.

See, Dennis began his NHL career with the California Seals in 1975. A year later, the franchise left Oakland and Maruk became a Cleveland Baron. Two years after that, the Barons folded. Maruk was dispersed to the Minnesota North Stars in the merger of the two teams. Soon after, on an October afternoon in 1978, Maruk got word he'd been dealt to the Caps.

Literally minutes later, his wife completed a 760-mile drive from their old Cleveland home to what they thought was going to be their new one in Minneapolis. As Maruk related in his autobiography, an athlete's nomadic existence also wears on their family. "My wife pulled into the driveway, excited and ready to start her new life," Dennis wrote. "I greeted her with, 'I just got traded.'" Joni Maruk recalled, "I can remember the G.M. (Max McNab) calling me and welcoming me to Washington, and I believe I burst into tears."

Four years into his D.C. term, the Caps almost went belly up. Dennis must have wondered how he'd offended the hockey gods. Just one season later, Maruk was on the move again, traded back to Minnesota. Fortunately, he was four years into retirement when the Stars franchise relocated to Dallas... meaning three of the four NHL teams Maruk played for *no longer exist!* Oh, and "Maruk's" restaurant? Yep, out of business within a year.

✪ The Last Word

Regardless of record or decade, selling Capitals hockey to the D.C. metropolitan area confronts a unique obstacle: so many of its residents come from somewhere else. The first-year season ticket base of 6,800 wasn't topped for a dozen years. Gary Loewen of the *Toronto Globe & Mail* wrote about the challenges in 1988. Loewen noted that in the six playoff years since 1982, season ticket sales had increased from 3,000 to 8,000. "It's an endless battle to keep those fans, however. The population is ever-changing because of the transient military presence, and because the political stage changes every four years. As a result, the Caps find that they must keep educating a new batch of spectators."

THE LEGENDS OF LANDOVER

David Poile, Capitals general manager, specified, "We have an attrition base of about 10 percent. We have to sell 15 percent more just to go up a step each year. We have the best, and I'm sure the biggest, marketing staff in the league."

The bottom line: four seasons after "Save The Caps," average attendance swelled north of 14,000. Full-price tickets, too, not the discount and free passes of previous years. A watershed was reached for a February, 1986 home game vs. the Oilers, when full and partial season ticket owners snapped up all 18,130 seats.

Owner Abe Pollin reflected on the skepticism he himself felt back in the summer of 1982. "Three or four years ago, if somebody had told me the paid attendance we'd projected for this year, I'd have said they were nuts." He made one more admission. "Basketball was always my first love and I knew little about hockey. I now like hockey as much as basketball." (*Washington Post, The Hockey News*)

THIRD PERIOD:
Capital Gains

The Capitals' First Playoff Era (1982-1990)

THE LEGENDS OF LANDOVER

13th Shift: *Montreal Seasoning*

Capital Centre president Jerry Sachs in 1975 pinpointed the root cause of lagging ticket sales. With the expansion Caps flailing, Sachs said to the *Baltimore Sun*, "It would help if we were a better team." Okay, not genius, but undeniably true; winning has always been the only sustainable method of moving tickets. The summer 1982 trade that brought Rod Langway, Brian Engblom, Doug Jarvis and Craig Laughlin from Montreal made the team a perennial playoff contender. That's what *really* Saved The Caps.

Newly-hired Caps general manager David Poile sparked the Montreal Four transaction. "I went to the Board of Governors meeting in Toronto because nobody was going from the Capitals," Poile recalled to *nhl.com*. "I said, 'That's important. That's a power position.' I walked into the room at age 32 scared to death and I sat down next to (Montreal G.M.) Irving Grundman."

Al Strachen of the *Toronto Globe & Mail* continues the story. "Poile heard that Larry Robinson and Guy Lafleur were dissatisfied with their contracts. Poile approached Grundman with an eye toward taking Robinson and Lafleur off Grundman's hands." As negotiations progressed, new players entered the discussion. So did agent Norm Caplan, who helped barter the six-man swap. "All the players involved were Caplan's clients. He arranged the deal, presented it to the general managers, and they accepted it."

Poile, at considerable professional risk, parted with defenseman Rick Green and center Ryan Walter. "I knew Ryan was Mr. Capitals, the captain and the leader," Poile said. "But I also knew that it was a deal which would tremendously improve our hockey club. I had to be objective and that's why we were able to consummate the deal." *(AP)* Walter was also Abe Pollin's favorite player. More than a decade later, a picture of Walter still occupied a wall in Pollin's office. "I said we've traded Ryan Walter," Poile told *nhl.com*, "and (Pollin) yelled back on the phone, 'You did what?' So I told him again, and he just said, 'Well, you better know what you're doing.'"

Remember the movie *Network*? The news anchor exhorts viewers to shout into their streets, "I'm not going to take it anymore!" After hanging up with Pollin, Poile had his own *Howard Beale* moment. He opened the window of his Toronto hotel and yelled out his boss' admonishment, "You better know what you're doing!"

One of the first outsiders to learn about the blockbuster was North Stars G.M. Lou Nanne. Shooting the breeze over the phone, Poile revealed, "I just traded for Rod Langway." Elliott Friedman of *Sportsnet* told what happened next. "Poile couldn't even say the rest of the names before Nanne yelled, 'What?! I gotta make a call!' and hung up on his buddy. 'I was going to call Montreal and make a better offer,' Nanne said."

THE LEGENDS OF LANDOVER

✪ Trade Talk

• "David Poile was as happy as a child swimming in a vat of chocolate… Imagine – a Washington G.M. leaving skate marks across the backs of the Canadiens!" (Bill Fleishman, *Philadelphia Daily News*)

• David Poile was having a hard time hiding a grin, stifling a gloat. He looked like the cat that swallowed the canary… fleecing Montreal… (for) a pittance, according to what the Caps got." (Rod Beaton, *USA Today*)

• "The feeling around the league was that Montreal's managing director, Irving Grundman, had his pocket picked." (E.M. Swift, *Sports Illustrated*)

• Grundman has established himself as a businessman, not a hockey man… It was Grundman who put together that disastrous trade." (Al Strachen, *Toronto Globe & Mail*)

• "It has not been uncommon for Washington players to complain, win or lose, about missing assists, plus-minus rulings, or even shots on goal. That self-serving foolishness is a thing of the past." (Robert Fachet, *Wash. Post*)

• "The Canadiens gave away too much for what they received. Far too much… Has the Canadiens' organization retrogressed to the point where it now must deal from weakness with a team which hasn't made the playoffs since entering the league in 1974?" (Red Fisher, *Montreal Gazette*)

• "At first, second, and third glance, the Montreal Canadiens were taken in their first major trade in ten years… No one can understand how the Canadiens could give up one of the best defensive pairs in the NHL." (Glenn Cole, *Hockey News*)

As Cole noted, parting with both Langway and Engblom didn't add up. While plus-minus has been devalued as a hockey analytic, consider that in the just-concluded 1981-82 season, only three players recorded a "plus" number equaling their games played. Unsurprisingly, one was Wayne Gretzky (80 games, +80). The other two were Engblom (76 games, +78) and Langway (66 games, +66). Rod himself went on the record about which team won the transaction: "Washington got a great deal."

✪ Not Just Another Hockey City

Langway and teammates were raised in the hockey hotbed of Montreal, with fanatical following and championship pedigree. It was a culture shock to find out the facilities and fan base in D.C. weren't in the same league. As Rod reminisced in a *WTEM Radio* interview, "I came in thinking this would be just another hockey city, but it was a Redskins city. I think we had a base of seven or eight thousand people. It was an eye-opener."

THE LEGENDS OF LANDOVER

Langway continued, "The facilities, the rink itself, I hate to say it, was really third-class compared to other teams. David Poile sat down with us and said, 'We're going to change the atmosphere, and the first thing we have to do is win on the ice. Everything else will take care of itself.' True enough. It became a first-class organization, and we won on the ice, also."

DEC. 23, 1982 — WAS 5 NYI 1 — UNIONDALE, NY

It's hard to overstate the magnitude of the Capitals' turnaround in 1982-83. Even NHL royalty couldn't believe it was the same franchise.

The Capitals' first 19 visits to Nassau Coliseum were ugly — 18 losses and one tie. Most of the games weren't competitive; a dozen times the Islanders scored five or more goals, eight times the Caps scored just once, and only four of the 18 losses were by as little as a one-goal margin. "It doesn't matter what happened in the past," said defenseman Brian Engblom, one of four Canadien transplants, as the new-look Caps ventured for the 20th time to Uniondale, N.Y. "We were really psyched," winger Mike Gartner would say later about facing the three-time defending champions. Why not? The Caps were riding a 13-game unbeaten streak.

That ride was a steamroller, and the Islanders got flattened. Dennis Maruk and Gartner scored before the game was four minutes old, the Caps fired 38 shots, and their forecheck pestered New York to distraction. After the 5-1 demolition, players and management alike noted its significance. "Everyone gets up for the defending champions," said Capitals G.M. David Poile. "Our dressing room was the most excited and happy of any win. They're still the best, and everyone wants to beat the best."

Added Gartner, who finished with two goals and an assist, "We realized how important this game was to our development. We've been down on the bottom for so long, just looking up, it's tough to think we're really up there." The win was Washington's ninth, plus five ties, in a now league-high 14 game unbeaten streak.

The despair – and sarcasm – was heavy in the home locker room. "Talking to them is like talking to a block of cement," said Islanders coach Al Arbour. "They outplayed us, outworked us, beat us to the puck, beat us in every department. They made us look like a last place hockey team, and our players accepted it gracefully." *(AP)*

Not *that* gracefully. From the *New York Times* game story: "With 29 seconds remaining, (Bob) Nystrom got into a tussle with Scott Stevens and appeared to have kicked him in the groin." Perhaps that was on Nystrom's mind after the game when he said, "We have to analyze ourselves." Good idea, Bob.

THE LEGENDS OF LANDOVER

✪ Turning Hab-Nots Into Habs

As much as talent, Langway & Co. brought a badly-needed injection of winner's swagger. "After one early loss," wrote *Sports Illustrated's* E.M. Swift, "the ordinarily quiet (Doug) Jarvis stood at his locker screaming about the value of team play." Jarvis knew his message was resonating when the Caps put together the 14-game unbeaten streak. "At the start of the year, the feeling in this room was very tentative," Jarvis said. "We went on that streak and, especially among the younger guys, confidence became very evident. They began to feel they could compete with anyone."

Mike Gartner quickly became a believer. "The guys we got from Montreal brought a winning attitude." Washington finished 39-25-16 for 94 points, 8th best in the league, and earned their first playoff berth. "It was the Montreal influence that ultimately pulled us through," Poile confirmed to *Sports Illustrated*. The Caps allowed 286 goals against, 5th best, and Rod Langway won the Norris Trophy as the NHL's top defenseman. Compared with the previous season, wins improved by 13, standings points by 29, and goals against fell by 55. Simply put, the franchise would never be the same.

✪ Trading Stars & Stripes For Bleu, Blanc And Rouge

What of the pair headed to Montreal? Rick Green and Ryan Walter helped the Canadiens win the 1986 Stanley Cup, so that's the short answer. Even so, Walter built deep roots in D.C. He told *nhl.com* after retiring, "I would have loved to stay in Washington for my whole career." Green wasn't as wistful. He'd suffered six years of losing, compared with Walter's four – as well as unrealistic demands placed on 1976's #1 overall draft pick. On trade day, Green told the *Montreal Gazette*, "I'm just glad to be getting out of here and with a winner. I view it as a promotion."

✪ The Best Trades The Caps Never Made, Part 1

Every team in the NHL had a crack at Rod Langway in the 1977 amateur draft; some had multiple cracks, because Montreal didn't snag him until the very last pick of the second round, number 36 overall. If you believe then-Boston coach Don Cherry – and I'm not certain you should – Bruins' brass rejected his advice to take Langway at #34, two spots ahead of the Canadiens. (Cherry made this claim on Twitter a mere 37 years later.)

Post-trade, one more surprising headline, from the *Montreal Gazette*: "Bruins Eyeing Langway." Rod grew up a half-hour ride from the Boston Garden, and the Bruins had been trying to pry the big defenseman away from Montreal for years. General manager Harry Sinden never succeeded with his archrival, but thought he might sweet-talk the still wet behind the ears Capitals G.M. Fortunately, David Poile stood firm, securing Langway's place as the vanguard of the Caps' bruising backline through the 1980's.

THE LEGENDS OF LANDOVER

✪ The Best Trades The Caps Never Made, Part 2

Everyone knows the Montreal Four trade between the Capitals and Canadiens in 1982. Forgotten is that the two teams discussed a different big deal just months earlier. Roger Crozier was the Caps' acting general manager at the time, early in the 1981-82 season. According to the *Gazette*, Crozier dangled his 1st round draft choice. In return, Crozier wanted two of Montreal's front-line players.

Sources named forward Doug Wickenheiser as one of those players. A former top draft pick himself, Wickenheiser suffered a tough rookie season under the glare of Montreal media and fans. Crozier was also interested in re-acquiring former Caps defenseman Robert Picard. Of course, the trade never happened. Wickenheiser finally arrived in Washington in 1989, where he scored the final three goals of his decade-long career. (At a bargain-basement salary, too: $25,000, plus $1,000 for each of the 27 NHL games he played in 1989-90.)

Keeping that 1982 first round draft pick proved wise, and so did the player Crozier selected: defenseman and future Hall-of-Famer Scott Stevens. A promise not to select Phil Housley as part of a larger trade with Buffalo helped land winger Alan Haworth and rights to acquire center Milan Novy. Roger's remarkable draft day haul also included a trade with Calgary for goalie Pat Riggin and forward Ken Houston. Stevens, Haworth, Novy, Riggin and Houston represented five players who would dress on the Caps' opening-night lineup.

Crozier would pay a high price for a trade later in the summer of '82. Not because of the players; winger Ted Bulley coming to Washington from Chicago for two draft picks didn't significantly impact either club. Roger's mistake was disobeying the boss. Owner Abe Pollin had ordered a trade embargo to avoid added payroll, an obstacle if the team was to be moved, merged or folded.

While Pollin retained the Capitals, he didn't retain Crozier, according to *AP*, because Roger ignored the directive. "I wasn't prepared to run upstairs every time a decision had to be made," Crozier told the *Toronto Globe & Mail*. "I did both jobs (general manager and assistant) for my old salary. I thought justice would be served, but it never was."

However, it wasn't clear how much justice Roger had shown the previous regime. *The Hockey News* indicated Crozier had been angling for the G.M. job while Max McNab was still his boss. Crozier tagged along on a road trip and *THN* speculated, "There was reason to believe that he had reported back to (Owner Abe) Pollin on the team's problems."

THE LEGENDS OF LANDOVER

APR. 4, 1982 | **MON 1 WAS 3** | **LANDOVER, MD**

Let's push rewind for a moment to the prior season's final regular season game, which just happened to match the Capitals and Canadiens. The finale was actually, in retrospect, a "prequel." No one at Capital Centre imagined they were watching six key players destined to swap uniforms over the summer.

Washington was playing out the string, having missed the playoffs for an eighth consecutive season. Montreal appeared to be flying high, concluding a 109-point campaign. Early in the second period though, star Habs defenseman Brian Engblom took a penalty, and the Caps scored. Ten minutes later, up-and-coming Habs defenseman Rod Langway took a penalty, and the Caps scored again for a 2-0 lead. This is probably *not* why the coveted pair were sent to Washington.

The next day's *Washington Post* published two game photos; one, of Montreal winger Craig Laughlin in a race with Washington's Bobby Carpenter. Craig, of course, was about to join Engblom, Langway, and Doug Jarvis in Landover. The other photo showed a board battle between Engblom and Ryan Walter, playing for the final time as Caps' captain before being shipped with Rick Green to the Canadiens.

If screenwriters had created Bryan Murray's "prequel" dialogue, it would be considered foreshadowing. Addressing the talent gap facing the Capitals, coach Murray noted, "We still have to get four or five hockey players. How we do it, or if we can do it, I don't know." Now we know Bryan and 12,753 Caps fans had just viewed the four players who would energize his lineup in the fall.

As long as we're time-traveling, consider the role another future Cap played in forcing Montreal's hand. Quebec's Dale Hunter scored an overtime goal in the deciding game of the Canadiens' opening round playoff series. The shocking early knockout led Montreal to decide a major personnel shakeup was necessary. Thanks, Dale!

✪ Taxing Relationship

Before the trade, Rod Langway threatened to retire over heavy federal and provincial Canadian taxes. G.M. Irving Grundman took that personally. "The Canadiens weren't built by keeping players that didn't want to play for them." Langway felt management had overreacted. "I wanted to renew my (Montreal) contract in U.S. dollars. I never expected to be traded. It was a shock."

THE LEGENDS OF LANDOVER

Rod hadn't forgotten the messy breakup as he accepted his first Norris Trophy. "I would especially like to thank Irving Grundman," Langway said at the awards ceremony. "Without his trading me, winning this award would never have been possible." *(UPI, Montreal Gazette)*

Langway's dig was mild compared to what Glenn Cole wrote in *The Hockey News*. "The Washington deal is the worst in team history... unforgettable and unforgiveable." The Canadiens agreed; Grundman (and his son) were let go at season's end.

✪ Bitter Coffey

Rod Langway won his second consecutive Norris Trophy in 1984, to the chagrin of Oilers defenseman Paul Coffey. "The petulant Coffey," Stan Fischler wrote in *Hockey Digest*, "considered staying home rather than accept the NHL's invitation to the league's awards fete." Paul groused "how hockey writers slighted him in voting," by overlooking his 40 goal, 86 assist season, plus Edmonton winning the Stanley Cup. Fischler wasn't buying, judging the comparison a choice between "Filet Mignon" (Langway) and "Lemon Ice" (Coffey). "Langway is a Leader with a capital L. Coffey's leadership qualities would fit on a needle point."

A sampling of league voices unanimously, and on the record, backed Stan. Bruins d-man Mike Milbury: "Langway (is) more of a team player with a lot more character." Devils goalie Chico Resch: "Langway has done so much for the Capitals." Blues coach Jacque Demers: "Rod plays from 35 to 40 minutes a game. He's the key to the blue line." Flames G.M. Cliff Fletcher: "Langway is the soundest defenseman in the league." North Stars coach Bill Mahoney: "Langway is the best because of his complete domination." Rangers d-man Tom Laidlaw: "Langway (is) a better all-around player."

To summarize: Coffey won his *Cup*, and Gretzky certainly wasn't a *grinder*, so Coffey had no *grounds* to complain. But because Coffey possessed a *perfect shot*, he worked himself into a *froth*. Instead of acting like a *drip*, Coffey needed to *filter* his comments. Trouble was *brewing* when Coffey stirred the *pot*, but he didn't know *beans*. Coffey was *roasted* by hockey people who knew *cream* rises to the top. Mr. Coffey, *percolate* on that.

(I apologize to everyone reading this, and will switch immediately to *decaf*.)

✪ Rick & Rod, Together Again For The First Time

Following the trade, Rod Langway played the rest of his NHL career in Washington; Rick Green played in Montreal through the 1988-89 season. Not many people realize they played two games together as teammates in February, 1987. What's more, they were paired on defense. What's more-more, they drew rave reviews.

THE LEGENDS OF LANDOVER

The event was "Rendez-Vous '87" in Quebec, a two-game series between NHL stars and the Soviet national team. Green wore the number 5 which both players used. Langway switched to number 4, while serving as an alternate captain.

"Playing the man and not the puck is vital against the Soviets," said Langway. "They pass so crisply and skate so fast that before you know it, they can blow right by you." Langway treated Rendez-Vous '87 with such respect, he was planning on paying to see the games if he hadn't been selected to participate.

Wayne Gretzky rejected critics who predicted Rick and Rod couldn't keep up with the fleet Soviets. "Some people say they're big and slow, but I say they're big and smart." Said Green, "I didn't know we'd be playing together until the first shift. He's fun to play with. I didn't have to worry about him being caught up the ice." The NHL and Russian squads each picked up one victory, and the Langway-Green duo won high marks. Capitals general manager David Poile noted, "They're a throwback to old-time hockey, the old, better-to-be-safe theory. It's a successful style." Team NHL goalie Grant Fuhr added, "Langway was the perfect defenseman, a stay-at home defenseman. He made my job easier." (Sources: *AP, Sporting News*)

THE LEGENDS OF LANDOVER

14th Shift: *The Playoff '80s*
Skaters

✪ **Gaetan Duchesne (1981-87)**

"Gaetan was as honest as the day is long." Admiring words from Capitals general manager David Poile about Gaetan Duchesne. The defensive specialist played 1,028 NHL games, which works out to 1,028 more than anyone expected when he was drafted in the 8th round by Washington in 1981. The 19-year-old, French-speaking Duchesne was a surprise addition to the roster for the '81-'82 season. "All he could say was, 'Muda, fada,' – he couldn't wait to find a phone to call his parents," said his first Caps coach, Gary Green.

Mom was listening in Gaetan's hometown of Quebec City when the rookie scored to help beat Montreal for only the second time in 41 tries. "Last year I see the Canadiens and Nordiques on television and now I'm on the ice," said Duchesne. "And the best is that my mother got a radio and can listen to the games." Mother Duchesne was picking up *WTOP's* 50,000-watt signal. She once implored broadcaster Ron Weber, "I wish you would speak in French, but if you must speak English, please go slower, so I can understand you." (*The Hockey News*)

Duchesne's mature-beyond-his-years play was turning heads. "Picking someone like that in the eighth round is like reaching in your pocket for a dollar bill and finding a hundred," said Whalers owner Howard Baldwin. Another New England observer gushed, "That kid's only 19?" Yes he was, Bobby Orr, thanks for asking. (*Baldwin, Orr quotes from The Hockey News*)

Duchesne blossomed the following season, when coach Bryan Murray created a checking threesome with Bob Gould and Glen Currie. Since the linemates all had a name starting with "G", they were dubbed the "Gee Whiz" line. "Gates is good getting the puck out of our end and he's an excellent forechecker," Gould said. Another teammate, Craig Laughlin, recalled his skating style. "He would get so low and battle and compete." Coach Murray noticed his players noticing Gaetan. "He's a good worker and he really seems to inspire our team with his efforts. A coach can't ask for more from a player."

The Gee Whiz line contributed timely scoring in 1982-83; all three of Duchesne's goals in the season's first 17 games were game-winners. In the final 89 seconds of a December victory over Pittsburgh, Duchesne broke a 1-1 tie on coach's orders. "Bryan Murray says the Currie line is next and tells us to get a goal, so we go out and get one," said Gaetan.

THE LEGENDS OF LANDOVER

Ten days later, all three Gee Whiz linemates scored in the third period to beat Pittsburgh once more, 6-3. Gaetan's goal came late, with the Pens' goalie pulled; defending deep in his own zone, he was rewarded with a fortunate bounce. "Duchesne fell in front of a shot and lay there as it caromed from his ribs and slid the length of the ice into the net." (*Pittsburgh Press*) "I wish I could tell you I practiced that," Gaetan joked.

His luck against a vacated cage apparently had limits. "I remember coming in on a breakaway," Duchesne recalled. "The goalie was way out of the net, but just as I shot, my blade broke and the puck went wide." Years later, Craig Laughlin added, "Bobby Gould and I were remembering how hard we were laughing on the bench."

Gaetan also spread joy playing Santa at the team's family Christmas party, which fits because he always made time for kids. "Every time a kid asks me for an autograph, I remember when I was his age, and how much of a thrill it would have been for me. I enjoy it. I really do." (*Capitals game program*)

His real forte, though, was making life miserable for the opposition's top line. In 1986, as the Capitals were finally besting the Islanders in a playoff series, "(Mike) Bossy knows it's going to be Duchesne against Bossy," said Gaetan. "I know it, too. You do the best you can." Bossy shared praise with his shadow in the handshake line, as he revealed to *The Hockey News*. "I told Gaetan that I hope he does as good a job on the rest of the right wingers in the playoffs as he did against me."

Duchesne died of cardiac arrest in 2007, at the age of 44. Tributes poured in from around the NHL, including from Bryan Murray. "He was always one of my favorite players."

(*Annapolis Capital, Frederick News-Post, Hockey News, Washington Post*)

✪ Greg Adams (1983-88)

"Getting Under The Opponent's Skin" doesn't appear on NHL scoresheets. But it was vital skill in the rough and tumble Patrick Division of the '80's. Rugged Greg Adams fit that bill for the Capitals. He possessed scoring touch – a career high 18 goals in 1985-86 – and made his reputation banging along the boards, corners, and crease. "He stood out when they played us," said Edmonton coach Glen Sather. "He's a good, hard-nosed winger who'll stand in front of the net."

During a 1986 Caps visit to Philly, Greg got shoved into Flyers goalie Bob Froese. A player named Froese shouldn't lose his cool, right? Well, Al Morganti of the *Philadelphia Inquirer* described Froese's violent retaliation on Adams as "Mad Goalie Beyond Thunderdome." Froese had a side-splitting, if skewed, explanation for aggression toward the Capitals winger.

THE LEGENDS OF LANDOVER

"Adams thought my head was a speed bag," said the Mad Goalie Beyond Thunderdome. "I know it's not pretty but it ain't no speed bag. He punched me in the head. Some guys are good at interfering without anybody knowing it. He's definitely no Picasso when it comes to that, he's more like modern art." The game story concluded, however, that, "Replays didn't show any punch by Adams." Froese later became a minister; did he decide the contact was an Immaculate Connection?

Greg had issues with one other NHL player – they shared the same name! Traveling city to city, the two Greg Adams would get each other's mail, sticks, even skates. "His size nine to my size 12s didn't work too well. I figured that out in a hurry," said the Capitals' Adams. "We've had a lot of mix-ups," said the not-Caps Adams. "One time I got his income tax forms."

Our Greg seized an opportunity after *their* Greg got off to a hot start in 1985. "When New Jersey's Greg Adams collected five assists in the opening game and was among the league scoring leaders for a while, (Washington's) Adams would show everyone the NHL statistics, with his thumb conveniently covering New Jersey." (*The Hockey News*)

At the 1989 trade deadline, Vancouver acquired one Greg Adams – and they already employed the other one! Helene Elliott's assessment, in the *L.A. Times*: "Unlimited potential for chaos." The former Cap said, "Sometimes, adults will ask me if Greg is my brother. After a while, my standard response would be, 'That wouldn't exactly make my parents neurosurgeons, now would it?'" *(Canadian Press, Sporting News)*

✪ Doug Jarvis (1982-86)

Hockey reporters in each NHL city nominate a player from the team they cover for the Bill Masterton Trophy. The award recognizes "perseverance, sportsmanship, and dedication." Selections in 1986 showed the respect accorded Doug Jarvis, who in midseason had been traded from the Caps to the Whalers. Hartford writers that summer nominated Jarvis for the Masterton. The choice of the D.C. press? Also Jarvis.

Even with the unique double nomination, Doug didn't win in 1986, but was the obvious Masterton choice in 1987. Jarvis became the NHL's all-time ironman, eventually playing 964 consecutive games. Modestly, Jarvis said, "If I get tapped on the shoulder to go out there, hey, I go out there."

Jarvis' record drew raves from former Caps teammates. Mike Gartner: "To say that Doug Jarvis is consistent would be an understatement. I can't ever remember Doug having a bad practice, much less a bad game." Rod Langway: "He's done so much, and look at the teams he's been on. He went from a champion (Montreal) to a team that was close to folding (Washington) and it became a contender."

THE LEGENDS OF LANDOVER

For most of the past three decades, Jarvis has served as an NHL assistant coach, most recently in Vancouver. Not surprising, because Doug was already taking on coaching assignments while playing with the Capitals. "All season (1983-84), he has dissected films of opponents' power plays, then furnished the tactics that have lifted the Capitals into the No. 1 ranking among NHL penalty-killing units." (*The Hockey News*)

Jarvis explained, "The easier thing to observe is the opponents' power play, because it's a structural thing. I've been editing tapes and building a library, so when we play teams again, we have something to go on." The Caps killed the final 25 penalties of the regular season, finishing at 86.7%, the best shorthanded success in the NHL in seven years. Jarvis acknowledged being a defensive specialist isn't a headline-grabbing style. "A lot of times it can be boring and you don't get a lot of recognition for it. But you need it and you have to do it if you're going to be successful." *(Sporting News)*

✪ Michal Pivonka, Hip Czech (1986-99)

Once the NHL embraced diversity, teams looked longingly at talent-rich Eastern Europe. However, Iron Curtain nations didn't allow defections, least of all their young, star athletes. Which brings us to the intrigue of Michal Pivonka becoming a Capital.

For two years, Jack Button, the Caps' director of personnel, crisscrossed the globe to keep tabs on the Czech teenager. Button arranged secret meetings in Austria, in Finland, in Sweden, in Canada, wherever Pivonka was playing in a tournament. Reports indicated Pivonka had first-round talent. Because getting him to North America would be difficult, Washington was able to wait and select him in the 3rd round of the 1984 draft.

By July of 1986, the 20 year old Pivonka, drawn by the lure of freedom – and a five year, $1 million contract – agreed to defect. Much easier said than done. As a ruse, Michal told Czech officials he and his fiancé were taking a Yugoslavian vacation. Instead, the couple crossed the border into Italy, where they were met by representatives of the Capitals. Staying ahead of armed Czech guards, the group raced on to Rome and into the U.S. embassy to seek asylum, which was granted. The heart-pounding excursion made Pivonka the 17th defector from the Soviet Bloc to the NHL. "If we had tried to negotiate Pivonka's release, he never would have gotten out," said Capitals G.M. David Poile.

Getting Michal on U.S. soil represented only half the battle. "When I came here," said Pivonka, "I had just one luggage, with the shorts and T-shirt from vacation. That's it." Poile added, "It was like somebody had a fire. Everything was gone."

THE LEGENDS OF LANDOVER

The G.M. took Pivonka and his fiancé into his home to ease the transition. "(We) played Parcheesi," Poile recalled for the book, *Breakaway*. "They started laughing and brought out their Czech version of Parcheesi. They were defecting and leaving for the rest of their lives and they brought Parcheesi."

Poile later helped the young couple get set up in their own apartment. What he couldn't provide were the parents and sister Michal left behind. "They cannot visit me," Pivonka said at the time. "I sent them an invitation, but the (Czechoslovakian) government said no." The Czechs further punished Pivonka's father by demoting him at his job.

Michael had to adapt on the ice as well as off. Count the ways for us, David Poile: "He has to adjust to the travel, the number of games, the type of hockey, the playoffs, the winning, the losing, the mental aspects." Is that all? Understandably, he scored all of three goals in his first 43 games, and endured a couple of trips to the minors.

The first real clue that all the scheming had been worthwhile came in the 1988 playoffs, when Michal scored four goals and six assists in the series victory over Philadelphia. He'd go on to an outstanding 12 year career in Washington, amassing 599 points in 825 NHL games. TV viewers got another early hint that Michal was adapting to American culture. Starring in his first clothing commercial, Pivonka donned sunglasses and a leather jacket, calling himself the "Hip Czech."

✪ Bill Houlder (1987-90)

Rookie defenseman Bill Houlder might not have been well-equipped to stop Gretzky & Lemieux. (Who was?) Bill was, however, well-*quipped*. When Houlder got called up, he hops over the boards for his first NHL shift... and sees Wayne Gretzky barreling down on him. "I didn't know whether to check him or ask him for his autograph," said Houlder, who even as a rookie belonged on the NHL All-Quote Team.

Just one month after his Gretzky encounter, Bill's facing a one-on-one with Mario Lemieux. Houlder recalled, "I kept seeing his arms going back and forth, moving the puck down by my feet. When I finally looked down, my feet were weaving so badly that I fell flat on my backside." Houlder had the good fortune to land on the puck, denying Lemeiux a clear path to the goal. "Lemieux said, 'Sorry about that, kid.'" Bill had a quick comeback ready. "I said, 'That's all right. I don't think you'll have to worry about seeing me out here too much more tonight.'"

The last laugh in each game also belonged to Houlder. The Caps beat Gretzky's Oilers, 4-2, and Lemieux's Pens, 5-3. (Quotes from *Los Angeles Times*, anecdotage.com)

THE LEGENDS OF LANDOVER

✪ Bengt Gustafsson (1979-89)

Bengt Gustafsson fascinated fans as hockey's answer to the Globetrotters, at a time when the skills of Europeans were uncommon in the NHL. Gus could dangle the puck like a yo-yo, and while virtually still, played keep-away from frantic opponents. "Gus doesn't have to be moving anywhere to fool people; he can stand still and fake out three guys," said admiring linemate Dave Christian to *The Hockey News*. Frank Orr of the *Toronto Star* put it this way: "Often, he appears to be doing little, when he really is accomplishing a large amount."

Gustafsson accomplished the largest amount in Philadelphia against the Flyers on January 8, 1984: a five goal game. Going 5-for-5 is rare enough in baseball. In hockey, it's unheard of. But that was Gus' line score - a goal on each shot. "Actually, I was lucky," he was quoted by *Allentown's Morning Call*. "Dave Christian told me after the fourth goal that I had to go for five," Gustafsson added. "He said (Willy) Lindstrom was the only other Swede to score five in the NHL. I wanted it." Bengt's 5-spot remains a Capitals record, tied a decade later by Peter Bondra.

Bengt, a tireless defensive worker, hounded Wayne Gretzky and Mario Lemieux to distraction. In the 1985-86 season, Gretzky was held to one goal in three games against Washington, Lemieux one goal in seven. Not coincidentally, the Caps won nine of ten against Edmonton and Pittsburgh. Explained Gus, "I try to analyze the opposition's play when they have the puck and then just move between them and where they want to go."

That method was put to the test on January 6, 1980, when Colorado came calling. By early in the third period, one Caps defenseman was out injured, and two more had been ejected for brawling. Gustafsson was asked to take defensive shifts for the final 18 minutes. The Capitals outscored the Rockies 4-1 the rest of the way, rallying for an 8-6 win.

Playing all three forward positions, he didn't shy from contact, throwing thunderous hits on fearsome forwards like Dave Brown (6-5, 210) and Dave Semenko (6-3, 215). For all his flashy playmaking, Gustafsson remained a Stoic Swede. His even-keel demeanor helped him take on the no-win job of assigning seats on team flights. He stayed cool with SOB Islanders goalie Billy Smith whacking at his shins.

Even if Gustafsson rarely showed emotion on the ice, his 555 career points in the NHL inspired plenty of passion. After Gus scored an overtime game-winner, owner Abe Pollin planted a big smooch on his forehead during a post-game TV interview. Don't worry, Abe, you weren't the only one with a man-crush on #16. And to think, Capitals fans would have missed out on all of Bengt's heroics if the team hadn't wrestled him away from the Edmonton Oilers.

THE LEGENDS OF LANDOVER

✪ Banned In Alberta

The rest of the hockey world really, *really* didn't want Bengt Gustafsson to play in Edmonton. The Oilers signed the Swedish rookie for the 1979 WHA final, and Bengt scored in his first game. Winnipeg protested on a roster technicality, terminating Gus' brief tenure as Wayne Gretzky's teammate.

The NHL months earlier had agreed to absorb four WHA teams after the season, including the Oilers. All players on those teams - save two skaters and two goalies - would return to the NHL clubs which owned their rights. Edmonton protected Gretzky, and they also chose to retain Gustafsson. The Capitals, who made Bengt a 4th round pick in 1978, objected, but NHL President John Ziegler ruled for the Oilers. That is, until Washington pointed out that during merger talks, the NHL had ordered a freeze on WHA contracts. Edmonton hadn't inked Gustafsson until the playoffs, after that freeze.

Considering the new evidence, Ziegler reversed himself, and awarded Bengt to the Capitals. Did this flummox the Oilers? Oh, could be a little; one executive called the decision, "Extremely unbearable." *(AP)* All of which added intrigue when the Caps made their first visit to Edmonton, on October 28, 1979. Just showing up had been an adventure - their first plane was grounded by lightning, and their second returned to the gate with electrical trouble. The team straggled into Northlands Coliseum barely two hours before puck drop.

Gus, probably dazed by jet lag, or maybe unsure which team he was playing for, removed his gloves on the ice so he could hitch up his pants - and promptly was whistled for a delay of game penalty! A forgiving coach Dan Belisle said, "The guy is entitled to loose suspenders once in a while. He certainly has loosened a few other suspenders the way he has played." (Trip story from *Washington Star, monumentalnetwork.com*.)

✪ Swedish Sabbatical

By the summer of 1986, Bengt Gustafsson had had enough. Enough of the interminable NHL travel; of being 4,000 miles from home; of the high crime rate – on and off the ice. He'd left family and friends behind in Karlskoga, Sweden, as well as a hometown hockey team which needed his talents.

Gustafsson felt less secure in the States. "You watch the news in D.C. and there is always somebody killed or raped," he told the *Washington Post*. "Nobody really remembers when Karlskoga last had a murder." So, after seven marvelous seasons, 479 games and 432 points playing in the U.S. Capital, Gus longed for home. Though the Caps tried to change his mind, Gustafsson was back in Sweden as the puck dropped on the 1986-87 NHL campaign.

THE LEGENDS OF LANDOVER

Gus may have been gone, but definitely not forgotten. In February, 1987, owner Abe Pollin, team president Dick Patrick, and G.M. David Poile made a clandestine trip to Karlskoga. Not that anyone would confirm it. Poile's secretary wouldn't. Poile's wife wouldn't. Even Poile's coach, Bryan Murray, wouldn't. Art Kaminsky, Gustafsson's agent, noted, "Hockey has become the most cloak-and-daggerish of sports." (This had been equally true of the Pivonka defection. While in Europe, a Caps executive tore a $5 bill in half, "keeping one half while giving the other to Pivonka so the two parties could identify one another," according to the book *Breakaway*.)

In their attempt to lure Gustafsson back, the Capitals offered more than 10 times what he was earning as a player and public relations executive in Karlskoga. They had precedent to believe that would sway the Swede. When a reporter asked Gus why he left Sweden the first time to play in the NHL, he boiled down the complex geopolitical issue to its essence: "Money," said Bengt with a grin. That, combined with the inferior quality of hockey in Sweden's second division, gave Caps management reason for optimism. "We had some good conversations with him," team president Patrick said. "I at least hold out hope we'll see him in a Washington uniform again. Of course, I don't know when that will be."

Patrick found out weeks later that Gustafsson's return wouldn't come during the '86-'87 season. The chance to captain the Swedish National Team for that spring's World Championships proved too tempting. "Money isn't everything," Gustafsson now said, and meant it – he'd accepted a $190,000 pay cut to move back home.

Satiated after leading Sweden to the World Championship, Gus held open the possibility of returning to Landover for the 1987-88 season. However, several factors complicated the decision. He already had an offer from a team in Sweden's top league, the Elite Division. He liked his off-ice public relations job, as well as playing and living in his native country. And he didn't count on his Swedish employer playing hardball.

NHL teams routinely paid European clubs a transfer fee for allowing players out of their contracts. The Capitals had originally gained rights to Bengt via a $100,000 payment in 1979, but balked at spending six figures for the same player a second time. "A holdup," Washington G.M. David Poile called it. Neither side appeared willing to budge.

Having decided to return to the NHL, Bengt set about untieing the Gordian knot. Gustafsson upped the stakes – announcing if he couldn't skate for the Caps in October, he'd forgo representing Sweden in September's Canada Cup tournament. Predictably, the Swedish hockey federation got involved, and after what the *Toronto Star* described as "48 hours of frenzied negotiations," an agreement was reached.

THE LEGENDS OF LANDOVER

So Bengt donned his Tre Kronor uniform once more for the Canada Cup. Then he traded it for the familiar #16 in stars and stripes, playing two more productive seasons in Landover from 1987-1989. Two sets of numbers convinced him to return to the States; one was a $1 million contract. The other? "I've been playing before 50 to 200 people," Gustafsson said. "18 thousand - that's what I missed most."

✪ Bobby Carpenter (1981-87, 1992-93)

The script was perfect: a U.S. teenage phenom jumps directly from high school to the NHL, in the Nation's Capital, no less. Oh, the fanfare! *Sports Illustrated* on its February 23, 1981 cover called Bobby Carpenter "The Can't Miss Kid." Former Caps coach Jim Anderson, now chief scout in Vancouver, gushed, "He's an exceptional puck handler and skater. And, geezus, he's got quick hands."

The Capitals leapfrogged Hartford to select him with the third overall pick in the 1981 draft, as detailed on page 104. "The Capitals announced his signing by opening up the raw bar and a ritzy room at the Capital Centre. Two U.S. Congressmen, one member of the White House staff, and dozens of members of the national media attended." *(L.A. Times)* Justifying the hype, the Massachusetts native poured in 92 goals his first three seasons, then erupted for 53 in 1984-85. The Caps touted Carpenter and fellow 50-goal scorer Mike Gartner as the "Goal Dust Twins."

At the time, the team issued a life-sized poster urging kids to "Drink Your Milk And See How You Measure Up To Bobby Carpenter." But his breakout season was followed by multiple breakdowns - contract squabbles, poor conditioning, feuds with coach Bryan Murray, declining production and injuries. In the words of the poster, Carpenter was no longer measuring up to the previous Bob Carpenter. *SI* acknowledged as much, derisively calling him the "Can't Play Kid." Maybe Bob had stopped drinking his milk.

Coach Bryan Murray wouldn't abide a lack of heart, his diagnosis of Carpenter's play. Oh, at the beginning they got along swell, saying all the right things. Bobby: "Mr. Murray is a real good coach." Bryan: "I could play him 40 minutes and he wouldn't complain." That was in 1981, when both were NHL rookies. By early in the 1986-87 season, the exasperated coach said, "I had 56 meetings with him last year and 15 more this season. I've tried to tell him just to forget his statistics. He's playing somewhat passive because he's down on himself."

Murray eventually came to question Carpenter's work ethic. "Physically, he's not as willing to be involved. Having success and not handling it," the coach said to *The Hockey News*. "He didn't work as hard. He wouldn't take the blame for anything."

THE LEGENDS OF LANDOVER

A defiant Carpenter said, "I'm glad I didn't listen to him." He was overheard saying, "I've got to get out of this (bleeping) organization." Sensing an increasing distraction, the Capitals suspended Carpenter, eventually granting his wish with a trade to the Rangers. For a deal they were forced to make, the Caps received a rich return. Winger Kelly Miller (931 games, 408 points) and center Mike Ridley (588 games, 547 points) were longtime mainstays of the forward corps in Washington.

When the dust settled, fellow Massachusetts native Rod Langway sided with his coach, not Carpenter. "Bobby has to look at himself in the mirror," said the Caps captain. "If you feel that way in your heart, obviously it's going to affect your play. But I didn't hear a lot of complaining when he was scoring 53 goals. You can argue with the boss all the time, but you'd better do your job. There aren't many guys who don't do what Bryan tells them." A neutral observer, Detroit G.M. Jim Devellano, knew who'd taken the low road. "Carpenter went out of his way to embarrass Bryan Murray."

Who could have imagined that after wandering through New York, Los Angeles and Boston, Carpenter would sign for one more season in D.C. in 1992, wearing the number 11 sweater made famous by Gartner, his former Goal Dust Twin. Carpenter, now a defensive specialist, moved on one more time to New Jersey. He helped the Devils win a Stanley Cup in 1995, hanging up his skates in 1999.

The Capitals could have put the Devil into Carpenter 14 years earlier, and in retrospect, probably wish they had. Jersey pursued Bobby, a restricted free agent, in the summer of 1985. Washington rejected a trade that would have sent winger Kirk Muller and defenseman Craig Wolanin to the Caps.

✪ Craig Laughlin (1982-88)

Craig Laughlin's specialty in six Capitals campaigns was the art of screening opposing goalies. Like a wide receiver tip-toeing the sideline, Laughlin kept track of the crease. "Most of the time, I can feel where the lines are, and I know not to go in too much," Craig explained to the *Washington Post*. Good screeners also master peripheral vision and timing. "You need to know when a player is getting ready to shoot, and if you see a check coming, you have to plant your feet and push back."

"He's willing to pay the price," said an approving coach Bryan Murray. "He's willing to take the contact and make the play." Laughlin took a lighthearted approach to the bumps and bruises inherent to his chosen specialty. "I figure they're just little things that go with the job. I'm not going to talk about them until I'm playing bad, then I'll tell you all about them." Laughlin added that the battle was mental as well as physical. "Goaltenders will try to hit you in the back of the ankles with their stick. It doesn't hurt, and I figure if they're whacking me, they're not thinking about the puck."

THE LEGENDS OF LANDOVER

Murray said Laughlin's contribution went beyond pain tolerance. "We look at Locker each season and figure him for a third- or fourth-line guy. But he had good hands, he's very creative, he shoots the puck a ton." Those skills reached their peak in his 30-goal season of 1985-86.

And Craig showed qualities which would later make him a beloved broadcaster. "He's a smart player," said the coach. "If we put something new in, he's one of the first to pick it up. He's a holler guy, a very positive guy, and he provides leadership and noise in the room."

Craig also had a TV analyst's way with words, long before trading a helmet for a headset. Consider his re-creation of a spectacular goal he scored to beat the Islanders in the last 62 seconds of a 1984 playoff game: "I took out the nine-iron and chipped it in. I saw it squirt loose. I tried to shoot and fanned, then tried again as I was going down. I said, 'Holy Smokes, it's in!'"

Even his divorce from the Capitals was amicable. In February, 1988, Craig was granted a trade to L.A. when the Caps reduced his ice time. "I didn't leave on a sour note," Laughlin confirmed. As fate had it, Washington visited the Fabulous Forum two weeks later, and Laughlin utilized his analyst skills to help his new team beat his old one. "We had a spy in here tonight," Kings coach Robbie Ftorek would say after the game. "Craig gave us a lot of scoops that proved beneficial." Laughlin remained well-liked by Caps players - too well liked, in the opinion of his former employer. "Bryan Murray was yelling at them, 'C'mon, he's not your friend any more, you can hit him,'" Craig recalled. (*L.A. Times, Toronto Globe & Mail*)

✪ Milan Novy (1982-83)

Milan Novy must be one of the few NHL players ever to simultaneously be a rookie *and* the oldest player on his team! Plus, he was the first NHL player to wear the high – and highly unusual – number 66.

How those came about is rooted in Cold War hockey relations. In the early '80's, Iron Curtain countries began allowing a trickle of aging stars to finish careers in North America. Milan qualified, having scored more than 400 goals during a distinguished tenure in his native Czechoslovakia. Buffalo G.M. Scotty Bowman signed Novy early in 1982, when Czech authorities confirmed his availability to play in the NHL.

At the '82 draft, Caps interim G.M. Roger Crozier fleeced Bowman, trading two picks who didn't pan out in exchange for Alan Haworth and rights to Novy. That made Milan, at age 31, the oldest player on the Washington roster, even though by NHL standards he was a "rookie." The number 6 sweater Novy wore as a Czech superstar belonged on the Caps to Darren Veitch; Milan asked for 66, but was assigned number 26 instead. "At the time," explained Milan, "only true stars could afford to have their way."

THE LEGENDS OF LANDOVER

Novy led the Caps to a 5-4 opening night victory in New York with a goal and two assists. Bryan Murray gushed, "Milan Novy is the greatest thing since sugar." Along with the coach's praise, he earned a number upgrade. "Before the next match," Novy recalled, "I was surprised (with his requested number 66 sweater). The club wanted to show appreciation for my efforts."

The language barrier presented problems for Milan – and opportunity for mischievous teammate Craig Laughlin. "He would nod and smile no matter what I said. I would trick him and say a whole bunch of bad stuff, and he would just say 'ja' and we would be laughing." For the year, Novy made the serious contribution of 18 goals, 30 assists, and a +1.

Yet Milan felt understandably out of his comfort zone - lacking a command of English, he lived in D.C. near the Czech embassy, and his kids attended a Czech school. Novy also wasn't fond of the rough NHL style, and Poile, feeling Milan didn't integrate with the team, wanted the roster spot for a younger player. So after one season, Novy returned to playing in Europe.

(Sources: Toronto Globe & Mail, Breakaway by Tal Pinchevsky, Pgh. Press, hockeydraftcentral.com, legendsofhockey.net, Sporting News)

✪ Dino Ciccarelli (1989-92)

In giving up Mike Gartner, their all-time offensive leader, to Minnesota for Dino Ciccarelli, the character-first Caps exchanged choir boy for frat boy. The upside was enormous - Ciccarelli channeled his cocky confidence to own real estate near the opposition net. Many of his 608 career goals came from in close while absorbing punishment. "We needed a type of guy who was going to be in traffic more," said Capitals coach Bryan Murray. "When (Ciccarelli) gets a chance around the net, it's in." (*Toronto Globe & Mail*)

Dino's dark side revealed itself in Minnesota on the ice (a stick-swinging incident), off the ice (an indecent exposure conviction), and a contract holdout in which he declared, "I'm just a number to them. Well, it's time this number moves on." At the 1989 trade deadline, Caps G.M. David Poile lauded Ciccarelli as one of the NHL's best, while acknowledging he "has made a few mistakes in his life that he regrets, that he's apologized for, and I believe that this will give him a fresh start." *(AP)*

His first full season in Landover, 1989-90, Dino poured in 41 goals and eight more in the postseason, fueling the Caps' first trip to the conference finals. The prolific forward contributed 209 points in 223 games as a Cap. Unfortunately, Ciccarelli couldn't outskate his frat-boy demons. The *Washington City Paper* reported, "In May 1990, a teenager accused Capitals players of raping her in a limousine after a team party." Ciccarelli, along with Geoff Courtnall and Neil Sheehy, sat before a federal grand jury, which ultimately declined to indict.

Legalities aside, even consensual sex with a 17-year-old in a car by three pro athletes is reprehensible behavior. Ciccarelli seemed unsure of his own culpability. On one hand, "He apologized on television and in the newspapers, and he talked to season-ticket-holders, calling two a day during the off-season to try luring some back." *(L.A. Times)* He also conceded to *Washingtonian* magazine, "I'm married. I shouldn't have been there."

So far, so contrite – except he went on to say, "If I was single, I would have stood up to the charges because, believe me, there's not a damn thing we did wrong." Though it didn't affect his play, the scandal contributed to Ciccarelli's trade to Detroit – for little return – following the 1991-92 season. "There's the unspoken but implied theory that ever since the alleged sexual assault, the team's image and marketing efforts were damaged badly," suggested the *Baltimore Sun*. Dino also claimed, "They didn't want to pay me. They've always made a big deal about loyalty around here, then they trade me."

Retired Numbers

Yvon Labre (No. 7, Page 25) also has his number retired. Let's hope by the time you read this, Peter Bondra (No. 12) & Olie Kolzig (No. 37) have joined them.

✪ 5 - Rod Langway, Secretary of Defense (1982-1993)

Unlike some of the obscure entries elsewhere in this book, Rod Langway's heroics are known to even casual Caps fans. He was a two-time Norris Trophy winner as best defenseman, longtime captain, a 2002 Hall of Fame inductee, and the Capitals averaged a robust 92 standings points during his 10 full seasons.

Yet none of these represent Langway's greatest achievement. After the 1981-82 season, financial woes caused owner Abe Pollin to consider moving or folding the team. Newly hired G.M. David Poile then engineered a blockbuster offseason trade with Montreal for Langway, Brian Engblom, Doug Jarvis, and Craig Laughlin.

Dividends were immediate. In 1982-83, goals-against went down 55; not coincidentally, wins went up by 13. In 1983-84, wins increased by another nine, while goals-against decreased a staggering 57. Langway's leadership and skill had lifted all his teammates, as Mike Gartner explained. "Our offensive capabilities have always been there. We used to score three goals and lose 5-3 or 6-3. Now we can score three goals and win. When we were losing all the time, I kept telling myself I was building character. I'm glad I don't have to build character anymore."

THE LEGENDS OF LANDOVER

"The thing I noticed most was how upset he gets when the other team gets a good scoring chance," said onetime defensive partner Mike McEwen. "He hates that. His intensity comes out, like a middle linebacker." (At the University of New Hampshire, Rod *did* play linebacker!) "He recognizes what he does best," coach Bryan Murray told *Sports Illustrated*. "He doesn't gamble. He plays very safe. He'll make the pass to the same winger time after time if the guy's open, and he's so strong that even when he's being leaned on he can get the puck to his man. He never gets in trouble in his own end."

"His biggest strength is his strength," goalie Pat Riggin concurred to the *New York Times*. "And, as the game gets tougher, Roddie seems to get tougher and stronger. He's got that great reach and a great mind for the game. The puck goes in the corner and in a couple of strides he's right on the guy. Or, if a guy's leaning on him when he's got the puck, he'll make the play with that reach - and the good play, the right play."

Even in the '80's, "throwback" described Langway. "My style is physical and simple," he wrote in a *washingtonpost.com* chat. "I focused on clearing the puck and quick transitions from defense to offense. I consider myself a proud player. I honor the game and the people who played before me. I like the physical hooking and holding. You made people work to score."

Throwback also described Rod's lack of headgear; he was one of the last to play without a helmet. During the 1985-86 season, Langway twice came close to suffering eye injuries. Did he consider a visor? "Never. I couldn't even wear a helmet. How could I get it down over my ears?" Rod Langway, man of no pretentions. After the Caps allowed three shorthanded goals in the 2nd period of a 9-4 loss at Philly: "I feel like I want to find a hole and bury myself in it." Rod again, after learning there could be a full overtime period in the 1985 All Star Game: "When I heard about the extra 20 minutes, I was going to wave the white flag."

Rod had a similar no-nonsense reaction to stardom. "It was simply my time," he told *legendsofhockey.net*. "If I had stayed in Montreal, I would have been the same, but I wouldn't have received the accolades. Larry (Robinson) was put on the ice during certain situations that I was getting in Washington. Being captain and being recognized as a key player with the Capitals, along with the way I played, helped me win the Norris Trophy."

As wins increased, so did interest in the team. Attendance peaked in 1989-90 at 17,251 per game - just a few hundred under capacity. And hockey in D.C. was safe. Laughlin later told *sportsfanmagazine.com*, "Rod Langway just about single-handedly saved the Washington Capitals. He put hockey on the map here." Hockey observers around the NHL agreed. In his book, *Who's Who of Hockey*, Stan Fischler calls Langway no less than a "Majestic franchise-saver."

THE LEGENDS OF LANDOVER

✪ The Tao Of Rod

Lao Tzu, Chinese philosopher and founder of Taoism, 2,600 years ago imparted this wisdom: *"Separate parts make no carriage."* More recently, Rod Langway, American defenseman, shared his interpretation: *"We had a saying in Montreal. 'Today a hero, tomorrow a zero.'"* Langway's *Tao* might not qualify as the height of Eastern enlightenment, even though he was born in Taiwan; then again, Lao Tzu never had to defend a 2-on-1 against Gretzky and Kurri.

Rod spread the wisdom of *hero vs. zero* to his new D.C. disciples. "What that means is that you don't just get up for the big teams, you do for the little ones, too. When we play a team like Hartford, those are two points that belong in our pockets. But you've still got to be ready to work to put them there, 'cause once they get away, it's tough to get them back."

Professor Langway was leading an on-the-fly course on culture change. "We'd lose 4-1, and the guy who scored the goal would be happy. Those of us from Montreal had never seen that before and it ticked us off. You play not to be scored on. It took a while to turn that around." A sluggish – and perhaps selfish – start in 1984 prompted Langway to set his teammates straight. "We've got to stop the bitching and moaning and looking for someone else to blame," Langway said at the time to *The Hockey News*. "It's time to get back to our normal selves, make the simple plays, and not worry about goals, assists, and plus-minus. Once you get a greedy attitude like that, you've got problems." Rod's tough love produced results, a sparkling 40-17-4 record for the rest of the '84-'85 season.

"He's very vocal, very exuberant, very assured," said teammate Randy Holt. "Before this year we'd come up against the good teams, and deep down we'd figure we were going to lose. Now when we play those teams, Rod tells us how he and the Canadiens beat them, and convinces us we can too. He's given us a lot more confidence and poise."

The last word on *The Tao of Langway* goes to the Sage himself. "If one guy starts loafing, he can infect a whole team. Someone who's working his butt off will notice the guy who's not and think, 'Hey, he's not putting out and he's getting away with it, so why should I?' Well, that's when you close that door and have some yelling and screaming."
(Quotes from *Philadelphia Inquirer, Christian Science Monitor, SI*)

✪ 11 - Mike Gartner, Mr. Consistent (1979-89)

Mike Gartner was the opposite of Forrest Gump's box of chocolates. With Mike, Caps fans always knew what they were going to get: 35 goals or more. In nine full seasons in D.C. (chosen 4th overall in the 1979 draft), Gartner's goal totals are staggering: *36, 48, 35, 38, 40, 50, 35, 41, 48.*

THE LEGENDS OF LANDOVER

An opposing coach called him "personable, talented and a strong team member." G.M. David Poile saw "Garts" as the complete package. "Mike has size, strength, speed and is smart. What more could you ask?" Well, David, he could stop making the rest of us look bad.

The *Edmonton Journal* published a photo of Gartner literally shoulder to shoulder with Wayne Gretzky as they battled for the puck, an image later immortalized on a hockey card. A mind-blowing 1,602 goals are rubbing shoulders in the image. Gretzky (1979-99) is the all-time leader with 894 goals, while Gartner (1979-98) ranks 7th with 708. "There aren't too many (records) Wayne doesn't own," Mike told *nhl.com*, "but I do own a couple - 15 consecutive 30-goal seasons and 17 total 30-goal seasons."

Mike's integrity matched his skills. "I always strove for consistency as a player and as a person," Mike said, and was he ever a straight shooter. Here's how straight: the Flyers often caught an illegal stick by an opponent, resulting in a minor penalty. Over a two-year period, they were only wrong one time – when they challenged the stick of Mike Gartner. *(N.Y. Times)*

Only a title eluded the 19-year NHL veteran. In his decade in D.C., the Caps won just three playoff series, and Mike's scoring touch sometimes eluded him in crucial situations. That said, Gartner was a first-ballot Hall of Fame selection in 2001. His retired #11 reminds fans of Mike's durability, work ethic, and notable totals with the Capitals - 397 goals, 392 assists.

✪ 32 - Dale Hunter, Tough, Talented, Allergic to Quitting (1987-99)

Lyrics to "The Dukes of Hazzard" TV theme fit Dale Hunter as perfectly as they did Bo and Luke. *Makin' his way, the only way he knows how, that's just a little bit more than the law will allow.*

A quintessential Hunter shift as a Capital came at his former home rink, Le Colisee in Quebec. As teammates enter the zone, Dale demolishes a Nordiques defender away from the play - in today's NHL, a blatant interference penalty. A lane to the net thus cleared, Hunter heads for the crease. Uncovered, because the defender is only now regaining his balance, Hunter bangs his stick on the ice no less than five times. Finally, the pass arrives, and Dale redirects it past the helpless goalie.

The New York Times labeled Hunter, "Tough, Talented, Allergic to Quitting." Bill Ranford, both a teammate and opponent of Dale's, gave his unique perspective to *washingtoncapitalslegends.blogspot.com*. "I assumed Hunter picked his spots to play the way he does, because nobody can play that way all the time. Then I found out he plays that way every game, every rink, against everybody."

THE LEGENDS OF LANDOVER

Hunter was an agitator par excellence. Other terms used by opponents and fans - not without admiration - included "pest," "warrior," "menace," and "dirty." Hunter is the only player in NHL history with more than 300 goals, 1,000 points, and 3,000 penalty minutes.

Above all, Dale was clutch - four overtime goals in the playoffs. One of the all-time great Capitals memories will always be Dale's overtime series-winning goal in Game 7 against the Flyers in the 1988 playoffs. For much more about that game, read the *19th Shift: Hunter's Shot.*

Dale might have remained a Nordique, if the Caps had consummated a different deal in December, 1986. Alan Haworth and Bobby Carpenter were headed north, for forward Anton Stastny and goalie Mario Gosselin. So close was the trade, that the Nords teased it on local radio, and Haworth's agent advised him to pack his bags.

The Caps backed out, but the teams resumed talks after the season. At the time, Hunter decided to attend the 1987 NHL entry draft at Joe Louis Arena in Detroit. While there, Dale learned of his trade from Quebec to Washington. "It's the first draft I've been to in a couple of years," said Hunter. "I'm staying at home next year."

Goalies

✪ Limited Partnership Suffers A Net Loss

If Al Jensen hadn't played so well, Pat Riggin might have won the Vezina Trophy in 1983-84. Of course, if Riggin hadn't played so well, Jensen could have won it. Instead, they cancelled each other in voting by general managers for the league's top goalie. Buffalo's Tom Barrasso captured the award, although Riggin and Jensen had equal numbers.

So smothering was the Caps' defense that Jensen once commented, "It was a good night to take off." No, Al wasn't the backup when he said it, he was the winning goalie! Jensen had faced just 20 shots in a 5-0 victory over the Kings, and the *L.A. Times* called the Kings' offensive half of the ice the "Dead Zone."

1983-84	GAA	Record	SO
Riggin	2.66	21-14-2	4
Jensen	2.91	25-13-3	4
Barrasso	2.84	26-12-3	2

Riggin posted the NHL's top goals-against, a stingy 2.66. Jensen's GAA of 2.91 was 3rd best; his .646 winning pct. was just below Barrasso's .671. What's more, Pat and Al each posted four shutouts. No other *team* finished with more than three!

THE LEGENDS OF LANDOVER

Barrasso's "advantage" was backup Bob Sauve, whose 3.94 GAA left him out of Vezina consideration. So while Capitals netminders garnered a combined 74 ballot points in G.M. voting – a landslide – neither Jensen nor Riggin could individually bring home the hardware. In fact, Calgary's Reggie Lemelin finished as runner-up. Al and Pat settled for the Jennings Trophy, given to the goalies on the team allowing the fewest goals.

✪ Al Jensen (1981-86)

For Caps coach Bryan Murray, Al Jensen was the exception. The rookie coach usually picked that night's goalie based on what he observed in practice. No wonder Jensen, also a rookie, once went 17 games between starts in 1981-82. "He's not the best practice goalie," Murray explained. Prior G.M. Max McNab traded for Jensen, explaining, "You can never have enough goaltending." I guess not – Al became the eighth goalie in the organization. And Murray wasn't eager to move him up the depth chart.

Jensen was demoted to Hershey to start the '82-'83 season. Yet Jensen always proved ready. "He sure plays in front of the crowd," Murray conceded to *AP*. "He's stepped in and filled the bill." Al's fine play (4-0-1 in his first five home starts) earned him a corrected nameplate above his locker, which at first read "Jenson." Later, he earned number-one-star honors in Detroit, the club which traded him away. Coach Murray admitted to *The Hockey News*, "We didn't think Al was this good; we're glad he is."

Though Jensen played parts of six seasons in Washington, compiling a gaudy 94-48-18 record, only during 1985-86 did he avoid time in the minors. Management thought Al became unreliable, especially distracted by aches and pains they considered minor. "He doesn't handle pressure," Murray said. "I know how nervous he was. He'd change skates between periods. Just hyper as could be." *(Washington Post)*

✪ Pat Riggin (1982-86)

Maybe another Capital was more disliked by teammates than Pat Riggin, but none come immediately to mind. It wasn't his play; Riggin once stopped Wayne Gretzky on a late-game penalty shot to preserve a 3-3 tie. Pat's play was stout enough to share that Jennings Trophy with Al Jensen.

Yet Riggin was ultra-competitive about playing time. He needlessly went on the record to compare records in 1984: "I've got over 70 wins. That's more than Al Jensen." Mike Gartner also felt Riggin's wrath, when the goalie objected to Gartner's high slapshots during practice. "Riggin slashed Gartner, Gartner swung his stick at Riggin's head, and they slugged it out." *(Toronto Star)* "I was probably the only guy who didn't shoot high on him in practice," said former teammate Bengt Gustafsson.

THE LEGENDS OF LANDOVER

Riggin in 1985 confusingly ignored the stars and stripes on his uniform, complaining, "Hey, it's our game and Americans are taking Canadian jobs." Pat also didn't care how the slight would be received by his half-dozen American teammates. "Evidently their rah-rah approach to Canada's game had made him sick," reported the *Free Lance-Star*.

Riggin had to realize there'd be blowback to his remarks, but Pat didn't take it as well as he dished it out. Bob Fachet in *The Hockey News* described the revenge of three American-born Capitals, who had been featured on a magazine cover. "They autographed the cover with appropriate comments and left it in Riggin's locker, then broke up laughing when he angrily tore it up." Management sent Pat packing soon after.

Once during his D.C. tenure, Riggin even turned his acid tongue on himself. Coach Bryan Murray assigned performance grades after every contest, and shared those grades with players at 20-game intervals. Riggin told *Sports Illustrated*, "My first two report cards were so bad, I had to take them home and get them signed by my parents."

✪ Anatomy Of A Goalie Swap

Early in the 1985-86 season, just as Washington concluded Pat Riggin would benefit from a change of scenery, Boston happened to be thinking the same about Pete Peeters. Riggin knew he'd been traded when he answered the phone just before 11 p.m. "David Poile (Caps G.M.) doesn't make a habit of calling me at home at this time of night."

Pat said things got weirder the next time his phone rang. "A voice at the other end asked, 'Is this David Poile?' Somehow, Pete Peeters had been given Riggin's phone number when he was told to get in touch with Poile." The goalies swapped pleasantries, though Riggin conceded, "It was a little awkward." (*The Hockey News*)

Rarely do teams simultaneously scan each other's roster and decide, "Hey, we'd be better off with *their* guy." Peeters, at $300,000, earned about twice as much as Riggin. Other than that, this was the nakedest of one-for-one exchanges; no prospects involved, no shoring up a weakness at another position. Just two players doing the same job, with similar age and resume.

The details took Pat by surprise. "The talk was that he wanted to trade for a goal scorer. I don't know how many goals Pete Peeters is going to score for the Capitals." Poile originally didn't care which of his tenders left, as long as offense arrived. "I thought I'd trade a goalie and maybe get a forward in return, since people keep telling me we need help scoring."

From the *Sporting News*: "Poile was close to a deal with Toronto for right wing Rick Vaive. When that trade fell through, he called Boston's Harry Sinden and the Peeters-for-Riggin transaction was the result."

THE LEGENDS OF LANDOVER

A quirk in the NHL schedule made this goalie swap especially awkward. Two days after the trade, on November 16, 1985, the Caps and Bruins met at Boston Garden. As new team faced old, Riggin and Peeters felt somehow they'd been placed in limbo. "Doesn't make any sense, does it?" said Pat. "It's just weird," said Pete.

Riggin, who admitted trouble focusing, watched from the Boston bench as the Caps and Bruins played a 2-2 tie. "It's just a very hollow feeling I have inside right now," Riggin explained. "I was hoping to win the Stanley Cup as a member of the Washington Capitals."

Even though Peeters was higher in altitude, watching from the press box, his mood mirrored Riggin's. "I love it here in Boston. I wanted to finish my career here," said Pete. "I was just so nervous, I just didn't know what to do. I had butterflies the whole time, I don't know why. Crazy, I guess."

The trade delivered an unexpected bonus to the Capitals: upgraded play from their other goalie, Al Jensen. "Pete's been great," coach Bryan Murray said. "He's always giving Al a pat on the back. He and Pete communicate so well and there's a good feeling between them." Murray termed the Jensen-Riggin tandem "an adversary situation. The goaltenders are approaching it differently now." Peeters explained, "When Al is in the net, I want him to do well, because then the team does well." It should be noted that Riggin exited with class, saying, "I wish (Al) luck and I wish the Washington Capitals luck."

(Boston Globe, Sporting News, Hockey News)

✪ Bob Mason (1984-87, 89-90): McNab, McVie Miss On Mason

G.M. Max McNab, coach Tom McVie, and goalie Bob Mason are key names from the first dozen years of the Capitals franchise. In fact, McNab and McVie had a lot to do with Mason coming to Washington in 1984. Nothing unusual about that... except they were a management pair in New Jersey at the time, not Landover.

McNab and McVie were hired in Washington in late 1975 to bring order and discipline to a chaotic organization. Although they succeeded admirably under the circumstances, McVie was relieved in 1978, McNab in 1981.

Undrafted goalie Mason, meanwhile, turned heads after joining the 1984 U.S. Olympic Team. Devils coach-G.M. Billy MacMillan appeared to have won the bidding for Bob's services – until Jersey cleaned house in November, 1983, deciding a McNab and a McVie were better than a MacMillan. (Should anyone be surprised that the team owner was John *McMullen*?)

THE LEGENDS OF LANDOVER

With the former Caps brain trust now in charge in the Meadowlands, Mason reconsidered. Caps G.M. David Poile swooped in and got the free agent signed in D.C. - just in time. Between Al Jensen's bad back and Pat Riggin needing a breather after 17 consecutive games, Mason got the call on March 1, 1984. Bob came within six minutes of a shutout in his debut, as the Caps crushed Pittsburgh, 9-1. "I would stop the first shot and the defense was always right there," the Olympian marveled. "I guess they've been playing like that for most of the year." *(Pittsburgh Press)*

Mason was solid, though sparingly used, for three seasons, compiling an 11-2-1 record. He became the go-to guy in 1986-87, finishing 20-18-5 with a 3.24 GAA. After losing the four-overtime finale to the Islanders in that year's playoffs, Mason bounced around with Chicago, Quebec, and Vancouver. He briefly returned to the Caps in 1989-90 - most notable because the goalie demoted to make room for Mason was a teen rookie named Olaf Kolzig. Oh, since we mentioned Olie anyway...

✪ Olaf Kolzig, "Olie The Goalie" (1989-2007)

(Kolzig barely qualifies as a Capital of the '80's, making his mark years later. He earns an entry because I admire him, and it's my book. – Glenn)

Olaf Kolzig earned a proud legacy during two decades in the Capitals organization - great performance on the ice, great class off of it. The NHL certainly took note of that rare and remarkable combination. Kolzig won the Vezina Trophy in 2000 as the league's best goaltender. He won the King Clancy Trophy in 2006 as "the player who best exemplifies leadership qualities on and off the ice and has made a noteworthy humanitarian contribution in his community."

It's no exaggeration to say that Kolzig embodied what we wish for in our sports heroes. A winner - 301 wins as a Capital; a vocal locker room presence and unofficial captain; articulate with the media; generous with fans; loyal to the organization; a devoted family man, who founded "Athletes Against Autism" on behalf of his son.

Longtime *Washington Post* Sports Editor George Solomon said it best, calling Kolzig "The ultimate mensch." (For those of you not versed in Yiddish, *mensch, n., a person of integrity and honor.*)

Quite the career for the Caps' #1 draft pick in 1989. Coach Bryan Murray was one of the 19-year-old rookie's first fans. "I told Olie that when he comes to camp next fall to bring his girlfriend with him and say all his goodbyes to his junior friends before he leaves," said Murray. "He's the goalie of the future." *(Toronto Star)*

THE LEGENDS OF LANDOVER

✪ Pete Peeters (1985-1989)

For four seasons in the 1980's, Capitals fans pinned their Stanley Cup hopes on the stick, glove and pads of Pete Peeters. Over the 1986-89 postseasons, Pete sported a 15-15 record. That fits, because as with stops in Philadelphia and Boston, Peeters was sometimes invincible, and other times… very vincible.

He could be abrasive; according to *bruinslegends.blogspot.com*, his nickname was "Grumpy." Robin Finn wrote in a *New York Times* profile, "If Peeters is having fun tending goal for the Capitals, he masks it well. Peeters is taciturn to the point of rudeness." Sample quote: "I don't like to talk about myself, or what I've done personally, or how I feel about it."

It's surprising, then, that Pete once produced a gem of an answer, on a night when he had reason to be grumpy. Peeters backstopped a playoff victory over the Rangers at Madison Square Garden, although he was hit in the left eye by a coin thrown from the stands. Pete's money quote: "I can't understand why so many people want to vent their frustrations on sports. We're entertainers, same as the circus, but nobody throws a shoe at the guy as he's swinging on the trapeze." *(AP game story)*

✪ "Pete, Get Up"

Six years after Wayne Stephenson starred as "The Reluctant Goalie," the Capitals staged a revival against Edmonton on February 15, 1987. For this performance, Pete Peeters played the Injured Starter, with Bob Mason as the Battered Backup, and Gaetan Duchesne as Winger In The Wings.

Peeters had neglected to follow his usual pregame regimen to prevent cramps, and it caught up with him in the third period. "I made a stretch and felt a cramp across the groin," Peeters told Bob Fachet of the *Washington Post*. "I reached back for the rebound and just toppled."

Mason watched from the bench, nursing an inflamed back. He'd used heat, ice, pills, and wraps, and still had trouble even walking the day before. "My heart was really beating when Pete was down," Bob admitted. "I was praying, 'Pete, get up.'" As Mason skated toward the crease to protect a one-goal Caps lead, coach Bryan Murray huddled with referee Bob Hall. Murray explained Mason's iffy status, and that winger Duchesne would have to play goal if Bob couldn't. (Murray didn't say if he informed Gaetan of this!)

Fortunately, Mason not only played, he made a series of sensational saves. Duchesne stayed at wing, setting up Bob Gould's clinching goal as the Capitals beat the Oilers, 5-3.

THE LEGENDS OF LANDOVER

✪ Butterfly Goalie

Might as well throw in one more Peeters story - he created a "Butterfly Effect" at the 1989 trade deadline. You know the "Effect" – a seemingly insignificant event that has unforeseen and wide-ranging impact. Well, it hardly appeared a leaguewide issue when Peeters injured his hip in a February game against Vancouver.

Percolating at the same time, a multi-player, three-team deal. Reportedly, the Capitals would send goaltender Don Beaupre to St. Louis. The Blues, in turn, would send a goalie to L.A. The Kings would deliver a pair of defensemen to the Blues. Finally, St. Louis would trade a defenseman to Washington.

The deal, like a carefully constructed house of cards, collapsed when Peeters got hurt. The Caps couldn't then afford to part with Beaupre – the same Don Beaupre who one year later would help the Capitals win two playoff rounds for the first time. (*L.A. Times*)

✪ Robbie Moore (1 Game, 1982)

The shortest career of any Capitals goalie – 19 minutes, 43 seconds - belongs to Robbie Moore. At the Spectrum on October 10, 1982, Moore tended goal in the 3rd period. The Capitals rallied for two late scores, then pulled Moore. But an empty net goal gave the Flyers a 6-4 win. Moore was also one of the shortest - just 5' 5" - though that was tall enough to record two shutouts playing for those Flyers in '78-'79.

Moore had a kindred spirit in 5-foot-8 netminder Don Beaupre. Don was anything but a one-game wonder, spending six strong seasons with the Caps during a 17-year NHL career. Asked if he was big enough to succeed in the NHL, Don replied, "I just have to stop the puck, not beat it to death."

Along with Moore, three others share the shortest Capitals goalie career - one game. Technically, less than one game; all appeared in relief: Alain Raymond, in a 5-4 loss vs. Hartford in 1987; Mike Rosati, in an 8-5 win vs. Ottawa in 1998; and Corey Hirsch, in a 6-5 win vs. Ottawa in 2001.

No discussion of Capitals one-game goalies would be complete without mentioning Shawn Simpson and Brett Leonhardt - although they only made it as far as the Caps' players bench. Simpson began the evening of April 23, 1990 in the broadcast booth at the Baltimore Arena, the third goalie for the AHL Skipjacks. Jim Hrivnak was playing, with Bob Mason dressed as his backup. Meanwhile, at Capital Centre, Don Beaupre was getting injured in the first period of a Caps playoff game. Mike Liut came on in relief, but what if he also got hurt?

THE LEGENDS OF LANDOVER

Shawn packed his gear, hopped in a car, and made it to Landover in time to suit up for the third period. Later, Caps G.M. David Poile wondered why Bob Mason hadn't been called. "All he had to do was take off his skates and get in the car."

Déjà vu struck for Leonhardt on December 12, 2008. The team's website producer, a former college goalie, took shots in warm-ups. He spent the first period as the backup on the bench, until minor-league callup Semyon Varlamov arrived from Houston to relieve him. Technically, Leonhardt worked his way off the one-game list, because he performed the same on-the-bench backup duty for a game in 2013. But what fun is being technical?

(Resources for this entry: Christine Brennan/Washington Post, Doug Norris/hockeygoalies.org, goaliesarchive.com, Viva la Repartee)

✪ Clint Malarchuk (1987-89)

The lives of Clint Malarchuk: Goalie; Victim; Hero; Horse Dentist (Horse Dentist?). Let's take those in order. Clint spent two years in Washington, including a remarkable stretch in February, 1988. Malarchuk, five weeks without a complete game victory, stopped 29 shots in a 6-0 whitewash in Winnipeg. One night later, he authored a 33-save, 3-0 win at Minnesota.

Clint, pulled in his next start, didn't expect to play on Long Island. Pete Peeters got injured in practice, though, so Malarchuk was inserted, saving 28 shots in a 3-0 victory over the Islanders. Wet blanket Bryan Trottier claimed the Capitals "didn't play well enough to deserve a shutout." Apparently, they did, Bryan. Malarchuk had backstopped his third shutout in nine days, all on the road!

Less than a week later, Malarchuk blanked New Jersey for 55 minutes, eventually "settling" for a 6-1 victory. He told *AP*, "I feel like I'm going to stop everything. No matter what they do, I'm going to stop it." What he didn't see coming was the 1989 trade deadline, when Clint was shuffled off to Buffalo. "Things were going good in Washington. I was with Pete Peeters, a good tandem. I was shocked."

He faced a life-threatening crisis days after joining the Sabres, cut by a skate blade and nearly bleeding to death. But that was far from his only health battle. Following a blowout playoff loss with the Caps, Malarchuk admitted, "I was depressed." In November, 1988, he hinted to *The Hockey News*, "If (people) knew the problems I had last year, they'd wonder how I ever played hockey." Clint was long retired before he was correctly diagnosed; he truly did suffer from clinical depression, as well as obsessive-compulsive disorder (OCD).

THE LEGENDS OF LANDOVER

In his courageous autobiography, *A Matter Of Inches*, Malarchuk wrote what no one knew about his time in D.C. "I suffered swirling bouts of anxiety that I didn't fully understand at the time. It'd been with me ever since I was a kid, and never really went away." Clint became a hero by sharing his diagnoses, first on his website, then with his book. Malarchuk spared no details in recounting his trauma, explosive outbursts, and failed relationships. "I received thousands of letters from people suffering from OCD who thanked me for being open," he wrote online.

And yes, the self-described "Cowboy Goalie" owns a degree from the Academy of Equine Dentistry.

✪ This Duck Didn't Mind Being Shot At

Clint felt compelled to wear a mask 24/7, and not the goalie kind. "I learned to live with it, acting like nothing was wrong in public. So I took advantage of every opportunity to let loose and forget the battles inside of me."

Unaware teammates merely found Malarchuk goofy - no, make that Donald Duck. They nicknamed Clint "Mallard" because of in-game impressions of Disney's Donald. "He quacks between periods. Actually quacks," marveled Garry Galley to *Sports Illustrated*. Greg Adams' take? "Clint is the mayor of Pluto." He meant the (former) planet, not Mickey's dog.

✪ Game Of Horse

On his most famous escapade, Malarchuk's partner in hijinks was Dale Hunter. Starting a California road trip, the team arranged a golf outing in Palm Springs. Teammates backed out on Dale and Clint's offer to go horseback riding first, so the duo set out on their own.

Two rented horses and several beers later, Hunter and Malarchuk rode within view of their teammates, who were on the hotel golf course. Clint wrote that he and Dale, neckties wrapped around their heads, "Charged down the canyon towards the course, hooting and hollering." As the players cheered, "We started pulling the pins out. Then we started jousting, riding at each other with the flags." Back at the stables, Butch and Sundance avoided jail only because the team paid for all damages.

Management was in for a greater shock, learning how Malarchuk spent his offseason in Alberta - rodeo riding! Caps G.M. David Poile viewed a press photo, then placed an emergency call to Calgary. "You're flying off a horse that's about ready to kick your head off," Poile shouted at Malarchuk. "What the hell are you doing?" Good thing Poile didn't see Clint participating in the Wild Cow Milking event (a real thing, and dangerous, too!)

THE LEGENDS OF LANDOVER

David should have granted Malarchuk's earlier, more productive request. From the book *Goaltenders Union*: "(Malarchuk) learned Soviet legend Vladislav Tretiak would be holding a hockey school in Montreal. When the Caps refused to expense the trip, he paid his own way." Clint recalled, "It was funny, because I was on the ice with 14, 15-year olds, and here I was in the NHL. But I tried to do anything and everything to be the best I could."

✪ "That's What Goalies Do!"

Coaches and G.M.s can be forgiven for not understanding goaltenders. You know, because, well, no one fully understands goaltenders. As Clint wrote in *A Matter Of Inches*, assistant coach Terry Murray lost confidence in him. Why? Because Malarchuk's pregame routine was to isolate himself. "That's what goalies do! The goalie is concentrating. He's focusing. It's the most essential part of the position."

Results-oriented coach Bryan Murray also took a hard line. "If you played great and lost, he was tough on you," Malarchuk said, while conceding, "(Coaching) feedback is rarely personal. But as a player, you're thinking, 'He hates me.'" Not hate, said the coach, tough love. "Sometimes I was accused of being too hard with players in the early days in Washington," Murray told the *Ottawa Sun*. "I always had great respect for them. I pushed them. I wanted them to accomplish what they could in their careers. Just give people a job, tell them what you expect and if they don't, do something about it, but help them along, compliment and help them do it better."

Clint was Murray's Exhibit A. "For everything Murray exposed in me - my lack of confidence and overpowering insecurities - he managed to bring out the best. He motivated me." The tough-love relationship reached its pinnacle, oddly enough, on the day Malarchuk was traded from the Caps. "(Murray) looked devastated. I was surprised to see him so emotional. He kept apologizing." Clint eventually had to console his coach. "Seeing how much he cared really meant a lot to me."

Coaches & G.M.

✪ Bryan Murray (Coach, 1981-90)

Knowledgeable sources on Capitals coach Bryan Murray:

"Murray has a lot of the old hardboot in him."
– *Toronto Star*
"Murray, the notorious bench baiter."
– *Philadelphia Daily News*
"Don't make Murray angry. You wouldn't like him when he's angry."
– *TV's Incredible Hulk*

THE LEGENDS OF LANDOVER

We can't confirm that Marvel Comics' Bruce Banner actually uttered the last quote. But it's smart thinking, regardless. If Rod Langway is the first name associated with the Capitals of the 1980's, Bryan Murray should be second. And if Langway is the man who made it toughest for Caps opponents in the '80's, Murray again isn't far behind. Armed with the courage of his convictions, Bryan never backed down during his decade in D.C., battling officials, opposing players and coaches, even his own charges.

✪ Player Hater

Coach Murray broke a taboo by heckling opponents. He pointedly advised L.A.'s Dave Taylor, "If you're going to go after people, take your mask off. Don't be pouncing on guys from the back while you wear a shield to protect yourself." Murray needled Montreal roughneck Chris Nilan, "Please don't get a penalty. We want you on the ice." Bryan chided Toronto's Rick Vaive for wrestling with Washington's Lou Franceschetti. "Vaive comes over to me and says, 'Murray, you so-and-so, you sent him out (to fight).' I said, 'You put a stick to a guy and he retaliates and you're upset at me. Go to the penalty box, Rick.'"

Murray didn't allow anyone to censor his commentary, or even suggest it. "I yelled at Bobby Clarke, 'Why don't you retire?' My brother Terry, our assistant coach, said, 'You can't be yelling at the players.' I said, 'You just coach the defense and let me worry about the rest.'"

One night, his verbal sparring partner was the Islanders' Duane Sutter – nicknamed "dog" for his yapping on the ice. Murray hit Duane with these barbs: "You're not as good as your brother Brent. You're not that tough, either. We can see right through you." Between periods, as Murray left the bench, Sutter slashed him on the shins. Murray grabbed a linesman who'd seen the contact, irate that a penalty wasn't assessed. Well, a penalty was assessed – against Murray, for touching an official. *(The Hockey News)*

Opposing players didn't realize that Murray's spontaneous outbursts… weren't. "Murray admitted the needling was planned," William Houston wrote in the *Toronto Globe & Mail*. "Those associated with him say he is a fiery but calculating manipulator." Houston said Murray would target players who were the "emotional backbone" of their team, to rattle them.

Combative Flyers goalie Ron Hextall was another target of Murray's verbal grenades. Fast-forward to 2014, Hextall is Philly's new G.M., and who sits beside him at a meeting of general managers but Bryan Murray. "I told Ron, 'You have to understand that when I yelled at a guy, he was a guy who was beating me or I wanted him on my team,'" Murray said. "I didn't care about guys who didn't compete. Ron smiled at me."

THE LEGENDS OF LANDOVER

✪ Official Biography

Murray spotted an official's goof in October, 1985, when a Devils player was sprung from the penalty box early. For protesting too vehemently, Murray was tossed by referee Andy Van Hellemond.

Virtually two years later to the day, the Van Hellemond ejection was commemorated with a more explosive dustup. At a game in Buffalo, ref Bill McCreary whistled a bench minor when Bryan argued a call. Murray believed his question about the original penalty was respectful, and he now wanted an explanation of both calls. As it happened, the officials' room at The Aud in Buffalo was adjacent to the visitors' locker room. So when the first period ended, Murray shouted down the hallway at McCreary.

As the team and officials re-emerged into the corridor for the second period, the coach resumed loudly expressing his dissatisfaction with referee McCreary. All of a sudden, linesman Ron Asselstine – a former football player and motorcycle-gang member – stepped toward Murray.

"We're both very emotional people, very involved," Asselstine told the *Worcester Telegram & Gazette*. "When push came to shove - that's what happened - we pushed each other. I got the impression from hearing some people talk about it that we were rolling around on the floor in the mud and blood and beer. But it was wrong. I stuck my nose into business that didn't concern me." Fortunately, the other linesman, Bob Hodges, had experience breaking apart combatants, and he separated shover and pusher. The NHL suspended both Murray and Asselstine for three games.

(Asselstine received higher marks for a 1989 confrontation at Boston Garden. A moron jumped onto the ice, running toward referee McCreary while his back was turned. Asselstine skated in from the blue line to deliver a check that sent the moron flying into the end boards.)

Lackadaisical effort was a charge Murray frequently hurled at referee Ron Wicks. The coach once told Wicks to "bear down." (Wicks in reply told Murray to *calm* down.) As the third period of a playoff game devolved into a wrestling match, coach accused ref of swallowing his whistle. "I told Wicks, 'Why don't you just go in and take a shower?'" Also incensed by an equipment penalty against Bobby Carpenter in the same game, Murray sought out Wicks for a postgame shouting match under the stands.

Similarly unimpressed by officiating at an October, 1984 home game, "Murray waited for Wicks at the visiting team's exit, then accompanied him toward the officials' dressing room," reported *The Hockey News*. A linesman went to close the door, but "Murray thought Wicks had made a disparaging comment to him and shoved it back open." After some more back-and-forth, Murray departed, along with a gross misconduct penalty.

THE LEGENDS OF LANDOVER

"It seems that every time (Wicks) says something to our bench he has a sneer on his face. Maybe I overreact sometimes when calls are so obviously wrong. But if a guy shows me he's working at the game, very seldom do I scream at him."

At least Bryan was an equal-opportunity arguer. The NHL socked Murray with a $1,000 fine for postgame shouting matches with referees Don Koharski and Wicks. Murray quipped about ref Ron Fournier, "He has good nights and bad nights. I'd just like to be around for one of the good ones."

Referee Paul Stewart wrote at his *hockeybuzz.com* blog, "Bryan was relentless. Bryan also had a tendency to refuse to send his players out on the ice until the referee skated over to the bench. I understand he's doing what he has to do. I don't engage with Bryan when he starts on me. I just skate to the other side of the rink and ignore him."

In Winnipeg, Stewart found turning a deaf ear wasn't an option. The Caps' coach, furious at a non-call, "Demanded I do something. The more Murray hollered, the more the spittle flew. 'Stop spitting on me!' I yelled. That made Bryan angrier. 'You can't disrespect me! I'm going to report this to (supervisor of officials) John D'Amico!' I bagged Bryan with a bench minor."

Paul had company; by the '89-'90 season, *every* current NHL referee had whistled Murray for at least one bench minor; G.M. David Poile kept a running tally. Murray even got tagged once while sitting in the stands! Between periods of an exhibition game vs. Calgary, Bryan spoke too much of his mind to game officials, and cost his team a bench penalty.

✪ Coaching Confrontations

Bryan Murray refused to be intimidated by anyone who took liberties with his Capitals players, or with their coach. Late in a 1984 playoff game, Murray thought the Flyers were throwing goons on the ice (nah, really?). Philadelphia coach Bob McCammon and Murray "shouted at each other, pointing fingers in obvious fury."

Murray especially objected to tough guy Dave Brown's stick work, which had nothing to do with controlling the puck. "(McCammon) said my players didn't have any guts," Murray said. "I suggested that there were a few people sitting on our bench or standing behind it that did."

Murray's opinion didn't change when Mike Keenan replaced McCammon. "I don't like the Flyers' game plan. If you score a goal, it's like gang warfare, with designated hit men out there trying to drag skill players of the other team into the penalty box."

THE LEGENDS OF LANDOVER

Murray told Pittsburgh's Bennett Wolf he didn't belong in the NHL. The coach was right; episodes of thuggery dominated Wolf's minor league resume. Bennett once chased a fan through the stands; while in street clothes, attacked an opponent; and threatened another, "I'll cut your eyes out." Murray had just watched Wolf sucker-punch one of his stars, Bengt Gustafsson. But Murray's verbal jabs at Wolf so enraged Pittsburgh assistant coach Mike Corrigan, that Corrigan threw a water bottle at Murray - and was promptly ejected.

Referee Paul Stewart, in a 1988 Caps game in Detroit, called a late penalty against the Red Wings. On the power play, Mike Gartner's goal with 58 seconds left tied the game. Detroit coach Jacques Demers' howled at the miscarriage of justice, which was funny, because before Stewart put on stripes, he played in the WHA and Demers was his coach!

As the *Detroit Free Press* reported, "Demers threw a tantrum that lasted throughout the overtime." Afterward, Caps coach Murray reviewed his opposite number's performance. "Jacques puts the act into it. He plays the fans pretty well." Like most actors, Demers frowned on critics. "(Murray) is one of the biggest talkers and complainers in this league. I've seen his act."

Former assistant Ron Lapointe shared lessons learned working for Murray. "Preparation and discipline." And something else. "I learned not to yell at the referees," Ron added with a smile. One time in Toronto, though, Lapointe became Murray's tag-team partner, and their wrestling names wouldn't have been Preparation and Discipline. Ron was first to turn around on the bench and return verbal fire from hecklers. Then Murray joined in, going so far as to take a couple of menacing steps toward the Maple Leaf Gardens loudmouths.

✪ Academic Approach

The '80's Capitals subscribed to the motto, *The job isn't finished until the paperwork's in*. Coaches determined game-by-game expectations for every player, then assigned a numerical grade based on whether that player met or exceeded his baseline. Grades were averaged into report cards at 20-game intervals, followed by individual interviews.

"This game is not just a matter of coming to the rink, putting on your skates, and going out there," said assistant coach Terry Murray. "It requires more thought than that." The first time report cards were issued, Terry Murray said, "Some players did a bit of swearing because they thought they deserved better marks." Terry, who spearheaded the system, and even did data entry on his home computer, conceded, "It was controversial at first, but that's what we wanted. The guys talked about it in the dressing room, and some of them talked about how they could get better marks next time."

THE LEGENDS OF LANDOVER

Rod Langway was one of those. "I think it's great to have someone taking down all the things you're doing right and wrong. We all know what our role is." Players traded to the Capitals also approved. David Shand, a 336-game NHL veteran when he arrived, marveled to the *Toronto Globe & Mail*, "I had never been told my role or had it defined so explicitly. Everybody else on the team had adapted, and I would have felt stupid if I didn't."

The academic approach was a natural, given Bryan Murray's background as a high school Phys. Ed. teacher. Murray, said the *Globe & Mail*, "sits down with each player on a regular basis to reinforce what has been taught and what is expected." He welcomed input from players, who answered questionnaires (almost 200 questions!) at 10-game intervals.

Topics ranged from individual performance (What skills do you need help to develop?), to group dynamics (What do you think your role with the team should be?), to what time practice or travel should take place, even to potential roster additions.

We think this is a sample question from the player form, but maybe it's not.	147. **What is Your Favorite Team?** A. **Washington Capitals** B. **Yeah, I'll go with Capitals** C. **I don't mind the AHL**

The innovation reflected Murray's highly regarded communication skills... which still faltered on occasion. Goalie Pete Peeters allowed three goals in the first period of a 1986 game at Quebec, and at intermission, Murray embarrassed Peeters in front of the entire team. Bryan, that's old school.

✪ Changing Of The Guard

By his ninth season as Capitals coach, no one was aware quite how tenuous Bryan Murray's job status was – except Bryan. Murray compiled an outstanding .572 winning percentage from 1981-1990, and was honored with the Jack Adams trophy as NHL coach of the year in 1984.

What he lacked was even one trip to the conference finals, so it figured the hot seat was warming. Still, players, media and fans thought Murray had signed a two-year extension, because that's what general manager David Poile said publicly. Only he and Murray knew the leash was really much shorter. As reported in the *L.A. Times*, Murray agreed to the deception "so players wouldn't be under the impression I was at the whim of them playing well or not playing well."

It didn't matter. After a midseason eight-game losing streak in 1990, Bryan became ex-coach of the Capitals.

THE LEGENDS OF LANDOVER

Like the phantom contract extension, what happed next surprised everyone except Bryan Murray. Poile replaced him with the team's AHL coach, younger brother Terry. "I was tremendously pleased, despite everybody saying everything, that Terry got the job," Bryan told *AP*. "Terry and I talked in the years leading up to when it happened, that, as a coach, you don't last forever. And that he would hopefully be the guy given the opportunity." Bryan recalled his exit conversation with Poile. "I was angry at David for firing me, but I said, 'At least you made one good decision today.'"

Despite all his heat-of-battle fireworks, Murray's legacy remains a proud one. As *USA Today's* Kevin Allen wrote in a 2007 profile, "He has respect around the league for his dignified approach to coaching." The high regard surprisingly included referee Paul Stewart. "A year or two (after Murray was let go), I ran into him. We talked about everything but hockey. We found we had a lot in common. I got a different slant on Bryan Murray that day. What a soft-spoken, intelligent gentleman he was!"

✪ Terry Murray (Coach, 1990-94)

A stay-at-home defenseman during his playing days, Terry was actually the first of the Murray brothers to reach Landover. He was claimed off waivers from Philadelphia by the Caps on Oct. 5, 1981. 37 days later, Bryan was promoted from AHL Hershey and became his brother's last NHL coach. Nothing new for the siblings; being eight years older, Bryan often doubled as mentor. Bryan, for instance, was Terry's high school basketball coach.

The player never expected favoritism from the coach, and the coach never provided any. Well, once. Two days after Christmas, the flight home from Buffalo was cancelled. Among the things Terry didn't pack extra of was cash, and Bryan floated him a loan.

In 1983, Terry began five seasons as Bryan's assistant, then went to Baltimore to coach the team's AHL affiliate. The relationship changed in January, 1990, when Terry agreed to replace Bryan as Caps coach. According to the *L.A. Times*, Terry phoned his older brother. "'Bryan, I'm really sorry the way things have turned out for you.' He said, 'Hey, I had a good run at it and now it's your time.'" Bryan had sacrificed wins to groom a crop of young players. Terry reaped the benefits, guiding the Caps to 1990 playoff wins over the Devils and Rangers, and their first conference finals.

For three of his five seasons as Capitals coach, Terry went head to head with Bryan, then coach-G.M. in Detroit. "I get excited coaching against him," Terry told *AP*. "We're competitive, so he wants to beat me as much as I want to beat him. I want to prove he taught me a few things." Bryan's deadpan response: "What does he know? He's the younger brother."

THE LEGENDS OF LANDOVER

✪ Coaching Brothers: Epilogue

Sibling rivalry? naturally; sibling tension? no way. "We're not going to let anyone drive a wedge between us," Terry Murray once said. "Bryan and I have gone through enough of that in Washington." More "of that" happened in January, 1994, when David Poile fired his second Murray brother.

Terry would follow Bryan as coach of another NHL franchise four years later. But that was OK, because the person hiring him was... Bryan Murray, who was also G.M. of the Florida Panthers, and wanted to step away from the dual role of coach. Bryan Murray told the *Philadelphia Daily News* that Terry worked so hard, "Even I have to make an appointment to see him."

(Sources for Bryan and Terry Murray entries: Washington Post, Los Angeles Times, Philadelphia Inquirer, Boston Globe, Toronto Globe & Mail, AP, Doylestown Daily Intelligencer, Annapolis Capital, Sporting News)

✪ David Poile (General Manager, 1982-97)

The Capitals almost missed out on hiring David Poile before the 1982-83 season. Poile, anxious to run his own shop, applied early in the offseason for the vacant top job in Detroit. The Red Wings in June ended up selecting Jim Devellano. (In his book, *The Road to Hockeytown*, Devellano suggests his winning edge was how well he got along with the owner's wife and her daughter!)

Poile, assistant G.M. in Calgary, was therefore still available when the Caps hired him on August 30, 1982. If Detroit had snagged him first, there might have been no Montreal Four trade, no winning, no spike in attendance, and after a while, maybe no Capitals in Washington.

✪ Devellano Vs. Poile, Round 2

Move ahead three seasons. In diving terms, Devellano is seeking to execute, not merely a splash, but a cannonball. "We're going to see if we can't trade a big name for a big name," said the Wings G.M. He contacted Poile, whose Montreal deal proved he, too, was comfortable swimming in the deep end of the trade pool. According to the *Sporting News*, "Devellano sought rookie Caps defenseman Kevin Hatcher for Ron Duguay, and either Bobby Carpenter or Mike Gartner for John Ogrodnick."

If true, no wonder Poile declined. Yet Devellano painted his Washington counterpart as the hard-liner. "He wants a ham sandwich for a cookie." Let me check; the sandwich is the prize in Devellano's comparison, right? Jimmy might not have been familiar with the concept of the "sweet deal."

THE LEGENDS OF LANDOVER

✪ Loose Lips Sink Trades

David Poile had a reputation as tight-lipped. No exceptions where trades were concerned, not even for David's own father. Keep in mind that "Bud" Poile wasn't just David's dad; Bud had been an NHL player and general manager, and an NHL Hall of Famer. Yet Bud told Kevin Allen of *USA Today* about one summer day in 1982, when he shared a cab with his son. The elder Poile asked, "Have you got anything going?" The G.M. responded, "Not much. Just talk."

Not exactly. Mere hours later, David Poile finalized the biggest trade in Caps history, bringing Rod Langway to Washington. Credit the younger Poile's world class poker face. Internally, as David told the *Boston Globe*, "I was shaking in my boots." Remember, Poile was just 32, the youngest G.M. in the league, and on the job for all of 10 days! How did Bud Poile find out about his son's blockbuster deal? Oh, when he opened his sports section the next morning. Blood may be thicker than water, but not the ink on trade documents.

✪ Unlisted Numbers

The fiercest competition in pro sports isn't televised. No arena necessary, because no tickets are sold. Yet the battles are bruising, often leaving permanent scars. It's the competition known as Contract Negotiations.

Washington's front office of the '80's looked for any edge, as Ed Frankovic, who compiled statistics for the Caps, told *stormingthecrease.com*. "The coaches got the stats - ice time, face-offs, hits. Those weren't published, weren't common knowledge. We were told by David Poile and the coaches, 'Don't let the players know what their ice times are, because this is sensitive information; the agents will use it for negotiating contracts.'"

Poile's "obsession with secrecy" rankled *Toronto Globe & Mail* columnist William Houston. "He is the only general manager in the league who sends his media-relations man into the dressing room after practices to listen to what reporters are asking his players." I'm not sure which reveals more, Poile's desire to know the content of media interviews, or Houston pouting in print about it. Then again, *Hockey News* writer Steve Simmons coined the term, "Poile-noia." Why? "Poile ordered his PR staff not to put players' game-by-game statistics in the game notes."

These days, ordinary fans can pour over a wealth of statistics at the click of a mouse - even while a game's in progress. Shot charts and salary-cap implications are frequent message board fodder. For followers of analytics, two important names in the league are Corsi and Fenwick. So it's revealing that basic numbers were once guarded as state secrets.

THE LEGENDS OF LANDOVER

✪ Capitals 2.0

The year before Poile's arrival, the Capitals dressed 44 players. The trend would continue to game one in 1982, when the Montreal Four were among 10 players - half the roster - making their team debut. In the *NHL Jeopardy* category "Familiar Faces," the answer was Dennis Maruk, Mike Gartner, Bengt Gustafsson, and Bobby Carpenter. The question: Who are the only four from the '81 Caps' opening-day roster to make it to the '82 opener? Poile tackled that transient image at training camp, according to Gary Ronberg of the *Philadelphia Inquirer*. "Poile emphasized that they need not feel the weight of Washington's losing image. 'Who's a Washington Cap?' he asked, then answered, 'Nobody's a Washington Cap. You haven't been around long enough to become one. So let's start our franchise today.'"

✪ Sobering Realizations

The shocking death of Flyers star goalie Pelle Lindbergh in November, 1985, rocked the NHL. Lindbergh, who liked driving his Porsche way too fast, got behind the wheel drunk, lost control, and fatally smashed into a concrete wall. While the tragedy was most severely felt by the Flyers, the crash posed an issue for executives on every team.

Capitals G.M. David Poile told the *Baltimore Sun* he wouldn't be lecturing on drinking and driving. "No, not at all," Poile said. "When an athlete does something like this, there's great public interest, way beyond the normal. Every one of our players is in shock, but we're not father figures. We'll continue to treat them like the men that they are. I've seen a lot of college-age kids, and they do a lot worse things. Our players' dedication away from the rink on a scale of 1-10 would be about a nine."

✪ Saving Face

Poile was decidedly more proactive regarding on-ice safety. He put pen to paper in March, 1983, after Mike Gartner and Brian Engblom suffered eye injuries. "All I did was issue a memo to the players saying that I did not want anyone to think it was macho to play without a helmet, and that it was not a sign of weakness to wear a helmet or a shield," the G.M. told the *Philadelphia Inquirer*. "We didn't want players to have any reservations about it, and if it made them feel better, we wanted them to wear one. And we wanted them to know that all of this was endorsed by management."

✪ Leave Your Criticism At The Beep

Overheard by the *L.A. Times*: "Answering the phone in his office one day, Poile tried to disguise his voice, making it sound as if the caller had reached a recording. 'Hello, this is David Poile and no, I don't have any answers for what's wrong with the hockey team.'"

THE LEGENDS OF LANDOVER

✪ Valuable Property

Trades aren't always about equal value; the Caps, for instance, gave Mike Palmateer back to Toronto in 1982 because the Leafs agreed to absorb most of the goalie's $200,000 salary. Poile told *The Hockey News* about the poor quality of trade offers at a time the Caps were slumping. "The best offer I've gotten was a two-week paid vacation in Hawaii for taking a player from another team they don't want because he's a problem."

Poile had an aging asset to move, so he contacted his old boss, Flames G.M. Cliff Fletcher. According to the *Syracuse Herald-Journal*, Poile offered to surrender a draft pick if Fletcher would take an underperforming property off his hands - Poile's house. David had purchased a home in Calgary when he was assistant G.M. there. Alberta's real estate market proceeded to tank, so the home remained unsold three years later. Poile lamented, "What is this game coming to when my house becomes a story?" Yes, David was kidding about the draft pick. Wasn't he?

✪ Tops In Integrity

We all wish to be described with words like honest, straightforward, responsible. The man who hired David Poile, Capitals president Dick Patrick, used those exact words for the G.M. "He's tops in integrity. He treats people the right way. Sometimes he has to do things like fire coaches. Things like that are never easy, but I think he's always approached the hard things in the correct manner and he was just really diligent and hard working."

Craig Laughlin, whom Poile brought to Washington in the 1982 Montreal trade, liked how the boss carried himself. "He was always loyal. He always talked to you. He wasn't a G.M. who would just walk by you, even if you were playing lousy. A lot of G.M.s would just kind of turn away (thinking), 'I might be dealing him or whatever. I don't want to talk to him today.' That was never David, and to me that was the reason that we had success. It was those dynamics that made the team."

(Patrick and Laughlin quotes from nhl.com)

THE LEGENDS OF LANDOVER

15th Shift: *'70's and '80's, By The Numbers*

✪ 1 – Patrick Division Banner

In the 24 years prior to joining the Southeast Division in 1998, the Caps won just a single regular season title. The 1988-89 Patrick winners were unusual among Capitals teams in several ways. For starters, they were defensively leaky, surrendering a lead of two or more goals 18 times. How did Washington still finish third-best in the league? The answer was the jolt to their traditionally pedestrian offense by a trio of 40-goal scorers, Geoff Courtnall (42), Mike Ridley (41), and Dino Ciccarelli (44, 12 with the Caps).

Seismic shakeups at the '89 trade deadline were also way out of character. The stability-first Caps had scuttled an early season mega-trade which almost sent Larry Murphy, Dave Christian and Michal Pivonka to Minnesota for Brian Bellows and Dave Archibald. G.M. David Poile told the *Sporting News* at the time, "If you're happy with the level of talent you have, a lot of times change can just be disruptive."

Yet March would bring significant changes. First, Clint Malarchuk and Grant Ledyard went to Buffalo for Calle Johansson, who would blossom into one of the great defensemen in Caps history. Minutes before the deadline, Poile triggered a blockbuster, reuniting with his earlier almost-trade-partner in Minnesota. The Capitals got defenseman Bob Rouse for Murphy, who had become a whipping boy of the Capital Centre faithful. What dropped jaws around the NHL was the swap of veteran right wings with Hall-of-Fame scoring prowess, Mike Gartner (397 goals, 392 assists) for Ciccarelli (332 goals, 325 assists).

If those numbers appear similar, the North Stars thought so too during contentious contract negotiations with Ciccarelli the previous summer. Since Gartner earned $200,000 per year plus incentives, Minnesota reasoned that was a fair offer to Dino. Ciccarelli eventually signed for closer to $350,000 per year. According to the *Toronto Star*, "When Gartner heard of the Minnesota scenario featuring his name and the numbers involved, he immediately requested that his contract - in year two of a four-year deal - be renegotiated upwards." Lingering hard feelings between player and management in both cities might have been a factor in the swap.

Dino's immediate, eye-popping dividends included four goals and three assists in an 8-2 romp at Hartford. At home March 26 against the Islanders, Dino's ninth shot of the game found the twine with 2:48 left to break a 2-2 tie. Not only did that propel the Caps to a dramatic eighth straight victory, it secured the franchise's first division title. Since the realignment of NHL divisions the year the Capitals were born, only the Flyers and Islanders had finished first in the Patrick.

THE LEGENDS OF LANDOVER

Owner Abe Pollin shared the joy of all long-suffering fans. "I screamed and jumped and hugged my wife," he told the *Post*. "To change the structure of the team with three weeks to go in the regular season, that takes something," said Winnipeg G.M. Mike Smith about Poile. "Give David credit for making those changes. He thought they were necessary and did it." Only one thing stayed depressingly familiar - the postseason flameout. Philadelphia bounced D.C. out of the playoffs in the 1st round.

✪ 107 – Standings Points In The Capitals' Underrated Season

The Capitals' best pre-Ovechkin regular season record actually came in 1985-86: 50-23-7. Philadelphia won the division with 110 points, three better than Washington. Next, some number-crunching reveals why '85-'86 deserves a ranking among the greatest regular seasons in Caps history.

An increase in the number of regular season games, plus changes in how the league awards standings points, complicates statistical comparisons. The 2009-10, 2015-16 and 2016-17 D.C. squads blew past all that came before in terms of wins and points; for this discussion, let's compare one of those teams against the '85-'86 Caps.

The 2009-10 Capitals smashed team records for wins (54) and points (121). The 1985-86 Caps, in contrast, earned 50 wins and 107 points. But just hold on a gol-darn minute. (Or is that goal-darn minute?) Back in '85-'86, teams played two fewer games, didn't earn a point for overtime losses, and there was no shootout. So which Capitals team actually had the more dominant regular season against the rest of its NHL competition?

The '09-'10 Caps, for example, earned *3* standings points during the extra two games at the end of the season (one win and one shootout loss). They won five games during the season via shootout, gaining *5* more points than if the games had ended in ties. Finally, the change in rules allowed them to collect *12* points for OT and shootout losses.

That adds up to 20 points not available to the 1985-86 team. So, here's the "point." By 1980's NHL computations, the 2009-10 Caps would have earned 48 wins and 101 standings points. That's fewer in both categories than the Landover squad of Gustafsson, Stevens, Langway, et al.

✪ 19 – Most Consecutive Periods Scoring At Least One Goal

Bobby Carpenter ignited a consistant six-game stretch with a power play goal in the first period of a 7-4 win vs. St. Louis on December 22, 1984. The Capitals scored at least one goal in 19 consecutive periods, including one in overtime.

THE LEGENDS OF LANDOVER

✪ 7 – Fewest Shots On Goal In A Game

Caps fans who love pouring over shots-on-goal statistics - and really, who doesn't? - should pay special attention to games with Philadelphia. (Okay, non-stat geeks may be excused.) These nuggets were culled by "Miami Screaming Eagles," a moderator on the *Hockey's Future* website:

• The Flyers held the Caps to a franchise-low seven shots in a 1978 game; The Caps held the Flyers to a franchise-low 13 shots in a 1990 game.

• The shot-clock operator had his thumb on the scale on March 7, 1982. Both thumbs. The final total was exactly 45 shots apiece in Philly's 7-1 win.

• Washington's first win in the rivalry was a 6-0 shutout authored by Mike Palmateer on Dec. 21, 1980 - despite 44 Philadelphia shots. Palmateer foiled a furious start by the Flyers, with 14 saves in the first seven minutes.

• The Flyers took 62 shots in a 1976 game; the Capitals responded with 52 in a 1988 tilt.

✪ 0 – Fewest Shots Allowed In A Period

The day after Christmas in 1975 started like an extra lump of coal in the stocking of the second-season Capitals. Greg Joly and Ace Bailey managed to both take penalties 53 seconds into the game, and 11 ticks after that, Minnesota scored a five-on-three goal.

Little could the 11,881 at Capital Centre have imagined that the North Stars offense was done for the night. Minnesota recorded six shots the rest of the first period, five in the second, and NONE in the third, when the Caps outshot them, 9-0. One of those nine was the tying goal by Nelson Pyatt, in what ended as a 1-1 draw. The Stars didn't even manage a shot on a third-period power play. Quite the turnaround from their most recent third period in Buffalo, when they surrendered a whopping 22 shots – and eight goals – to the Sabres. News accounts say Washington goalie Bernie Wolfe stuck around for the final 20 minutes, though he didn't really need to.

✪ 35 – Games Without A Regular-Season Overtime Loss

An overtime loss in Winnipeg on February 19, 1984 is notable for ending a Capitals' 14-game unbeaten streak. No one knew it was the demarcation line for a new streak. The Capitals would not lose in their next 35 regular season overtime games, winning 10 and tying the rest. The streak lasted three years, until a 5-4 OT loss to the Rangers on Feb. 7, 1987. The Caps fell two short the NHL record set by the 1930's Bruins, who went 37 overtimes without losing. (Overtimes weren't played from 1941-1983.)

THE LEGENDS OF LANDOVER

The final victory of the streak came on New Year's Day in 1987 against Pittsburgh. Mike Gartner, playing with a bum elbow, netted a breakaway for a 4-3 victory. Necessity was the mother of a game-winner. "The way I was taped up, I couldn't extend my arm," Gartner said. "So I used a wrist shot to place the puck instead of trying to put it through the goalie." The Caps only made it to overtime because a shot ricocheted off Gaetan Duchesne's leg to tie the game with 48 seconds left.

Other lucky bounces helped the Caps maintain the streak. The 25th and final OT tie of the stretch, a 3-3 deadlock with the Islanders, came courtesy of two Mike Gartner goals in the final six minutes. The *Canadian Press* explained the lucky part: "With the Islanders on a power play in the extra period, Ken Leiter's soft flip shot was deflected by teammate Brent Sutter, who raised his stick thinking the puck had gone into the net. So did goalie Bob Mason, who started skating away dejectedly. However, the puck clanged off the post and remained in play. 'I thought it was in,' Mason said. 'I was as surprised as the guy who tipped it.'"

OT success involved reversing a defense-first philosophy. "We try to win in overtime," coach Bryan Murray told *AP*. "A lot of teams play for the tie. We have a lot of confidence going in because of our goaltending and defense." "It's funny, but for some reason we play much more responsible when we go into overtime," winger Bobby Gould said to the *Annapolis Capital*. "We pick our spots to take chances and don't give up many three-on-twos. I don't know why we can't do that in the first period."

✪ $50 – The Price Of Losing

For the 1984-85 season, Caps coach Bryan Murray added new meaning to the phrase, "Costly Losses." Murray decreed that the Capitals should achieve a minimum of 12 standings points for each 10-game chunk of the season. "Failing that," explained *AP*, "each player will be asked to donate $50 to charity." Coincidentally - or not - the Caps earned exactly 12 points over the first 10 games of the season.

Then they relaxed the grip on their wallets, winning just two of their next ten games. Not only did coach Murray collect the charity donations, he upped the ante: the next 12-point quota would have to be earned in nine games instead of 10.

The team responded with a 7-1-1 stretch. In fact, they went 27-5-3 after paying the penalty. Murray wielded financial carrots as well as sticks. For meeting pre-set team goals, players and their partners would be treated to dinner, or flowers sent to the significant others. Murray credited the improvement to more physical play. But was it possible they were just being more economical?

THE LEGENDS OF LANDOVER

✪ 50 – Minutes Of Robert Picard's Single-Game Ice Time

"I've been down on myself," defenseman Robert Picard confessed in December, 1978. "I've been miserable for the last two or three weeks, not playing as much as I wanted to, not getting the ice time I need to be effective." How much would that be, Robert? "I'd like to play 45, 50, even 55 minutes every game. The more I play, the better I get."

When you're 21 years old you wish for such things, and coach Danny Belisle was happy to oblige. Picard barely visited the bench during a January 9, 1979 home game against the Flyers. He scored one goal, assisted on another, and while the Caps lost 5-2, Robert's play was regarded as outstanding. Belisle on his ironman: "He said he wanted to play 50, even 55 minutes a night. I'm just trying to accommodate him." (*Quotes from Washington Star*)

✪ 23-2-2 – Dominant Early '80's Record vs. Pittsburgh

Since recent history with Pittsburgh (pre-2018) is unpleasant, it's soothing to reflect on the early '80's. The Capitals routinely beat the Pens, dare we say, *like a rented mule.* David Fink of the *Pittsburgh Post-Gazette* wrote admiringly about the Caps' stifling defensive style. "There are more enjoyable ways to kill time than playing the Capitals. A trip to the dentist, an IRS audit, a week on the rack."

Some highlights: Washington extended an unbeaten streak in the series to 15 wins and one tie on November 20, 1985 at Pittsburgh. "We're not the Edmonton Oilers," said Craig Laughlin, who scored twice in a 3-1 win. "We don't do anything fancy. But once we pull ahead, it's tough to come back."

The Pens got an especially cold reception at Capital Centre in the 1984-85 season. Squashed 9-1 by the Caps on December 2, 1984, there was also no hot water for the visitors' postgame showers. Blown out 6-2 on January 17, 1985, there *still* wasn't any hot water for their showers.

A sellout in Landover on April 1, 1986 saw the Capitals win again, 5-3. Larry Murphy scored his 20th goal and added two assists, and Pete Peeters stopped 24 of 27 shots. That gave Washington a remarkable 23-2-2 record against Pittsburgh, dating back to December, 1982.

"They are disciplined, and love to grind it out, wear you down, and beat you at the end," said Pens coach Bob Berry, Added defenseman Doug Bodger, "More than any team, they wait for you to make a mistake, and then beat you by a goal." Concluded Fink of the *Post-Gazette*, "To appreciate how committed the Caps are to defense, their brightest star is Rod Langway. He handles the puck flawlessly and prevents goals with an almost religious fervor."

THE LEGENDS OF LANDOVER

✪ 3,314 – Games Needed to Rise Above .500 All-Time

1974 OCT. 9 −1

1982 NOV. 5 −216

2010 APR. 9 +1 ?

2017 FEB. 4 +1 ✓

Back in 1978, Capitals beat writer Russ White landed a long-range prediction damn close to the pin. "The Capitals may have to play 50 years to come even close to a .500 lifetime record after their dismal entry into the National Hockey League." The Capitals could've owned a winning all-time record at least once – if they'd beaten the Rangers in their first-ever game. Instead, it wouldn't happen for 35 years. (Don't tell the NHL, but it actually took 42 years!)

The low-water mark came early in the 1982-83 season. When the Capitals lost a 4-3 home decision to St. Louis, the franchise dropped 216 games under .500 since their inception. Langway, Hunter, Bondra, Kolzig, et al. undertook the long trek to respectability; Ovechkin & Co. completed the Everest-like climb with a 5-2 home victory over Atlanta on April 9, 2010. Their all-time record at the final horn: 1,215 wins, 1,214 losses, 303 ties, and 71 overtime defeats.

A mere 2,944 games and 12,935 days later, the Capitals had reached the heights of one game above .500 for the first time ever. Um, wait. What about those 71 OT defeats? Doesn't that mean the Caps were still actually 70 games underwater? Not according to the New Math, NHL style.

The Caps couldn't truly lay claim to being a winning franchise until a 3-2 victory in Montreal on February 4, 2017 (an additional 370 games and 2,493 more days!). As Marv Albert would say, the Caps were now 1,506 up and 1,505 down, plus those 303 pre-shootout deadlocks.

✪ 4 – Most Capitals In An All-Star Game

Four players represented the Capitals at the 1985 NHL All-Star Game in Calgary. No, that wasn't the most for any one team; Edmonton placed eight players, plus coach Glen Sather. You know how popular that must have been with the Flames' fans!

Three of the Caps were winger Mike Gartner, center Bobby Carpenter, and defenseman Scott Stevens. The fourth, defenseman Rod Langway, earns special mention for his entrance at the Saddledome. As each player was announced, he put on a cowboy hat, symbolizing the western Canadian theme. Bucking (get it?) tradition, the fun-loving Langway put his Stetson on sideways. We can only assume, though this is unconfirmed, that Rod recognized the vast North American TV audience, and wanted to promote his upcoming tour-de-force, "Napoleon On Ice."

THE LEGENDS OF LANDOVER

✪ 8 – Consecutive Games With Multiple Power Play Goals

The NHL in 1987-88 got one of its periodic pangs of conscience, declaring a crackdown on clutching and grabbing. The Caps took advantage of the rise in hooking, holding, and interference penalties. During an eight game November stretch, 11 of their 17 goals were scored with the extra man.

Following a shutout loss to Detroit, Washington's power play ramped up again, collecting two or more PPGs in eight games in a row. Notable in that stretch, November 27 against Pittsburgh, with Mike Ridley scoring on a power play for the third consecutive game; and December 1, as PPGs by Ridley and Bengt Gustafsson led a 4-2 victory over Edmonton, the sixth win over the powerful Oilers in their last seven meetings.

The power surge reached maximum on December 6, a 10-3 home rout of L.A. Kevin Hatcher scored two, Gustafsson and Ridley one apiece; four extra-man goals in the game, raising the Caps' success rate for the season to 25%. (In the third period, Washington couldn't miss. Bob Gould, Dale Hunter, Dave Christian, Ridley, and Hunter again scored on five consecutive shots past Kings goalie Roland Melanson!)

In all, the Capitals scored at least one PPG in 12 straight games. Ridley (five goals), Gary Galley (eight assists), and Mike Gartner (11 points on four goals, seven assists) were offensive leaders in the streak. The only thing sour about the power: the Caps went 5-6-1 in those dozen games.

✪ 11 – Consecutive Games Without Allowing A 3rd Period Goal

An amazing defensive lockdown by the Caps began in Buffalo on January 25, 1984. Ron Langway scored the lone third period goal in a 2-2 tie, starting an 11-game streak of third period shutouts. Most impressive of all was a 9-2 beatdown of mighty Edmonton on February 5, in which the Caps scored as many third-period goals (six) as the Oilers had shots.

Washington went 10-0-1 during the run, outscoring opponents in the third period by a combined 26-0. Only twice did the opponent even reach double digits in shots during the final 20 minutes: 8-6-12-6-7-6-6-8-13-4-8.

The final game of the streak came February 18 in St. Louis, when third period tallies by Alan Haworth, Bobby Carpenter and Doug Jarvis erased a 2-1 deficit. "In a game like that," Caps coach Bryan Murray told the *St. Louis Post Dispatch*, "We can be patient enough to give ourselves a chance to win. When you adopt a (defensive) style of play, it's nice to be rewarded." Blues coach Jacques Demers added simply, "They're the best defensive team in the NHL."

THE LEGENDS OF LANDOVER

✪ -1,103 – A Mountain Of Minuses

The expansion Capitals of 1974-75 provided a numerical cornucopia of misery; Medusa numbers so hideous, that staring directly at them could turn the viewer into stone. How to choose just one for this chapter?

From the five-star smorgasbord of awful, numbers we bypass include the losses (67), goals allowed (446), and shots allowed (3,064, or 38+ every night). Caps goalies made more saves per game on average (32.7) than NHL teams took shots (30.8). Our eyes are starting to sting, so let's settle on the obscure but revealing *-1,103* as our representative number. Negative eleven-hundred-and-three is the insane cumulative plus-minus rating for all Caps skaters in their inaugural season.

✪ 6 – Wedding Bells Chimed In 1987 Off-Season

Hockey Cupid worked overtime between the end of the '86-'87 campaign and next season's training camp. Six Capitals got hitched: Dave Christian, Kelly Miller, Larry Murphy, Michal Pivonka, Mike Ridley and Scott Stevens.

For Christian, tying the knot silenced nosy teammates. As a bachelor, Dave remembered being teased about a late night, post-game date. "We won the night before. I rolled out of bed early the next morning, only to find the guys (at practice) laughing at my very red, bloodshot eyes. They wanted to hear how it happened." (*Profile Network Magazine*)

The Caps organization made a great first impression on Kelly Miller's new bride, Shelby. "As soon as we heard about the trade, the next day I had a bouquet of flowers sent to me, wishing me luck in the hard endeavors I was going to have in front of me. There's just nothing like that on any team I've ever heard of. It's very classy and very family oriented." *(WDCA-TV)*

✪ 1 – Seasons Finishing First Quarter In The Black Through 1989-90

From their inception through the 1980's, the Caps always seemed to hit the snooze alarm at the start of the season. A 6-10-4 opening in 1989 ensured that only once in their first 16 seasons would Washington have a winning record at the one-quarter-pole (11-6-3 in 1985-86). The solution, mentioned to general manager David Poile, would be to trick the players by erecting Christmas trees at training camp. According to the *Chicago Tribune*, an amused Poile responded, "Not a bad idea. I'll have to think about that." The Capitals, sluggish out of the gate, proved to be remarkably fast closers. For the last eight of those 16 seasons, they rallied to make the playoffs.

THE LEGENDS OF LANDOVER

16th Shift: *More Stuff Legends Are Made Of*

✪ Mike's Money Matters

Giveaways are a negative statistic, except in this case. For each goal he scored in the '86-'87 season, Mike Gartner pledged $50 to Children's National Medical Center, and got local businesses to match that amount – times 20. Gartner's 41-goal campaign netted the hospital a combined $43,050. Off the ice, Gartner knew all about rugs. Not hairpieces – *rugs*. "Mike always treated hockey like a business," noted linemate Bobby Carpenter. "I used to go over to his house for dinner and I noticed he had a lot of area rugs. He said he could take those with him if he got traded."

For his last contract negotiation with the Caps, Gartner ditched his agent. "I feel I know my work," he said to *The Hockey News*. "I know basically what I'm worth, so I don't feel I should be paying someone to do that for me. But knowing what you're worth and getting that – well, that's a different story."

✪ Black Marks

On another negotiating front, Gartner can attest that black scuff marks carry more weight with baseball umpires than hockey referees. The 1957 Braves and 1969 Mets each won World Series in which a baseball scuffed with shoe polish was presented as evidence that one of their batters had been hit on the foot with a pitch.

Against the Rangers in 1982, Gartner's pleas for similar relief went unanswered, despite his presentation of the evidence. "Can you believe what they got away with out there? Take a look at my sweater," Mike said to reporters. *The Hockey News* confirmed that "Gartner's white jersey was covered with black marks on the chest and sleeves, the imprint left by New York sticks that had hooked and hacked him most of the night." Gartner confronted referee Bob Myers about the New York defender's stick between his legs which dragged him down on a breakaway. "He told me he was about to call it, but he figured I was taking a dive."

✪ Sartorial Solution

Gartner came up with a novel approach for making sure opponents' illegal stickwork didn't go unpunished. The plan relied on custom alterations to his number 11 sweater. "I used to shorten it up, and I got it a size or two bigger, because I wanted it loose. If I could get a defenseman hooking me and (the referee) seeing my jersey swinging in the wind with the hook, I felt I could draw more penalties." *(Gartner, on a Capitals Social podcast)*

THE LEGENDS OF LANDOVER

✪ Minor Penalties

For former Caps, the road from Landover to the minors was strewn, not just with broken dreams, but also broken promises. Rueful comments were collected by *The Morning Call* reporter Joe Kitka, who tagged along on a 1984 road trip with the Hershey Bears, the Caps' AHL farm team.

Rugged winger Lou Franceschetti: "I've played some in the NHL and what keeps you going is what they say to you. They might say we're going to give you a shot but then they never do." Chris Valentine, one-time 30-goal scorer: "I grew up thinking the top 20 players with the most talent make it. But that's not the way it is at all. There's a lot of politics involved."

Do players overestimate their value? Likely. Does management make decisions based on factors beside skill? Also likely. Goalie Dave Parro, winner of 21 games with the Caps: "I've been through this many times. Naturally when they send you down you're depressed, but you can't get frustrated because that will affect your play."

D-man Paul MacKinnon, who bounced between Landover and Hershey for three seasons: "No matter what guys say, it's an easy life. For seven months, all arrangements are taken care of. All we do is play hockey." But not for the Capitals. Just weeks after their interviews, when the '83-'84 season ended, MacKinnon, Parro, and Valentine were released from the organization. None of the trio ever again set skate to NHL ice.

Franceschetti's wife Diane, on being a hockey spouse: "I worry a lot about his safety. After a game, he's bruised pretty well, and I hope 10 years down the road it doesn't add up." Lou thought the "road closed" sign would appear sooner. "At my age (26), I'm over the hill," Franceschetti said in the 1984 article. Hardly! Lou played 285 more games as a Capitals fan favorite. When Franceschetti finally hung 'em up in the late '90's, Lou had dressed for 20 teams in nine different leagues, including two roller hockey leagues!

✪ Recipe For Success

The following morsel came from *Sports Illustrated*, or maybe *Bon Appétit*: "G.M. David Poile was concerned that younger Capitals, particularly the bachelors, weren't eating properly, and he tried to get them all to take cooking lessons." The team turned to a surprising instructor: P.R. director Lou Corletto. Lou was "an experienced cook known to dabble in gourmet foods." (*Chicago Tribune*) Corletto's bone fides apparently weren't affected by the team's nickname for him – "Cupcake".

(Despite a team executive doubling as nutritionist, there's no evidence the Caps combined other job descriptions; coaches weren't recruited to drive the team bus, or healthy scratches asked to sell programs.)

THE LEGENDS OF LANDOVER

After morning practices, young unmarried players headed, notebooks in hand, to Corletto's kitchen. Explained Lou, "There's always a concern when you have players away from home for the first time." Like 20 year old Scott Stevens. "The class really helped me. I was one of those players who ate at fast-food restaurants," said Stevens. "My mother did all the cooking at home, and I didn't know the first thing. I didn't even know that pasta was good to eat before a game." Under Corletto's tutelage, Stevens transitioned from Big Macs to baking chicken breasts marinated in teriyaki sauce.

Another pupil, winger Gaetan Duchesne, also had tutoring from his new Italian bride. "My wife is a good cook," said Duchesne. "I eat a lot of fettuccine and a Caesar salad, and then I feel great by game time."

✪ "Randy" Reading

Caps defenseman Randy Holt possessed a briefcase more enigmatic than the one in *Pulp Fiction*. Teammate Dennis Maruk described it in Maruk's autobiography: "On a flight… Randy opened up his briefcase… pulled out the Bible and started reading it. He looks over the Bible for a few minutes and then puts it back. Then he reaches into another pocket in the briefcase and pulls out *Hustler, Playboy*, and *Penthouse* magazines."

✪ Czech, Please

Rookie Michel Pivonka had a surprise waiting for him in the corner, during a 1986 game against the Canucks. Vancouver's Rick Lanz, whose family had also fled Czechoslovakia, spoke about his countryman to the *Toronto Star*. "(Pivonka) pinned me up against the boards," said Lanz, laughing at the memory. "My mouth was wired because of a broken jaw and I couldn't speak too well. But I said something in Czech like 'take it easy. Don't be a dirty Czech.' He looked at me in surprise and, when we lined up for the faceoff, he stared at me again before he moved in for the draw."

✪ Glove-ly

Michael Jackson's famous single white glove debuted on a Motown TV special in 1983. Five years later, Caps forward Michael Ridley showed off a single left glove at an October, 1988 home game against Pittsburgh. While Ridley's glove wasn't adorned with silver sequins, The King of Pop never used his to complete a hat trick.

When Ridley's right glove fell off behind Pittsburgh's net, cheater Paul Coffey swept it all the way out to the blue line. "I thought about skating out to get it," Ridley told *The Hockey News*. Meanwhile, another Michal (Pivonka) was teeing up a shot. "I moved in front with the play, and the puck hit my left glove and went in. That was real lucky, because if it had been my right hand, I might have been out for a month."

THE LEGENDS OF LANDOVER

✪ After You; No, After You

Capital Centre fans waiting for game two of a 1984 playoff series noticed a problem – no players. The *Annapolis Capital* reported on mind games between coaches Bob McCammon of the Flyers and Bryan Murray of the Caps. "McCammon tried to psyche his opponent out" by making the Caps take the ice first. "When Murray refused to let his counterpart get away with that bit of one-upsmanship, the game was delayed almost 10 minutes. Finally, referee Bryan Lewis made both teams enter at the same time." Despite the stall, the Capitals won the game, 6-2, and the series.

✪ Peter (Half A) Puck

Slices are best avoided in golf - and hockey, as Mike Gartner can attest. Mike sheared a puck in half during a 1982 Caps-Jets game. Reyn Davis wrote about it in the *Winnipeg Free Press*. "Gartner shot so hard, barely missing (goalie Doug) Soetaert's head, the puck broke in two after striking the glass. Players headed for each piece before referee Bruce Hood stopped the action. 'I've never seen that happen before,' said Soetaert, who turned to see two pieces of puck littering the ice after Gartner's shot."

Amazingly, the scene was repeated a year later at Capital Centre. As Bill McGraw of the *Detroit Free Press* recounted, "The puck split in two pieces during one rush over the Washington blue line, and the Wings continued to play both pieces until the whistle."

Only Monty Python could have anticipated such an absurd scenario, with their song, "Eric The Half A Bee." We've substituted "puck" for "bee."
Half a puck, philosophically, Must, ipso facto, half not be.
But half the puck has got to be, Vis-à-vis, its entity. D'you see?

✪ Talk About High Sticking

Until records are kept for the slowest shot ever to wind up in the net, consider this nominee from an October, 1983 game in New York. As the Rangers' Dave Maloney fired a left point slapshot, his stick exploded. The shaft rocketed up, way up, toward the Madison Square Garden roof – the only hockey stick ever tracked by NASA. Maloney skated toward the bench, which is where players normally go when their stick breaks in two.

Meanwhile, the puck began a leisurely journey slower than Manhattan rush hour traffic. Somehow, the seeing-eye disc avoided a tangle of players. It reached Caps goalie Pat Riggin, who attempted a poke check, and missed. The puck, unhurried and unfazed, rolled on, nestling inside the right post. Hearing cheers, Maloney turned, realized his good fortune, and jumped in celebration. Amazingly, he landed before his stick did! Broadcaster Dan Kelly exclaimed, "A weirder goal you won't see."

THE LEGENDS OF LANDOVER

✪ Oh Say, Can You See?

As everyone with side-view car mirrors knows, objects on right and left wings may be closer than they appear. Or become hidden in the blind spot, the problem for forwards Greg Adams and Alan Haworth. Teammate Craig Laughlin explained on a *Capitals Talk* podcast, "They had blinders on. They both had right eye problems, they couldn't see to the right side. No one knew that."

The Capitals did enlist Maryland vision specialist Harvey Ratner. Ratner told the *Chicago Tribune*, "We measure hand-eye coordination, quickness, tracking skills, speed of recognition, depth perception." In the late '80's, vision training was a new science, with unorthodox tools; for one, the "Jugglestick," a plastic baton with three wiffle balls. Ratner's equally unusual sales pitch: "I like to think of this program as a toothbrush for your eyes." Ewww.

✪ Practice Wasn't Dynamite, But Game Was The Bomb

Drills are a routine part of morning practice. Not fire drills, though. While Caps' players went through their paces on March 11, 1989, a Capital Centre employee came upon a box labeled "explosives." A peek inside revealed what looked like dynamite. Soon, fire officials were evacuating the arena. Players didn't return until that night's game with the Rangers, which they won 4-2, Dale Hunter scoring the game-winner with 4:42 left. And the dynamite? Actually harmless road flares. (*Toronto Star*)

✪ Not So Easy Come, Not So Easy Go

Sports trades often are made at the speed of molasses. Sources estimated it took two years and roughly 100 conversations for the Capitals to finally pry defenseman Larry Murphy from Los Angeles in October, 1983 (for Bryan Engblom and Ken Houston). The most pivotal conversation may have been Murphy's pay-me-or-trade-me request with the Kings' G.M.

Six seasons later, Larry was certain his tenure with the Caps was coming to an end. Or was it? On a *Capitals Social* podcast, Murphy recalled the feeling in hockey limbo. "We were in Montreal, we had scheduled practice for three o'clock that afternoon, which was the trade deadline. I'm in the dressing room beforehand, I'm quite sure I'm getting traded, but I haven't got the word yet. It's getting like 10 (minutes) to three, so I race and get my equipment on. I step on the ice at three o'clock, I do half a lap." Murphy looked over to the bench, where coach Bryan Murray was motioning to him. "I turn around, go back to the dressing room, he tells me I've been traded (to Minnesota). That was probably the quickest practice of my career, lasted about four seconds."

THE LEGENDS OF LANDOVER

✪ Quick Hits

▷ One morning in Chicago, Murphy found the hotel bed a little too comfortable. "I woke up early and sat up in bed. My roommate was going down for breakfast, and I must have fallen back asleep. The next thing I knew, I was looking at the clock. My five-minute snooze lasted over an hour, and I missed the plane home."

▷ Goalie Bob Mason will remember January 3, 1985 as a day of ups and downs like no other. For winning all six of his December starts, the NHL named Mason co-winner of its Rookie of the Month. The "down" was literal, as the Caps demoted Mason to the minors on the same day, so they could recall veteran netminder Al Jensen.

▷ Here in the Internet age, "status" is listed on social networking sites. Back in the '80's, the Caps offered a round pin called the "Fun Meter," including a hockey net, a dial, and three settings. Denis Potvin has the puck? Set the Fun Meter to "Lo". Mike Gartner steals and scores? Move that needle to "Hi"! Fans stopped wearing the pin; perhaps moms scolded them that too much touching their Fun Buttons could make them go blind.

▷ Exceptional performance; Rod Langway demanded it of himself, of his teammates, even of his... *skate laces*? Why, yes. In the locker room after a loss, Rod would use scissors to snip his skate laces, explaining, "Those ones were losers; better get a different pair."

▷ For a short time, all of America owned a piece of the Caps. In April, 1985, D.C. businessman Edward Markowitz pled guilty to a $445 million tax fraud. As the *L.A. Times* reported, "He will turn over to the government his 2.5% ownership of the Washington Capitals, worth as much as $250,000."

▷ Before a 1989 game at Boston, defenseman and Harvard graduate Neil Sheehy arranged for ice time at the school's rink. But the team flight was delayed 90 minutes, so after a half hour of practice, the Caps were pushed off the ice by a women's hockey game.

▷ Revealed! The Caps' avian logos since 1995 are actually a tribute to visitors at their former arena. "Over the years (at Capital Centre), you'd see birds flying around fairly regularly," said Mike Fitzhugh, a Capitals season-ticket holder. "Pigeons and starlings and sparrows."

▷ Talk between opponents isn't always of the trash variety. During a 1985 game against visiting St. Louis, the Caps' Alan Haworth accidentally - but painfully - slashed the Blues' Brian Sutter on the chin. "He was apologizing to me the rest of the game," Sutter said. "He was saying, 'I'm sorry, I'm sorry,' when we were in the penalty box."

THE LEGENDS OF LANDOVER

▷ There are workout fanatics, and then there's Pat Riggin, hero to couch potatoes everywhere. Asked in 1984 if conditioning played a part in a personal 27-game hot streak of 20-5-2, Pat said, "I'm not in shape now, and I've never been in shape."

▷ Dave Christian's pregame routine in 1983-84 included a curious assignment: playing a cassette tape as the team got revved up by listening to *Break On Through* by Jim Morrison. Strange Days, weren't they?

▷ Rookie coach Bryan Murray could attest that knee-jerk sports opinions existed long before today's social media. "I received dozens of letters, with people listing section and seat number, that were very uncomplimentary. They hurt my feelings badly at the time. I just tore them up."

▷ In the early '80's, Redskins owner Daniel Snyder – then a teenager – "got his father to help him sell travel packages to fans of the Capitals, to take the bus to see the team play in Philadelphia. It proved a tough sell."

▷ Capital Centre showed better synergy at a December, 1984 Caps-Red Wings game. The NFL team's cheerleaders and band were in attendance, and the Redskins at Cowboys game was shown on Telscreen when hockey was done. Both D.C. teams won, 4-0 and 30-28.

▷ Bengt Gustafsson returned to Sweden for good in 1989, but two NHL teams still acquired his NHL rights. First, Detroit in the '90 Waiver Draft, then San Jose in the '91 Expansion Draft. That's right, Gustafsson was involved in a paper transaction between the Wings and Sharks, while playing for Färjestad. As James Thurber would say, you could look it up.

▷ Can a defense be *too* efficient? Goalie Clint Malarchuk might say so. In a 3-2 win at New Jersey, Malarchuk wasn't forced to make a save for 16 minutes in the middle period – and battled leg cramps from lack of motion! "A goaltender feels a lot better when he's busy," said Clint. "But how do you complain about something like that?"

▷ The best-dressed crowd ever at a Capitals game came in the 1986 preseason in Hamilton, Ontario. Most of the 15,050 spectators arrived at Copps Coliseum in tuxedos, hoping to convince the NHL to award the city a franchise. The *Boston Globe* called it "The Prom Night Game." Like many on prom night, the Caps didn't score, losing to the Bruins, 7-0.

(Stories on pages 268 and 273-274 from: Washington Post, Canadian Press, St. Louis Post-Dispatch, The Argus-Press, washingtoncaps.com, N.Y. Times, Montreal Gazette, nhl.com, In The Crease by Dick Irvin, Wash. Capitals by David Smale, musingsofahockeyenthusiast.com, War Without Death by Mark Maske, The Hockey News, Toronto Globe & Mail)

THE LEGENDS OF LANDOVER

17th Shift: *Games Of Note 1982-1989*
Regular Seasons of the Playoff Years

| JAN. 2, 1983 | WAS 7 QUE 4 | QUEBEC CITY, QC |

Two dozen Gaetan Duchesne well-wishers cheered their native son as Washington's flight landed in Quebec City. (It helped that Gaetan grew up with 10 siblings.) When Duchesne tore away from his fans and belatedly boarded the team's bus, teammates good-naturedly applauded as well.

The homecoming celebration was just beginning. Prior to the game with the Nordiques, Gaetan was honored by a local hall of fame. There to enjoy it was an entire cheering section in the upper deck at Le Colisee, many in Caps' apparel. They cheered again when Duchesne scored the first goal, and stayed rowdy whenever No. 14 in red touched the puck.

| JAN. 11, 1983 | LAK 9 WAS 7 | LANDOVER, MD |

If goal judges got paid by the score, they would have been rich men by the end of the 2nd highest-scoring game in Capital Centre history. Even the august *L.A. Times* couldn't keep a straight face, with this lead paragraph: "The Kings gave up almost as many goals as owner Jerry Buss has girlfriends." Caps Coach Bryan Murray said simply, "I'm embarrassed."

By 2:12 of the 1st period, the score was already 2-1 Kings. Within a five minute span to start the 2nd period, Washington scored on a power play, shorthanded, and at even strength, to take a 4-3 lead. Most remarkable, poor goalies Mike Blake and Pat Riggin endured the entire game. No one could blame Pat for staying in the training room postgame to avoid reporters. "That was exciting for the fans," Marcel Dionne told the *Canadian Press*, "But it was nerve-wracking for everyone else."

| FEB. 3, 1983 | MIN 1 WAS 3 | LANDOVER, MD |

Baseball fields contain so many quirks – some intentional, some not – managers and umpires meet before each game to discuss the ground rules. While NHL rinks don't have as much variance, they, too, add to hometown advantage. Here's one: Minnesota Coach Murray Oliver noted caroms off the boards at Capital Centre acted strangely. "When you miss on the short side, the puck comes right out in front rather than ring around to the other side. Washington knows how to play their own boards."

THE LEGENDS OF LANDOVER

Winger Ted Bulley thought that might be giving players too much geometry credit. His line was expected to do dirty work, not make finesse bank shots. "We work hard, we're a mucker line," Bulley said. "The Redskins had their hogs, we've got the dogs." Early in the 3rd period, this dog mastered a new trick. Bulley played the angles, corralling the rebound of Brian Engblom's off-target shot to score the game-winner. "I happened to be in the right place at the right time," said Ted, adding, "It was just a lucky play." Bulley may have known more than he was letting on, telling *AP*, "My parents were down from Canada. I told my father I'd get him one and I did."

| FEB. 24, 1983 | WAS 4 CGY 2 | CALGARY, AB |

Calgary was a sweet location for the Capitals to clinch their first playoff berth. Defenseman Randy Holt, wingers Bobby Gould and Ken Houston, and winning goalie Pat Riggin all began the previous season as members of the Flames. G.M. David Poile, plucked from Calgary's front office over the summer, also celebrated in his Alberta homecoming. When he decided to accept the Caps' job, Poile called the Flames owner. "I told him I was in the shower scrubbing the logo off my butt." (*washingtoncaps.com*)

The reunion would take place at the most unusual building in the NHL. The Stampede Corral rodeo arena held 7,242 for hockey, had shoulder-high boards, and was already three decades old when the Flames moved from Atlanta. As for the game, Riggin asked to start; he'd left Calgary on sour terms. Coach Bryan Murray explained why playing Pat wasn't a *gamble*. "I haven't had any trouble with him. Maybe it's that we feel the same about horses and the track." (Pat Riggin fun fact: one of the racehorses he owned was named "Riggette.") Riggin finished in the money, stopping 26 of 28 Calgary shots.

Alan Haworth's hat trick, a goal per period, powered the victory. In a low-key locker room, he told the *Calgary Herald*, "If it had been last year, guys would be jumping around and carrying on. But this isn't the team that didn't make the playoffs." Indeed, unlike the 1980 and 1981 squads which each missed the playoffs on the final night, this Caps team clinched with a comfy six weeks left in the regular season.

| MAR. 17, 1983 | WAS 2 BOS 1 | BOSTON |

It's time for another exciting game of "Playing a Hunch." Today's contestant is Capitals coach Bryan Murray. Bryan, your goalie Al Jensen beat the Bruins four days ago. Al's on a winning streak. Now you're playing the Bruins again. Who do you start in goal? What's that, Bryan? Pat Riggin? Not Jensen? Really? Is that your final answer? Bryan, you're a Winner!

THE LEGENDS OF LANDOVER

Now let's reveal the clues that helped coach Murray win "Playing a Hunch." The date of the game was March 17 – *St. Patrick's Day*. The location of the game was *Boston*. His goalie *Pat* said of himself, "I'm as Irish as they come. St. Patrick's Day is one of my favorite days."

Honoring the legend of St. Patrick himself, Riggin banished pucks from his net, repelling 39 of 40 shots. News accounts called his netminding "sharp" and "masterful." Boston coach Gerry Cheevers stopped short of calling Pat magically delicious, but couldn't explain how "Our scorers missed point-blank shots." Riggin joked, "I'm surprised they got a goal at all. St. Patty's Day in Boston is an exciting thing." Murray said, "He was ready to play. He was really up for the game."

So was Bengt Gustafsson, who scored both Caps goals. Significantly, the win completed a three-game season sweep of the Bruins, which had the NHL's best record at the time. And Washington won for just the second time in 19 tries at Boston Garden. *Faith and Begorrah!*
(Quotes from the Annapolis Capitol)

`OCT. 22, 1983   PHI 1 WAS 4   LANDOVER, MD`

The legend of the "Mulligan," or do-over, is credited by *pga.com* to a 1920's Canadian golfer named David Mulligan. One day, he blamed his rotten first tee shot on numb hands; you see, driving his touring car to the course, bumpy roads naturally required him to keep a crushingly tight grip on the steering wheel. The others in David's foursome, a forgiving lot, allowed him a second try at his tee shot, and the "Mulligan" was born.

Early in the 1983-84 NHL season, another Canadian named David created what we'll call the "Champagne Mulligan." Poile, the Caps G.M., wanted to relieve the tension from a season-opening seven game losing streak. He dreamed up a postgame event Poile admitted was "corny," but to execute it, the Caps had to win a game. Washington came through against the Flyers, with Alan Haworth and Darren Veitch scoring on the power play, Gaetan Duchesne scoring shorthanded, and Al Jensen making 22 saves.

Then the G.M. surprised the team with a champagne party. "We all laughed about it," said Mike Gartner, who had opened the scoring. "Imagine, a 1-7 team drinking champagne." Craig Laughlin got the point. "We cracked the bottles and said, 'Now the season has really started.'" As Poile explained, "It was a chance to say, 'Can you believe that this happened to us? Now it's over. Let's get on with it.'" Did they ever, posting a sizzling 48-20-5 record following the losing streak - a rare instance when bubbly helped *cure* a hangover. Cheers!

(Quotes from Boston Globe, Sporting News)

THE LEGENDS OF LANDOVER

OCT. 29, 1983 | WAS 6 MIN 1 | BLOOMINGTON, MN

Even Olympic heroes don't get special favors in the NHL. Back in 1980, Warren Strelow had mentored Jim Craig, "Miracle on Ice" goalie for the gold-winning U.S. Olympians. Now it's 1983. Strelow is the Caps' goalie coach, while Craig, after stops in Atlanta and Boston, is attempting a revival with Minnesota.

Before the Caps-Stars game at the Met Center, Wayne Coffey writes in *The Boys of Winter*, "Craig saw Strelow in the hallway and hurried over to talk to him." Craig was after "some insight into his game." Strelow declined, telling his former pupil, "Jimmy, I'm not your goaltending coach anymore." In fact, "Strelow told the Caps to shoot low on the stick side on Craig."

The advice was quickly put to use. Dave Christian gave Washington the lead 51 seconds into the game; Gaetan Duchesne scored three minutes later. Craig surrendered five goals before being benched after two periods. (He'd sustain a career-ending injury in his next, and final, NHL game.) A box score footnote: Assisting on the only North Stars goal, former Cap Dennis Maruk, and future Cap Dino Ciccarelli.

NOV. 6, 1983 | DET 2 WAS 3 | LANDOVER, MD

Did a dirty play decide this game? Depends who you listened to afterward, and how strongly you believe that goaltenders should be off-limits to contact. Rod Langway scored the winner 12 ticks into the 3rd period, while Detroit goalie Ed Mio lay motionless behind the cage. Washington's Bobby Carpenter pled guilty after the game - except he didn't feel at all guilty. "Mio came out to get the puck, and I just took his skates out from under him." About Mio, who suffered bruised ribs on the play, Carpenter said, "I didn't feel bad for him. When he's out of the net, he's just like any other player."

Mio, mad enough to bite through a puck, predicted pain for the rematch. "That's OK. He'll get his. They better be looking for a stick in the face." Fortunately, when the teams next met on December 28, Ed thought better of performing a Zorro impression. Mio saved his stickwork for legal purposes – he didn't even draw a penalty – in a 3-2 Wings victory.

FEB. 15, 1984 | WAS 4 LAK 2 | INGLEWOOD, CA

A confident Pat Riggin said, "Right now, I don't feel like the puck is going to go in." And even when it did go in, it didn't count. An apparent 2nd period goal by L.A. was waved off, keeping alive Riggin's team-record road shutout streak.

THE LEGENDS OF LANDOVER

Pat's away-game whitewash reached 241 minutes, 45 seconds, before Pat was pierced by a Brian MacLellan tap-in. (The same MacLellan who would become Washington's general manager in 2014.) MacLellan's power play goal snapped another impressive Caps mark – 35 straight penalty kills.

Ex-King Larry Murphy's game-winner assured that two Washington streaks would continue to grow: consecutive wins (nine), and games unbeaten (13). Those were the numbers that mattered to Riggin. "The scoreless streak doesn't mean a thing," he said. "The 'W' is what keeps the family together." As any respectable marriage counselor will tell you.

Riggin backstopped the Capitals to another "W" two nights later in St. Louis, raising the team's win streak to 10, the unbeaten streak to 14. A remarkable personal turnaround for Pat, who didn't win his first game of the season until January, and spent two weeks in the AHL. "I thought for sure I would be traded while I was in the minors," Riggin said. "They tried to give me away but couldn't get a ham sandwich. I'm still mad David Poile sold out on me when he went looking for another goalie."

For the record, Pat did start the season 0-8-1, with a GAA just under five. "People tell me, don't get mad, get even. That's what I want to do. I want to make him (Poile) regret what he did. They seemed to forget me in a real big hurry. I never thought I could be washed up at 24 years of age. I have a lot of faults, but there's definitely no quit in me." Or in the Caps team, as Dave Christian noted. "Early in the season, when we lost our first seven, we went into a slump because we actually believed that winning was automatic," he said. "Winning is contagious and so is losing. Fortunately, we did our losing early." *(Sporting News)*

| NOV. 17, 1984 | BUF 2 WAS 3 | LANDOVER, MD |

By 1979, the Capitals had a Scotty Bowman problem. In five seasons of trying, they'd never beaten the Bowman-coached Canadiens. Scotty had his own problem; despite four consecutive titles, the Habs wouldn't hand him their G.M. job. With Bowman eager to move on, Caps owner Abe Pollin saw an opportunity to kill two problems with one hire. "Bowman, however, wanted more than a coaching job and said no thank you. Instead, he went to Buffalo as director of hockey operations." (*Washington Star*)

Scotty brought his mastery of the Capitals with him to upstate New York. By early in 1984-85, Bowman's unbeaten string against D.C. stood at 42 wins, 3 ties, zero losses. The Caps finally broke through against Bowman in their 46th try, as Bobby Carpenter and Bryan Erickson scored 68 seconds apart. The victory was rare in another way; in their first 14 years and 53 meetings with the Sabres, Washington recorded a measly five victories. A measure of retribution was finally achieved in 1988-89, when the Caps won all three sets, 6-2, 6-4, 5-3.

THE LEGENDS OF LANDOVER

JAN. 23, 1985 | WAS 3 CHI 2 | CHICAGO

In this edition of "NHL Court," *The Case of the Breakaway Pick*. Facts already in evidence: Washington's Bryan Erickson scored a power play goal in the second period to tie the game, which proved crucial in a one-goal victory. Chicago, you maintain Scott Stevens illegally detained Blackhawks defenseman Doug Wilson, allowing Erickson to skate in unimpeded on his breakaway.

Call your witnesses. "It was a pick," said Wilson. "It was blatant," said teammate Bill Gardner. Permission granted to impugn the consistency of referee Bob Hall. Mr. Wilson? "10 minutes later, he called Stevens for the same thing." Mr. Gardner? "Hall tried to make up for it with the next call. It doesn't work that way when it was probably the difference in the game. Against a tough defensive team like Washington, one goal makes a big difference."

Washington coach Bryan Murray, rebuttal? "Wilson was trying to push Stevens offside. He was way out of position. He was playing Stevens instead of the other way around. I'm sure they thought it should have been called, but you have to say something when you look that bad."

This court finds Mr. Murray's testimony convincing – snide, but convincing. Therefore, Mr. Stevens is not guilty of obstruction of ~~justice~~ Blackhawk, and Bobby Carpenter's goal with 1:51 left will stand as the winning tally. We're adjourned.

OCT. 16, 1985 | WAS 6 TOR 5 | TORONTO

The Capitals rallied from an apparent two-goal deficit in the final seconds, thanks in part to the keen eyes of referee Kerry Fraser. And it was only the second-most heartbreaking result of the night for Toronto sports fans.

When Greg Terrion scored into an empty net for a 6-4 Maple Leafs lead, Washington was staring at a fourth straight loss to start to the season. The despondent Caps' bench didn't hear Fraser's whistle, blown because Terrion had tripped Larry Murphy to steal the puck.

The call erased the empty net insurance marker, reducing the deficit back to 5-4 Leafs. Though the visitors went on the power play, they still only had 17 seconds to force overtime. The Caps once more pulled Al Jensen to gain a six-skaters-to-four advantage, and Mike Gartner's wrist shot tied the game with four seconds left. Gaetan Duchesne completed the improbable comeback 47 seconds into overtime, sliding an Alan Haworth pass into the net.

THE LEGENDS OF LANDOVER

A miniscule gathering at Maple Leaf Gardens witnessed ecstasy turn to agony. "If the Leafs ever had a smaller crowd, no one around the Gardens could remember it," reported the *Toronto Star*. "Attendance was announced at 13,602, but the guessing was that it was closer to 5,000." Leafs great Johnny Bower, who broke into the NHL in 1953, added, "I've never seen a crowd this small in this building."

The city's sports focus was 2½ miles to the south, on game seven of baseball's American League Championship Series at the Skydome. The Blue Jays were in the process of blowing a 3-1 series lead to the Kansas City Royals.

| OCT. 28, 1985 | WAS 4 CHI 2 | CHICAGO |

Chicago's Troy Murray joined the pantheon of Famous Last Words, sports division: "We seemed to be ready during the warm-up." Ready, willing, and unable, as the Caps' Gaetan Duchesne converted in close, 23 seconds into the game. Six ticks later, a lucky break doubled the lead. Mark Taylor sent a long blast wide, except Hawks goalie Bob Sauve deflected the puck into his own net. The Caps were due against Sauve, 9-0-2 against them in 11 prior starts. "I guess I can't beat a team forever," Sauve mused to the *Chicago Tribune*.

A pair of goals in the game's first half-minute, and then the Caps stopped shooting altogether - just one shot on net for almost 19 minutes of the 2nd period. If not for Al Jensen's 37 saves, the lightning-quick two goal lead would have evaporated. "Al really played well," said Caps' coach Bryan Murray. "We had some excellent saves when they could've turned it around. They missed a few, too, and that didn't hurt."

| NOV. 12, 1985 | EDM 2 WAS 5 | LANDOVER, MD |

A sellout crowd witnessed two record-setting performances against the champion Oilers. When Alan Haworth scored just 2:09 into the game, it marked his 9th straight contest with a goal. Alan told *UPI* that injuries to teammates played a part in the streak. "I started getting more ice time, and a regular shift on the power play. The more I score, the better I feel about my game, and I guess it shows."

Later in the period, against the NHL's top-ranked power play, Mike Gartner scored shorthanded. Early in the 3rd period, down a man to Wayne Gretzky & Co., Dave Christian also scored shorthanded. In the final minute, with the Caps killing yet another penalty, Christian scored again, into an empty net.

THE LEGENDS OF LANDOVER

Three shorties in one game! "I've never played on a team that scored three shorthanded goals," Christian told *AP*. "Edmonton probably sees it all the time, but they get them." Exactly right. The mighty Oilers, who scored 61 times while killing penalties over the previous two seasons, were being fed their own medicine. It wouldn't have been possible without Bobby Carpenter, in the box for two of the Capitals goals.

Haworth's nine-game goal streak set a team record (tied a season later by Mike Gartner) that's lasted more than a quarter-century, and three goals shorthanded has been equaled just twice. As Rod Langway observed, "Everything we did seemed to work."

JAN. 14, 1986 — CGY 4 WAS 3 — LANDOVER, MD

Try as they might, the Capitals couldn't bail out defenseman Scott Stevens, not even once. Stevens was penalized in the first period for cross-checking, and the Flames scored. Stevens was nailed for elbowing in the second period, and the Flames scored. Stevens was whistled for hooking in the third period and – stop me if you've heard this – the Flames scored again.

Remarkable, because over the prior six weeks, Calgary went 7-for-84 with the extra man, an anemic 8.5% success rate. Against the Caps, Calgary scored all four of their goals on the power play. "We have a way of turning teams around," said a clearly frustrated coach Bryan Murray. Little solace that Washington tallied three times on its own power plays, meaning that all seven goals in the game came with an opponent in the box.

The Caps actually put a fourth puck home with an extra skater, appearing to forge a tie with 24 seconds left and goalie Al Jensen on the bench. But as the *Baltimore Sun* reported, referee Andy Van Hellemond waved it off. "Calgary's Jim Peplinski appeared to knock the goal off its moorings as Craig Laughlin's shot settled into the net." For the only time in a night of 19 power plays, Van Hellemond failed to call a penalty. "I would never do that on purpose," claimed Peplinski afterward. "It wouldn't be fair." For the record, Jim wasn't under oath.

JAN. 21, 1986 — MIN 5 WAS 7 — LANDOVER, MD

Fans who showed up fashionably late missed a big opening act, starring Dave Christian. He collected three points in three minutes, assisting on goals by Bengt Gustafsson at 3:47 and Craig Laughlin at 4:12, then scoring one of his own at 6:32. In all, the Capitals scored four times in the first seven minutes. Fans who left early almost missed a Caps collapse. Scott Bjugstad drew Minnesota within 6-5 with eight minutes to play. Only Bobby Carpenter's empty net goal with nine seconds left assured the outcome.

THE LEGENDS OF LANDOVER

Referee Ron Wicks helped keep the game interesting, early in the 3rd period. Although the red light never went on, Wicks – standing behind the net – ruled the North Stars' Brian Bellows' close-in try had scored. "It didn't go in," Caps goalie Al Jensen told the *Annapolis Capital,* citing the Telscreen for evidence. "I saw it on the replay. I tried to get my body up as much as possible and it hit me and went down. I don't know how Wicks could call that a goal."

"We got trapped," coach Bryan Murray said. "The goals came easy early on and instead of being disciplined and working hard to put them away, we went for more - even in the third period when we harped on them about playing defense."

FEB. 2, 1986 | WAS 5 HAR 4 | HARTFORD, CT

The single most eventful period of a Capitals game happened at the Hartford Civic Center, and not just because the Caps rallied from a four goal deficit. In the 3rd period, coach Bryan Murray made three goalie changes! Starter Al Jensen had yielded four Whalers scores over the first 40 minutes, so final period mop-up duty was assigned to backup Bob Mason, playing just his 15th NHL game.

But Mason remained as much a spectator as he had been on the bench, with the ice tilting sharply to the Hartford end. Over a whirlwind seven minutes, Bobby Carpenter scored twice, Bengt Gustafsson and Craig Laughlin once each - the Caps lit the lamp four times to tie the game, 4-4.

Soon after, Scott Stevens took a penalty. With a newly competitive game, Murray made the unorthodox move to re-insert his number one goalie. Mason came off, Jensen went back in, and Washington killed the penalty. On another Whaler power play with six minutes left, Jensen made a painful save off his boot. Al gamely played on until the next whistle, when he fell to one knee. He hobbled to the bench, replaced by Mason for a second time in the same period!

A night earlier, the Caps rallied from two down to beat New Jersey, 5-4. Emboldened by that success, they completed a grander comeback when Larry Murphy gave D.C. its first lead with 1:15 to play. Washington received one final break, Kevin Dineen hitting the crossbar with 18 seconds left and Mason out of position.

As the victorious Caps mobbed each other, coach Bryan Murray explained, "When we were down 4-3, we were playing to protect the lead." Hey Bryan, how can a team protect a lead it doesn't have? "We knew we were going to win," said Murray.

THE LEGENDS OF LANDOVER

MAR. 25, 1986 | BOS 3 WAS 6 | LANDOVER, MD

When ornery Pat Riggin returned to Capital Centre for the first time since a trade to Boston, it had all the warmth of a Hatfield-McCoy reunion. On separate plays, Craig Laughlin and Steve Leach made sure to bump their former teammate while heading to the net.

After a 2nd period whistle, Riggin exacted retribution on mild-mannered Bengt Gustafsson. As reported by the *Reading Eagle*, Riggin shoved his goalie stick under Bengt's visor. When Gustafsson asked, "What are you trying to do?" Riggin took a swing at him. Later, Pat played coy. "I was just playing hockey. I have nothing against Gus." Well, maybe one thing. Bengt scored the breakaway game-winner past Riggin with six minutes to play, then paused for a satisfied glance at the goalie on his way to the bench.

MAR. 28, 1986 | NYI 4 WAS 3 | LANDOVER, MD

Chris Webber famously called a timeout his team didn't have during an NCAA basketball final. He could have used a T.O. lesson from Capitals coach Bryan Murray. In the 2nd period, Murray called his timeout. Then, in the 3rd, he called another one. No one – not the officials or any of the Islander coaches or players – remembered that with NHL timeouts, it's supposed to be one to a customer. In the end, Bryan was just prolonging the agony, as the Caps couldn't score a late tying goal.

DEC. 6, 1986 | MON 1 WAS 3 | LANDOVER, MD

Montreal feasted on the expansion Capitals, and since they played in the same division, the dinner bell rang often. Even in Landover, the Habs won the first 14 meetings, until the Caps managed a 2-2 tie on March 5, 1979. If you'd predicted then that the Canadiens wouldn't win again at Capital Centre for eight years, vendors would have cut off your Busch Beer access.

Yet that's what happened; following their 14-game road winning streak in Washington, Montreal went winless in its next 14. "I wasn't even aware of it," Caps winger Alan Haworth said. Rod Langway, whose trade with three Montreal teammates had a lot to do with the reversal of fortunes, said, "Because of their status, we're always ready to play them. They have a dynasty, and when you beat the Canadiens you have to play well."

The final game of the unbeaten streak came before a sellout of 18,130. A member of the Montreal Four trade, Craig Laughlin, haunted his old team with two goals and one assist. Remember, the Caps weren't beating pushovers - the victory completed a three-game season sweep over the defending Stanley Cup champions.

THE LEGENDS OF LANDOVER

| JAN. 5, 1987 | WAS 6 STL 4 | ST. LOUIS |

The middle of the first period paid homage to Beatles' song "Eleanor Rigby" – *No one was saved*. First, John Barrett scored on a breakaway for Washington at 6:18. The Blues didn't have a shot at all until Brian Benning tied the game at 7:30. Craig Laughlin took the next shot on goal 30 seconds later, and it went in, too. The Caps weren't done, as Dave Christian connected on the power play at 9:42. Four goals on consecutive shots with zero saves in between, creating a 3-1 Caps lead.

Caps goalie Pete Peeters wasn't in a position to lend sympathy to Rick Wamsley, his St. Louis counterpart. Pete had just returned from rebuilding his confidence in the minors, and this was his first start for the Capitals in a month. It appeared the ice might be cracking underneath him when the Blues scored twice in the first minute of the second period. At that point, Peeters had allowed three goals, and made a grand total of two saves.

Fortunately, the calendar was working in Washington's favor. The Caps had won their previous three road games on Mondays. (On other days of the week, their road record was 1-11-5!) Plus, they were unbeaten in their last half-dozen visits to the St. Louis Arena. Of more concrete value, three expatriate New York Rangers – Kelly Miller, Mike Ridley, and Bobby Crawford – were playing their first road contest in Washington sweaters, after being traded for Bobby Carpenter.

The first of Miller's 162 career Capitals goals restored the D.C. lead, and Mike Gartner also scored before the middle period ended. Meanwhile, Peeters stabilized, stopping all 15 Blues shots over the final 34 minutes. "I think the team wanted to win the game for me," Peeters said. "I made mistakes and I'm thankful we won anyway." Blues coach Jacques Martin had kinder words. "Peeters came up with big saves in the third period."

One other note – think Dale was the only mischief-making Hunter brother? Hardly. When Michal Pivonka got into a fight near the St. Louis bench, Mark Hunter reached out and grabbed Pivonka's sweater – and the officials didn't catch it! (Quotes from *Washington Post, Associated Press*)

| JAN. 17, 1987 | WAS 6 HAR 1 | HARTFORD, CT |

The Capitals' early-game shooting rivaled an NBA team on a good night. Mike Gartner hit the bulls-eye on a penalty shot 90 seconds into the game. Washington took more than six minutes to register a second shot, and they scored on that one, too, by Kevin Hatcher. Dave Christian converted a breakaway later in the first, making three Caps goals on five shots.

THE LEGENDS OF LANDOVER

They weren't poured past some minor-league call-up, either. The Whalers' Mike Liut was leading the league with three shutouts. Liut eventually departed in the middle period, having surrendered five goals on 12 shots.

The team had endured a tortuously slow ride to Hartford from Long Island the night before. So pleased was coach Bryan Murray with the 6-1 victory, however, he proclaimed, "All trips are by bus from now on." (*Wash. Post*)

| FEB. 24, 1987 | DET 2 WAS 8 | LANDOVER, MD |

The Capitals exercised a road-ice advantage all season, most recently ravaging western Canada with wins, 4-3 in Edmonton, 6-3 in Vancouver, and 5-2 in Calgary. The head-scratcher was that Washington owned the circuit's second-worst home record. Coach/psychologist Bryan Murray had an idea how keep that good on-the-road vibe going; when the Caps returned home, they wouldn't return home. Instead, as the visiting Detroit Red Wings checked into the Greenbelt Hilton Towers, Capitals players did, too. (No reports exist of any pushing and shoving at the hotel ice machine.)

Coach Murray, motivational guru, explained, "Coming off the road, we asked the team to move the puck and concentrate on forechecking." The ploy worked wonders. Bob Gould scored on the team's first shot; Dave Christian scored on the team's second shot. 22 minutes in, the Caps had built a 6-0 lead. Mike Gartner tallied twice, making 16 in his last 20 games. "We learned so much from those games on the road," Gould said. "We were more disciplined." *(AP)*

| MAR. 13, 1987 | TOR 2 WAS 10 | LANDOVER, MD |

For a three-minute stretch in the 3rd period, the Capitals produced the most prolific power play in the history of the NHL. If that sounds like hyperbole, read on. With 4:36 left, Toronto's Wendell Clark was assessed a 5-minute fighting major. The power play parade began with Mike Gartner lighting the lamp at 16:07. 45 seconds later, the Leafs' Bob McGill got his own fighting major. Because major penalties never end early, the Caps were about to gorge on an all-you-can-score 5-on-3. The carnage: Gary Galley at 17:14, David Jensen at 17:52, Jensen again at 18:24, and Ed Kastelic at 19:10.

That's right: five power play goals in 3:03! For the team, believe it or not, holding the league's worst power play percentage. The *Toronto Star* found the display "almost ghoulish… right out of a horror movie." Come to think of it, the date *was* Friday the 13th. The Caps outscored the Leafs 7-0 in the 3rd period, on 22 shots - and finished the game with seven extra-man tallies. In fact, the Caps generated so much power, observers reported the Capital Centre was actually glowing. (Now *that's* hyperbole.)

THE LEGENDS OF LANDOVER

Defenseman Larry Murphy kept the rout in perspective. "That will help our shooting percentages," Murphy joked to the *Baltimore Sun*, while admitting, "We didn't take it very seriously. It's kind of an unrealistic situation."

The only Cap unable to join the fun was goalie Bob Mason, who faced just 20 shots (10 after two periods) and felt like the Maytag Repair Man. "I kind of like to see more shots. It was tough mentally. I tried to take a few skates around and follow the puck."

| DEC. 22, 1987 | WAS 2 QUE 1 | QUEBEC CITY, QC |

The Nordiques discovered in one evening what the rest of the NHL had experienced for seven years: the receiving end of Dale Hunter bad-assery.

Hunter came from Quebec to Washington along with goaltender Clint Malarchuk in an off-season trade. Returning for the first time to Le Colisee, Malarchuk wouldn't play – he said later his biggest concern was finding the visitors' locker room. For his part, Hunter admitted to butterflies, "Playing against people who saved my rear a few times."

"I left on good terms, not like I asked to be traded," Hunter added. "I think the fans understand that." Indeed they did; Nordiques fans honored him with a 15-second ovation on his first shift. So, would Hunter, for old-times' sake, put a muffler on his trademark mayhem? The answer came 7:12 into the game, the moment he flattened Quebec goalie Mario Gosselin with a cross check. Ex-Cap Robert Picard came to Gosselin's aid, and Hunter tangled with him, too.

Dale remained feisty in the second period, drawing matching roughing penalties with Alan Haworth, one of the players (along with Gaetan Duchesne) he was traded for. Haworth did his best to steal the show, firing a team-high five of the Nordiques' 25 shots. But Pete Peeters stood tall, also repelling two Peter Stastny breakaways, and fending off a 5-on-3.

Hunter inflicted the most severe damage to his former team in the third period. First, he won a faceoff with the Caps shorthanded. Mike Garter exited the penalty box, sped down ice, and scored at 3:34 to tie the game, 1-1. Hunter's second assist came three minutes later. Drawing the defense to him, Hunter found Gartner on a breakaway. Mike deked and backhanded home his second goal, the eventual game-winner. "I was playing against friends of mine," Hunter observed postgame. "As hard as that was for me, I'm sure it was just as hard on them."

(Quotes from *Washington Post, Associated Press*)

THE LEGENDS OF LANDOVER

JAN. 11, 1988 | **WAS 2 EDM 3** | **EDMONTON, AB**

A fan held up a ref-baiting sign at the Spectrum during a 1988 Capitals-Flyers game: "Does Your Eye Dog Skate?" A few days later, the Caps surely wished they'd borrowed the sign, when they lost a one-goal decision to Edmonton, and referee Ron Hoggarth.

Questionable call #1: Bengt Gustafsson stuffed the puck past Edmonton goaltender Grant Fuhr in the second period. "The puck was loose, there's no question about that," said linemate Mike Gartner, who was standing near the crease in view of the play. Except referee Hoggarth ruled Fuhr had smothered the puck. "Well, his glove was on the ice," countered Gartner, "but the puck wasn't anywhere near it."

Questionable call #2: In the third period, the Caps possessed the puck during a delayed Edmonton penalty. The Oilers clearly failed to gain control as Bobby Gould put a rebound in the net. Hoggarth whistled down the play a moment earlier, though, believing an Oiler had touched the puck.

Questionable call #3: Edmonton's Mark Messier wasn't called for standing in the crease, or kicking the puck into the net. His power play goal proved to be the game-winner. Messier admitted he kicked the puck but said he touched it with his stick before it crossed the line. TV replays didn't support that view, however. "He (Hoggarth) took two goals away from us earlier," said Caps goalie Clint Malarchuk. "Then there's a situation like that where the guy is in the crease and kicks the puck in and he doesn't call either one." *(Game stories from Associated Press, Canadian Press)*

JAN. 13, 1988 | **WAS 8 LAK 3** | **INGLEWOOD, CA**

As the goals-against mounted, the Forum crowd made its displeasure known. New Kings coach Robbie Ftorek realized he needed to deliver a pep talk between periods – to the fans! "Ftorek requested time on the Kings' radio broadcast, which could be heard at the concession stands," the *L.A. Times* reported. "He asked fans not to verbally abuse goaltender Glenn Healy, who was having enough problems with the Capitals. 'If you believe in something strongly, you should speak your mind,' Ftorek said."

If only Kings skaters had provided such a spirited defense. Washington's Greg Adams scored 81 seconds into the game; Yvon Corriveau followed with two goals 13 seconds apart; The Caps scored four on the power play. This all felt familiar. The Caps pasted L.A. 10-3 in Landover a month earlier, including six third-period goals on seven shots! L.A. goalie Rollie Melanson, who surrendered all 10 tallies in that game, said, "It was like a freeway out there - guys just skating through."

THE LEGENDS OF LANDOVER

Ex-Kings coach Mike Murphy, fired hours before that debacle, returned to the Forum on this night to watch his former charges. Joining the Capitals' *WMAL* broadcast, Murphy quipped, "Not much has changed," after a Caps goal.

| JAN. 31, 1988 | PHI 0 WAS 1 | LANDOVER, MD |

The Capitals and Flyers played their typically rambunctious 1980's game. Which is to say, slashing, roughing, cross-checking, spearing, and fighting. Remarkably, a combined 16 power plays led to zero goals; The Caps went 0-for-9, Philly 0-for-7. Even in the brief moments with a full complement of skaters, nobody could score. Into the last two minutes of OT, the Caps' Pete Peeters recorded 28 saves; Philly's Ron Hextall turned away 35.

As a Capital Centre sellout looked on, Kelly Miller skated into an impromptu meeting with teammate Bob Gould behind the Flyers net. "I don't know how Gouldy got back there, but I ran into him," said Miller. "I came back the other way and just put it towards the net." Miller's try went fortuitously toward Kjell Samuelsson. The puck hit the defenseman's skate and trickled past Hextall, forging a 1-0 Caps overtime win.

| MAR. 2, 1988 | NJD 1 WAS 6 | E. RUTHERFORD, NJ |

The Caps beat the Devils 5-3 at Capital Centre one night earlier, a contest which turned nasty toward the end. Before the Meadowlands rematch, N.J. assistant Doug McKay sought out Caps coach Bryan Murray. Wagging a finger in Murray's face, McKay boasted, "It's going to be different tonight." McKay forgot to tell his team. Mike Ridley, Dave Christian, and Greg Adams scored in the first 15 minutes, as the Caps cruised, 6-1.

At the other end, goalie Clint Malarchuk took the advice of Fernando, Billy Crystal's *Saturday Night Live* character: "It is better to look good than to feel good." The *AP* game story noted that "Malarchuk's legs were weak and his stomach was doing flips" with the flu. He still stopped 19 of 20 shots. Imagine if he'd been in good health – Clint probably could have juggled sticks and practiced the tango along with tending goal.

The postgame wound up being more hotly contested. Murray shouted down the hall to McKay, "You were right. It was a different game. Smart comment." The language got nastier and the men closer, until Devils coach Jim Schonfeld raced out of an interview to confront Murray between the locker rooms. Schonfeld in a hallway confrontation? Sounds familiar. Oh, right. This was a limbering exercise. Schonfeld's "Have another doughnut" dustup with referee Don Koharski came in the playoffs a few weeks later.

THE LEGENDS OF LANDOVER

MAR. 16, 1988 | WAS 8 NYR 4 | NEW YORK

"The thing about (Dale) Hunter," said Washington coach Bryan Murray, "is that you're never quite sure what he'll do to beat you, legal or otherwise." The "otherwise" by Hunter proved the undoing of the Rangers. New York held a 3-2 second period lead when goalie John Vanbiesbrouck vacated his crease to clear the puck. Hunter became a shark zeroing in on chum. "I saw him coming," Vanbiesbrouck said, but "I didn't brace for such a big hit."

A brawl ensued, Hunter was assessed a charging penalty, but he'd achieved his purpose. With more than half the contest remaining, Vanbiesbrouck didn't make another save. Greg Adams scored at 14:47, Scott Stevens at 15:50, Lou Franceschetti at 17:13 - three goals in under three minutes - and the Caps skated off after two periods with a 5-3 lead.

In the 3rd, Washington took just three shots, and scored on all of them, making six straight goal-scoring shots. Kevin Hatcher gave the Capitals a 6-4 lead at 8:48; with Vanbiesbrouck pulled for an extra skater, Hunter put the puck in the empty next at 18:49; the Rangers goalie returned between the pipes, and wished he hadn't, as Yvon Corriveau became the eighth different Washington goal-scorer at 19:09.

Despite evidence to the contrary, Vanbiesbrouck denied the Hunter collision altered the game. "It looked like it (the change of momentum) had something to do with that play, but it didn't," Vanbiesbrouck said. "They just took advantage of my poor play."

Coach Murray knew Hunter had played a key role in the Capitals' 13th win in their last 16 games. "We gave up two really good kids (Alan Haworth and Gaetan Duchesne) to get Hunter. But we thought he'd help us when things got tough and that he'd add pizzazz to our lineup. It makes another team uncomfortable. We've never had anybody like that before."

MAR. 25, 1988 | PHI 3 WAS 5 | LANDOVER, MD

Perhaps the Caps were getting paid by the shot. 12 minutes in, they'd peppered Flyers goalie Mark LaForest with 20 – count em', 20 – shots on goal. (On pace for 100!) Only problem, LaForest made all 20 saves. It took the unlikeliest Capital to finally pierce the twine.

Ed Kastelic, all 6-feet-4, 215 pounds worth, dressed for 35 games during the season, whenever tough-guy insurance was called for. Such insurance was always called for against the Broad Street Bullies. Kastelic was exiting the penalty box (where else?) when play headed toward him. Ed skated down ice with Yvon Corriveau, took a return pass, and scored his only goal of the season on shot number 21 of the first period.

THE LEGENDS OF LANDOVER

Since it was Kastelic, the goal naturally included a measure of punishment. As Corriveau celebrated, his stick clipped linesman Ron Asselstine in the mouth. Ron needed medical attention to continue, as coach Bryan Murray no doubt anxiously looked on. (See page 251.) The shooting gallery never closed, as Washington finished with 52 shots, including 3rd period scores beating LaForest by Garry Galley and Grant Ledyard.

| DEC. 11, 1988 | WAS 0 MON 0 | MONTREAL |

During the 2nd period, Montreal general manager Serge Savard placed an unusual phone call - to game referee Paul Stewart.

For the first half of the game, the Canadiens repeatedly bumped, elbowed, and otherwise jostled Caps goalie Pete Peeters. Trying to ward them off, or exact revenge, Peeters was called for hooking midway through the middle period. Pete told the *Washington Post* it was a "bad call." Peeters' opinion of the officiating improved three minutes later. Referee Stewart waived off a Montreal goal; Mike Keane, standing in the crease, trapped Peeters' stick against his body. "It was a good call and took a lot of guts," said the goalie.

The Habs' G.M. saw it differently, as Stewart recalled at *hockeybuzz.com*. "I skated to the scorer's table to explain that the goal would not count. The phone on the bench rings. 'It's Serge Savard,' the scorer said. I reached for the phone. 'Stewy, you have to allow that goal,' Savard said. 'He wasn't in the crease. He jumped out of the way.'

"'C'mon Serge,' I said. 'You know that the crease area extends from the ice to the height of the crossbar.' 'If you're so sure of what happened, why would you even take the phone?' Savard demanded. 'Well, Serge,' I said, 'I thought you were going to tell me you were bringing me pizza after the game and asking what I wanted on it.'"

The game ended 0-0, the first scoreless tie the Caps had ever played. In the officials' locker room, Stewart answered a knock on the door. "It was Serge Savard, holding a box in his hands. 'I brought you a pizza,' he said. 'But I forgot to ask what you wanted on it.'"

| DEC. 21, 1988 | WAS 4 CHI 3 | CHICAGO |

The middle period was crazy: seven penalties by the Capitals; three goals a side; the Hawks scoring once each 5-on-5, 5-on-4, and 5-on-3; the Caps scoring once each at 5-on-5, 5-on-4, and 4-on-4. And the second period was only the second wildest of the game. A culprit would prove to be Blackhawks trading cards, a promotional giveaway distributed as fans had entered entered Chicago Stadium.

THE LEGENDS OF LANDOVER

Kelly Miller's goal 51 seconds into the third period put the Caps ahead for good. Restless fans at Chicago Stadium, whose heroes had won just eight of their first 33 games, soon grew feisty - soccer hooligan feisty. Tempers flared as Mike Eagles committed a hockey no-no. Eagles rocketed down the slot, colliding with Capitals goalie Pete Peeters. It took a few moments for referee Rob Schick to determine Peeters was left woozy by his left post.

When Schick whistled Eagles for interference, many in the crowd of 14,968 littered the ice with cups, wrappers, and hundreds of those trading cards. A full six minutes elapsed before play could resume. When it did, Caps defenseman Grant Ledyard decided valor was the better part of discretion. Ledyard took revenge on Eagles, affording Chicago a late power play. Not only did the Hawks fail to get a shot on the man advantage, Peeters was forced to make only one save during the final seven minutes of play.

JAN. 7, 1989	CHI 3 WAS 6	LANDOVER, MD

Mike Ridley was the gift that kept on giving, with teammates only too happy to accept. In the first period, Ridley assisted on Larry Murphy's power play goal. He then had helpers on both of Mike Gartner's middle period goals, the second by faking Chicago goalie Ed Belfour out of position, then sliding the puck to Gartner with an open net.

In the third period, Ridley won a faceoff and fed Kevin Hatcher for the eventual game winner. Then he assisted on late power play goals by Dale Hunter and Scott Stevens. Six assists - one on every goal the team scored! Ridley became only the third NHL player to pull that off; six assists is still a Caps record. "I like setting up other guys," Ridley told the *Washington Post*. "I've always played that way. I'm not much of a shooter."

True, he registered just one of Washington's 34 shots. Still, he finished the '88-'89 campaign with 41 goals, so perhaps he was *something* of a shooter. Not bad for a player who was never drafted.

JAN. 24, 1989	LAK 4 WAS 4	LANDOVER, MD

The Kings scored three middle-period goals in a three minute span, two assisted by Wayne Gretzky. By the 3rd, thousands in the Capital Centre sellout had departed, sure the Caps couldn't recover from a 4-1 deficit.

Even Caps goalie Clint Malarchuk kept leaving, which proved crucial in a glorious and unorthodox Capitals comeback. With seven minutes left, a sixth attacker replaced Malarchuk as a delayed penalty was being called on L.A. Mike Millar scored to cut the deficit to 4-2. In the final minute, Malarchuk again left for an extra skater, with the Caps already on a power play. Scott Stevens' point shot at 19:11 closed the gap to 4-3.

THE LEGENDS OF LANDOVER

When Washington gained possession, Clint left one final time for an extra forward. Dave Christian, while shoved down to the ice, pushed in the tying goal with five seconds left. Three goals in the final 6:37 - two in the final 49 seconds - all with a pulled goaltender! "My view from the bench was pretty good," Malarchuk joked. "The guys were playing great, really taking it to them. That was a victory in a sense." Stevens added, "We came back and stuck together and threw everything we could at them."

When the Caps cut the deficit to one, coach Bryan Murray outfoxed his counterpart. "I anticipated that Washington would call timeout," admitted Kings coach Robbie Ftorek. "When they didn't, I felt that cost us (by failing to slow their momentum)." Murray also had a message for fans that departed before the comeback. "They can criticize us, but they shouldn't quit on us." (Quotes from *Washington Post*)

| MAR. 5, 1989 | VAN 0 WAS 3 | LANDOVER, MD |

Glass-half-full types would applaud this game for its magnificent penalty killing; a combined 20 of 21 extra man opportunities were foiled. Three times the teams faced 5-on-3 disadvantages without surrendering a goal. The doom-and-gloom crowd might describe it differently; not since the great Northeast Blackout of 1965 had anyone witnessed such a sustained lack of power. Washington went 1-for-10 on power plays. Amazingly, Vancouver proved more inept, failing on 11 chances; two were 5-on-3's.

Assessing his squad, Capitals coach Bryan Murray sounded like he was describing two different teams. On defense: "We're getting back, getting the third man back, playing with contact, moving the puck well." On their power play: "Absolutely no confidence." The Capitals did connect once per period by Kelly Miller, Neil Sheehy, and Dave Christian. Goaltender Don Beaupre faced 11 total shots the final two periods on the way to a shutout.

| FEB. 14, 1990 | WAS 4 EDM 3 | EDMONTON, AB |

For once, the Capitals were merely spectators in a netminder crisis (see pages 166, 245). Former goalie John Garrett, the Oilers' TV analyst, watched as a first period collision knocked starter Pokey Reddick out of the game. Replacement Bill Ranford proceeded to twist his ankle, playing hurt until intermission. Meanwhile, Edmonton G.M. Glen Sather got league permission for Garrett to play if neither Reddick nor Ranford could answer the bell for the second period. Garrett, five years into retirement, headed for the locker room, although Reddick ultimately returned to finish the game. "It would have been a hoot," Garrett said later. "Do you think I could have talked the Capitals into a no-slapshot, no-contact game?"

✪✪✪✪✪✪

18th Shift: Playoffs: Faceoff Circle of Hell
AKA Eternal Playoff Suffering, with apologies to Dante's *Inferno*

Inferno, Dante Alighieri's 14th century epic poem, describes travels through increasingly horrific levels of Hell. When Dante and his guide arrive at the ultimate 9th Circle of Hell, far from an inferno, it's actually a frozen sheet of ice. Look it up! Better yet, I'll do it for you, aided by *worldofdante.org.*

Dante writes, "We passed beyond, where frozen water wraps, covering still other sinners." Then they spy Satan. "The emperor of the despondent kingdom... so towered from the ice... Beneath each face of his, two wings spread out... and he was agitating them... and all Cocytus (a river in the underworld) froze before those winds." In other words, Satan is encased up to his chest in what's commonly considered the central zone of the 9th Circle, i.e. *Center Ice.*

Nearby is the much less well known "Faceoff Circle of Hell." This is where the annual playoff hopes and dreams of the Capitals and their fans go after they die, to suffer in eternal misery. (Of course, heavenly balm was applied in the form of the 2018 Stanley Cup championship! We touch on that on page 305.)

Because of its gruesome nature, the Capitals' playoff history of the 1980's has been quarantined from the rest of this book, to be contained, like nuclear waste, inside this chapter. Those with heart conditions, pregnant, or with easily triggered depression are encouraged to skip this section. For everyone else, the courageous are invited to descend into the nether world of the "Faceoff Circle of Hell" on the following pages. Before continuing, for your own safety, please lock up sharp objects, store away toxic liquids, and secure prescription medications.

You've Been Warned!

✪ It Happens Every Spring

The playoff history of the Capitals is painful – not just *that* they lose, but the excruciating *ways* they find to lose. In the words of the *Philadelphia Daily News,* "Only cholesterol has broken more hearts than the Washington Capitals." While it's the defining characteristic of the franchise, the gory details won't be found on these pages. Why? For the same reason you don't stick a fork in your eye: it would hurt – a lot – and serves no useful purpose. How pithy can you be about 4-overtime losses, or evaporating 3-1 series leads, or key injuries that stymied runs at the Stanley Cup?

THE LEGENDS OF LANDOVER

Pat Calabria of the *Sporting News* put it this way: "Once upon a time, when (G.M. David) Poile began transforming the Capitals from also-rans to respectability, he said: 'The book has been started, but the final chapter hasn't been written.' In the Caps' case, the book is a mystery." Pat, the 1980's book is more like a Stephen King novel. Former general manager Max McNab certainly didn't dismiss a supernatural curse, observing, "There seems to be a black cloud hanging over that franchise."

Each spring in the '80's (and beyond), even armed with painful memories, Capitals fans remained eternally optimistic. Maybe it's amnesia. Maybe masochism. For whatever reason, fans re-enacted the fraternity pledging scene from *Animal House*. As playoff opponents whacked painfully away, we exclaimed, "Thank You! May I Have Another!"

Perhaps an even better movie metaphor is *Groundhog Day*. Of course, many people refuse to stop playing the lottery, for fear they'll miss their number coming up tomorrow. Likewise, at playoff time, we plunked down our emotional savings year after year for the elusive chance at victory.

Psychologists call this the "Sunk Cost Effect." Tony Kornheiser called it the "Choking Dog" Effect. The former *Washington Post* columnist sinfully ignored the Caps most of the time. But he did speak for the fans in a damning 1989 column: "They do it to me every spring. First, the forsythia blast out, then the Capitals. Why do I continually fall for this? It's a disease. It has to be a disease. As soon as you put on the uniform, you lose in the playoffs. But you can't hurt me anymore. I'm washing my hands of you. You're on your own... Unless you win."

✪ Great Expectations

Here's a refresher on why hopes each spring ran so high. Consider that Mike Gartner, Rod Langway, and Scott Stevens - three future Hall of Famers - played *in their prime* on the same Caps teams. That's equal parts remarkable and frustrating. The 1980's Capitals thrilled fans by piling up monster regular season win totals. But Gartner, Langway and Stevens ultimately were all dressed up with nowhere to go - not one appearance in a Stanley Cup Final. How could that be?

Langway said, "It's on our minds. We have the ability. We have the talent. We've even had the opportunities. We just can't seem to get out of the division." A fourth future Hall member, defenseman Larry Murphy, disputes that these Caps teams failed to meet expectations. "We just didn't have the complete personnel," Murphy told *USA Today*. "(We) got the most out of what we had. I never considered us underachievers." Langway revealed that when the Caps did reach the conference final in 1990, both he and Stevens were playing with separated shoulders.

THE LEGENDS OF LANDOVER

✪ My Kingdom For A Goalie

Langway has also suggested that stellar goaltending was a missing piece. Year after playoff year, the Capitals hoped in vain for a stud performance from one of their goalies. You know, the kind that would make the *other* team say, for once, that *they* had run into the hot netminder, the kind who can steal a series.

It never happened. In the seven postseasons from 1983 to 1989, the Capitals lost seven of 10 series, never advancing past the second round. A parade went between their pipes over the years, solid goalies all, stoking hopes with sparkling regular season resumes. None elevated his game when it counted most, evidenced by their post-season records: Pat Riggin, 2-5; Al Jensen, 5-5; Bob Mason, 2-2; Clint Malarchuk, 0-2, Pete Peeters, 15-15.

With Pete, Al Strachan of the *Toronto Globe & Mail* heard his fatal flaw was the five-hole. "Scouting reports stress the point forcibly - make him move, then shoot for the opening. The ability to close those legs quickly... is an asset that Peeters does not possess."

Don Beaupre and Mike Liut, each acquired for a pittance, finally backstopped a conference final appearance in 1990. Minnesota dealt Beaupre for Claudio Scremin, a 10th-round draft choice who played 17 NHL games. At the time Liut was dealt in March, 1990, he had the 2nd best GAA in the league. The Caps gave up Yvon Corriveau, producer of 23 goals over five seasons. The Whalers liked his C.A. - Contract Affordability - just $90,000, compared with Liut's $455K.

✪ Proceeding With Caution

Like a recipe that looks better than it tastes, the Caps never could get the mix of ingredients quite right. For instance, the 1988-89 edition was the NHL's heaviest, averaging 204 pounds, and second-tallest, averaging six-foot-three. Size didn't matter, as the Flyers bounced the Caps in the playoffs' first round. "This gets more painful every year," Mike Gartner confided to hockey historian Stan Fishler. "I don't want to be building a foundation my whole career. Someday I'd like to get to put on the chimney."

When he was first hired, general manager David Poile stated the mantra that would define the franchise. "In this league, all they remember is how you did in the playoffs." *(Philadelphia Inquirer)* Yet management never pulled the trigger on a risky, bold, mortgage-prospects, "Future is Now" move to get over the top. One glaring example: early in the 1984-85 season, the L.A. Kings shopped high-scoring winger Charlie Simmer. "They wanted a first-round pick. The price was too high," Poile said to the *Sporting News*.

THE LEGENDS OF LANDOVER

I know, hindsight, yada, yada, but Simmer went to Boston and scored 98 goals with a +48 rating in three seasons with the Bruins. Couldn't he have provided badly needed playoff scoring? The 1st rounder kept by the Caps became the aforementioned Yvon Corriveau.

Poile elaborated on his measured approach to *The Hockey News*. "The easiest thing in this business is to go for it today, with no caring for the future. This is a business and I want to stay here for a lot of years. I want the fans to enjoy a competitive hockey club for many years. The moves I've made have been looking to the future." Fair, reasonable, logical. But juxtapose it with Poile's lament after one playoff ouster. "I thought we were going to win," Poile said in 1984. "I thought it was our year. I felt we'd built this team to be ready for this moment." A sentiment which could have been placed on a torturous loop and played every April.

While the Capitals' roster churned through the '80's, Bryan Murray suffered each and every playoff sting. In Jason Farris' book, *Behind The Moves*, Murray suggested, "To me, it's not about the player being traded or acquired all the time; it's the message you send to your players. When you get the better player or you make a trade that you can tell as being a positive for the team, that message is very loud in the room. I don't know that David Poile and I totally understood that with the Capitals, and it affected our playoffs on a couple of occasions."

✪ "We Just Haven't Won"

Following one playoff exit, Craig Laughlin smashed his stick on the goal until the shaft was reduced to splinters. His words resonated for every one of the Caps' playoff fizzles. "They made the most of the few breaks we gave them. We couldn't capitalize on their 65,000 mistakes." Added coach Murray, "We've done the right things. We've outplayed teams and outshot them. We just haven't won."

Sigh

THE LEGENDS OF LANDOVER

19th Shift: *Hunter's Shot: 1988 Playoffs*

Prior to the Stanley Cup Final run of 1998, there was no debate about the single most thrilling moment in Washington Capitals history. It came at Capital Centre, late on the night of April 16, 1988. "It" was Dale Hunter's overtime goal in Game Seven of Washington's opening round Stanley Cup playoff series with Philadelphia.

Drama in the vein of Hunter's heroics typically needs no embellishment. In this case, even the phrases "Game Seven" and "Overtime Goal" don't adequately tell the story. The Capitals had trailed in the series three games to one, and fell behind in the seventh game, 3-0, before rallying to forge a 4-4 tie at the end of regulation. Even that doesn't provide full context. The season before, it was the Caps who had taken a 3-1 series lead over the Islanders, only to lose games five and six. Then, on the same Capital Centre ice, they lost game Seven in the fourth overtime.

Now here they were again. The first five minutes of OT packed a game's worth of glorious scoring chances - mostly by the Capitals. Mike Gartner failed by inches, hitting the post from in close. "If it hadn't been for Dale Hunter, I would have been hearing pucks ring off crossbars for about the next year," Gartner said to the *Toronto Star*. With Ron Hextall hopelessly out of position, the rebound of Gartner's shot bounced by Hunter's stick, as he swung and missed at an empty net. Hextall's sliding save robbed Peter Sundstrom on a 2-on-1, and he foiled Bobby Gould on a bang-bang backhander in close. At the other end, Pete Peeters stoned Philly's Brian Propp on a shorthanded breakaway.

Suddenly, there was Hunter, splitting the defense, taking Larry Murphy's pass, and sliding the puck between Hextall's pads to win the series. He raised his stick, jumped in the air, and awaited the welcoming committee of teammates to mob him in the near corner. Caps fans - 18,130 in the arena, watching on *HTS* or *ESPN,* or listening on radio - exploded with the cheer stifled and swallowed for an entire year.

The Flyers' Rick Tocchet, who had engaged in a profane hallway shouting match with Hunter earlier in the series, gave him the ultimate opponent's compliment. "We would love to have Dale Hunter; every team would love to have Dale Hunter," Tocchet said to the *Toronto Star*. "He's in your face all night and he scores the winning goal."

To be sure, there was playoff heartbreak in the years before the Hunter goal, and in the years that followed. On this one night, though, the emotion of the moment was captured beautifully by Jim Hughson, calling the game for Canada's *TSN*: "The Washington Capitals finally, finally, won the big one."

THE LEGENDS OF LANDOVER

✪ Caps Radio Broadcaster Ron Weber, to *washingtoncaps.com*

"As I phrased it, 'Washington lives to play again.' It wasn't something I had planned, just the words that came to me and I still almost get goose bumps.

"The fans didn't leave. Everyone stood around, clapped, high-fived each other, applauded the players. It wasn't the finals, but it was a very precious series win. Marv Brooks, the public address announcer, said, 'We will see you Monday.' It was a Saturday night game and that meant we had qualified for the next round of the playoffs and we would host a game two days later. When he said, 'We will see you Monday,' they roared again."

✪ Excerpts From *The New York Times* Game Story By Joe Sexton

When he arrived from Quebec last June, Dale Hunter gave the Capitals a quality they had sorely lacked. He was tough, talented and allergic to the notion of quitting. Tonight, Hunter gave the club's legions of loyal but consistently disappointed followers something they had craved for more than a decade. He gave them a supremely clutch overtime goal, drama that ended in delight and relief from the oppressive label of losers.

"He will absolutely do anything to win," said Rod Langway, a veteran of five seasons of Capital collapses. "He sacrifices his body. Look at him, stitches and cuts everywhere. But he knows how to give it, too."

✪ Closing Comments From *ESPN's* Game Broadcast

Bill Clement, game analyst: "Ron Hextall needed one more 10-bell save to keep this game alive. But on a breakaway right up the middle, the man that has the heart about as big as this Capital Centre, Dale Hunter, puts it by Ron Hextall."

Mike Emrick, play-by-play: "What these fans, some of whom wore black armbands before game five recall is going up 2-nothing in a best of five with the Islanders in '85 and going out three straight. Being up 2-1 in a best of seven to the Rangers in '86 and going out three straight. Being up 3-1 on the Islanders last year and going out three straight.

"This year they were the ones down, they gave away the fourth game. (Washington led 4-1 with 10 minutes left before bowing 5-4 in overtime.) But they came back. They outhit the Flyers in game five, humiliated Philadelphia in the Spectrum, 7-2 (in game six). And tonight, before a full house of fans who were ready to resume their cynicism or thrill to a comeback, based on one score of one game, there it is" - referring to the final score filling the screen. "You have seen a label change."

THE LEGENDS OF LANDOVER

✪ Excerpts From Michael Wilbon's *Washington Post* Column

"I'm not going to kid you," (Rod Langway) began. "When it was 3-0, I thought we'd be blown out. As a veteran, you know you're scared, but you try to act confident. A great play by Hunter got it turned around." The great play was a game-changing pass from Hunter to Gary Galley for the Capitals first goal; (it) helped eliminate fear of being blown out that so many of the Capitals must have been feeling.

Here was Hunter bearing down on Flyers goalkeeper Ron Hextall. "He's got to do something before I can do something. But he didn't do anything. I made a little deke because I didn't see room to shoot. Finally, he opened his legs and it was just enough room for me to put it in." Larry Murphy, who started the play, called it, "The biggest goal in the history of the franchise."

✪ Excerpts From Frank Orr's *Toronto Star* Column

David Poile eased his way into a small anteroom, away from the dressing quarters' bedlam, admitted to being in a major league daze and, arm around his young son, said softly, "Well, maybe we won't have to hear it again for at least four games." Poile is the general manager of Washington Capitals, who have had the terms "losers" and "chokes" jammed down their throats so often that they were fortunate not to strangle.

"I doubt if anyone in the world figured we had a chance to come back when we were down 3-1 in the series," said coach Bryan Murray, whose future was the subject of the heaviest number of rumors. "But I knew there was an enormous amount of character on my team and I really believed we did have a chance," Murray added. "Where we were in the series and in the seventh game, too, was the spot for our players to answer all the questions about their guts or heart or courage. After what we did, no one can doubt any of those things again."

✪ Excerpts From Jay Greenberg's *Hockey News* Column

Atheists were delighted because their point, that there is no God, was being proven. If the Caps, having rallied from a 3-1 deficit in the series and 3-0 score in the deciding game, were still not going to win, then He had died and been replaced by Ron Hextall. Lord, what was it that Yvon Labre did so long ago that caused you to forsake the Washington Capitals?

It was not until His messenger, the angelic Dale Hunter, was in alone on a breakaway that everything was perfect. The Caps' triumph was one of Murray's patience, of Poile's judgment, of the perseverance of players like Langway, Gartner and Gould. It was nice to see good losers finally become great winners. For all they've been through, the Caps deserved it. (Greenberg's full-time gig was Flyers' writer for the *Phila. Daily News*)

THE LEGENDS OF LANDOVER

✪ **Excerpts From Tony Kornheiser's** *Washington Post* **Column**

What tender poetry in the way they won. Not only to come back from 3-1 in games, but to come back from a 3-0 deathtrap in the seventh game. To go to overtime in the very building where they went so many agonizing overtimes one year ago in similar circumstances.

When overtime came the Capitals were the aggressors. How many shots did they fling at Hextall? Does 100 sound like too many? How close were they? So close that if they were any closer, you could shave with them.

And when Hunter finally pinched through and pierced him, there was the noise of 20,000 sleepless nights, 20,000 muffled screams, 20,000 broken hearts all freed from the grasp of history and exploding into joy. "Tonight was meant to be," Rod Langway gushed. "It had to be that we won this game."

OVERTIME:
Still Crazy – About the Caps

The odds had to be astronomical: that I would be contacted by two people I'd never met, more than 30 years after we all happened to attend our first hockey game on the same night.

As I wrote at the beginning of this book, the Caps beat the Kansas City Scouts that night, 3-0. Among the 14,214 at Capital Centre on February 16, 1975, were me and my dad - and, as it turned out, a kid named Dan and his dad. It was the first NHL game for either of us. Dan e-mailed me after visiting my website devoted to the Capitals, and attached a pair of *Montgomery Sentinel* game photos.

More recently, I received an e-mail from another fan named Warren, saying he also attended his first Caps game that night, with *his* father! I can't improve on Warren's eloquence, so here's part of what he wrote:

"I will *never* forget the first time I looked through the portal opening and saw THE ICE. Of course "we" won and I, like you, was hooked. Who knew I'd still be here, more than 3 decades later. My Verizon Center seats are much better than dad got me back on February 16th, 1975. I don't have my ticket stub from my first-ever Caps game; but, I *do* have the ticket from my son's first ever Caps game: Feb 9, 1992 (San Jose). I saw you got an email from someone named Dan, who also saw his first game with his dad that day back in 1975. Amazing. Just amazing."

WARREN   DAN

Warren continued to correspond with me, as did Dan. Then they decided to meet at the Capitals Convention in October, 2010. In the photo they sent me, Warren and Dan are pointing to a timeline noting our fateful shared game. The caption reads, "Feb. 16, 1975: Goaltender Ron Low notches the first shutout in franchise history."

This long-ago game said a lot about us now graybeard Capitals fans... though Warren, Dan and I don't actually have gray beards (do we?). For starters, 14,000 paid to see a team which had won just five of its first 57 games. As Russ White wrote in the *Washington Star*, "With the last seconds of the game ticking away... a crescendo of cheers built. Yvon Labre marvels at the crowds that the Capitals draw at home, and the way crowds back the Capitals. 'All we hear are cheers. Don't think we can't hear,' Labre said later. 'There is nothing wrong with our ears.'"

THE LEGENDS OF LANDOVER

The Capitals averaged 10,004 per game in their woeful first season, more than the Flyers drew in their first year. White in the *Star* called it, "The most peculiar love affair any city has ever had with one of its sports teams… The Capitals weren't just another bad team. They were downright ridiculous. But you looked at them as you did your first car. Somehow, you were too wrapped up in the ecstacy of the moment to care about the performance."

This devotion was essential, allowing the franchise time to outgrow its troubled youth. Without the fan support, Washington likely would have joined Kansas City, Oakland, Cleveland, Atlanta, and Denver, all cities which lost NHL teams between 1976 and 1982.

To a man, the Caps expressed admiration – make that awe – for their faithful followers (quotes collected by *The Hockey News*). G.M. Milt Schmidt: "More than anything, we are grateful for our fans, who stuck by us in the troubled times." Winger Bill Lesuk, calling Capitals fans "the only good thing" about the season: "I think they deserve more for their money." Labre, taking the mic after the final home game: "I never saw better fans anywhere." Center Stan Gilbertson, noting thousands of autograph-seekers and picture-takers on the ice at season's end: "These fans are tremendous. In time this will be an exciting franchise."

Nailed it, Stan.

I haven't lived in the D.C. metropolitan area since 1984. The players, coaches, owner, home arena, uniform and logos have all changed. Yet the team remains near to my heart. Perhaps it's because I remember the joy of that downtrodden Mets team winning it all. When the Miracle Capitals finally capture that elusive Stanley Cup, it'll be sweetest for those of us who were there from the beginning. I just hope I live long enough to see it.

Yep, that's how I originally ended this book.
Fortunately, the events of Spring, 2018 required I add additional pages.

THE LEGENDS OF LANDOVER

DOUBLE OT:
From Stanley Can To Stanley Cup

> When the Capitals played their first home game at Capital Centre in October, 1974, Russ White wrote this in The Hockey News: "The Hockey Hall of Fame brought the Stanley Cup to Washington. It'll take some doing for the Cup to return."

No kidding. Tickets to my first Capitals game in 1975 were a 14th-birthday present. Which made me, in the spring of 2018, *old*. So the prospect of the Capitals winning a title in my lifetime was anything but certain – especially with the general manager's self-proclaimed two-season "championship window" having closed with yet another heartbreak one spring earlier.

Like a lot of you, I felt that window had repeatedly been slammed shut on my fingers, and I was growing weary of hanging on. Regretfully, in the summer of 2017, my three framed sweaters from the various eras of Capitals' hockey were re-homed from my den to the backyard shed.

✪ The Hottest Team In Hockey

Tongue in cheek - or not - a Toronto radio host predicted in 1975 that "The planet will be a cinder when the Capitals win the Stanley Bauble." *CFKH*'s Dick Beddoes didn't specify if he meant the Capitals' Cup celebration wouldn't come for five billion years, the estimated wait until our Sun becomes a red giant and fries the solar system; or whether a Caps reign as NHL champs would, in and of itself, cause the planet to self-immolate.

It would have been fitting for the hardships of the expansion years to be avenged when Langway, Gartner, and Gustafsson brought home a championship, but they couldn't. And for Bondra, Hunter and Kolzig to add another, but they didn't. And for Ovie's Young Guns to make it three.

Al Strachen of the *Montreal Gazette* was among the first to notice the black cloud which hovered over the franchise for decades. The indignities of a 1970's trip to Montreal began early, as the Caps' chartered plane broke down. When they finally reached the Forum, the Canadiens torched Washington for four goals in a 1:47 span, and glided to a 7-0 victory. A compassionate Strachen reasoned, "The beleaguered Capitals must be getting the impression they have been damned to eternal misery."

THE LEGENDS OF LANDOVER

The misery didn't disappear in the '80's, just relocated to the postseason. "The law of averages decrees some blessings are owed the Capitals," Robert Fachet wrote in a 1987 *Hockey News* story. "Their history of misfortune is probably unmatched in sports." Thomas Boswell concurred in a *Washington Post* column, headlined, "Heartbreak Is Spelled With Capitals." The lede: "Of all the teams in pro sports, perhaps one club stands above all others in its capacity, year after year, for combining obvious talent and realistic high expectations with slapstick frustration and postseason perplexity. The Washington Capitals."

See what we were up against? And that was 30 years ago!

✪ Happy Ending

Much as I wanted to distance myself from the 2017-18 Capitals, the desire to follow their fortunes grew like an addiction. This is what Michael Corleone meant in *Godfather III* when he lamented, "Just when I thought I was out, they pull me back in!" So by the playoffs, again I was back in, watching the games on TV, scanning the web before and after. Naturally, the Caps lost their first two games, at home, both in overtime. Lucy had once again tricked Charlie Brown into believing that *this time*, he would get to kick the ball.

Who would have guessed then, that even eternal misery has an expiration date. In the case of the Capitals, 44 years, because they rallied to eliminate Columbus, then vanquished Pittsburgh, Tampa Bay, and Vegas to win the 2018 Stanley Cup. Comments on message boards, not to mention my own email, revealed the legions of long-suffering Caps fans – and former players – who shared the elation of victory, the first championship, at long last.

In a *Post* chat, Boswell gladly revisited his three-decade-old thesis. "The Caps had The Curse of All Curses. The fact that so much post-season failure could be piled on top of so much regular-season success in a mere 35-year time period, an experience that large numbers of fans experienced in its entirety and held in common, made the Caps unique. And that they finally won in exactly the season when ALL sports logic said that they were finally dead as a true SC contender, and dead for years to come, just made it mind-bogglingly wonderful. It will be a long time before that whole experience is forgotten."

Sylvain Cote, a 622-game defenseman with the Caps beginning in 1991, posted this to Twitter: "I'll say this in a very emotional way. Every (Caps) alumni has earned a very small piece of this." Abe Pollin's widow, Irene, wished her husband could share the joy. "You remember all the decisions, everything it took to get to this point, it's just very exciting. And to think, everyone told us Washington would never be a hockey town."

THE LEGENDS OF LANDOVER

1970's Caps Bill Riley and Mike Marson reveled in the contributions of newly minted hero Devante-Smith Pelly, a fellow player of color. Said Riley, "Gives me goosebumps. Wicked." In the depths of the team's misery – March 20, 1976 to be exact – goalie Bernie Wolfe had defiantly promised, "In the years to come, the Capitals will win the Stanley Cup." When the Ovi-led Caps delivered on that promise, Wolfe celebrated with his 11 year old grandson. "He said, 'I've waited 10 years for this.' Well, I said, 'Grandpa's waited 44.'"

Hall of Fame defenseman Rod Langway was "beaming with pride, and said he has felt the same from fellow alumni." Another d-man, original Capital Yvon Labre, is still a season-ticket holder. "I was very happy for the organization. I don't have a tattoo of them, but it's on my heart," Labre said.

Ours too, Yvon. I'd like to write more, but I need to visit my backyard shed. There's three framed Capitals sweaters that need re-hanging.

(Quotes from colorofhockey.com, sudbury.com, washingtonjewishweek.com, capitalgazette.com, Associated Press, Washington Post, Washington Star.)

About the Author

Glenn Dreyfuss is proud of his wife (Katie), son and daughter (Alex and Rachel), dogs (April and Sailor), and TVs (Aquos, Toshiba, Panasonic and Sharp).

Seven of them live in suburban Seattle, while the now-grown kids have their own homes in the Northwest.

Glenn's sister Dana and her family also live nearby. They get together often to discuss Jim Bedard.

Glenn hosts a weekly YouTube show, *Hockey Time Machine*. Past guests have included Lanny McDonald, Scotty Bowman, Ed Belfour, and the cast of *Slap Shot*, as well as former Caps Dennis Maruk, Guy Charron, Bernie Wolfe and Bill Mikkelson.

He writes for *The Fischler Report*, part of *The Hockey News* online, and is a member of the Society for International Hockey Research.

In addition to local TV sportscasting, Glenn has produced network shows for PBS, HGTV, Versus, DIY and Food Network, as well as serving as Director of Programming for two satellite TV networks.

Glenn's e-mail: notapwplfan@yahoo.com

www.ingramcontent.com/pod-product-compliance
Lightning Source LLC
Chambersburg PA
CBHW070301010526
44108CB00039B/1439